THE

Bible in the Public Schools.

ARGUMENTS

IN THE CASE OF

John D. Minor et al.

Versus

The Board of Education of the City of Cincinnati et al

SUPERIOR COURT OF CINCINNATI.

WITH THE

OPINIONS AND DECISION

Of the Court.

CINCINNATI:
ROBERT CLARKE & CO.
1870.

Superior Court of Cincinnati.

John D. Minor, Samuel P. Bishop, Charles W. Rowland, James F. Irwin, William Clendenin, William M. F. Hewson, David Judkins, Charles Bonsall, Nathaniel Goldsmith, R. P. Bradford, William J. Dunlap, James F. Cunningham, Andrew Miller, William H. McReynolds, August Hoeltge, John M. Brown, Edward Betty, Martin B. Coney, O. N. Bush, Matthew Addy, John L. Talbott, John Richards, Philip Hinkle, Charles M. Rankin, J. B. Chickering, Addis E. Chamberlain, James W. Sibley, Anthony H. Hinkle, John E. Bell, Enoch T. Carson, John W. Williams, John J. Hooker, James H. Laws, John Pfaff, Abraham Springett, Pitts H. Burt, and John Simpkinson, on behalf of themselves and many others, citizens and tax-payers of Cincinnati, PLAINTIFFS,

Against

The Board of Education of Cincinnati, W. J. O'Neil, J. H. Brunsman, J. W. B. Kelley, Peter Gibson, Edgar M. Johnson, C. C. Campbell, Benjamin J. Ricking, D. J. Mullaney, Henry W. Poor, W. I. Wolfley, Joseph P.

Carbery, F. Macke, H. P. Seibel, C. F. Bruckner, Stephen Wagner, C. H. Gould, Joseph Kramer, F. W. Rauch, Henry L. Wehmer, William Kuhn, Thomas Vickers, Howard Douglass, J. C. Krieger, A. Theurkauf, John Sweeney, George D. Temple, G. W. Gladden, Henry Mack, Abner L. Frazer, A. D. Mayo, John P. Story, Francis Ferry, J. L. Drake, Samuel A. Miller, Louis Ballauf, Henry Bohling, Herman Eckel, J. F. Wisnewski, James T. Fisher, J. H. Rhodes, W. F. Hurlbut, and the City of Cincinnati, DEFENDANTS.

Petition

Filed November 2, 1869.

The plaintiffs, who bring this action on their own behalf, and on behalf of many others, say that they and those on whose behalf they sue, are citizens and tax-payers of the city of Cincinnati. That on the 1st day of November, A. D. 1869, the Board of Education of said city, at a regular meeting thereof, then held, passed the following resolutions by the vote of a majority of the members, to-wit: by the votes of W. J. O'Neil, J. H. Brunsman, J. W. B. Kelly, Edgar M. Johnson, Benjamin J. Ricking, D. J. Mullaney, Henry W. Poor, Joseph P. Carbery, F. Macke, H. P. Seibel, C. F. Bruckner, Stephen Wagner, Joseph Kramer, F. W. Rauch, Thomas Vickers, A. Theurkauf, John Sweeney, George D. Temple, John P. Story, Samuel A. Miller, Herman Eckel, J. F. Wisnewski, defendants, and members of said board:

"*Resolved*, That religious instruction, and the reading of religious books, including the Holy Bible, are prohibited in the Common Schools of Cincinnati, it being the true object and intent of this rule to allow the children of the parents of all sects and opinions, in matters of faith and worship, to enjoy alike the benefit of the Common School fund.

"*Resolved*, That so much of the regulations on the course of study and text books in the Intermediate and District Schools (page 213, Annual Report), as reads as follows: 'The opening exercises in every department shall commence by reading a portion of the Bible by or under the direction of the teacher, and appropriate singing by the pupils,' be repealed."

Plaintiffs state that the entire rule quoted from is in the words following:

"The opening exercises in every department shall commence by reading a portion of the Bible by or under the direction of the teacher, and appropriate singing by the pupils. The pupils of the Common Schools may read such version of the sacred scriptures as their parents or guardians may prefer, provided that such preference of any version, except the one now in use, be communicated by the parents and guardians to the principal teachers, and that no notes or marginal readings be allowed in the schools, or comments made by the teachers on the text of any version that is or may be introduced."

Plaintiffs say that the rule last above quoted was adopted by the Board of Education of the city of Cincinnati, said board then being known as the Board of Trustees and Visitors of Common Schools, in the year 1852, and has ever since that time been in full force and effect, as one of the rules for the conduct of the schools of the said city, and that the version of the Holy Bible generally used in said schools, and referred to in the rule last above quoted as "the one now in use," is that published by the "American Bible Society," and commonly known as King James' version. Plaintiffs further say that the reading of the Holy Bible without note or comment has been one of the daily exercises of said schools from the time of their first establishment under the general school laws of Ohio, to-wit: from about the year 1829, till now, and that instruction in the elemental truths and principles of religion has always been given in said schools, but no sectarian teaching, nor any interference with the rights of conscience has at any time been permitted. That in the year 1842 the School Board of said city, by unanimous vote, provided that no pupil of the Common Schools of said city should be required to read the Testament or Bible if his parent or guardian should desire that said pupil should be excused from that exercise; that said provision has never been repealed, but the same is yet in full force.

Plaintiffs further say, that a large number of the text books used in said schools contain selections and passages from the Holy Bible, and from other books, and from writings which inculcate religious truths; that this is especially true as to the readers in common use in said schools; that every series of school readers accessible for use in said schools recognizes and inculcates religion, and that text books which omit all religious instruction, and yet contain the principles and teachings of those branches of knowledge usual and necessary for the instruction of the youth in said schools, are not extant, and can not be had. That the enforcement of the rule proposed by said Board of Education, and so passed as aforesaid, will exclude from said schools large numbers of valuable text books which have been recently purchased by parents or guardians for the use of children attending said schools in compliance with the requirements of said Board of Education, and will require the preparation and publication of new text books, and their purchase at great expense by said parents or guardians, without any corresponding benefit to said children or said schools, but, on the contrary, to their great detriment and injury.

Plaintiffs further say, that a large majority of the children in said city who receive any education are educated in said schools, and of said children large numbers receive no religious instruction or knowledge of the Holy Bible, except that communicated as aforesaid in said schools, and that the enforcement of the resolutions first aforesaid will result in leaving such children without any religious instruction whatever. And the plaintiffs allege that such instruction is necessary and indispensable to fit said children to be good citizens of the State of Ohio and of the United States: and is required by the third article of the act passed by the Congress of the United States, July 13, 1787, entitled "An ordinance for the government of the territory of the United States north-west of the river Ohio," to be forever encouraged.

Wherefore, the plaintiffs allege that the action and resolutions aforesaid of said Board of Education are in violation of law and against public policy and morality, and are an abuse of the authority vested by law in said board; that said resolutions are in contravention of the true meaning and intent of the constitution of the State of Ohio, and, if carried into operation, will greatly injure the Common Schools of said city, which, under the rules and system of instruction above set forth and heretofore adopted, have been in the highest degree successful and useful to the children of said city, and have contributed and are contributing largely to the welfare and prosperity of the city itself. And plaintiffs further allege that the enforcement of said resolutions will have the effect to make said schools deistical and infidel both in their purpose and tendency. Plaintiffs further allege that said resolutions have not yet been promulgated to the teachers of said schools, nor put in operation therein, but that said Board of Education, unless restrained by order of this Court, will proceed immediately to enforce the same, to the great and irreparable injury of the plaintiffs and those for whom they sue, and of said schools and said city.

Plaintiffs further allege, that the individuals who are named as defendants are, with the exception of W. F. Hurlbut, members of said Board of Education, duly elected and qualified, and, by virtue of their election and qualification, are acting as Trustees and Visitors of said Common Schools, and that the defendant W. F. Hurlbut is Clerk of said Board of Education, and the rules of the board require him to furnish principal teachers copies of all rules and resolutions adopted for the regulation of the schools. Plaintiffs further allege, that the corporate authorities of the city of Cincinnati are authorized and required by law to provide for the support and regulation of the said schools in the manner prescribed by said act.

Plaintiffs further allege, that they have requested the City Solicitor of said city to apply for an injunction upon the case herein stated, and he has failed and refused, and still refuses, so to do.

Wherefore, plaintiffs pray that the defendants, each and all of them, be restrained from promulgating, putting in operation or enforcing said resolutions, passed November 1, 1869, as above set forth, or either of them, and from authorizing, directing, or requiring any officer, or agent, or employe of said board, or any teacher in any of said schools, to promulgate, put in operation, enforce, or obey said resolutions, or either of them, or any of the prohibitions therein contained; that upon final hearing said injunction be made perpetual, and said resolutions be adjudged null and void, and such other and further relief granted as, the premises considered, may be just and proper.

SAGE & HINKLE,
WM. M. RAMSEY,
KING, THOMPSON & AVERY,
Attorneys for Plaintiffs.

State of Ohio, Hamilton County.

Charles Bonsall, one of the plaintiffs, solemnly affirmed, says that the allegations of the foregoing petition are true.

CHARLES BONSALL.

Affirmed to before me, and subscribed in my presence, this 2nd day of November, A. D. 1869.

[SEAL.] JULIUS DEXTER,
Notary Public, Hamilton County.

RESTRAINING ORDER.

Superior Court of Cincinnati, November 2, 1869.

JOHN D. MINOR *et al.*, Plaintiffs, *v.* THE BOARD OF EDUCATION OF THE CITY OF CINCINNATI *et al.*, Defendants.	*Minutes*, 323.

"On the application of the plaintiffs that a restraining order be allowed to issue against said defendants upon the matters alleged in the petition and affidavit filed, it is ordered that the defendants show cause on Thursday, November 4, at 10 o'clock, in Room No. 3, of the Superior Court, why the said application be not granted, and that in the meanwhile the resolutions of the defendants, as charged in said petition, be not further acted on until the hearing of this application."

ORDER OF NOVEMBER 4, 1869.

Minutes, 325.

By consent, the hearing of the cause upon the order hereinbefore made, is continued until Saturday, November 7th, 1869, at 10 o'clock, A. M., and the order of restraint hereinbefore made is continued and to remain in full force and effect until otherwise ordered.

[On the 7th of November the Court, with the consent of all parties, assigned the case for hearing before the full bench on Monday, November 30th, and it was agreed that the answers of the defendants should be filed, and the order of reservation made, at the convenience of counsel. No minute entry was made on the 7th.]

ANSWER OF THE DEFENDANTS NAMED THEREIN, FILED NOVEMBER 26, 1869.

Superior Court of Cincinnati.

JOHN D. MINOR *et al.*,
Plaintiffs,
v.
THE BOARD OF EDUCATION OF THE CITY OF CINCINNATI *et al.*,
Defendants.

The Board of Education of the City of Cincinnati, the City of Cincinnati and W. J. O'Neil, J. H. Brunsman, J. W. B. Kelley, Edgar M. Johnson, Benjamin J. Ricking, D. J. Mullaney, Henry W. Poor, Joseph P. Carbery, F. Macke, H. P. Seibel, C. F. Bruckner, Stephen Wagner, Joseph Kramer, F. W. Rauch, Thos. Vickers, A. Theurkauf, John Sweeney, George D. Temple, John P. Story, Samuel A. Miller, Herman Eckel, J. F. Wisnewski and H. L. Wehmer, defendants in the above entitled action, in answer to the petition say: That it is true that on the 1st day of November, 1869, said Board of Education passed the resolutions in said petition set forth; that these defendants also believe it to be true that the rule abrogated by said resolutions was adopted by the Board of Trustees and Visitors of the Common Schools in 1852; that it is also true that the version of the Bible generally in use in the common schools of Cincinnati is that known as King James' Version; that these defendants are not informed as to the truth of the allegation in the petition respecting the action of the School Board in 1842, but that if said allegation be true the rule claimed in the petition to have been adopted in 1842 has long since ceased to be acted upon or to be recognized as of binding force, the same not being found among the standing rules published and promulgated by the School Board, or Board of Education, during the last twenty-five years; that the sole version of the Bible which has been read in the common schools at any time within the knowledge of the defendants is that known and described in the petition as the King James' Version; that it is true that there are books other than the Bible now in use in the common schools of Cincinnati, which contain passages and selections from the Bible, and from writings inculcating truths which by many persons are designated as religious truths, but that such books are not religious books, and are not used for the purpose of conveying religious instruction; that these defendants believe it to be true that a number of children, who are educated in the common schools, receive no religious instruction or knowledge of the Bible except that communicated in said schools; that while the defendants do not deny that religious instruction is necessary and indispensable to fit said children to be good citizens of the State of Ohio, and of the United States, they deny that such instruction can or ought to be imparted in the schools established by the State; and these defendants say that it is true that the individuals named as defendants, are, with the exception of W. F. Hurlbut, members of said Board of Education, duly elected and qualified, and that said W. F. Hurlbut is clerk of said board, and that his duties are correctly described in the petition; and these defendants deny each and every other allegation of the petition which is not hereinbefore admitted.

And said defendants further answering, say that the citizens of Cincinnati, who are taxed for the support of the schools under the management of said Board of Education, and all of whom are equally entitled to the benefits thereof by having their children instructed therein, are very much divided in opinion and practice upon matters connected with religious belief, worship and education; that a considerable number thereof are Israelites who reject the Christian religion altogether, and believe only in the inspired truth of what is known as the Old Testament, and this only in the original Hebrew tongue, and such other religious truths and worship as are perpetuated in their body by tradition; that also, many of said citizens do not believe the writings embraced in the Bible to be entitled to be considered as containing an authoritative declaration of religious truth; that a still greater number of said citizens together with their children are members of the Roman Catholic Church, and conscientiously believe in its doctrines, faith and forms of worship, and that by said church the version of the scriptures referred to in the petition, is taught and believed to be incorrect as a translation and incomplete by reason of its omission of a part of the books held by such church to be an integral portion of the inspired canon; and furthermore, that the scriptures ought not to be read indiscriminately, in as much as said church has divine authority as the only infallible teacher and interpreter of the same, and that the reading of the same without note or comment, and without being properly expounded by the only authorized teachers and interpreters thereof, is not only not beneficial to the children in said schools, but likely to lead to the adoption of dangerous errors, irreligious faith, practice and worship, and that by reason thereof the practice of reading the King James' version of the Bible, commonly and only received as inspired and true by the Protestant religious sects, in the presence and hearing of Roman Catholic children, is regarded by the members of the Roman Catholic Church as contrary to their rights of conscience, and that such practice as heretofore pursued has had the necessary effect to prevent the attendance of large numbers of children of those who are members of said church, who, in consequence thereof have erected, and now maintain, separate schools at their own expense, in which there are enrolled and taught a number, about two-thirds of the number of those who are enrolled and taught in the schools under the management of said Board of Education; that also there are other religious sects and denominations and bodies of citizens who either do not regard the Bible as the authoritative source of religious truth, or who regard themselves as possessed of the only true sense thereof; that furthermore, a large number of persons in this community who are ready and qualified to act as teachers in said public schools object to the reading of the Bible in the version in use (or, indeed, in any version without note or comment) on conscientious grounds, and are thereby precluded from employment as teachers in said schools; that in consideration of these facts said Board of Education has concluded that it was not possible for it to take upon itself any instruction in religion, and that it is neither right nor expedient to continue in use in said public schools the reading of any version of the Bible as a religious exercise, or any other religious exercise whatever, and therefore has passed the resolutions now complained of by the plaintiffs.

These defendants pray to be dismissed with their costs.

WALKER & CONNER,
Solicitors for City.
S. & S. R. MATTHEWS,
GEO. HOADLY,
STALLO & KITTREDGE,
Attorneys for other Defendants.

State of Ohio, Hamilton County, ss:

Henry L. Wehmer being duly sworn, deposes and says that he is the President of the Board of Education of the city of Cincinnati, one of the defendants in the above entitled action, and that he believes the statements contained in the foregoing answer to be true.

H. L. WEHMER.

Sworn to before me, by said Henry L. Wehmer, and by him subscribed in my presence, this 23d day of November, 1869.

[L. S.] ED. H. KLEINSCHMIDT,
Notary Public.

ANSWER OF WM. F. HURLBUT.

Superior Court of Cincinnati.

JOHN D. MINOR *et al.*, Plaintiffs,
v.
THE BOARD OF EDUCATION OF THE CITY OF CINCINNATI *et al.*, Defendants.

Filed Nov. 27, 1869.

The defendant, William F. Hurlbut, admits that he is the clerk of the Board of Education of the city of Cincinnati, and says that he has been such since the 23d of March, A. D. 1857.

He further admits that the statement of his duties in the petition is correct, and that the Board, on the 1st day of November, A. D. 1869, passed the resolutions set forth in the petition, and that the same are in his hands for promulgation, subject to the order of the Court in this cause.

As to the other facts set forth in the petition, this defendant says he is not advised, and consents that this cause be heard and decided as to them upon the issues made up by the plaintiffs and his co-defendants.

W. F. HURLBUT,
Clerk of the Board of Education of Cincinnati.

State of Ohio, Hamilton County:

William F. Hurlbut, the above-named defendant, being first solemnly sworn, says that he believes the allegations of the foregoing answer to be true.

W. F. HURLBUT,
Clerk of the Board of Education of Cincinnati.

Sworn to before me, and subscribed in my presence, this 27th November, 1869.

T. BISHOP DISNEY,
Clerk Superior Court Cincinnati.

ANSWER OF THE MINORITY OF THE BOARD OF EDUCATION.

Superior Court of Cincinnati.

JOHN D. MINOR *et al.*, Plaintiffs, *v.* THE BOARD OF EDUCATION OF THE CITY OF CINCINNATI *et al.*, Defendants.	*Filed Nov.* 29, 1869.

The defendants, A. D. Mayo, Abner L. Frazer, C. C. Campbell, Louis Ballauf, Henry Bohling, W. I. Wolfley, J. L. Drake, Peter Gibson, G. W. Gladden, Howard Douglass, C. H. Gould, William Kuhn, Henry Mack, and J. H. Rhodes, for answer say: That the resolutions in the petition set forth were adopted by a majority of said Board of Education against the open and persistent opposition and over the votes of these defendants against said adoption, as will appear by the journal of said Board.

And the defendant, Francis Ferry, says, that at the time of the submission of said resolutions to vote, he was absent from the meeting of said Board, but that he afterward caused his vote to be entered on said journal as against said resolutions.

And all said defendants disclaim all connection with and responsibility for said resolutions.

A. D. MAYO,	LOUIS BALLAUF,
ABNER L. FRAZER,	C. H. GOULD,
J. H. RHODES,	C. C. CAMPBELL,
G. W. GLADDEN,	WM. I. WOLFLEY,
FRANCIS FERRY,	J. L. DRAKE,
HENRY MACK,	H. BOHLING,
WM. KUHN,	PETER GIBSON.
HOWARD DOUGLASS,	

Verification waived.

SAGE & HINKLE, *for Plaintiffs.*
STALLO & KITTREDGE, *for other Def'ts.*

AGREED STATEMENT OF TESTIMONY.

Superior Court of Cincinnati.

JOHN D. MINOR *et al.*,
Plaintiffs,

THE BOARD OF EDUCATION OF THE CITY OF CINCINNATI *et al.*,
Defendants.

Filed Nov. 27, 1869.

Be it remembered that at the hearing of the above-mentioned action, at special term of November, A. D. 1869, the plaintiffs to maintain their case offered and read in evidence a certified copy of the proceedings and resolutions passed by the Board of Trustees and Visitors of the Public Schools of the City of Cincinnati, at a meeting on August 29, 1842, which is hereto annexed and marked Exhibit 1.

Also, certified copy of an extract from the annual report for the year ending June 30, 1853, published by said Board, which is hereto attached and marked Exhibit 2.

Also, certified copy of an extract from the annual report for the year ending June 30, 1862, published by said Board, which is hereto annexed and marked Exhibit 3.

And they also offered and read in evidence six books, herewith filed and referred to, as part hereof, marked respectively Exhibit 4, Exhibit 5, Exhibit 6, Exhibit 7, Exhibit 8, and Exhibit 9, and marked with the style and number of this cause.

Exhibit 4 being entitled "McGuffey's New First Eclectic Reader."

Exhibit 5 being entitled "McGuffey's New Second Eclectic Reader."

Exhibit 6 being entitled "McGuffey's New Third Eclectic Reader."

Exhibit 7 being entitled "McGuffey's New Fourth Eclectic Reader."

Exhibit 8 being entitled "McGuffey's New Fifth Eclectic Reader."

Exhibit 9 being entitled "McGuffey's New Sixth Eclectic Reader."

And plaintiffs offered evidence tending to show that said six readers are, and for more than twenty years have been, used in the several grades of the public schools of said city as the regular and only authorized text books for lessons in reading.

And the defendants offered evidence tending to show that the rule referred to, as above adopted in 1842, has long since ceased to be acted upon or recognized as of binding force, and that the same is not found among the standing rules published and promulgated by the School Board of Education during the last twenty-five years.

This being all the testimony offered on either side, the case was submitted upon the pleadings and evidence to the Court, all of which is certified by the Judge presiding at special term.

B. STORER [SEAL].

EXHIBIT 1.

Extract from the Minutes of the School Board of Cincinnati:

"COUNCIL CHAMBER, *August* 29, 1842.

"The Board met pursuant to adjournment. Present—Mr. Perkins, President, and Messrs. Bonsall, Mulford, Meader, Symmes, Morrison, and Poor.

"The President having informed the Board that the Bishop of the Catholic Church had told him, in private, that certain objections existed to the English common schools, and also to the German common schools, on the part of the Catholics, viz:

"1. That the books used contained obnoxious passages.

"2. That the Catholic children are required to read the Protestant Testament and Bible; and

"3. That the district libraries contain objectionable works, to which the Catholic children have access without the knowledge of their parents.

"Thereupon, the following resolutions were submitted by him and adopted:

"*Resolved*, That the President of this Board be requested to inform Bishop Purcell that he is invited by the Board to examine the books used in the English common schools and the German common schools, or to cause them to be examined, and all obnoxious passages pointed out.

"2. *Resolved*, That no pupil of the common schools be required to read the Testament or Bible, if its parents or guardians desire that it may be excused from that exercise.

"3. *Resolved*, That no child shall be allowed to take books from the district libraries, unless at the beginning of each session its parent or guardian make the request, in writing or in person, that it may have that privilege."

I hereby certify that the foregoing is a correct copy from the Minutes of the School Board, under the date above mentioned.

W. F. HURLBUT,

Clerk of Board of Education.

CINCINNATI, *November* 26, 1869.

EXHIBIT 2.

I also certify that the following is a correct extract from the Twenty-third Annual Report of the Common Schools of Cincinnati, for the school year ending June 30, 1853 (page 19).

W. F. HURLBUT,
Clerk of Board of Education.

CINCINNATI, *November* 26, 1869.

"But to the charges, on one hand, of using sectarian or obnoxious text books, which render the schools intolerable by violating the rights of conscience, and upon the other hand, that we are indifferent to religion and morality, and devote our schools too much to mental instruction merely—to charges of this nature, very freely, and as it seemed to us, inconsistently used in the late discussion respecting the schools, we must be expected to answer, as the culpability, if any, attaches to this Board.

"Avowing this responsibility, we take occasion to say again that everything in our power has been done to obviate the first of these complaints, so that our schools may be in fact what they are in law, free and common to all. Whatever in the text-books or administration of the schools is justly offensive, we have again and again consented, if it be inconsistent with the truth, or even though true, if immaterial in its character or matter, to abrogate, whenever it is pointed out."

EXHIBIT 3.

I further certify that the following is a correct extract from the Thirty-third Annual Report of the Common Schools of Cinnati, for the school year ending June 30, 1862 (see pp. 12 and 13).

W. F. HURLBUT,

Clerk of Board of Education.

CINCINNATI, *November* 26, 1869.

"We are forced, very reluctantly, to notice intimations from an influential quarter, that the division of the school fund must and will be again agitated and demanded. We should be relieved from any necessity of reply as to this point by the fact that the Constitution of the State imperatively prohibits the right or control of any part of the school funds by any religious or other sect. The threat is accompanied, however, by reproaches against our schools, so groundless and so easily refuted, that we need only state as facts that for twenty years our standing request that any offensive exercises, or books, or passages in books, used in our schools, be made known to us, has never been answered; that for nearly ten years we have offered to supply teachers and schools in every orphan asylum whatever having a sufficient number of children to warrant the employment of a teacher; that we have always carefully excused pupils whose parents desired it from attending the religious exercises with which our schools are daily opened, and that, in order to encourage pupils to attend the religious teachings which their parents prefer, we have expressly required that they shall be excused from school one half day, or two quarter days each week. It has also been suggested, and, doubtless, such an arrangement may be effected, if sufficient numbers encourage it, that at the hours so allowed children of different denominations of religion might receive the instructions of the clergy in school-rooms temporarily set apart to them."

ORDER OF RESERVATION.

Superior Court of Cincinnati, November 27, 1869.

JOHN D. MINOR *et al.*, Plaintiffs,	
25,245.]	*Minutes*, 438.
THE BOARD OF EDUCATION OF THE CITY OF CINCINNATI *et al.*, Defendants.	

This cause came on to be heard upon the petition, answers, agreed statement of testimony, and exhibits filed, and upon the plaintiffs' motion for injunction, was thereupon reserved to the General Term of this Court for hearing by the full bench, on Monday, November 30, at 10 o'clock A. M.

Monday, November 30, 1869.

The parties, by their attorneys, appeared before the Court in General Term, Judges Storer, Taft, and Hagans upon the bench. The pleadings and agreed statement of fact having been read, it was announced that the Court would hear three counsel on each side; and it was arranged that Mr. Ramsey should open the argument for the plaintiffs, that Judges Stallo and Hoadly should follow for the defense, then Mr. Sage for the plaintiffs, and that Judge Matthews should close for the defendants and Mr. King for the plaintiffs. The argument then proceeded in the order indicated.

Argument of W. M. Ramsey,

For the Plaintiffs.

May it Please Your Honors—I approach the discussion of the questions involved in this cause with great diffidence. These questions had not been, prior to the inception of this cause, the subject of especial reflection or investigation upon my part, and they are not within the scope of ordinary professional study or experience. Profoundly conscious as I am that we are entering upon an inquiry of a very high order, in the ultimate determination of which the welfare of this community, and, perhaps, of the State and nation, is deeply involved, I can not but regret that the part which has been assigned to me had not devolved upon one more able to maintain it.

So far, however, as I shall be permitted to address your Honors, I will endeavor to keep constantly in view that this is a court of law, and not a popular assemblage—a court, convened to administer a well-defined system of jurisprudence, under solemn responsibility, and I will, therefore, address to the Court only such considerations, drawn from the statute books, and from the historical and judicial records of the State and nation, as shall seem to have a legitimate place in a discussion of such a character.

Your Honors have heard the facts of the case, as set forth in the pleadings of the parties, and the further agreement as to evidence, and I need not repeat them. It is proper to say that it has been the wish of the defendants, as well as of the plaintiffs, to strip the case of all technicalities, and mere questions of practice, in order that a complete and satisfactory decision upon the merits of the questions involved should be had.

The important questions that might arise in another form of action, touching the organization, and involving even the existence of the School Board, will not be presented here. These questions courd hardly be properly raised in an action of this nature. The Board is, at all events, assuming to exercise certain powers under authority of law—the validity of the claim to general power is properly the subject of inquiry in proceedings of *quo warranto*, which may be instituted by the proper authority in pursuance of the statute in that behalf. No question has been made by the defendants as to the jurisdiction of the Court, or the legal capacity of the plaintiffs to bring the action.

I desire to say, however, because there has been some misapprehension upon the subject, that the power of courts of equity to arrest and forbid the illegal action of public officers, is as familiar, as unquestioned, and as freely exercised, as any other. It is the duty of courts to interpret and administer the laws, and in the exercise of these high functions they may enjoin and forever prohibit even the execution of an act of the Legislature, if, in the judgment of the Court, it contravenes the fundamental law. It is their duty to preserve and protect the rights of individuals or communities, no matter by whom or by what asserted authority they are assailed, and they will, and do, lay their hands upon the State itself, when, through its agents, it attempts the exercise of power it does not possess. No surprise was felt when your Honors forbade the execution of a contract between the city, acting by its Common Council, the municipal legislature, and an individual who proposed to use the lamp-posts in the streets for advertising purposes. No surprise was expressed when the District Court enjoined the execution of a contract to supply the city of Covington with water. It is the glory of our institutions that we have no where lodged any absolute discretionary power. These public officers are appointed to the work of executing the law, not their own will. Municipal corporations, as well as private corporations, are invested with certain well defined powers, beyond which they can not go. Even the discretion with which the Court itself is invested, which is not ordinarily reviewable upon error, may be reviewed if it appears to be exercised wantonly or capriciously. The Board of Education of the city of Cincinnati, the city itself, is amenable to the process and the decree of this Court, in the same manner and to the same extent as the humblest citizen.

There is, then, nothing to hear in the present case but its merits. I address myself, therefore, directly to the question: "Are the plaintiffs entitled to the relief prayed for?"

I choose to anticipate and to concede all that will be claimed upon the part of the defendants, as to the general nature of the case which must be presented by the plaintiffs. It will not be sufficient to show that the defendants, in taking the action complained of, committed a mere error of judgment. It must be shown that the action is illegal, either by reason of positive prohibition, or the entire absence of statutory authority, or that, in the exercise of power over a subject within their general control, they have acted so capriciously, so wantonly, so injuriously, as to warrant the Court in holding that their action was not directed by a proper sense of duty, and that it is, therefore, unlawful and void. The plaintiffs must make a strong case—the right must be clear—the threatened injury great, with the entire absence of any other remedy than that which is here invoked.

To show themselves entitled to the relief prayed for, the plaintiffs must establish two propositions:

First. That religious instruction is, in contemplation of law, an essential element in our common school system of education.

Second. That the Board of Education of the city of Cincinnati has not power to prohibit all religious instruction in the schools of the city.

These propositions will be met, it may fairly be anticipated, by—

First. A general denial.

Second. The affirmation that, irrespective of any action upon the part of the School Board, religious instruction is unlawful.

I respectfully submit that religious instruction is an essential part of our common school system of education.

Our common school system was organized under the Constitution of 1802. Schools were established by the Legislature, in obedience to the direction of the Constitution itself. That direction is contained in the following words, constituting the concluding sentence of the third section of the Bill of Rights:

"Religion, morality and knowledge being essentially necessary to good government and the happiness of mankind, schools and the means of instruction shall forever be encouraged by legislative provision, not inconsistent with the rights of conscience."

This is not the announcement of a mere abstract principle for the information of the people. It is the solemn and authoritative declaration of organic law. It is a command to the legislative department of the State government to accomplish certain ends by certain means, and clearly indicating both means and ends.

The school established by the Legislature is, it will scarcely be denied or doubted, the school contemplated by the Constitution. There was no power to establish any other. Let, then, the language of the Constitution be fairly analyzed, that it may be fairly interpreted, for by the result of that analysis and consequent interpretation must this cause be determined. We find here the declaration that "religion, morality and knowledge" are "essentially necessary to good government and human happiness." "Religion, morality and knowledge" are, therefore, to be promoted—how? By the establishment of "schools and the means of instruction." These three things are equally desirable; they are to be equally fostered, and by the same instrumentality. I care not what may be included in the words "the means of instruction." They undoubtedly mean all the places and all the ways in which and by which "religion, morality" and general knowledge are disseminated.

They may, and doubtless do, include the churches. It only strengthens the view which I now present, to hold that religion was to be taught in the schools even as it was to be taught in the churches. But, it is said, there is limitation upon the Legislature, imposed by the words "not inconsistent with the rights of conscience." And that is true. Of the extent of that limitation I do not now care to speak, but shall do so directly. I desire now to call the especial attention of the Court to these words, with reference to their bearing upon the construction of the preceding language. If religion was not to be taught in the schools at all, whose "conscience" was in danger? I know how sensitive some of these consciences are; but the most sensitive would scarcely be offended if there should be no religious teaching, and it would scarcely have occurred to the framers of the Constitution to provide a safeguard for them, if none had been contemplated. Can it be supposed that the framers of the Constitution intended to command the Legislature to establish schools, in which instruction should be given in "reading, writing and arithmetic," "not inconsistent with the rights of conscience?"

It will not be argued, I know, by the learned counsel for the defendants, that the latter part of the sentence destroys the meaning of the entire sentence—that while the opening part of it provides for schools in which religion is to be taught, the concluding part contains a declaration which, in effect, precludes all religious teaching, and renders the entire provision nugatory.

Manifestly, then, schools were to be established for the purpose of disseminating religious, as well as general knowledge and the principles of morality, but in the teaching of religion regard was to be had to the rights of conscience; that is to say, sectarianism was to be avoided.

Following the adoption of this Constitution, several acts were passed by the Legislature making provision for the distribution of the school fund arising from the Congressional grant of lands, but it was not until January 22, 1821, that the first law was passed providing for the establishment of a system of common schools. It will be found on pages 1176–8 of Chase's Statutes. This act was followed by a very large number of laws, enacted from time to time, all, or nearly all, of which were repealed by the general law passed March 14, 1853, still in force. It is not necessary that I should enumerate these laws, or consider their provisions in detail, with reference to the aspect in which I now desire to present them.

These laws do not prescribe the course of study to be pursued, the text books to be used, the mode of discipline, the qualification of teachers, the duration of the period of pupilage, or anything else relating to the practical administration of the system thus established. They provide for appropriate division of the territory of the various counties and townships into districts and sub-districts, for the election of directors, and the organization of the board of directors, for suitable taxation for the support of the schools. These laws simply provide for "schools." They afford no more light as to the purpose to which they were to be devoted, or the manner in which that purpose was to be effected than would have been done by the words, "It is hereby declared that common schools shall be established and maintained in Ohio."

The various legislatures that have acted upon the subject have been content to allow the general declaration of the object of the schools contained in the Constitution to stand as the single and sufficient declaration of that object. And these remarks apply to the special law affecting the schools of Cincinnati.

Will it be said that this silence of the legislative enactments leaves the whole subject within the control of the various local boards of directors? Undoubtedly they are invested with large discretionary power with respect to the management of the schools. But it is equally free from doubt that that discretion is subject to the general purpose for which the schools were established and controlled by it. There must be a limit to this discretion. It is readily found. Would it be claimed that the School Board could lawfully require teaching only in the higher branches of learning, to the exclusion of elementary instruction? Could they give instruction only in a foreign tongue, to the exclusion of our own? As to discipline, how often it has been held that rules upon the subject must be "reasonable." Could they teach positive infidelity or immorality? Certainly not, because these things would defeat, not the declared object of the schools, but the well understood object. And, in any of the cases here supposed, the power of a court of equity to interfere would scarcely be controverted.

And, therefore, if the construction which I am now claiming for the Constitution and laws be the true one, the Board of Education possesses as little authority to proscribe the teaching of religion and morality as they have to require the positive teaching of immorality and irreligion.

But I affirm with entire confidence, as a proposition of law, that had the Constitution been as silent as these laws as to the purpose for which schools were to be established; had it simply declared that it should be the duty of the Legislature to establish schools, the construction would be precisely the same—that religious instruction would be as clearly contemplated as it is now by the express language of that instrument.

In that event, called upon to give a judicial definition of the term, the Court would examine the history of "schools" and ascertain what had been their character, what had been taught in them, and having thus ascertained what it was that had presented itself to the minds of the framers of the Constitution under that title would be amply prepared to declare their meaning. I need scarcely refer to authorities to maintain this proposition.

It has been decided that, in the absence of any declaration in the Constitution as to the number of persons required to constitute a jury, a jury of twelve men was intended, because juries had been so composed prior to the date of that instrument, and because the term had a well known signification.

Now I by no means intend to argue that the term "school" has such a technical legal signification as the term "jury" or the words "*habeas corpus*." I claim only that in the absence of express provisions upon the subject, the *general features* of the school will be determined by reference to the understanding and practice of mankind at and before the date of the enactment.

Viewed in this light, then, it must have been within the contemplation of the framers of the Constitution that the teaching of religion had been a leading object in every school establishment preceding our own, and the sole object of many.

The schools of the Grecian philosophers were chiefly devoted to the dissemination of knowledge concerning the nature of the gods and the spiritual nature of man. The public teaching of Pythagoras was but the expression of his "speculations concerning the harmony of the universe, of his profound conviction of man's immortal destiny, and the paramount import of his moral nature;" for Pythagoras, during his sojourn among the Egyptians, had been told something of the true God, which he more than half believed; and Aristotle, when he had instructed the Macedonian prince in ethics, rhetoric, and politics, repaired to the lyceum to teach a philosophy to the Athenian youth in which theology bore the most conspicuous place.

In the third century of the Christian era the Church turned its attention to the subject of the education of youth, and to this day in all the Catholic countries of Europe this interest is committed almost exclusively to its care. And in all the Protestant countries, and even in states and communities divided in religious sentiment as widely as Catholic and Protestant are divided, religious instruction is regarded as of the first importance, and is vigilantly maintained in every school system. Whether we regard the catechetical schools at Alexandria, the imperial schools at Rome, the itinerary schools of the monks, the later schools of the Jesuits, or those of Charlemagne, or the Benedictine convents, in which for five long centuries nearly all that remained of literature and the arts was sacredly preserved, or the schools of modern Europe, we find religious teaching the predominating element in most of them, and in none of them deemed less important than instruction in the arts and sciences. "*Religionibus et artibus sacrum*" has been written over the portals of all of them. And I desire briefly to call the attention of the court to the character of the systems of education of the various states of Europe as they existed at a recent date. From a report made to the Ohio Legislature in 1839 upon "Elementary Public Instruction in Germany," by Rev. Dr. Calvin E. Stowe, then Professor of Biblical Literature in Lane Seminary, I gather the following account of the primary schools of Germany, particularly of Prussia and Wurtemburg:

"The system embraces a course of eight years. In the first division, comprising two years, for children from six to eight years, is taught four branches, the first one being logical exercises or oral teaching in the exercise of the powers of observation and expression, including religious instruction and the singing of hymns.

"In the second division of the period of time, intended for children from eight to ten years, instruction is given in seven branches, the third one in the enumeration being 'religious instruction in select Bible narratives.'

"In the third division, including children from ten to sixteen years old, is 'religious instruction in the connected Bible history.'

"In the fourth division, including children of the same age, is given 'religious instruction on the religious observations of nature, the life and discourses of Jesus Christ, the history of the Christian religion in connection with the contemporary civil history, and the doctrines of Christianity.'"

The learned author of this report gives a brief and interesting account of this religious instruction.

In a report upon the same subject, made by Horace Mann to the Massachusetts Board of Education, he points out the methods by which, in the mixed schools, the pupils receive combined literary and separate religious instruction; the Protestant and Catholic children being separately instructed in the tenets of their respective churches. And Mr. Kay, in his work on "The Social Condition and Education of the People in England and Europe," speaks with enthusiastic admiration of the concessions made and forbearance exhibited by all religious sects and parties in all the German states, to the end that the harmony and success of the system should be secured.

In Barnard's "National Education in Europe," page 92, in treating the subjects and methods of instruction in Prussia, it is stated that every complete elementary school in that country gives instruction in religion—morality—established on the positive truths of Christianity.

In the public schools of Berlin instruction is given in "the Bible, the catechism, the positive truths of Christianity."

In Saxony, under laws established in 1836, religious instruction is given, but the pupils are not required to take part in it. The certificate, however, granted at the end of the term of pupilage, is only granted if the child gives satisfactory evidence to a committee composed of clergymen and teachers that he has received a certain amount of religious instruction. (Page 266, Barnard.)

The Austrian system, which is like that of Prussia, compulsory, is "based on religion and governed and molded by the State." (Page 324, Barnard.)

In Switzerland no one is allowed to exercise the vocation of a teacher without a certificate from a clergyman of his own church that he is fitted both by character and education to conduct the religious education in the school for which he is designed.

The system of France, formed on the Prussian model after its careful examination by Cousin in 1833, embraces moral and religious instruction.

The system of Holland, established in 1801, contains the following regulations:

"SEC. 22. The instruction shall be conducted in such a manner that the study of suitable and useful branches of knowledge shall be accompanied by an exercise of the intellectual powers, and in such a manner that the pupils shall be prepared for the practice of all social and Christian virtues.

"SEC. 23. Measures shall be taken that the scholars be not left without instruction in the doctrinal creed of the religious community to which they belong, but that instruction shall not be exacted of the schoolmaster.'

In Russia, it appears from a report made to the emperor in 1851, that in that country "it is assumed that religious teaching constitutes the only solid foundation of all useful instruction."

Of the Italian states, Portugal, and Spain, I need not speak. The Catholic Church still adheres to the view with which it began upon this subject.

The view of the subject which has prevailed in England is well illustrated by a judicial opinion which I will now cite.

In *The Attorney General* v. *Cullum*, 1 Young & Collyer, 411, decided in 1842, soon after the attention of the people of England had been so powerfully directed to the subject of popular education by Lord Brougham, the Vice Chancellor said: "Courts of equity in this country will not sanction any system of education in which religion is not included."

In the matter of *The King's grammar school, in the borough of Warwick*, reported in 1 Phillips, page 563, Lord Lyndhurst left the subject of religious instruction in the school to the master, being satisfied to do so when it appeared that he was required to be an undergraduate and in holy orders.

It does not at all impair the validity of the argument which I seek to draw from these citations to say that they are the examples of states and countries in which there is a union between Church and State, because,

First. In all these States and countries there are dissenters from the State religion, and the utmost care is taken to avoid injury to the just views of the different sects, and the injury is avoided by means of combined literary and separate religious instruction. But the pupil in a school is absolutely required to have some religious instruction from some person.

Second. These examples are cited to show the understanding of enlightened Europe upon the subject of the office of "schools," and they must be presumed to have been in the contemplation of the framers of our Constitution and laws upon the subject. And especially when considered in connection with the language of the Constitution, which clearly contemplates religious instruction, restricted only by the rights of conscience.

I am not informed with sufficient accuracy to speak of the extent to which instruction of this character has been given in the common schools of the other states of the Union. The laws of the different states upon the subject are very similar to our own.

So far as relates to those institutions in which the higher branches of learning are taught—colleges, academies, and seminaries—with perhaps the single exception of the University of Virginia, religious instruction is and has ever been regarded as of the first importance, and nearly all of these institutions are in the enjoyment of aid from the various states in which they are situated. In all of them Paley's and Alexander's Evidences of Christianity, Butler's Analogy, and works of a similar character, are regular text-books. Very early in the history of the colonies they laid the foundations of those great institutions that are now among the chief objects of the pride and glory of the nation, the colleges of Yale and Harvard. The propagation of the Christian religion was the chief end in view in the establishment of these institutions, as avowed by their individual promoters and in their grants of state authority.

But the law-making power of the State of Ohio has spoken directly and distinctly upon this subject in at least three instances: On the 9th day of January, A. D. 1802, the General Assembly passed an act for the establishment of the university at Athens, under the name of the "American Western University." The preamble to the act and the first section thereof are as follows:

"WHEREAS, Institutions for the liberal education of youth are essential to the progress of arts and sciences, important to morality, virtue, and religion; friendly to the peace, order, and prosperity of society," etc., "therefore, *be it enacted*,

"SECTION 1. That there shall be a university established in the town of Athens, in the ninth township of the fourteenth range of townships within the limits of the tract of land purchased by the 'Ohio Company of Associates,' by the name and style of the 'American Western University,' for the instruction of youth in all the various branches of the liberal arts and sciences, for the promotion of good education, virtue, *religion*, and morality, and for conferring all the degrees and literary honors granted in similar institutions."

The twelfth section of the act provides that the rents and profits of the corporate property should be "appropriated to the endowments of the said university in such a manner as shall most effectually promote virtue, morality, piety, and the knowledge of such of the languages and of the liberal arts and sciences as shall hereafter be directed from time to time by the corporation."

The fourteenth section exempts the property of the university from taxation.

On the 18th day of February, 1804, the Legislature passed an act upon the same subject changing the name of the proposed university to that which it now bears. This act contains the same recitals in the preamble, and the first section is identical with that of the act of 1802.

On the 9th day of February, A. D. 1809, the act for the establishment of Miami University was passed. The first section of that act is follows:

"SECTION 1. That there shall be a university established and instituted in the manner hereinafter directed, within that part of the county known as John Cleves Symmes' purchase, which university shall be designated by the name and style of the Miami University, for the instruction of youth in all the various branches of the liberal arts and sciences, for the promotion of good education, virtue, religion and morality, and for conferring all the literary honors granted in similar institutions, and the benefits and advantages of the said university shall be open to all the citizens within this State."

Here, then, is the public policy of Ohio. Here are the expressions of the understanding of the people of the State upon the subject now under consideration. It is to be observed that these are institutions for the education of youth; that they are State institutions; the land with which they were endowed was the gift of the Federal government, but vested in the State in trust, with discretionary power as to the manner in which it should be applied to the general purpose for which it was designed, and they received the further support of the State in the exemption of their property from taxation.

In these State institutions—in these "schools" for the "instruction of youth"—"religion," "virtue," "piety," "morality," are to be carefully taught. These acts were passed when the Constitution was fresh in the minds of the people; one of them, indeed, a few months before its adoption. The men who made the Constitution made these laws, and they understood that these things could be taught consistently with "the rights of conscience."

They stipulated by law that these universities should be equally open to all the citizens of Ohio, and yet required the teaching of "religion," "piety," and "morality," not dreaming that there was any incompatibility between the two provisions.

The *power* of the State to make the provision which was thus made for religious teaching in the universities was never questioned. The Federal government, by its acquiescence, signified its approval; the people of the State—and all were equally entitled to the benefits of the institutions—gave to these enactments their sanction; and it has never been whispered that, because religion has been made the basis of all instruction in them, the conscience of any one was offended, or that any person in the State was deprived of his right or interest in them.

Let it not be argued that because the Legislature had provided for religious teachings in the universities, and omitted to make such provision in relation to the common schools, it is to be implied that none was intended to be given them. The university acts provided that the liberal arts and sciences should be taught in the universities, but the common school acts make no corresponding provision in relation to the common school. If the argument should be held good, it would prohibit, or excuse, the teaching of the alphabet or the multiplication table, at the same time that it would prohibit, or excuse, the reading of the Bible. Had the University acts omitted to make any declaration of the purpose for which the universities were established, there would

4

still have been no doubt in the mind of any one as to that purpose. They would have been readily understood as directing the establishment of institutions in which "religion and the arts" were to be taught.

Nor let it be said that there is no analogy between the university and the common school in this respect, on the ground that religious subjects may properly engage the attention of the young men who attend the universities, but not that of the young minds receiving instruction in the common schools. These schools are to some but schools of preparation—to many more they are the only means of instruction—but, if religion be at all desirable to any one at any time, it is important to both these classes to receive instruction in it here—in the time of early youth, when the mind is most open to the reception of faithful teaching—before the slumbering passions have been aroused—hate, revenge, unhallowed ambition—the promptings of evil appetites—here, where the preparation must be made, and while it may be made, for the great succeeding struggle between inclination upon one hand and duty upon the other, a struggle in which none may engage with confidence, but they who are panoplied in "the whole armor of God."

The courts of this State have not been called upon hitherto to give a definition of the meaning of the Legislature as expressed in the school laws. But the people gave them an interpretation, and for more than twenty years prior to the adoption of the present Constitution, acted upon it. They understood that religious instruction was a part of the system, and hence, as your Honors have been made aware by the petition, the daily sessions of the schools of this city have been opened by the reading of the Bible, and by "appropriate singing."

In cases of private contract the Court will always construe the written instrument, where the meaning is not clear, as the parties have understood it, holding that to be good evidence of the intention. So, the construction which the people of a state place upon its laws, and upon which they act, will be regarded by the Court as of great significance, when called upon to solve a doubt upon the meaning of the laws, especially where the action appears to have been general and unquestioned.

The subject occupied this attitude at the adoption of the present Constitution, in 1851. A separate article of that instrument is devoted to the subject of education. The second section of article 6 is as follows:

"SEC. 2. The General Assembly shall make such provisions, by taxation or otherwise, as, with the income arising from the school trust fund, will secure a thorough and efficient system of common schools throughout the State; but no religious or other sect or sects shall ever have any exclusive right to or control of any part of the school funds of this State."

This is manifestly a guard against any division of the school fund for sectarian purposes. So far from being, as has been claimed, an evidence of a divorce between the schools and religion, it is an additional recognition of their intimate union. It is in furtherance of the design to exclude sectarianism from the schools. Why should such a provision be made if the schools are to be confined to secular teaching? If the seventh section of the Bill of Rights is effectual to prohibit all religious teaching, this provision is superfluous. If no religion is to be taught, surely the peculiar tenets of a sect can not be taught.

In the presence of this provision I find additional evidence that the seventh section of the Bill of Rights does not affect the question under consideration, and that this is a clear recognition of the intimate and necessary union between religion and the schools. There can be no doubt that this is the true construction of this provision, when it is read in the light of the concluding sentence of the seventh section of the Bill of Rights, which is, in substance, the same as the third section of the Bill of Rights in the Constitution of 1802.

"Religion, morality and knowledge, however, being essential to good government, it shall be the duty of the General Assembly to pass suitable laws to protect every religious denomination in the peaceable enjoyment of its own mode of worship, and to encourage schools and the means of instruction."

I have thus called your Honors' attention to these considerations:

1. That the Constitution of the State, in force at the incep-

tion, and during the full development of the common school system, required the establishment of schools in which "religion, morality and knowledge" should be promoted.

2. That the common school laws are silent as to the purpose for which they were established, necessitating a reference to the Constitution, and an inquiry into the general understanding of civilized and enlightened nations as to the functions which such schools perform—eliciting the clear response that religious instruction is one of their chief objects.

3. That the Legislature of the State, in a series of enactments upon the subject of education, declared the purpose to be the promotion of "piety," "religion," "morality," and "knowledge," thus clearly indicating the policy of the State in that behalf.

4. That the new Constitution contains a provision similar to the old one, with an additional provision against sectarianism, which is a clear recognition of the near connection between religion and the schools.

It would scarcely be denied that these considerations would make good the proposition with which I began, to-wit: That religious instruction is, in contemplation of law, an essential element in our common school system of education, if it were not for the reliance which is placed upon that part of the seventh section of the Bill of Rights, which I have not read, and which is as follows:

"All men have a natural and indefeasible right to worship Almighty God according to the dictates of their own conscience. No person shall be compelled to attend, erect or support any place of worship, or attend any form of worship, against his consent; and no preference shall be given by law to any religious society; nor shall any interference with the rights of conscience be permitted. No religious test shall be required as a qualification for office, nor shall any person be incompetent as a witness on account of his religious belief."

It has been claimed, and will doubtless be argued here, that this clause renders any religious instruction in the schools, unlawful, irrespective of any action of the School Board upon the subject. Unless this position can be made good by the learned counsel for the defendants, it would seem that the restraining order in this case must be made perpetual.

It seems to me that nothing connected with the public discussion of this general subject is so striking as the total failure upon the part of so many really intelligent persons to apprehend the history, the purpose, the spirit, or the scope of this provision, and its counterpart in the Federal Constitution. It is really supposed by many persons to be the declaration of the utter indifference of the State to all religion, and as such deplored by them. The infidel points to it with exultation as the charter of his liberty to scoff and sneer at all sacred things. The procurement of the recognition of the principle, if not its authorship, is attributed by many to Thomas Jefferson, a man who deliberately wrote that he did not allow himself to have religious opinions, because he could not certainly know that they were correct. Your Honors well know how utterly mistaken are these views.

Your Honors well know that the principle involved in this section was firmly established in the government of this country an hundred years before Thomas Jefferson was born; that it was established and proclaimed by men who had been persecuted, not for infidelity, but for religious opinions, in the just sense of that expression. They intended to secure freedom of conscience, which they never defined in any other way than the right to "worship" God according to the dictates of the conscience. I do not mean to deny that the principle is broad enough to include the right to omit all worship, or even to disbelieve in the existence of God, but it was so established because they were wise enough to know that no man could be legislated into the enjoyment of religious opinions, or a devout spirit. The very essence of the English Reformation, the very essence of Puritanism, no matter how much Puritanism may now be misrepresented or misunderstood, was the utter denial of the authority of the political government over matters of religious faith or worship. This was the teaching of Martin Luther. This principle never had a more powerful advocate than it found in the pen of John Milton.

Was William Penn indifferent to all religion, or without religious opinions? No. Yet the first care of William Penn was to establish this principle in the laws of Pennsylvania. The most convenient account of this is found in the case of *Updegraph* v. *The Commonwealth of Pennsylvania*, 11 Serg. & Rawle, 394,

The decision recites a law promulgated by William Penn, as follows:

"Almighty God, being only Lord of conscience, Father of lights and spirits, and the Author as well as object of all divine knowledge, faith, and worship, who only can enlighten the minds and persuade and convince the understandings of people in due reverence to his sovereignty over the souls of mankind. It is enacted by the authority aforesad, that no person at any time hereafter living in this province, who shall confess and acknowledge one Almighty God to be the creator, upholder and ruler of the world, and that professes him or herself obliged in conscience to live peaceably and justly under the civil government, shall in any wise be molested or prejudiced for his or her conscientious persuasion or practice, nor shall he or she at any time be compelled to frequent or maintain any religious worship, plan or ministry, whatever, contrary to his or her mind, but shall freely and fully enjoy his or her Christian liberty in that respect, without any interruption or reflection; and if any person shall abuse or deride any other for his or her different persuasion and practice in a matter of religion, such shall be looked upon as a disturber of the peace, and be punished accordingly."

And to the end that looseness, irreligion and Atheism may not creep in under pretense of conscience, it provides for the observance of the Lord's day, punishes profane cursing and swearing, and further enacts, for the better preventing of corrupt communications, that

"Whoever shall speak loosely thereof and profanely of Almighty God, Christ Jesus, the Holy Spirit, or Scriptures of Truth, and is thereof legally convicted, shall forfeit and pay five pounds, and be imprisoned for five days in the house of correction."

Judge Duncan, commenting on this enactment, says:

"Thus this wise Legislature framed this great body of laws for a Christian country and Christian people, Infidelity was then rare, and no infidels were among the first colonists."

And to this day Christianity is held to be a part of the common law of Pennsylvania, with liberty of conscience to all.

In the Constitution of the State of Massachusetts, in which

the Protestant religion is expressly declared to be the subject of the care and support of the State, this liberty of conscience is fully secured.

"ART. 2. It is the right as well as the duty of all men, in society, publicly, or at stated seasons, to worship the Supreme Being, the great Creator and Preserver of the universe. And no subject shall be hurt, molested or restrained in his person, liberty, or estate, for worshiping God in the manner and season most agreeable to the dictates of his own conscience, or for his religious profession or sentiments; provided, he doth not disturb the public peace, or obstruct others in their worship.

"ART. 3. As the happiness of a people and the good order and preservation of civil government essentially depend upon piety, religion and morality; and as these can not be generally diffused through a community but by the institution of the public worship of God and of public instructions in piety, religion and morality; therefore, to promote their happiness and to secure the good order and preservation of their government, the people of this Commonwealth have a right to invest their Legislature with power to authorize and require, and the Legislature shall, from time to time, authorize and require the several towns, parishes, precincts, and other bodies politic, or religious societies, to make suitable provision, at their own expense, for the institution of the public worship of God and for the support and maintenance of public Protestant teachers of piety, religion and morality, in all cases where such provision shall not be made voluntarily."

The Constitution of Vermont is the most happy in the form in which this principle is expressed, to-wit:

"That all men have a natural and inalienable right to worship Almighty God according to the dictates of their own consciences and understandings, as in their opinion shall be regulated by the Word of God; and that no man ought to or of right can be compelled to attend any religious worship, or maintain any minister contrary to the dictates of his conscience; nor can any man be justly deprived or abridged of any civil right as a citizen on account of his religious sentiments or peculiar mode of religious worship; and that no authority can or ought to be invested in or assumed by any power whatever that shall in any case interfere with or any manner control the rights of conscience in the free exercise of religious worship. Nevertheless, every sect or denomination of Christians ought to observe the Sabbath, or Lord's Day, and keep up some sort of religious worship, which to them shall seem most agreeable to the revealed will of God."

Notwithstanding the differences in the form of expression between the various constitutions, it is apparent that they intend the same thing—protection to the various forms of religious belief, and thereby the encouragement and promotion of religion.

The Constitution of New Hampshire contains in the fifth section the amplest provision securing the rights of conscience, and yet in the sixth section the Legislature is authorized to empower the establishment of churches and schools for the promotion of "morality and piety, rightly grounded on evangelical principles."

"ART. 5. Every individual has a natural and inalienable right to worship God according to the dictates of his own conscience and reason, and no subject shall be bereft, molested or restrained in his person, liberty or estate for worshiping God in the manner and season most agreeable to the dictates of his own conscience; or for his religious profession, sentiments or persuasion: *provided* he doth not disturb the public peace or disturb others in their religious worship.

"As morality and piety rightly grounded on evangelical principles may give the best and greatest security to government, and will lay in the hearts of men the strongest obligations to due subjection, and as the knowledge of these is most likely to be propagated through a society by the institution of the public worship of the Deity and of public instruction in morality and religion, therefore to promote those important purposes the people of this State have a right to empower, and do hereby fully empower, the Legislature to authorize from time to time the several towns, parishes, bodies corporate or religious societies within this State to make adequate provision at their own expense for the support and maintenance of public Protestant teachers of piety, religion and morality."

I do not care to make a further reference to the various state constitutions. They are uniform in substance, though various in form, and they are well illustrated by the commentary of Judge Story upon the similar provision of the Constitution of the United States:

"The real object of the amendment was not to countenance, much less to advance Mohammedanism, or Judaism, or Infidelity, by prostrating Christianity, but to exclude all rivalry among Christian sects, and to prevent any national ecclesiastical establishment, which should give to a hierarchy the exclusive patronage of the National government. It thus cut off the means of religious persecution (the vice and pest of former ages), and of the subversion of the rights of conscience in matters of religion, which had been trampled upon almost from the days of the apostles to the present age."

In Rawle on the Constitution, pages 116 and 117, the same view is presented concerning these provisions, to-wit: That they are for the protection of "religious opinions and worship."

"The first amendment prohibits Congress from passing any law respecting an establishment of religion, or preventing the free exercise of it.

"It would be difficult to conceive on what possible construction of the Constitution such a power could ever be claimed by Congress. The time has long passed by when enlightened men in this country entertained the opinion that the 'general welfare' of a nation could be promoted by religious intolerance, and under no other clause could a pretense for it be found. Individual states whose legislatures are not restrained by their own constitutions, have been occasionally found to make some distinctions, but when we advert to those parts of the Constitution of the United States which so strongly enforce the equality of all our citizens, we may reasonably doubt whether the denial of the smallest civic right under this pretense can be reconciled to it. In most of the governments of Europe,some one religious system enjoys a preference, enforced with more or less severity, according to circumstances. Opinions and modes of worship differing from those which form the established religion, are sometimes expressly forbidden, sometimes punished, and in the mildest cases only tolerated, without patronage or encouragement. Thus a human government interposes between the Creator and His creature, intercepts the devotion of the latter, or condescends to permit it only under political regulations. From injustice so gross and impiety so manifest, multitudes sought an asylum in America, and hence she ought to be the hospitable and benign receiver of every variety of religious opinion."

Chancellor Kent, commenting upon the subject of these provisions, in vol. 1, p. 657, says:

"The free exercise and enjoyment of religious profession and worship may be considered as one of the absolute rights of individuals, recognized in our American constitutions, and secured to them by law."

No, these provisions are not the evidences of indifference to religion. They are not the charters of Infidelity or the work of infidel hands. They are the monuments of Christian philanthropy —of Christian statesmanship; they are the offspring of the free spirit of Christianity; they are designed for the promotion of true religion, the very essence of which is the accountability of man to God, and to God alone, for his religious faith and practice.

The State of Ohio is not an infidel State, nor indifferent upon the subject of religion. And in this connection, I desire to call your Honors' attention, hastily, to some further legislation bearing upon that subject:

The fifth section of the act relating to apprenticeship, volume 1, Swan & C., page 77, provides that the master or mistress shall give the apprentice certain instruction, and at the end of his or her service, shall furnish the minor with at least two suits of wearing apparel, and "a new Bible." The minor is thus to go forth into the world clothed in suitable wearing apparel, and "clothed and in his right mind"—subject, I dare say, to "the rights of conscience." I commend this law to the careful attention of a distinguished divine, who is also a member of the School Board, and who, in the transport of the joy that he experienced when the end of religious instruction in the schools was supposed to have been reached, declared that the work then and thus consummated was but the beginning of a series of pious labors looking to the more complete divorcement of Church and State.

If the Bible ought not to be read in the schools, it ought not to be given to the homeless child going out into the world with naught else, without the presence of some judicious person to point out to him, at least, the immorality of the fifth chapter of Matthew.

On page 1440, Swan & C., will be found the law exempting from taxation "all public school-houses and houses used exclusively for public worship, the books and furniture therein, and the grounds attached to such buildings necessary for the proper occupancy, use, and enjoyment of the same."

"This exemption is accorded," says Judge Caldwell, *Cincinnati College* v. *The State*, 19 Ohio, 110, "because the purposes to which said property is devoted are beneficial to the community."

On page 447, Swan & C., will be found an act which his Honor, Judge Thurman, in *Bloom* v. *Richards*, calls "a mere civil regulation," but which, if it be so, is in very bad company, for it is classed among the "crimes," and there are "crimes" before it, and "crimes" just behind it. It was passed February 17, 1831, and is really described as "an act for the prevention of certain immoral practices."

It provides, in the first section, that "if any person shall be found on the first day of the week, commonly called Sunday, sporting, fishing, shooting, or at common labor," he or she shall be punished. If this act merely provides a "day of rest," and does not regard the sacred character of the day, it seems to me that it was injudicious to carry it so far. A quiet seat by the bank of a pleasant stream, with a fishing-rod, would be an admirable disposition of one's self for a day of rest and reinvigoration after six days of toil!

The third section of the act provides that "if any person or persons shall, at any time, interrupt or molest any religious society, or member thereof, or any meeting for the purpose of worship, or performing any duties enjoined on, or appertaining to them as members of such society," shall be punished.

The fourth section is as follows:

> "That if any person of the age of fourteen years and upward, shall purposely curse or damn, or profanely swear by the name of God, Jesus Christ, or the Holy Ghost," he shall be punished.

On page 911, Swan & C., will be found the Penitentiary act.

Section 5 requires the employment of a chaplain to the penitentiary, who shall hold his office one year, and receive an annual salary; that he "shall be a minister of the gospel in good standing in some one of the denominations of this State," and that he "shall devote his entire time and ability to the welfare of the convicts."

In addition to this provision, the thirty-fifth section of the act of 1835 requires the warden to "furnish each convict with a Bible, and shall permit, as often as he may think proper, regular ministers of the gospel to preach to such convicts."

The statute upon the subject of "marriages," passed in 1824, Swan & C., page 855, is very significant.

The second section declares that "it shall be lawful for any ordained minister of any religious society or congregation, within this State, who has or may hereafter obtain a license for that purpose," in the manner prescribed by the act, to solemnize marriages.

This is a very broad provision apparently. Standing alone, it would open a wide door to those who should desire to make a broad claim as to what constituted a "religious society." But it will be observed that the "minister" must obtain a license.

The third section points out the mode of obtaining a license, and describes with more accuracy the class of persons who may obtain it. Any "minister of the gospel," upon producing satisfactory evidence of his regular ordination as such, may obtain licensend, a none other.

Thus the Court is called upon to consider the express declaration of the Constitution of the value of religion to the individual, to society, and the state, with a large body of legislation looking to its promotion. And thus we are led to the question, "What religion is contemplated by the Constitution and laws?" and, in the same connection, "What religious instruction shall be given in the schools?"

The answer to both questions is simple and obvious: The religion of the Bible is the only religion known to the Constitution and laws of the State of Ohio, and instruction in its elementary truths should be given in the schools.

What "Bible" is referred to in the Apprentice act? Do your Honors doubt that it is the Old Testament and New, treated as one book? What "gospel" is meant in the Marriage and Penitentiary acts? Have your Honors any question upon that subject? Of what "welfare" is the chaplain to be mindful? The spiritual "welfare" of the inmates, of course. Do the Blasphemy acts refer to any of the gods of the ancients? Would the act exempting from taxation property used for "public worship" be held to embrace a place used for the worship of pagan deities? No espectable lawyer would make such a claim.

The *power* of the State to enact these laws, and put them in force, has never been questioned. And it will not avail the defendants to argue that these are mere regulations looking to the preservation of the public peace and welfare, as has been decided with reference to the Sunday law. *That is precisely the basis upon which the common school system itself rests.* It is a political maxim that the welfare of a republic is dependent upon the virtue and intelligence of its citizens. It is upon this ground that the State assumes the right to educate its youth. It is in recognition of its supreme importance, its overwhelming necessity. Nothing but this necessity could justify for one moment the levy of a tax for educational purposes. Viewed in any other light, the State has no more right to assess such a tax than it would have to provide for food and raiment for all the children of the State—it would simply be an agrarian law. The high and responsible duties of American citizenship require not merely intelligence in the person performing them, but virtue and intelligence—intelligence, that he may know the right; virtue, that he may do it. The same qualification is required for the performance of his various social duties, and these are equally within the cognizance of the State—if, indeed, there be any line of distinction between public and private obligations. Intelligence, without virtue, is a positive evil. It simply increases the power to do evil. It is the recognition of this truth that has made "religion and the arts" inseparable in the estimation of all faithful teachers and of all wise statesmen. The right of the State to give secular instruction can not be admitted, and its right to give religious instruction denied, upon principle. They must stand or fall together. The State asserts the right to "*educate*" the youth of the State, and the right is conceded.

Education is defined by Horace Mann in these words:

"All intelligent thinkers upon the subject now utterly discard and repudiate the idea that reading and writing, with a knowledge of accounts, constitute education. The lowest claim which any intelligent man now prefers in its behalf is, that its domain extends over the threefold nature of man; over his body, training it by the systematic and intelligent observance of those benign laws which secure health, impart strength and prolong life; over his intellect, invigorating the mind, replenishing it with knowledge, and cultivating all those tastes which are allied to virtue; and over his moral and religious susceptibilities also, dethroning selfishness, enthroning conscience, leading the affections outwardly in good will toward man, and upward in gratitude and reverence to God."

This is the view of the subject which prevailed in the constitutional conventions of 1802 and 1851. This definition, or one substantially the same, would have been given by those bodies, had they given any. It is the definition that was present to the minds of the framers of the university acts and the common school laws. It is the definition that would be given by the people of Ohio. I put the question to the Court, and it touches the very heart of this case: *Is it possible to educate youth in schools where these resolutions are enforced?* I unhesitatingly declare that it is *impossible!*

In this connection, I call the attention of the Court to the resolutions of the School Board, that their full scope and effect may be observed:

"*Resolved*, That religious instruction and the reading of religious books, including the Holy Bible, are prohibited in the common schools of Cincinnati, it being the true object and intent of this rule to allow the children of the parents of all sects and opinions in matters of faith and worship, to enjoy alike the benefit of the common school fund.

"*Resolved*, That so much of the regulations on the course of study and text-books in the intermediate and district schools (page 213, annual report), as reads as follows: 'The opening exercises in every department shall commence by reading a portion of the Bible by or under the direction of the teacher, and appropriate singing by the pupils,' be repealed."

Here is an absolute, positive prohibition of all "religious instruction," and of the "reading of religious books," "including the Holy Bible." It requires some effort of the mental faculties to enable one to fully grasp the scope of this enactment. You must consider the state and condition of those most directly affected by it—the nature and object of schools, as hitherto universally agreed upon—the object of education, as always understood—the nature of religion.

These resolutions forbid all religious instruction, direct or indirect. They forbid all incidental teaching upon the subject.

The teacher is limited to "facts and figures." Talk of the practical difficulty of giving religious instruction without giving offense! That is possible, even if difficult.

But, with a literature such as ours, religion interwoven with every fibre of it, the great theme of its best examples—dealing with human souls, conscious of their immortality—God help the teacher upon whom the task is imposed of carrying out these resolutions. That is simply impossible.

The "religion" to which the Constitution refers is, as before remarked, the religion of the Holy Bible. A familiar rule of interpretation would lead to that conclusion, even in the absence of the express declarations in the various statutes to which I have referred. The history of the country, of the State, the most prominent facts in the social life of the people, would conclusively establish it. Now, to teach "religion," even from the Bible, does not necessarily require the admission of the authenticity of every part of the Bible according to the King James, or any other version; nor does it involve the necessity of putting any construction upon such portions of it as may be the subject of differences of opinion between the various sects or denominations of religious bodies in this State. The God of this Bible is the God of the Christian—be he Catholic or Protestant—of the Unitarian—of the Jew! The general truths of the religion of this Bible are admitted by all who recognize the existence and authority of Almighty God. The term "religion," used in the 7th section of the Bill of Rights, refers to the relation between man and the Almighty God, who is also referred to in the same section. The legislature can not prohibit the exercise of that religion. But the legislature could prohibit the worship of "stocks and stones." The legislature may, and ought to, should the necessity arise, prohibit the erection and maintenance of pagan temples.

The religion of our Constitution is thus defined:

"Religion—Virtue, as founded upon reverence of God, and expectation of future rewards and punishments."—*Dr. Johnson.*

"Religion, or virtue, in a large sense, includes duty to God and our neighbor; but, in a proper sense, virtue signifies duty toward men and religion duty to God."—*Dr. Watts.*

"Directed against God it is a breach of religion; if as to men it is an offense against morality."—*Dr. South.*

"An acknowledgment of our *bond* (*a religando*) or obligation, as created beings, to God, our Creator; a consequent return of duty and obedience; godliness, holiness, piety toward God; reverence toward Him and to things sacred or consecrated to Him; a strict and conscientious discharge or observance of our duties or obligations to each other as fellow creatures, or creatures of the same God."—*Richardson's Dictionary.*

"An acknowledgment of God as our Creator, with a feeling of reverence and love, and consequent duty and obedience to Him; duty to God and His creatures; practical piety, godliness, devotion, devoutness, holiness."—*Worcester.*

It does not matter which one of these definitions is most accurate. They may all stand. Religion, according to all of them, is the theme of the Bible. Religion, according to these definitions—not theology, not dogmas, not creeds—is to be taught in the schools; and it is to be taught to the end that the pupils may become intelligent and virtuous citizens, competent to discern the path of duty in all the relations of life, and strong in the resolution to walk in it!

"It is difficult to avoid forming a false conclusion," says Abbe de Mably, in the letters addressed to John Adams concerning the government and laws of the United States, "respecting the relations of religion to our God, because they are enveloped by a multitude of mysteries; but the relations of religion *to society* are ascertained beyond the possibility of dispute. Who can entertain a doubt whether God hath intended to unite all mankind by the ties of morality and virtue; ties whereon is founded the welfare of each citizen and of society."

Cousin, in recommending to his countrymen the Prussian system of popular instruction, had expressed himself with the greatest enthusiasm with reference to the religious teaching which is so prominent a part of that system. Afterward, in a letter to a friend upon the subject, he said that this would probably occasion some surprise in France, where it was well known that he was anything but a devout believer; but that, whatever might be his individual opinions, he recognized the inestimable blessings that religion conferred upon individuals, society and the state.

I am not required to indicate the precise extent to which religious teaching in the schools should be carried. These resolutions forbid all teaching. But there could not be any and be less than has been hitherto afforded. The reading of the Bible and the incorporation of extracts from it, and from religious writings into the books used in giving lessons, is religious instruction. I grant the justice of the claim that it is but little. Unaccompanied by suitable exposition, and unaccompanied by the commendation of the teacher, the pupil, doubtless, fails to receive the complete and lasting impression that he otherwise would receive. I thank God that it is no fault of mine that it is thus limited.

But the pupil is at least advised that the Bible exists, and he will hardly fail to receive the impression that it deals with the great problems of his existence. He will doubtless comprehend that it teaches that he is an immortal being; that there is a Supreme Being to whom he is accountable. He will doubtless learn valuable moral truths which will not only be conducive to his spiritual welfare, but will qualify him for the various duties of society and citizenship. Above all, the spirit of inquiry will be aroused.

What offense against "conscience" is here? The Jew believes the existence and authority of God. He believes in the immortality of the human soul. The Catholic makes no question concerning these things. But, say the defendants, there are persons in this city who can only recognize the Bible when printed in the Hebrew language; and there are others who do not quite like King James' version, but who are well satisfied with another.

To all of this, I answer: "*De minimis non curat lex.*" I yield to no man in respect for the rights of conscience. If there is a spark of bigotry or intolerance in my nature I am wholly unconscious of its presence. But even conscience may become too tender. It may become so delicate in its sensibilities and manifestations that it will elude the grasp of even the most liberal Bill of Rights, and place itself beyond the pale of its protection! Nay, its possessor may become so vigilant and so persistent in the assertion of his own right that he will forget the rights of others.

The right of conscience, sacred as it is, must receive a sensible, practical construction, such as is consistent with a state of human society, and the existence of human government, preserving the general welfare by the enforcement of general laws.

If there are persons in this country who do not recognize the Bible, when printed in the vernacular of the country, while such persons may be entitled to the jury trial, and the *habeas corpus*, and all the safeguards that the laws throw around the citizens of this country—and may be excellent citizens withal—yet I apprehend that the laws of this country will hardly concern themselves with this question of taste. The State of Ohio will continue to give the poor apprentice boy a Bible—the James version—printed in the language spoken in this country.

But the action of the Jewish people of this city, in dissolving their own schools, and placing their youth in the public schools when the rule requiring the Bible to be daily read was in full force, speaks louder upon this subject than the words of any who profess to speak in their name.

No, the Israelites did not invoke this action. It is not even alleged in the answer that they did. If I believed that they had done so, I would, in the kindliest spirit, remind them that there are countries in the world with laws in force to this day, limiting the length of the period during which one of their race may remain within their borders, and making that period brief. I would ask them to rejoice with me that such discrimination and oppression can have no place in this land. I would point them to their elegant warehouses, to their palatial homes, their costly and magnificent temples, to the positions of honor and trust to which their chief members are frequently called, and I would ask them if, after all, there was not religious as well as civil liberty in this country.

So with reference to the difference between the version of the Scriptures read in the schools, and any other version. It is a refinement of which the law will not take notice. Especially when it is considered that there is no sectarian or doctrinal teaching in the schools, and no attempt to give a construction to that which is read.

I can not believe that this question of "version" is regarded as vital by those who uphold the action of the School Board. I am assured that a large majority of the names appended to the petitions addressed to the Board, in favor of the result which was reached, were signed with the cross, or "X," which usually indicates an indifference in literary matters, and whieh certainly would not suggest the presence of the power to pass judgment upon the merits of respective translations.

I call upon your Honors to witness that I do not rely upon the rule of the School Board, giving to the parents of each child in the schools, the right to determine what version the child shall read. If there were otherwise a valid ground of complaint, this rule would meet it, but I must be candid with myself, and I can not recognize any just, or reasonable, or lawful ground of complaint, and do not believe that any complaint has been sincerely made.

Infidelity always fights under a mask. David Hume left some infidel manuscripts, with directions that they should be printed and published after his death. "He loaded a blunderbuss," said Dr. Johnson, "directed it against Christianity, and sneaked into the grave, leaving another to fire it off." So it is here. On behalf of the Catholic Church, I utterly deny that it wants a school system without religion. It would be false to the traditions of sixteen centuries if it were so. To show that it is a reflection upon that Church, utterly unwarranted, I quote the language of the Archbishop of Cincinnati, in a communication to a committee of the School Board, having this subject in charge, the result of whose labors was the bringing forward of these resolutions.

"The entire government of public schools in which Catholic youth are educated can not be given over to the civil power.

"We, as Catholics, can not approve of that system of education for youth which is apart from instruction in the Catholic faith and the teaching of the Church."

In view of that parting declaration upon the part of the Archbishop, it requires a considerable degree of hardihood to place any of the responsibility for these resolutions upon the Catholic people of this city.

Just what the Catholic people do want to do with the schools it is unnecessary to consider here. It is sufficient to show that they do not want to send their children to any school where no religious instruction is given.

But, says the answer of the defendants, there are many persons in this city who deny the divine authority of the Scriptures, and they ask to be protected.

I have no embarrassment with this question. The law will not compel the infidel to believe—it will not compel him to support, or erect, or attend, any place of worship, or to maintain any form of worship. Thus far, and no further, will his rights of conscience be respected. For him, the Bill of Rights will be fully and fairly construed. He may teach infidelity, if he can find pupils, but shall he forbid the State to teach religion? He may have a system of morals derived from Epictetus or Seneca, and he may practice it, and teach it. But shall he deny the right to the State, representing the body of society, to prefer the lessons of the Bible, as the best means of raising up wise and good citizens? He may denounce the Bible, but the law of the State will yet give a Bible to the poor apprentice boy. The Constitution will yet require the promotion of "religion, morality, and knowledge," by the use of "schools and other means of instruction;" the law will yet enforce outward respect to religion, and the keeping of the Sabbath, and he can not stand in the way of these things. Whatever he may think upon the subject, the State thinks that "religion" is "essential to good government and human happiness," *and has formed its policy upon that conviction!* There are persons who think that legal restrictions upon rates of interest are wrong, yet have we the usury laws? There are persons who think that laws restraining the sale of intoxicating liquors are in excess of the just power of government, yet the liquor laws are upon the statute-book; there are many persons who dispute the justice of the right of eminent domain, holding it to be an unwarranted invasion of the sacred right of property, and yet even a cherished homestead must be surrendered upon the demand of a railroad or a turnpike company. Mere difference of opinion among the people, does not alter the policy of the State. That policy is fixed by law, in accordance with prevailing sentiment.

There are, doubtless, persons who do not think that "religion is essential to good government," but the State, giving authoritative utterance to the sentiment of its people, declares that it is, and will act upon that assumption, and if, perchance, while the laws of the State are being administered—while the institutions of the State are performing their several appropriate functions—even the child of the unbeliever should receive the impression that these laws and institutions are all founded upon religion, and that they are rightly founded, it would be simply the result of his presence in a society of which religion is the chief bond, and a State which is but the expression of the spirit of that society.

No man appeals to sympathy more strongly than the honest, earnest, thoughtful doubter. Such an one, in the person of Thomas, appealed to the Savior of men, and did not appeal in vain; but it seems to me that if I believed the Bible to be a fable and God a myth, I would not seek to disturb my fellow-men in their delusion, and I can not refrain from saying that the common schools of this country owe their existence to this Bible—that they were organized and are principally maintained by men who adhere to its teachings. Carry these resolutions into effect, and their interest in them and their duty toward them ceases.

These resolutions forbid all religious instruction, as I before remarked. They are, in substance, a repudiation, not only of Christianity, but of all religion, in the broadest sense of which the term is susceptible. They clearly constitute such a case as was supposed by the Court in pronouncing the opinion in the Girard will case, but from which that case was distinguished. I desire to adopt and to submit to the Court as part of my argument every word of the great argument of Mr. Webster in that case—an argument that was not answered or denied by the Court, so far as its conclusions were concerned. The holding of the Court that Christianity might be taught in the orphans' college by pious laymen, avoided his conclusion without controverting his premises.

These resolutions carried into effect signalize the complete surrender of the modern conception of education. The intellectual and moral faculties of man are so intimately blended that they can not be separately cultivated and developed. A being endowed with cultivated intellect without enlightened moral faculties would be a monster.

Upon this subject, I beg to quote the language of a profound thinker, an eminent scholar, and a devoted teacher, Dr. Thomas Arnold:

"Physical science alone can never make a man educated; even the formal sciences, invaluable as they are with respect to the discipline of the reasoning powers, can not instruct the judgment; it is only moral and religious knowledge which can accomplish this, and if, habitually removing such knowledge from the course of our studies, we exercise our thoughts and understanding exclusively on lower matters, what will be the result, but that when we come to act upon these higher points, in our relations as citizens and men, we shall act merely upon ignorance, prejudice, and passion? For notions of moral good and evil of some sort we must have; but if we take no pains that these notions shall be true and good, what will our lives be but a heap of folly and of sin? This should be borne in mind carefully; and if these merely scientific or literary institutions appear to us to be sufficient for our instruction, if, having learned all that they can teach us, the knowledge so gained shall hide from us our moral ignorance, and make us look upon ourselves as educated men, then they will be more than inefficient, or incomplete; they will have been to us *positively mischievous*."

I now submit the cause to the court, so far as I am concerned. I can not take my seat, however, without submitting the inquiry: Where will the demand for the rights of conscience end? We are educated not only in schools, not merely by books, by painting, by sculpture, and by music, but by the experience and observation of daily life, by contact with men and things. The contemplation of a stately and beautiful church edifice, with its tall spire pointing heavenward, the solemn intonations of its Sabbath bell, borne out upon the quiet morning air, may awaken thoughts of God, of immortality, of accountability; may arouse a slumbering conscience, and ultimately lead a bleeding and contrite heart to the foot of the throne of God! If this be so, ought the children of the unbeliever to be thus exposed to this constant, silent teaching? And how long will it be until the demand will come that the church edifice shall be withdrawn from the public thoroughfare, or, erected in the similitude of the private dwelling, with its spiral shaft displaced, and its muffled bell, to the end that the child on its way to the school in which the name of God is never heard, shall not see the one nor hear the other?

Argument of J. B. Stallo,

For the Board of Education.

MAY IT PLEASE YOUR HONORS—I thank my friend who has opened the debate on behalf of the plaintiffs in this cause, for the example of ability and thorough research which he has set me in the treatment of the subject under discussion, as well as for the frankness and candor so conspicuously displayed by him in stating the positions assumed by the plaintiffs and that large and respectable part of the community which they profess to represent. I can not hope to equal his ability, eloquence, and learning; but I will not be behind him, I trust, in candor. It is my purpose, as it is my duty, to reply to his argument, and thus to advance such of the propositions relied upon by us as are antagonistic to his own,—after briefly indicating, however, certain other positions about to be assumed on behalf of the defense, of which the argument of my friend is not an anticipation. There is a branch of the subject to which he has referred very cursorily, but which is, nevertheless, in my judgment, a very important topic in the discussion of the merits of his cause. I refer to the attitude of this Court to what has been termed the main question at issue.

What is this case? It is an application by the plaintiffs to this Court to inhibit by its restraining order the carrying into effect of certain resolutions passed by the Board of Education of Cincinnati, abrogating a rule, or rules, established by the same Board (or its predecessor, the Board of Trustees and Visitors of the Common Schools) some eighteen years ago. The injunction prayed for is obviously mandatory in its nature; it is in substance an order commanding the School Board to enforce the reading of the Bible and the teaching of religion in the public schools. If it is within the power and among the duties of the Court to make such an order now, it would manifestly have been the right and duty of the Court to make a similar order, upon the application of the proper parties, if the School Board had never established a rule prescribing the reading of the Bible and other religious exercises in the schools committed to their care and supervision.

It is plain that what your Honors are asked to do is nothing less than this: to wrest from the Board of Education the discretionary power vested in them by law; to usurp the functions of the School Board.

Upon what ground are your Honors asked to do a thing so dangerous and subversive of the very foundations of our government and laws? I say dangerous and subversive of government and law, because at the very base of the structure of our government lies the principle of the mutual independence of, and non-interference between, its several branches. There is an article in the Constitution of Massachusetts—one of the oldest now in force—which expresses this so clearly and emphatically that I beg leave to quote it. It is the thirtieth article of the first part of that instrument, and reads as follows:

> "*In the government of this Commonwealth the legislative department shall never exercise the executive or judicial powers, or either of them; the executive shall never exercise the legislative or judicial powers, or either of them*; AND THE JUDICIAL SHALL NEVER EXERCISE THE LEGISLATIVE OR EXECUTIVE POWERS, OR EITHER OF THEM: TO THE END IT MAY BE A GOVERNMENT OF LAWS, AND NOT OF MEN."

My learned friend on the other side has taken it for granted that the case at bar is one of the ordinary cases in which courts restrain the action of corporate bodies, when that action exceeds their delegated powers, is *ultra vires*, or is in contravention of law, or in which they annul legislative acts on the ground that these acts violate the express provisions of the Constitution, or their necessary implication. He refers to the injunction granted by your Honors in what is known as the Lamp-post case, and to the injunction recently made perpetual by the District Court, restraining the city of Cincinnati from executing a contract with the neighboring city of Covington for the supply of that city with water from our reservoirs. My friend forgets that the government of our public schools is not the exercise of corporate power at all; that the Board of Education is not a corporate body; that its action is in its nature legislative, the legislature of the State acting in this matter through a particular instrumentality, created by it for a particular purpose. To show the authority of this Court for invalidating, by its judgment and order, the resolutions of the School Board, he would have to place his finger upon some provision of the Constitution of the State, or of the United States, of which these resolutions are violative; and this he does not even attempt to do. He merely refers to a series of past legislative acts (all of them, by the way, anterior to the adoption of the present Constitution of Ohio), such as the Apprentice act, which prescribes the presentation of a Bible by the master to the apprentice at the end of his term, in order to exhibit what is termed the policy of the past legislation of the State. Now, has it ever been heard of before that an act of legislation was any the less valid because it was a departure from past legislative policy, so long as it did not transcend constitutional limits? What need is there of continued legislation, if there is to be no departure from antiquated policy, as well as from the letter of obsolete laws?

Whatever view your Honors may take of the action of the School Board, whether you regard it as the exercise of corporate or other delegated power, or as being in the nature of legislative authority, in either case you can not interfere with it. It is at least the exercise of a discretion vested in the Board by law, and no principle is better settled by the unbroken current of decisions in England and in the United States, by the unanimous declaration of the Federal as well as the State courts, than this: that such a discretion, however unwisely exercised, can not be judicially interfered with.

[Here Judge Stallo cited a number of cases in support of the proposition just announced.]

I claim, therefore, with confidence, that the matter brought to the attention of this Court by the plaintiffs is within the sole, exclusive control of the Board of Education, and that your Honors have not the right to substitute your judgment for that of a majority of the members composing it.

But now, having briefly discussed this preliminary part of our inquiry, I make bold to claim that the action of the School Board complained of by the plaintiffs is right; that it is wise; that it is both just and expedient; that it is a simple application of the theory of our republican institutions, and an enforcement of the express provisions of the Constitution of our State; and that if this Court had jurisdiction of the matter at all, its chancery powers ought to be invoked for the purpose of preventing the reinstatement at any time hereafter of the old rule, which prescribes the reading of the Bible and the celebration of religious rites in our public schools.

The new Constitution of Ohio, in the seventh section of its Bill of Rights, provides:

"All men have a natural and indefeasible right to worship Almighty God according to the dictates of their own conscience. No person shall be compelled to attend, erect, or support any place of worship, or maintain any form of worship, against his consent; and no preference shall be given, by law, to any religious society; nor shall any interference with the rights of conscience be permitted. No religious test shall be required as a qualification for office; nor shall any person be incompetent to be a witness on account of his religious belief; but nothing herein shall be construed to dispense with oaths and affirmations. Religion, morality, and knowledge, however, being essential to good government, it shall be the duty of the General Assembly to pass suitable laws to protect every religious denomination in the peaceable enjoyment of its own mode of public worship, and to encourage schools and the means of instruction."

Again, the second section of the sixth article of the same organic law reads

"The General Assembly shall make such provision, by taxation or otherwise, as, with the income arising from the school trust fund, will secure a thorough and efficient system of common schools throughout the State; *but no religious or other sect or sects shall ever have any exclusive right to, or control of, any part of the school funds of this State.*"

Phraseology more emphatic, more explicit, more unmistakable in its import, it would be difficult to devise. And yet my friend on the other side has cited these very provisions in support of his claim and that of his colleagues, that religious instruction, conveyed by reading a book repudiated wholly or in part by a large class of citizens of this community, ought to be enforced in common schools which are supported by the taxation of all citizens alike, without distinction of creed! Claims of sectarian privilege are preferred on the strength of enactments which were made canons of the Constitution for the express purpose of placing upon a surer foundation, than the variable will of legislative majorities, the equal civil rights of all men of whatever sect or creed! The reasoning by which our opponents draw such a conclusion from the constitutional premises is as remarkable as the conclusion itself. Their reasoning, if I correctly appreciate it, is based upon the assumption that the sense of the constitutional provisions, which I have adduced, is narrower than their abstract and literal import; that these provisions must be construed in the light of the history of our country, the character of its civilization and the genius of our national culture; that the founders of our institutions and the framers of our Constitution meant simply to secure an equality of civil rights as between the various professors of Christianity, our institutions being founded upon Christian civilization, and our laws presupposing and deriving their sanction and binding force from the truths of the the Christian religion, as recognized alike by all the denominations of the christian community, and from the system of morality based upon these truths; and that the reading of the Bible, without note or comment, in whatever version the parents of the children in our public schools may prefer, is not, and can not fairly be obnoxious to the adherents of any Christian sect or denomination.

Before discussing the question as to the validity of this assumption I must be permitted to express my surprise at the persistency, no less than apparent sincerity, with which our opponents urge the claim that the reading of the Bible in the public schools is not sectarian, because it may be read either in the ordinary Protestant version or in any other version preferred by the parents, and because it is read strictly without note or comment. What will the Catholic say to this claim? He will say that the relation of the Bible, in any version, to his faith, is wholly different from its relation to the faith of a Protestant; that the Catholic seeker after religious truth turns to his church and not to the Bible, which is only one of many sources of religious truth, and which indeed is not such a source at all, unless it is resorted to as a means of instruction, with appropriate comment and exposition, by the Roman Catholic Church; that the reading of the Bible, even in the Douay version, without note or comment, involves the right of private judgment, a right which, in the sense in which it is asserted by the Protestant, the Catholic denies; that the practice of reading the Scriptures without comment is an essentially Protestant practice, and a symbol of the Protestant faith. More than this, the Catholic apprehends danger from the uncommented and indiscriminate reading of the Bible, not only to what he regards as sound religious doctrine, but also (and here he is joined by many who are not Catholics,) to good morals. "It may be possible," he says, "to derive, if not all, at least a great part of the canons of Christian morality from the teachings of the Bible. It may be possible to extract the principles of Christian purity from the lives of the patriarchs, as related in the Old Testament,—from the stories of Abraham, or Isaac, or Jacob, or of Lot, or of King Solomon, or of David. It may not be very difficult to enucleate maxims of honesty and good faith from the practices of Jacob and his sons, as set forth in the Bible. It may be practicable to realize a worthy conception of the Deity from Biblical accounts, which not infrequently represent the Lord as subject to very human and apparently very ignoble passions; but to this end surely something more is necessary than a mere sticking to the letter of the Bible; to this end the infant mind, at least, must be aided by appropriate comment and exposition."

It is not necessary, however, to confine our attention to the Catholics in order to see that the reading of the Bible in any version, without note or comment, by or under the direction of a teacher in the common schools has the natural tendency to being perverted, intentionally or unintentionally, so as to subserve sectarian ends, and that it involves serious peril to the morals of the pupils. This may be seen as well if we forget the Catholics, and bring other Christians—*Protestant* Christians—into the fore-ground of our vision. To speak first of the tendency to sectarianism: nothing could be more illusory than the supposition that the making of improper comments is the only or chief mode of using the text of the Bible for sectarian purposes. The teachers in our public schools, by whom or under whose direction the Bible is read, are not abstract, non-denominational Christians; they are or may be, some or all of them, Lutherans, Presbyterians, Methodists, Baptists, Trinitarians, Unitarians, etc. Each one has his religious bias, of which he will find it difficult to divest himself when he comes to read the Bible, with some parts of which he is peculiarly familiar, and parts of which he holds in peculiar esteem, according to the teachings of his peculiar church. He selects the passages to be read. If he be an Old School Presbyterian, he may fall upon those parts of the Scriptures which seem to him to teach predestination, total depravity, justification by faith, effectual calling, the perseverance of the saints, and eternal damnation. If he be a Baptist of one school, he may single out such chapters as appear to militate against the practice of infant baptism, and uphold the doctrine of regeneration. The Trinitarian may prefer the texts upon which he bases his belief in the Trinity; and the members of Rev. Mr. Mayo's church may omit the reading of passages such as the ninth verse in the fifth chapter of the first epistle of St. John.

Judge Storer: It is admitted by all Biblical critics that that passage was interpolated after the book was written.

Judge Stallo: That is one reason why the Bible should not be read in the schools without comment. If it be read at all as the exponent of religious truth, explanations of a critical nature, showing what parts are or are not authentic should be added.

Judge Storer: That has been done.

Judge Stallo: Here is precisely the trouble. We require a great deal of commentary and critical learning to make the Bible a proper vehicle for sound religious and moral instruction. But to resume. It is but natural that a teacher who believes it to be true, what these plaintiffs allege in their petition, that the Bible ought to be read in the public schools in order that religion may be taught there, if he be a sincere and pious adherent of his faith, will endeavor as far as he can without a violation of the rule prohibiting doctrinal comment, to hedge and guard against the errors of other denominations. And without adding a word to the letter of the book, he may inculcate the doctrines of his particular faith almost as effectually as though he preached a dogmatic sermon from the pulpit of his church. Zoologists teach us that nature produces the several genera and species of the vertebrates by taking the fundamental vertebrate type and developing a particular organ or set of organs in each case while dwarfing the others, without adding to the original complement of parts in the common vertebrate structure. Similarly, I apprehend, denominational differences may be evolved by emphasizing or bringing into relief certain truths or doctrines taught or believed to be taught by the Bible, and throwing the others into the background. If the whole body of Protestant Christian faith (and such the Bible is claimed to be by most Protestants, as I am told,) is placed in the hands of the teachers and children in the public schools, these schools inevitably become denominational schools, though of the poorest possible sort. I say of the poorest possible sort, for what religious culture can be imparted by the hurried, mechanical "dog-trot" (to borrow the somewhat irreverent expression of a distinguished Protestant divine) mumbling of scriptural passages, translated from writings which, granting that they are inspired, nevertheless embody, or at least reflect, the imagery and modes of thought of other ages of various degrees of remoteness, and of races and nations whose mental physiognomy is as strange to us as their physical aspect? And it is not to be forgotten that the language of the translation even is the language of more than three centuries ago. It is not necessary to be a philologist in order to know what changes of meaning and import words have undergone during this long period of rapid moral and intellectual progress and development.

So much as to the tendency of Bible reading, without note, to lend itself to sectarian teaching. The peril to the cause of good morals is no less obvious from a variety of considerations, of which I will mention only one. Thus far, I believe, the Board of Examiners has not asked any applicant for a certificate of competency as a teacher, the question whether he believed in Christianity or not, and what he thought of the character and inspiration of the Bible. And there are men of culture quite able to pass the prescribed examination who believe that the Bible is by no means a proper standard of belief or morals. Suppose one of these men, employed as a teacher in our public schools, and compelled to read the Bible, should, for the purpose of quietly enforcing his view of the character of the Scriptures, so select his texts that the first lesson would be the story of a fratricide; the second the account of the drowning of all mankind as incorrigible sinners; the third a fraud practiced by a son upon his blind father; another, the drowning of hundreds of infants, or the slaying of an Egyptian by Moses, or of three thousand Israelites at his command, or the killing of a thousand Philistines by Samson, or the meditated attempt upon the life of David by Saul, or David's task of procuring the heads of a thousand Philistines, or the treacherous assassination of Uriah at the instigation of David, not to speak of the infamous acts of immorality and sensuality attributed to patriarchal and saintly personages. Suppose I say that an unbelieving teacher should thus comply with the letter of the rule which prescribes the reading of the Scriptures without comment, while doing violence to its spirit, who, in case of complaint, would be on the defensive, the School Board or the teacher?

It may not be amiss, before I take leave of this subject, to call the attention of your Honors to another reason assigned by citizens who have the right to be heard, why the naked text of the Bible should not be presented to their children in the schools, or even to adults, as the authoritative exposition of God's whole truth. The citizens I refer to constitute a large and I believe growing class of sincere and devout Protestants, yea, of Protestant divines. While believing, in a modified sense, in the inspiration of the Bible, in its character as a revelation of God to man, they insist that the Scriptures should be read and interpreted with a view to the mental, moral, and physical condition and culture of the races and nations, whose history they relate, or whose life they portray, or with whose morals they profess to be concerned; that there are precepts and commands both in the Old and New Testament, which it would not be proper to obey, and examples which it would not be wise to follow at the present day. And there are Protestant divines who hold tenets respecting the character and origin of the Scriptures which would seem wholly to preclude the propriety of presenting them to infant minds as a sacred book containing absolute truth. I will not speak of such men as Bishop Colenso, who is still a bishop of the Established Church, even after his trial before an ecclesiastical tribunal, or to the authors of *Essays and Reviews*. I will simply read, as an exemplification of modern Protestant thought upon this subject, the concluding page from the *Introduction to the New Testament*, by Rev. Samuel Davidson, D. D., a Presbyterian clergyman, I am informed, in good standing. "The following propositions," says Mr. Davidson, "are deducible from an impartial survey of the history of the first two centuries:

"1. Before A. D. 170, no book of the New Testament was termed Scripture, or believed to be divine and inspired. On the contrary, even after that date, different books were believed to be human compositions, having none other authority than their contents warranted.

"2. No certain trace of the existence of the fourth Gospel can be found till after Justin Martyr, *i. e.* till after the middle of the second century. That Gospel came into use in the first instance among the latter Gnostics, the followers of Basilides, Valentinus, and Marcion, who do not seem to have ascribed it to John. Toward the end of the second century, and not till then, it was assigned to the apostle by fathers of the Catholic Church and by canons. On what ground this opinion rested can not be ascertained. One thing is clear, that the fathers, who believed in its Johannine authorship, neither assert nor hint that they relied on historical tradition for their opinion.

"3. The canonical Gospels of Matthew and Mark can not be identified with the *logia* of Matthew and the things said and done by Jesus, which Mark wrote, mentioned by Papias. That writer does not himself identify them. It is also noteworthy that he put oral tradition above written documents.

"4. The writings of Paul were either not used or little regarded by the prominent ecclesiastical writers of the first half of the second century. After A. D. 150, they began to be valued.

"5. The canon, as far as it relates to the four Gospels, was not settled at the close of the first century, as Tischendorff supposes.

Not till the latter half of the second century did the present Gospels assume a canonical position, superseding other works of a similar character, and receiving a divine authority.

"6. No canon of the New Testament, *i. e.*, no collection of New Testament literature like the present one, supposed to possess divine authority, existed before A. D. 200."

It is not a little curious to see how nearly this summary of the Presbyterian divine agrees with certain propositions advanced by a Jesuit father, in a lecture on the Bible, recently delivered in this city, though the ulterior conclusions drawn by the two gentlemen, if they had an opportunity to compare notes, would probably prove to be widely divergent.

It is not necessary, I hope, to remark that I do not cite the opinions and conclusions of Mr. Davidson and others for the purpose of urging them upon this Court or any member of this Court for adoption. It is of no consequence to my argument, whether your Honors agree to or dissent from these conclusions. As a Court, indeed, you have no right to any opinion upon the subject, for it is your duty to expound the law and not the Gospels. I cite the opinions and conclusions referred to simply to show, that they are held by a number of citizens, whose sincerity you have no more right to question than the sincerity of those, who proclaim the belief that the books of the Bible constitute God's sacred archives, containing the whole body of his revelation to man, and that every word contained in them is of direct divine inspiration. I cite them, because at the bar of this Court they are of as much weight—no more and no less—as the opinions of the plaintiffs, and because those who hold opinions called heterodox have precisely the same right to have them enforced by the State, which the plaintiffs may claim for the enforcement of their orthodox belief.

It must be evident, I think, to every candid mind, from the preceding considerations, that the reading of the Bible, in any version, without note or comment, can not possibly be anything else than a sectarian exercise. And it must be further evident to all whose vision is not completely obstructed by their prejudices that the hurried, perfunctory reading of the Bible in the schools, of necessity tends more to impede than to promote religious culture; that, indeed, its only office is to serve as a badge of a particular faith—as the symbol of Protestantism, (or as a Protestant minister, who insists upon its continuance, has recently expressed it) as the flag of Protestantism on our school houses. And I insist that every flag, of whatever glorious achievements on the field of religion it may be emblematic, if it tends to drive nearly one-half of our children from the colleges of the people, which their parents have helped to establish and maintain, must come down.

To show how idle it is to assert that the reading of the Bible in the schools ought not to be offensive to reasonable Catholics and others, let me suppose a case. It is entirely possible that the time is not far distant, when the Catholics in this city will be in the majority. Now up to the days of the reformation, every Christian, from time immemorial, symbolized his faith in the doctrine of redemption, by making the sign of the cross before and after every secular act of his life, after rising and before going to sleep, before and after meals, etc. This practice is commemorated by innumerble authorities, some of which are not wholly spurned, even by Protestants. "Ad omnem promotum," says Tertullian (*De Cor. Mil.* III) "ad omnem progressum, ad omnem aditum et exitum, ad vestitum, ad calceatum, ad lavacra, ad mensas, ad lumina, ad cubicula, ad sedilia, quandocunque nos conversatio exercet, frontem crucis signaculo terimus." Similarly Cyril (*Hieros. Catech.* IV). "Fac hoc signum, sive edas, sive bibas, sive sedeas, sive stes, sive loquaris, sive ambules, sive in omni negotio, et seq." The cross is the sacred symbol of Christianity, and the making of the sign an inveterate practice, for the refusal to renounce which many of the early professors of the faith have suffered the death of martyrdom. What would the Protestants say if a Catholic majority in the School Board should enjoin this practice upon the teachers and children in the public schools? Would they listen to the plea that no believer in the death of the Redeemer on the cross could reasonably object to the emblem of universal salvation? Would not their instant reply be: It is enough for us to know that the sign of the cross is now the peculiar symbol of Catholicism, and it can not be tolerated in the schools established by and for Protestants and Catholics alike? And has not the Catholic the right, for the same reason, to say: reading the Bible without comment is the peculiar symbol of Protestantism, and it is not to be tolerated in the schools established by Catholics and Protestants alike?

Thus far I have considered the main question at issue on the hypothesis that the theory of our opponents, according to which the equality of all forms of belief before the law is applicable only to Christian beliefs, is tenable. I have argued the question as it stands between the various Christian denominations, leaving out of account the large body of citizens who are not Christians, the Jews, and those persons whose faith is not formulated in the writings and professions of any of the Christian sects, those who have lately been indiscriminately denounced as atheists and infidels. That as against the belief or non-belief of these citizens, and in view of the presence of their children in the public schools, the Bible, embracing the Old and New Testament, is not a sectarian book, can not, I am sure, be seriously contended. If they have equal civil rights with the orthodox Christians, the Bible must of necessity be excluded from the State schools, and sent to the Christian houses, Sunday schools and churches. The objection of the Israelites and freethinkers to the reading of the Bible in schools, which they have helped to erect and still help to maintain equally with orthodox Catholics and Protestants, can be successfully met only by the assertion, which I understand to be distinctly made on the other side, that Christianity is part of the fundamental law of the State and that the Bible is an organic instrument behind the Constitution, for the reason, that both our social life and our political institutions rest upon the broad substratum of Christian civilization.

The doctrine thus seriously (and in view of the exigencies of their case *necessarily*) broached by our opponents, that Christianity is part of the common law of our State, because this law has its roots in Christian civilization, is a momentous doctrine. It is pregnant with the most serious consequences. It draws in question the civil rights, as I believe, of nearly one-half of our citizens. I propose to examine it therefore candidly, fearlessly, and as far as I may thoroughly. If this is a Christian country, in the sense that the non-Christians have no rights which the Christians are bound to respect, or in the narrower sense, that the Christians enjoy rights and privileges, which the law denies to the non-Christians, the time has come for the refluence of the wave which has brought so many millions of European thinkers and laborers to the shores of the new Western world.

While entering upon the inquiry into the truth or falsity of this great fundamental theory of our opponents, I am puzzled *in limine* to understand, what is meant by the sounding phrase, that Christianity is part of the common law of the State. The law—positive civil law—either imposes duties or it confers rights. If Christianity is part of the law of the State, then, there must be certain duties enjoined upon the citizens, which are peculiarly Christian, or certain rights, which none but Christians possess. Now the duties enforced by the State, the duty to respect your neighbor's life, his person, his property, his good name, to refrain from murder, robbery, theft, defamation, etc., are not peculiarly Christian duties; they are enforced or at least enjoined by all States, whose citizens are civilized in any modern sense. They are enjoined and enforced because their observance is essential to the very existence and good order of society, and not because they are Christian virtues. I know of no duty which the State recognizes as a merely Christian duty. Similarly I know of no civil right which the Christian holds in preference over the professors of another creed or of no creed. The Jew for instance, can hold property. He can acquire it by inheritance, or by devise, or by purchase. He can sue and be sued. There are the same remedies, civil and criminal, for wrongs inflicted upon a Jew, as for those done to a Christian. The Jew can be a witness in a court of justice, for the Constitution provides, that "no person shall be incompetent to be a witness on account of his religious belief." The Jew has the right to vote. He can hold any office, for again the Constitution provides, "that no religious tests shall be required as a qualification for office." A Jew may sit upon the bench, and administer justice "*without respect of persons*," between Christians, as a Jew now sits upon the bench in New York. A Jew may not only administer the law, but help to make it. A Jew sat last winter, in the Ohio Legislature, and there is nothing in the Constitution to hinder that the majority of the Legislature may be Jews—a case which, according to the theory of the plaintiffs, would present the remarkable anomaly of a body of Jews making

Christian laws. A Jew was recently appointed, by this Court, commissioner of the Southern railroad. Jews have sat in both Houses of Congress. A Jew may be President of the United States, if he has the requisite other qualifications and can obtain the requisite number of electoral votes. A Jewish temple or synagogue is exempt from taxation no less than a Christian church. I might proceed indefinitely with this enumeration of rights, but I have gone far enough to show, that there is no particular, definite civil right, which Jews, Christians and non-believers do not share in common. And in view of this I am not able to see the force of the assertion so frequently and so confidently made, that Christianity is part of the law of the State. It is strange, that any one should at this day refer to the nebulous deliverances of Judge Story in his *Commentaries of the Constitution* (secs. 1870–1879), and seek to discredit as an *obiter dictum* the emphatic language of our own Supreme Court in the case of *Bloom* v. *Richards*, 2 Ohio State Reports, 387, which I now beg leave to quote.

"The Constitution of Ohio," says Judge Thurman, in deciding that case, "having declared that all men have a natural and indefeasible right to worship Almighty God according to the dictates of conscience; that no man shall be compelled to attend, erect or support any place of worship, or to maintain any ministry against his consent; and that no preference shall ever be given by law to any religious society or mode of worship, and no religious test shall be required as a qualification to any office of trust or profit, it follows that neither Christianity or any other system of religion is a part of the law of this State. We sometimes hear it said that all religions are tolerated in Ohio, but the expression is not strictly accurate. Much less accurate is it to say that one religion is a part of the law, and all others only tolerated. It is not by mere toleration that every individual here is protected in his belief or disbelief. He reposes not upon the leniency of Government or the liberality of any class or sect of men, but upon his natural, indefeasible rights of conscience, which, in the language of the Constitution, are beyond the control or interference of any human authority. We have no union of Church and State, nor has our Government ever been vested with authority to enforce any religious observance, simply because it is religious."

"Of course it is no objection, but, on the contrary, is a high recommendation, to a legislative enactment, based upon justice or public policy, that it is found to coincide with the precepts of a pure religion, but the fact is, nevertheless, true, that the power to make the law rests in the legislative control over things temporal, and not over things spiritual. For no power over things merely spiritual has ever been delegated to the Government, while any preference of one religion over another, as the statutes would give upon the above hypothesis, is directly prohibited by the Constitution. Acts evil in their nature, or dangerous to the public welfare, may be forbidden, and punished, though sanctioned by one religion and prohibited by another; but this creates no preference whatever, for they would be equally forbidden and punished if all religions permitted them. Thus, no plea of his religion could shield a murderer, ravisher or bigamist; for community would be at the mercy of superstition if such crimes as these could be committed with impunity, because sanctioned by some religious delusion."

It is to be observed that this opinion was the unanimous judgment of the whole Court, that the propositions here quoted were necessary premisses for the conclusion arrived at by the Court in deciding the case, and that they were made authoritative by being incorporated into the syllabus by the Court itself. And the same doctrine has been emphatically reaffirmed by the whole Bench in a subsequent case, with which your Honors are familiar.

My friend on the other side has referred to the case of *Vidal et al.* v. *Girard's Executors*, 2 Howard, 127, which is supposed to be in conflict with the decision of our Supreme Court; and he has adopted the "great and immortal" argument of Mr. Webster in that case, as his own. When he comes to read the opinion of Judge Story, who sustained the will of Mr. Girard and upheld his bequest, my friend will be as much at a loss as I am, to determine what Judge Story means by saying that Christianity is part of the law of Pennsylvania. For, after stating this proposition in general terms, the Judge proceeds carefully to evacuate it of all intelligible meaning. As he himself, if he had appreciated the real force of his reasoning, would have said, quoting from Papinian: "*Derogat generi per speciem.*" As to the argument of Mr. Webster, which has been so much eulogized by Christian laymen and presbyters, opinions may differ among those who regard it, not as a mere oratorical display, but as a defense of Christianity, and an exhibition of its spirit in the fierce duel with infidelity. Let us see for a moment under what circumstances and to what end that great argument was made. Mr. Stephen Girard, who appears to have been one of the unfortunate men to whom my Christian friend vouchsafes his tender commiseration, devised and bequeathed the bulk of his property (several millions of dollars) to the mayor, aldermen and citizens of Philadelphia, for the establishment and maintenance of a college for the education of "poor white male orphan children." Hating the sectarian wrangles of which he had been a witness in Philadelphia, but expressly disclaiming any intention to reflect upon Christianity, or any sect or person whatever, he provided, that no ecclesiastic or minister should enter the precincts of his college, expressing it as his desire "that all the instructors and teachers in the college shall take pains to instil into the mind of the scholars *the purest principles of morality, so that on their entrance into active life they may, from inclination and habit, evince benevolence toward their fellow-creatures, and a love of truth, sobriety and industry*, adopting, at the same time, such religious tenets as their matured reason may enable them to prefer."

The trust was accepted; the college was founded; orphans were gathered under its roof, and trained by good men in the ways of truth, honesty and charity. But presently it was found that Mr. Girard's will was, to use the expression of my Christian friend, a "blunderbuss loaded with infidelity to be fired off by other men, after the malevolent heathen Girard had sneaked into his grave." And, thereupon, came Mr. Webster, to empty that blunderbuss of its dangerous contents. How did he come, and in what way did he seek to interpose the shield of Christianity between the posthumous machinations of the infidel and the precious welfare of humanity? Did he come at the head of poor Christian orphans, such as that other Frenchman, St. Vincent of Paul, used to gather about him in the streets of Paris or Marseilles, and did he propose to drive infidelity out of Girard College, putting Christianity in? Not at all. He came at the head of a number of rapacious heirs (who, if they were average modern Frenchmen, must have been strange representatives of the Biblical Christianity of my enthusiastic friend), and in their name, and for their and his benefit, he proposed, by the aid of the Supreme Court of the United States, to tear Girard's will into fragments, to demolish the noble edifice of the Orphans' College, to turn the fatherless children into the street, and to parcel out the orphans' legacy among Francois Fenelon Vidal, John F. Girard, with other heirs-at-law of Stephen Girard, and Daniel Webster! Fortunately, the judges of the Supreme Court, while they listened to the eloquence of the distinguished advocate, were not duped by his sophistry. They sent him and his clients out of court with an opinion which may be summed up in the few lines of an English poet, who was cursed by the pious "evangelical" Christians of his day alternately for his popery and his infidelity:

"In faith and hope the world will disagree,
But all mankind's concern is charity;
All must be false that thwart this one great end,
And all of God that bless mankind, or mend."

Devotion to Christianity sometimes breaks out in very extraordinary manifestations. Some weeks ago I saw in an evening journal of this city a series of resolutions passed by a Christian association, shortly after the adoption of the resolutions by the School Board which purify the State schools from sectarianism, and throw their doors wide open for the entrance of the children of all citizens alike. In those resolutions the Christian association called upon all Christians to direct their prayers to Almighty God "during the continuance of the present emergency," that He might soften the hearts of those who sought to exclude the Bible from the common schools, and convert them, "even as Saul of Tarsus was converted into the believing Paul." And prayers have been said, I am told, in many of the churches, and, no doubt, in many houses, ever since. Whether your Honors were included in these prayers, so that the Lord might enlighten your understandings, I can not say. Now, what was the real burthen of these petitions, so devoutly addressed to the God of justice and right? What did these plaintiffs (some of whom were, no doubt, among the petitioners), when they approached the Throne of Mercy with their supplication, pray for? Looking beneath their form of words to their true meaning, their prayer may, without irreverence or injustice, be paraphrased into an imploration like this: "O Lord, deliver us from the necessity of educating our children at our own expense; help us to take money out of the pockets of the Jew and the unbeliever, so that we may train our youth in Thy ways; harden the hearts of our legislators and judges, so that they may shut the doors of our common schools at the approach of the poor children of those who sign their names with a significant cross or a mysterious X!" Up to this moment, I believe, there is no evidence that these humble prayers have been answered, and I trust that the answer will not come in the form of a judgment of this Court! I trust that your Honors will not overrule the solemn decision of our Supreme Court and do violence to the spirit of our liberties, no less than the words of our Constitution, by deciding that Christianity—Protestant Christianity—being the the law of the State, the rights of Jews, Catholics, and free-thinkers need not be considered. I point to the history of our country, to the spirit and language of our Constitution, to the decisions and practice of our courts, to the necessities arising from the condition of our society, and say that Christianity is not and can not be the law of the State. Christianity was part of the common law of Massachusetts two hundred and thirty-three years ago, when Roger Williams was cited before the General Court for preaching the doctrine of liberty of conscience, and was sent into the wilderness in midwinter for that offense—when Quakers were banished and Quakeresses hanged; it was part of the law of the State of New York when the penalty of death was threatened to be inflicted on Catholic priests for bringing the sacrament to the dying faithful; it was a part of the common law of Virginia when dissenters were required to build the churches of the Anglican cavaliers; but it is not to-day, thanks to the followers of the Protestant Roger Williams, and the Catholic Charles Carroll, and the Infidel Thomas Jefferson, a part of the common law of Ohio, or, indeed, of any State in the Union I know of.

Having now shown, or attempted to show, that the current doctrine, according to which Christianity is a part of the common law of the State, has not only been emphatically denied and repudiated by our Supreme Court, but has no intelligible meaning and practical import in view of our Constitution, and of our law as found in the statutes and administered in the courts, I desire to proceed a step further, and inquire whether or not it be true, as has been so repeatedly and tenaciously claimed, that not only our social life, but also our free political institutions, are grounded in Christian civilization.

I desire to examine this question, because it is one of the premisses from which the conclusion (which I have already shown to be erroneous in fact) is drawn that Christianity is the fundamental law of the State. It is the minor premiss in the syllogism, by which that conclusion is reached, the major premiss being that the law of necessity perpetuates the state of civilization in which the institutions, to which the law is subservient, have arisen. It is true that, in a strict sense, the inquiry upon which I am about to enter, is unnecessary and irrelevant. If the major premiss of the syllogism is untenable, there is no need to examine into the validity of the minor. And I deny the truth of the general proposition that the life of the past imposes itself in the form of law as a limitation upon the life of the present and future. It does not follow from the prevalence of Paganism or Judaism at the time when Christianity took its origin, that Paganism or Judaism was the fundamental law of the empire under Constantine; it does not follow that Catholicism was the law of the northern states of Europe at the time of the Reformation, because up to that time the civilization of Europe had been preëminently Catholic, or that Monasticism must everywhere remain intact, inasmuch as the learning and culture of that age had been fostered in monastic institutions.

Nevertheless, the minor premiss, above referred to, has of late been so strenuously insisted upon, and seems to be regarded as so important a part of the argument in favor of the enforcement by the State of the religion of the Bible, that I deem it proper to challenge its truth. In view of the momentous issue before us, it is best to dig up the pestilent doctrine which seeks to inject ecclesiastical dogmatism into civil law, by all its roots.

Before proceeding to say what I desire to say upon this subject, I beg leave, at the outset, to disclaim any intention to derogate from the just claims of Christianity for its achievements in history. I yield to no man in reverence for the institutions and forms which have perpetuated the great moral traditions of the human race, which have developed its blind, groping instincts of right into consciousness of duty, and by their discipline hardened the precepts of God or man into habits of virtuous life. I revere Christianity as being one of these institutions, and, in the days of its purity, the noblest of them. I revere it, because to Christianity I owe a part, at least, of that little moral culture which enables me to-day to bow with becoming humility under the commiseration so tenderly expressed for the unbelievers by my Christian friend on the other side. Above all, I revere Christianity because, in proclaiming the spiritual dignity of man, and asserting the accountability of the human soul for agreement between life and conviction, it has established—in theory, at least—beyond the possibility of denial, the freedom of thought and conscience. Having said this in all sincerity, I hope to be pardoned when I say, with equal sincerity, that I do not believe the spirit incorporated in our political institutions, the spirit which caused our fathers to found them and causes us to uphold them, to be the spirit of Christianity. While I recognize to its fullest extent the importance of cultivating Christian virtues in a republican community, I hold it to be an error to maintain that our republicanism is due to the Christian elements in the culture of our people, whether you look to the dogmas or the ethics of Christianity, its theory or its practice.

What is the fundamental theory of Christianity? A total denial of the value of the things of this life as compared with the inestimable value of the possessions in another. Christianity writes an infinite denominator under the finite numerator of this world, and thus reduces the value of the fraction to zero. In the words of Christ, and generally in the words of his followers, it asserts the equality of all men; but the equality upon which it insists is a *spiritual*, not a *temporal* equality. It is equality before God, not before the law. Whenever, in history, the teachers of Christianity, the Bible or the Church, have spoken of the realization of that equality, they have pointed to the world beyond. In the view of the Christian, the equal brotherhood of all men is to find its vindication, not before the throne of an earthly king or the bar of a republican tribunal, but before the throne of God. And it is a necessary consequence of this depreciation by Christianity of all earthly affairs, that the virtues inculcated by Christianity are the virtues of resignation, humility, meekness, obedience, self-denial, charity, etc.—noble virtues, indeed, but not such virtues as lead to the establishment or maintenance of a democracy or a republic.

Neither Hampden nor the patriots who fought at Concord or Lexington were men who tendered their right cheek after they had been smitten on the left. The truth is (however sad it may be in the eyes of my friends on the other side) that political freedom is born of the spirit of stalwart and manly self-assertion; of the readiness to do battle for personal right; of the disposition to quarrel about a penny or pound which is wrongfully exacted; and to resent—mortally to resent—every injury or insult to the person. If the founders of our liberty had been thoroughly imbued with the teachings of St. Paul, in the thirteenth chapter of his epistle to the Romans, written during or shortly after the massacre of the Christians by Nero, in Rome, they would never have inaugurated the Revolution.

Christianity discourages interest in political life, preaches submission to constituted authority, and stifles the impulse of resistance to wrong. It is doing no injustice to Christianity to say, that for more than twelve hundred years it was everywhere the faithful handmaid of despotism, whenever this was willing to avail itself of its services.

Now, for this reason, and for the further reason that Christianity inculcates uninquiring faith and undoubting belief, and represses that spirit of free and courageous thought which challenges dogmatic assertion no less than despotic behest, and which, together with the spirit of manly vindication of personal right already alluded to, integrates the spirit of modern political liberty, it can not be true that Christianity, as against the generically human elements in our culture, is the foundation of our republican institutions.

Let me not be misunderstood. While I do not believe, for the reasons already assigned, and for further reasons, which I am about to assign, that the rise and progress of our republicanism is due to

Christianity, I have no intention whatever to claim that Christian virtues are superfluous in a republican state. I do not at all mean to deny that those virtues, which Christianity, by reason of its genius has had the preëminent tendency to foster—humility, meekness, charity, forbearance, obedience, etc.—are necessary in order to temper the generically human virtues or instincts, or passions, or whatever else you choose to call them, and thus to prevent the lapse of freedom into anarchy. Such Christian virtues cement the fabric of the State and tend to uphold it. But, as all history shows, their sedulous cultivation is far more favorable to the maintenance of despotism than of republican liberty.

It is sometimes said that the establishment of free institutions in the north of Continental Europe, in England and in the United States is due to Protestantism. In a certain sense this is perfectly true, but in the sense in which the claim is now made it is the reverse of the truth. Protestantism embraces two elements which may be designated as the negative and the positive elements. Its negative element is the spirit of denial, both of dogmatic assertion and of constituted authority, the spirit of resistance to the dictation of the Church no less than the arbitrary commands of the temporal ruler, the spirit of independent belief and private judgment—the same spirit which is now denounced in this Court as the progenitor of atheism and disbelief. Its positive element, on the contrary, is its tendency to erect the transitory opinions of its adherents into permanent and binding articles of faith, to maintain forever positions temporarily assumed during its antagonisms with the ecclesiastical system from which it emerged, to substitute the authority of the dead letter of a book for the authority of the Church, or the authority of reason, and to execrate and anathematize those who seek to keep alive the spirit from which Protestantism itself was born, in terms as fierce as those with which it had spurned the traditions of the past. If we look to the former, the negative element, it is unquestionably true, that the freedom of our institutions is the child of Protestantism; but if we leave this out of view and only regard the latter, the positive element, it is as indisputably true that our freedom is in its very nature a protest against Protestantism. Dogmatic Protestantism is less fatal to civil liberty than dominant Catholicism only because it is less powerful.

To illustrate and enforce my assertion that Christianity, Protestant as well as Catholic, Christianity as it stands forth in history—is destructive of that mobility and independence of thought, without which free institutions can not endure, I beg leave to quote a passage from an author, who is justly distinguished for his truthful candor and judicial impartiality. Mr. Lecky, in his *History of Rationalism in Europe*, vol. ii., p. 90 (Appleton's American edition), says:

"Until the seventeenth century every mental disposition which philosophy pronounces to be essential to a legitimate research was almost uniformly branded as a sin, and a large portion of the most deadly intellectual vices were deliberately inculcated as virtues. It was a sin to doubt the opinions that had been instilled in childhood before they had been examined; it was a virtue to hold them with unwavering, unreasoning credulity. It was a sin to notice and develop to its full consequence every objection to those opinions; it was a virtue to stifle every objection as a suggestion of the devil. It was sinful to study, with equal attention, and with an indifferent mind, the writings on both sides; sinful to resolve to follow the light of evidence wherever it might lead; sinful to remain poised in doubt between conflicting opinions; sinful to give only a qualified assent to indecisive arguments; sinful even to recognize the moral or intellectual excellence of opponents. In a word there is scarcely a disposition that marks the love of abstract truth, and scarcely a rule which reason teaches as essential for its attainment, that theologians did not for centuries stigmatize as offensive to the Almighty.

"By destroying every book that could generate discussion; by diffusing through every field of knowledge a spirit of boundless credulity, and, above all, by persecuting with atrocious cruelty those who differed from their opinions, they succeeded, for a long period, in almost arresting the action of the European mind, and in persuading men that a critical, impartial, and inquiring spirit was the worst form of vice. From this frightful condition Europe was at last rescued by the intellectual influences that produced the Reformation, by the teaching of those great philosophers who clearly laid down the conditions of inquiry, and by those bold innovators who, with the stake of Bruno and Vanini before their eyes, dared to challenge directly the doctrines of the past. By these means the spirit of philosophy or of truth became prominent, and the spirit of dogmatism, with all its consequences, was proportionately weakened."

These words of Mr. Lecky, the truth of which no one with the book of history before him can successfully question, sufficiently show how erroneous is the assumption that human freedom is the product of Christian civilization; that Christianity has nursed the growth of spiritual or temporal independence. Christianity, like every other institution, must submit to the judgment of history; it must be tried by what it has done and avouched when it had the power to assert itself. I have already admitted that Christianity proclaimed the universal brotherhood of men; if this, its cardinal principle, had in time proved to be the principle of its development as an institution, as an authoritative and efficient teacher and disciplinarian of men, as a producer of human civilization, its history would have been a continued assertion of liberty, and our opponents would be right in maintaining that our free institutions are founded upon Christian civilization. But unfortunately the history of Christianity has been, in all its phases, and at all times, the continued assertion of despotism. This is true not only of Christianity in the middle ages, but of Christianity in the earliest as well as the most recent times. Upon this subject I again invite your Honors to hear Mr. Lecky. Speaking of early Christianity, when it was yet in the throes of emergence from Paganism and Judaism, he says (op. cit. p. 22):

"From the very moment the Church obtained civil power under Constantine, the general principle of coercion was admitted and acted on, both against Jews, heretics and pagans. The first had, at this time, become especially obnoxious on account of a strong Judaizing movement, which had produced one or two heresies and many apostasies; and they were also accused of assailing 'with stones and other manifestations of rage' those who abandoned their faith. Constantine provided against those evils by a law, in which he condemned to the flames any Jew who threw a stone at a Christian convert, and at the same time rendered it penal for any Christian to become a Jew. Against the Arian and Donatist heretics his measures were more energetic. Their churches were destroyed, their assemblies were forbidden, their bishops banished, their writings burnt, and all those who concealed those writings threatened with death. Some of those Donatists were actually condemned to death, but the sentence was remitted, and any blood that was at this time shed seems to have been due to the excessive disturbance of the Circumcelliones, a sect of Donatists whose principles and acts appear to have been perfectly incompatible with the tranquility of the state."

And, in a note, referring to Milman's *History of Christianity* and Palmer *On the Church*, he adds:

"The Arians had to pay ten times the taxes of the orthodox. The first law that has come down to us in which the penalty of death is annexed to the simple profession of a heresy, is law 9, *De Hæreticis* in the Theodosian code."

Such was Christian civilization, Christian fostering of freedom in the times of early Christianity—not in the period of mediæval Catholicism, upon which Protestants are wont to charge all the sins of persecution, but at the epoch of that primitive neutral Christianity, the paternity of which must be recognized by all Christian sects and denominations.

I forbear to speak of the middle ages—of the time when the Church was the State, and no one dared to question her authority in temporal matters. Every one within the hearing of my voice is familiar with the horrors of that period.

But, it may be said, we are dealing in this case with Protestant Christianity. Well, I turn to Protestantism and again quote Lecky (op. cit. p. 46):

"While the preëminent atrocity of the persecutions of the Church of Rome is fully admitted, nothing can be more grossly disingenuous or untrue than to represent persecution as her peculiar taint. She persecuted to the full extent of the power of her clergy, and that power was very great. The persecution of which every Protestant church was guilty, was measured by the same rule, but clerical influence in Protestant countries was comparatively weak. The Protestant persecutions were never so sanguinary as those of the Catholics, but the principle was affirmed quite as strongly, was acted on quite as constantly, and was defended quite as pertinaciously by the clergy. In Germany, at the time of the protestation of Spires, where the name of Protestant was assumed, the Lutheran princes absolutely prohibited the celebration of mass within their dominions.

"In England a similar measure was passed as early as Edward VI. On the accession of Elizabeth, and before the Catholics had given any signs of discontent, a law was made prohibiting any religious service other than the Prayer Book, the penalty for the third offense being imprisonment for life; while another law imposed a fine on any one who abstained from the Anglican service. The Presbyterians, through a long succession of reigns, were imprisoned, branded, mutilated, scourged, and exposed in the pillory. Many Catholics, under false pretenses, were tortured and hung. Anabaptists and Arians were burnt alive.

"In Ireland the religion of the immense majority of the people was banned and proscribed; and *when in 1626 the Government manifested some slight wish to grant it partial relief, nearly all the Irish Protestant bishops, under the presidency of Usher, assembled to protest in a solemn resolution against the indulgence.*"

Judge Storer. It is not necessary to consume time by enlarging upon these things with which we are all familiar. We all know that persecution is not Christian.

Judge Stallo. Certainly, persecution is against the spirit of Christianity, as your Honors understand it. And I am aware that your Honors are perfectly familiar with many things to which I have been constrained to advert in view of the extraordinary positions taken by my friends on the other side. I have felt all along as though in facing these positions, I was bringing an ancient catapult to batter down the walls of a fortress which was successfully stormed under the fire of the heaviest siege guns, a hundred years ago. But my friends choose to take these positions, and I am referring to history to show that unfortunately Christianity, whenever it had the power, practiced and preached persecution, and that this is true of evangelical Protestantism as well as of any other form of Christianity. Hear what Mr. Lecky says (page 61):

"It is often said that Protestantism, in its earlier days, persecuted because it had inherited something of the principles of Rome, but that persecution was entirely uncongenial with its character, and was therefore in course of time abandoned. In a certain sense this is undoubtedly true. Protestantism received the doctrine of persecution from Rome, just as it received the Athanasian creed, or any other portion of its dogmatic teaching. The doctrine of private judgment is inconsistent with persecution, just as it is inconsistent with the doctrine of exclusive salvation, and with the universal practice of all sections of early Protestants in its dealing with error.

"If man is bound to form his opinions by his private judgment, if the exercise of private judgment is both a duty and a right, it is absurd to prescribe beforehand the conclusion to which he must arrive, to brand honest error as criminal, and to denounce the spirit of impartiality and of skepticism as offensive to the Deity. This is what almost all the Protestant leaders did in the sixteenth and seventeenth centuries, and what a very large proportion of them still do, and it was out of this conception of the guilt of error that persecution arose. Nothing can be more erroneous than to represent it as merely a weapon which was employed in a moment of conflict, or as the outburst of a natural indignation, or as the unreasoning observance of an old tradition. Persecution among the early Protestants was a distinct and definite doctrine, digested into elaborate treatises, indissolubly connected with a large portion of the received theology, developed by the most enlightened and far-seeing theologians, and enforced against the most inoffensive as against the most formidable sects. It was the doctrine of the palmiest days of Protestantism. It was taught by those who are justly esteemed the greatest of its leaders.

"It was manifested most clearly in those classes which were most deeply imbued with its dogmatic teaching. The Episcopalians generally justified it by appealing to St. Augustine, and Calvin and the Scotch Puritans by appealing to the Old Testament; but in both cases the dominating and controlling cause was the belief in exclusive salvation and in the guilt of error; and in all countries the first dawning of tolerance represents the rise of that rationalistic spirit which regards doctrines simply as the vehicles of moral sentiments, and which, while it greatly diminishes their value, simplifies their character and lessens their number."

One more passage in the same connection (page 50):

"As late as 1690 a synod was held at Amsterdam, consisting partly of Dutch and partly of French and English ministers, who were driven to Holland by persecution, and in that synod the doctrine that the magistrate has no right to crush heresy and idolatry by the civil power, was unanimously pronounced to be false, scandalous, and pernicious. When Descartes went to Holland, the Reformed clergy directed against him all the force of their animosity, and the accusation by which they endeavored to stir up the civil power against the author of the most sublime of all modern proofs of the existence of the Deity was Atheism. The right of the civil magistrate to punish heresy was maintained by the Helvetic, Scottish, Belgic, and Saxon confessions. Luther, in reply to Philip of Hesse, distinctly asserted it. Calvin, Beza, and Jurieu, all wrote books on the lawfulness of persecution. Knox, appealing to the Old Testament, declared that those who were guilty of idolatry, might justly be put to death. Cranmer and Ridley, as well as four or five other bishops, formed the commission, in the reign of Edward VI, for trying Anabaptists, and if we may believe Fox, it was only by the long and earnest solicitation of Cranmer that Edward consented to sign the warrant that consigned Jean Bocher to the flames. The only two exceptions to this spirit among the leaders of the Reformation seem to have been Zwinglius and Socinus. The first was always averse to persecution; the second was so distinctly the apostle of toleration that this was long regarded as one of the peculiar doctrines of his sect."

It is needless to quote further. Every intelligent student of history knows that Christianity, as the architect of states, or mother of civilizations, has never, during the whole period of its ascendancy and vigor, either practiced or taught anything but despotism; that it has promoted the cause of freedom only by the violence of its attempts to repress it, which roused the irrepressible spirit of manly independence. I have not the time to delineate the history of Christianity—Protestant Christianity—from the pristine days of the Reformation to the present age so as to make it evident that its intolerance has invariably found its measure in the extent of its power; the literature and legislation of Europe during the last three centuries afford overwhelming proof of the fact, that the seeming alliance between freedom and Christianity in some cases was merely an accident attributable to other causes. Christian sects and denominations have been tolerant at times—when they were in the minority; but as soon as the temporal power was within their grasp, they did not hesitate a moment to wield it so as to crush out the spirit of liberty. Early Christian writers, such as Lactantius, preached toleration—under the Roman emperors; a few Puritan roundheads advocated freedom of conscience—under Charles I, before his head rolled in the dust at White Hall; even Anglicans proclaimed the rights of independent belief—during the supremacy of the Puritans in England, as Calvert and Baltimore established religious freedom in Maryland when they were fugitives from the persecutions of their native land, where Englishmen were "hanged, boweled, and quartered," for saying a mass, or repeating the Lord's prayer without the ascription. When you hold up John Milton's immortal defense of the rights of conscience, in his *Areopagitica* to an Anglican churchman, he tells you that there is in the literature of his church a defense equally noble, the *Liberty of Prophesying*, by Jeremy Taylor. But it is a sad fact that this book was written while Taylor was an exile in Wales, after the dethronement and decapitation of Charles I, and before the Restoration, and that he recanted his doctrines when Charles II made him an Irish bishop. "If Jeremy Taylor," says Mr. Coleridge (*Notes on English Divines*, i, 209), "had not in effect retracted after the Restoration—if he had not, as soon as the Church had gained power, most basely disclaimed and disavowed the principle of toleration, and apologized for the publication by declaring it to have been a *ruse de guerre*, currying pardon for his past liberalism by charging, and most probably slandering, himself with the guilt of falsehood, treachery, and hypocrisy, his character as a man would have been almost stainless."

"But," my friends on the other side will interject, "you are speaking of the history of Christianity in Europe; we point to the history of Protestant, liberal Christianity in this country." Alas! this American Protestant Christianity has not been recreant to the teachings and practices of its European precursors. All honor to the Puritans! all honor to the earnestness of their belief! all honor to the virtue and purity of their lives! They came, victims of the persecutions of the established church of England, but they lost not a moment in establishing the equally intolerant church of puritanism. Need I appeal to history, to cite the pages of Bancroft or Hildreth, or quote from the *New England Tragedies* of Longfellow, to show what freedom—religious and civil freedom—was in Puritan times?

"It was," says Prof. Gammell, in his *Life of Roger Williams*, p. 14, "to escape oppression for themselves, not to secure the boon of freedom to others; to carry into practice their own views of Christian worship, and their own doctrines of civil liberty, not to open a temple for the disciples of every faith and the adherents of every creed, that they had braved the ocean and the wilderness, and begun to plant their civil and religious institutions beneath these unpropitious skies. To secure the accomplishment of this object, the dearest which their hearts could cherish, all their legislation was designed, and all the arrangements of their society were framed.

"It was in accordance with this that they reserved to themselves the right of admitting only whom they pleased as freemen of the colony; and within a little more than a year after their arrival, they 'ordered and agreed that, for time to come, no man should be admitted to the freedom of the body politic but such as are members of some of the churches within the limits of the same.'

"It was the aspiration of the Puritans to form a Christian republic after the model of the Jewish theocracy, in which the laws of Moses should constitute the rules of civil life. Their system, thus educed from the highest sources of authority, tolerated no contradiction and allowed of no dissent. The mandates of public sentiment, not less than the enactments of the General Court, in the infant colony, were as stern and unyielding as had been the statutes of uniformity, from whose tyrannical operation they had fled when they embarked for the shores of the new world.

"Wrapped in their singular and somewhat original social system, there lay the germs both of immense good and immense evil; of a moral energy that was to bless the world by the results it has produced, and of dissensions that were to rend their youthful republic, and kindle the fires of intolerance and fanaticism even upon the spots most sacred to freedom."

I will not stop to refer to the legislation of the Colonies—to the legislation, not only of the New England Puritan colonies, but of the colonies settled by Christians of various Protestant denominations, to make it appear that the Christian element in the civilization of our country was not the progenitor of that "Christian statesmanship" to which my friend Mr. Ramsay so confidently attributes the freedom of our institutions. It is sufficient for my purpose to point to the constitutions of the several colonies, in force at the time of the American Revolution, in which the Christian spirit of our fathers is unmistakably reflected. Hear what Mr. Hildreth says in his *History of the United States*, (vol. iii, 1st series, p. 382):

"The provisions of these early constitutions," writes Mr. Hildreth, "on the subject of religion, betrayed a curious struggle between ancient bigotry and growing liberality. On the eve of the Revolution, Congregationalism still continued the established religion in Massachusetts, New Hampshire and Connecticut. The Church of England enjoyed a similar civil support in all the southern colonies, and partially so in New York and New Jersey. It was only in Rhode Island, Pennsylvania and Delaware that the equality of all Protestant sects had been acknowledged—an equality in the two latter colonies extended also to the Catholic religion, the public exercise of which was illegal in most or all the others, Catholic priests being liable, in Massachusetts and New York, to perpetual imprisonment, or even death.

"The Constitution of Massachusetts seemed to guarantee entire freedom of religious opinions and the equality of all sects; yet, the Legislature was expressly authorized and implicitly required to provide for the support of ministers, and to compel attendance on their services—a clause against which the people of Boston protested and struggled in vain.

"The Legislature also took upon itself to subject to heavy penalties any who might question received notions as to the nature, attributes and functions of the Deity, or the divine inspiration of any book of the Old or New Testament; reviving, in fact, the old colonial laws against blasphemy.

"Similar laws remained in force in Connecticut, and were re-enacted in New Hampshire. Favored by the Legislature, and still more so by the Courts, Congregationalism continued to enjoy in these three States the prerogatives of an established church, and to be supported by taxes from which it was not easy for dissenters to escape, nor possible except by contributing to the support of some other church on which they regularly attended. The ministers once chosen held their places for life, and had a legal claim for their stipulated salaries unless dismissed for causes deemed sufficient by a council mutually chosen from among the ministers and members of the neighboring churches.

"The Church of England, the majority of whose members were loyalists, lost by the Revolution the establishment it had possessed in the southern colonies, and the official countenance and the privileges it had enjoyed in New York and New Jersey. But it retained its parsonages, glebe lands and other endowments which, in some of the States, and especially in the city of New York, were by no means inconsiderable.

"By the second Constitution of South Carolina the 'Christian Protestant religion' was declared to be the established religion of that State.

"All persons acknowledging one God and a future state of rewards and punishments were to be freely tolerated; if, in addition, they held Christianity to be the true religion, and the Old and New Testaments to be inspired, they might form churches of their own, entitled to be admitted as a part of the establishment. The election of their own ministers was secured to all the churches, which were to be entirely supported out of their own funds and the voluntary contributions of their members.

"The Constitution of Maryland contained an authority to the Assembly to levy a 'general and equal tax' for the support of the Christian religion, to be applied to the maintenance of such minisister as the tax-payer should designate, or, if he preferred it, to the support of the poor; but no attempt was ever made by the Maryland Assembly to exercise the authority thus vested in it.

"No mention was made of the subject of religion in the Constitution of Virginia, but the question came up in the first Assembly.

"By the influx of Scotch-Irish Presbyterians and other dissenters, especially Baptists, into the upper counties, the Episcopalians had become a minority of the people. But they still had a majority in the Assembly, and it was only after warm debates that Jefferson and George Mason procured the passage of a law repealing all the old disabling acts, legalizing all modes of worship, releasing dissenters from parish rates, and suspending their collection until the next session; a suspension made perpetual in 1779, and the more readily, as most of the clergymen of the Church of England were tories.

"By the Religious Freedom act of 1785 all parish rates were abolished and all religious tests abrogated. This act, of which the passage was procured by the earnest efforts of Jefferson and Madison, seconded by the Presbyterians, Baptists and other dissenters from the late established church, seemed to them the more imperatively called for in consequence of an attempt the year before, supported by Washington and Henry, and nearly successful, to pass a law in conformity to the ecclesiastical system of New England, compelling all to contribute to the support of some minister.

"By the Constitutions of New York, Delaware and Maryland, priests or ministers of any religion were disqualified to hold any political office. In Georgia they could not be members of Assemblies. All gifts to pious uses were absolutely prohibited by the Constitution of Maryland, except grants of land not exceeding two acres each, as sites for churches and churchyards.

"In several of the States religious tests were still kept up, and they were even to be found in some constitutions which, in other respects, were among the most liberal. The old prejudice against the Catholic religion could not so easily be got rid of. In New Hampshire, New Jersey, North Carolina, South Carolina and Georgia the chief officers of State were required to be Protestants.

"In Massachusetts and Maryland all office holders must declare their belief in the Christian religion; in South Carolina they must also believe in a future state of rewards and punishments; in North

Carolina and Pennsylvania they were required to acknowledge the inspiration of the Old and New Testaments, and in Delaware to believe in the doctrine of the Trinity.

"Though somewhat softened from the harshness of former times, religious bigotry and intolerance were by no means extinct. The French alliance had, however, a powerful effect in diminishing the deep-seated prejudices against Catholicism, and Rhode Island presently set an example of liberality in this particular by repealing the law, so contrary to the spirit of her charter, by which Catholics were prohibited from becoming voters. The old colonial laws, for the observation of Sunday, continued in force in all the States.

"Only the Constitutions of Pennsylvania, North Carolina, Massachusetts, Georgia and the second one of New Hampshire, made any mention of the all-important subject of education, and except in Massachusetts and New Hampshire the clauses on that subject, by which the Legislature were required to establish schools for general instruction, remained, in fact, a dead letter."

In view of the state of facts thus exhibited I think I have the right to protest against the assertion of my friend that the freedom of our institutions is the outgrowth of Christianity—even of American Protestant Christianity. This does not, of course, constrain me to become the champion of the counter-proposition held in so much horror by my friend, that "the charters of our liberties are the charters of infidelity." It is one of the lessons of history, however, that when mankind during the last fifteen hundred years, has made any decided progress toward civil or religious freedom, the epoch is invariably marked by inroads upon Christianity by non-Christian influences. The age of the Reformation was also the age of the Humanists, the age of Reuchlin and his compeers, who renewed the acquaintance of Europe with the letter and spirit of Greek and Roman literature; it was, moreover, the age of those independent thinkers who first dared to look beyond the Bible and the text-books of theology into the books of nature and history. The epoch of our revolution was the epoch of French and English skepticism, the effluence of whose spirit pervaded the air of the colonies no less than the atmosphere of Europe. When my friend proclaims indignantly that the charter of our liberties "is not the work of infidel hands" I can not refrain from reminding him that the Declaration of Independence was written by Thomas Jefferson, whom he, himself, denounced as an infidel, in terms as bitter as is consistent with his Christian charity, that the "pious old heathen," Benjamin Franklin, helped him, and that the fathers of the Revolution read the "Rights of Man" of "infidel" Thomas Paine. And I beg leave further to remind him that the men who assembled in Philadelphia to frame our Constitution were, many of them, imbued with the spirit of free thought then prevalent. I am not without apprehension that this will be found to be true, to a certain extent, of *George Washington—clarum et venerabile nomen*—who presided in that Convention; that when you turn to the reliable accounts of his life, and not to the accounts of the rhetoricians, who have seen fit to meddle with it, the suspicion will arise that he would hardly have subscribed to any of the dogmatic creeds of the day, though in the noblest ethical sense of the term, no man had a better right than he to call himself a Christian.

Judge Storer. He was a member of the Episcopal Church.

Judge Stallo. I know it; but your Honor also knows what he is reported to have said to the quarrelsome wardens of his church. If the traditions of the day do not do him great injustice it was fortunate for him that our laws against blasphemy, to which my friend referred, were not in force in Virginia.

Judge Storer. There is no doubt of that.

Judge Stallo. Assuredly not; and I do not think it is the greatest of crimes now and then to let off a truth *ore rotundo.*

There is a curious illustration of the spirit which pervaded the Constitutional Convention in an incident recorded by Mr. Madison. I find it in Elliott's abbreviation of the Madison Papers—(Elliott's *Debates*, v. 254). It seems that there was a time in the deliberations of the Convention when Dr. Franklin feared lest its labors should not be brought to a successful close, and proposed—with what degree of sincerity I do not undertake to say—to call in the clergymen of Philadelphia and request them to preface the discussions with prayer. Mr. Sherman seconded the motion, but Mr. Hamilton and others expressed doubts as to the propriety of the measure. And I am sorry to be obliged to say that the resolution was tabled upon the remark of Mr. Williamson, that "the true cause of the omission (to have prayers said) could not be mistaken. *The Convention had no funds.*" And no prayer was said at any time before, during or after the deliberations of the Convention, and I may add that the name of God does not occur anywhere in that charter of our liberties except in the formal date of the signatures. Our Jacobin friend, Mr. Groesbeck, was not there to legislate the Lord into existence by expressing "gratitude to Almighty God for our freedom," after the manner of his predecessors of the first French revolution, who prided themselves in alternately establishing and annulling the existence of God by their decrees. In this connexion it is worthy of note that the customary conclusion "so help me God" is omitted from the formula of the oath, which the Constitution prescribes the President to take. All this certainly does not prove that the Constitution is a "monument of infidelity;" it only proves that its framers understood civil government to be a purely secular institution, and to have no direct concern with things spiritual. It was in obedience to this conviction that Thomas Jefferson, while he was President, persistently refused to proclaim days of thanksgiving and prayer, and that James Madison even hesitated when called upon to sign a bill for the incorporation of a church.

"*Fuit hœc sapientia quondam,*
Publica privatis secernere; sacra profanis."

And this brings me to the great fundamental proposition of our defense, which most effectually disposes of the claim of the plaintiffs that Christianity is part of the law of the state—to the proposition that, since the establishment of our republican liberty, the divorce of the State from the Church, of civil government from religion, is not merely a divorce *a mensa et thoro*, as Judge Story and some New York and Pennsylvania judges have thought, but a divorce *a vinculo matrimonii.* But, before I proceed to make a few observations upon this all-important head, permit me to say another word in the line of discussion which I have pursued during the last hour.

I deny, not only that Christianity is the law of the State, and that the freedom of our institutions is grounded in Christian civilization, but I deny, also, that our modern European and American civilization can in any just sense be called Christian. By the term civilization we designate the materials and forces of the physical, intellectual, and moral culture of a people. Now, in the first place, the intellectual possessions which make up the stock of our culture, and their corresponding material possessions, are not only not the gains and emoluments of Christianity, but have been acquired in spite of its resistance and recalcitration. It is not Christianity which has expanded our mental and physical horizon to coextension with spatial infinity, which has revealed to us the laws according to which the stellar, planetary, and satellitic orbs form or develop themselves in the ethereal expanse, and in obedience to which they rotate and revolve, under the invisible guidance of immutable attraction, in their perennial courses; it is not Christianity which has unveiled the mysteries of our planetary history, or armed us with the power by the aid of which we subject the elements to our dominion. Copernicus dedicated his immortal book to a pope, but a pope sealed it to the eyes of all faithful believers; and his inquisitors interposed the walls of a prison between the heavens and Galileo, because he had dared to look into their depths through a telescope, and to open his mind to the truth of the heliocentric theory. Nor was it the pope or the Catholic church alone who sought to extinguish the dawning light of the new era, or to obstruct the vision of awakening humanity. Luther and Melanchthon denounced the Copernican system as fiercely as the inquisitors of Rome; and John Kepler, the discoverer of the laws of which Newton's *Principia* are but the mathematical verification, had to turn his back upon a Protestant university—his *alma mater*—because of his heliocentric belief, and to seek employment as a tutor in a Catholic Austrian college. There is hardly one of the eminent investigators to whose labors we owe the sciences of astronomy, physics, chemistry, geology, physiology, etc., who has not been under the ban of the churches and proscribed by the monopolists of salvation. When in the lapse of ages, after the first centuries of the Christian era, has Christianity baptized or stood sponsor to any of the new truths which were born into the world to redeem it from a part of its miseries and woes, or when has it welcomed them with a benediction? Whenever, of late as of yore, the precursory glimmer of an unwonted light has brightened the skies, the surest and readiest way to discover its source has been to look in the direction in which the pope and his church have driven their latest anathema, or a Protestant ecclesiastic has sent his loudest curse. At this very moment Europe is in a roar from the discharge of ecclesiastical artillery at the zoologists and physiologists who seek to refer the evolution of organic beings to the same immutable laws which preside over the genesis of all the phenomena of this universe.

Judge Storer. Do you allude to the man who thinks that our ancestry runs into the animal creation?

Judge Stallo. I allude to the followers of Charles Darwin, who has formulated (and, I think, imperfectly formulated) the doctrine that man, too, was not placed miraculously on the highest round in the ladder of organic progression, but in some way had to scale that ladder, step by step.

Our planet has not described a quadrant of its annual orbit since the day, when its hills glowed with bonfires and its valleys resounded with festive clamor in centennial commemoration of the natal hour of a great and good man, who, seeing at a glance, what had dawned upon the ages before him, and resuming in one thought the meditations of centuries, proclaimed, that in the lines, which are the true graphic representations of the laws of this Universe, is written the word, which he adopted as the title of the noblest book of our century: the word signifying immutable order and indelible beauty. It was the natal day of *Alexander Humboldt.* Whoever wished to find the places, which were dark, and to see the men who were silent and gloomy, on that day, had but to look at our churches and the persons who entered there. I am proud to be able to say, for the honor of my clients, the Board of Education, that among those whose hearts were glad on the 14th of September, to whom Humboldt's birthday was a holiday, were the boys and girls of the Common Schools of Cincinnati.

Christianity does not, in any of the brilliant constellations which appear in the firmament of our modern culture, read the words: "*In hoc signo vinces;*" and it calls no light blessed which promises to dispel the mystic haze of former days. Nor does it vouchsafe its benignity to the deeds of the great benefactors of our times, who make their knowledge and skill the common property of the age. The instances are rare, indeed, where it has hallowed the vigils and toils of genius in its endeavor to devise new engines for the lightening of human labor or the easing of human poverty. It is not to Christianity that we owe the steam engine, or the telegraph, or the spectroscope, or any of the other appliances by means of which we shorten the roads to knowledge or to wealth.

"But," it is whispered, "the ethical part, at least, of our culture is incontestably a contribution of Christianity. We are a moral people, so far as we are a Christian people. It was Christianity which planted the dicotyledonous seed of love of God and love of man, and from this double germ has sprung the noble tree whose fruits of benevolence and mercy have made the word 'Christian' a term descriptive of everything generous and lofty in our moral nature."

Far be it from me to deny or disparage the inestimable blessings which Christianity has conferred upon man (whether you regard him as having fallen from primeval grace or as struggling up from primeval barbarity), by bringing him the gospel of love and charity and justice. Far be it from me to refuse my homage to the spirit which animates layman or priest, when he visits the sick, or clothes the naked, or feeds the hungry, or shelters the wandering stranger, or consoles the dying sinner. I cheerfully admit that sublimer words, or words of greater import, can not be found in the religious or other books of any people, than the simple words of Christ, which, according to Him, are all the law: "Whatever ye would that men shall do to you, do ye even so to them;" or, "Love thy neighbor as thyself."

But it must not be forgotten, that the maxims embodied in these words did not originate with Christ or Christianity; that they are as old as the traditions of the Aryan and Semitic families, or indeed, as the traditions of the human race. Even the Bible contains evidence of this; for we read in the Old Testament, in Micah (vi, 8): "And what does the Lord require of thee, but to do justly and to love mercy, and to walk humbly with thy God." Nor must it be overlooked, that the influence of Christianity upon morals has not consisted solely in the inculcation and enforcement of the injunctions of Christ, but in a large and perhaps even greater degree in the inevitable effect of the methods and sanctions resorted to for this purpose. Christianity taught men to love their neighbors, but also to regard them as utterly lost, if they could not or would not believe in its doctrinal tenets; it taught them to do unto others as they would be done by, but it also burned the heretic at the stake, and led Christian hosts against peaceful nations to exterminate them, if they could not exterminate their beliefs. Christianity incrusted the simple principles of charity and justice with innumerable layers of dogmatic assertion, and held up devout acquiescence in these as conditions of salvation more essential than conformity of life to the eternal principles of right. Of what avail is it, in the eyes of most Christians, to lead a virtuous and upright life, if you do not believe in the Trinity or justification by faith?

In one sense Christianity, though not, as is sometimes claimed, the only source from which the living waters of virtue and morality flow, has nevertheless sweetened and purified these waters; but in another sense it has tainted and polluted them. And I give expression to an obvious truth, when I say, that humanity has, in some measure, paid the debt of gratitude which it owes to Christianity for refining and ennobling it, by reacting in its turn with its progress—I mean that progress which is due to agencies in which Christianity has no part—upon Christianity, emancipating its ethics from the shackles of dogmatism. This is so beautifully expressed by Mr. Lecky, whom I have already laid so largely under contribution, that I can not forbear to quote him again (*History of Rationalism*, i, 200).

"If we were to judge the present position of Christianity by the tests of ecclesiastical history, if we were to measure it by the orthodox zeal of the great doctors of the past, we might well look upon its prospects with the deepest despondency and alarm. The spirit of the Fathers has incontestably faded. The days of Athanasius and Augustine have passed away—never to return. The whole course and tendency of thought is flowing in another direction. The controversies of bygone centuries ring with a strange hollowness on the ear. But if, turning from ecclesiastical historians, we apply the exclusively moral tests which the New

Testament so invariably and so emphatically enforces; if we ask whether Christianity has ceased to produce the living fruits of love and charity and zeal for truth, the conclusion we shall arrive at would be very different. If it be true Christianity to dive with a passionate charity into the dark recesses of misery and of vice, to irrigate every quarter of the earth with the fertilizing stream of an almost boundless benevolence, and to include all the sections of humanity in the circle of an intense and efficacious sympathy; if it be true Christianity to destroy or weaken the barriers which had separated class from class and nation from nation, to free war from its harshest elements, and to make a consciousness of essential equality, and of a genuine fraternity, dominate over all accidental differences; if it be, above all, true Christianity to cultivate a love of truth for its own sake, a spirit of candor and of tolerance toward those with whom we differ; if these be the marks of a true and healthy Christianity, then never since the days of the Apostles has it been so vigorous as at present, *and the decline of dogmatic systems and of clerical influence has been a measure, if not a cause, of its advance.*"

Having proceeded to this length, I have no hesitation in adding, that the standards of morality are by no means all of Christian erection. Indeed the proclamation of a truth or the distinct affirmance of an ethical principle by the founders of a philosophical or religious system never *precedes* but always *succeeds* the recognition of that truth or the appreciation of that principle by society; it is but a summing up and formulation of the outward or inward experiences of mankind. "It is only in the dusk, when the day has passed," says a German thinker, "that the owl of Minerva begins its flight."

That the origin of our system of ethics can not be referred to the writings held sacred by Christians and that no complete code of morality can be eliminated from its contents, has been often shown. Let me read a few sentences from the pen of a writer, with all of whose opinions I do not agree, but whose conclusions are of as much weight, as those of any thinker of the age. Mr. John Stuart Mill in his *Essay on Liberty*, page 94 (Boston edition), says:

"Before pronouncing what Christian morality is or is not, it would be desirable to decide what is meant by Christian morality. If it means the morality of the New Testament, I wonder that any one who derives his knowledge of this from the book itself, can suppose that it was announced, or intended, as a complete doctrine of morals. The Gospel always refers to a pre-existing morality, and confines its precepts to the particulars in which that morality was to be corrected, or superseded by a wider and higher, expressing itself, moreover, in terms most general, often impossible to be interpreted literally, and possessing rather the impressiveness of poetry or eloquence than the precision of legislation. To extract from it a body of ethical doctrine has never been possible without eking it out from the Old Testament—that is, from a system elaborate, indeed, but in many respects barbarous, and intended only for a barbarous people. St. Paul, a declared enemy to this Judaical mode of interpreting the doctrine and filling up the scheme of his Master, equally assumes a pre-existing morality, namely: That of the Greeks and Romans; and his advice to Christians is in a great measure a system of accommodation to that, even to the extent of giving an apparent sanction to slavery. What is called Christian, but should rather be termed theological, morality, was not the work of Christ or the Apostles, but is of much later origin, having been gradually built up by the Catholic Church of the first five centuries, and though not implicitly adopted by moderns and Protestants, has been much less modified by them than might have been expected. For the most part, indeed, they have contented themselves with cutting off the additions which had been made to it in the middle ages, each sect supplying the place by fresh additions, adapted to its own character and tendencies. That mankind owe a great debt to this morality, and to its early teachers, I should be the last person to deny; but I do not scruple to say of it, that it is, in many important points, incomplete and one-sided, and that unless ideas and feelings not sanctioned by it had contributed to the formation of European life and character, human affairs would have been in a worse condition than they now are. Christian morality (so-called) has all the characters of a reaction. It is, in great part, a protest against Paganism. Its ideal is negative rather than positive; passive rather than active; innocence rather than nobleness; abstinence from evil, rather than energetic pursuit of good; in its precepts, as has been well said, "thou shalt not" predominates unduly over "thou shalt." In its horror of sensuality, it made an idol of asceticism, which has been gradually compromised away into one of legality. It holds out the hope of Heaven and the threat of hell, as the appointed and appropriate motives to a virtuous life; in this, falling far below the best of the ancients, and doing what lies in it to give to human morality an essentially selfish character, by disconnecting each man's feelings of duty from the interest of his fellow-creatures, except so far as a self-interested inducement is offered to him for consulting them. * * * * * And while, in the morality of the best Pagan nations, duty to the State holds even a disproportionate place, infringing on the just liberty of the individual; in purely Christian ethics, that grand department of duty is scarcely noticed or acknowledged. It is in the Koran, not the New Testament, that we read the maxim, "A ruler who appoints any man to an office, when there is in his dominion another man better qualified for it, sins against God and against the State." What little recognition the idea of obligation to the public obtains in modern morality, is derived from Greek and Roman sources, not from Christian; as, even in the morality of private life, whatever exists of magnanimity, high-mindedness, personal dignity, even the sense of honor, is derived from the purely human, not the religious part of our education, *and never could have grown out of a standard of ethics, in which the only worth, professedly recognized, is that of obedience.*"

There is a still graver error, however, than that involved in the claim, that a complete system of ethics sufficient for all time can be erected upon the foundation laid in the Bible. I allude to the common assumption, according to which sound morality can thrive only as an efflorescence of dogmatic belief, and can not be sustained except by the props of a theological system. It is quite possible to be honest without a belief in the immaculate conception, to be charitable without acquiescence in the doctrine of eternal damnation, to be just without assent to the tenet of justifiy cation by faith, and generally to be virtuous without adherence to the notion of vicarious atonement. More than all this: the stamina of our moral nature rest upon a far surer foundation, than the inculcation of a few precepts by an external authority. The ethics of human society are a part of the grand order of the universe, by virtue of which it shines in beauty and exuberates with the fruits of righteousness and bounty. That order asserts itself, whenever the immortal spirit of humanity is not obstructed in its self-revelation, and the conceits of passing time do not clothe themselves in the habiliments of everlasting authority. There is an eternal law, according to which industry tends to develop the virtues of frugality and honesty, the social commerce between men fosters charity, mutual forbearance and truthfulness, and the very conflicts of society generate fortitude and the sense of honor. It is in this law of the evolution of morals, that we must seek the explanation of the consoling fact, which meets us in our daily intercourse with our fellow men, that their practices are often better than their professions, and the morals of their lives more exalted, than the morals of their creeds. I have many valued friends, in whom the man is preferable to the religionist. Take my friend on the other side, for example, in whom I cherish not the Christian less, but the man more—disrobe him of the panoply of his Christian zeal, and set him up before a meeting of Democratic citizens—even of Catholic and unbelieving citizens—and I am sure he will speak of the infidel Thomas Jefferson with far more charity and respect, than he has done here.

The vigorous evolution of society strengthens the vital forces which control that evolution; and this is the most trustworthy safeguard against social perdition. The only true preservative from corruption and decay in the moral as in the physical world is activity and growth. The only reliable antiseptic is life. The untrammeled action of the forces of society sustains its integrity as surely, as the unhindered flow of a river preserves the sweetness of its waters.

I have spent so much time on this part of the discussion, which your Honors will perhaps regard as a digression, that I have but a few moments left, in which I can attempt to refute what I regard as the most fatal error of my friend on the other side: his theory of the relation between the State and society. He refers to the systems of education prevalent in ancient and modern Europe, and seems to deplore the possibility, that our educational system, if the action of the Board of Education is upheld, will be an anomaly. He betrays no consciousness of the radical difference between the theories of the past and the teachings of the present day as to the nature and functions of the State. The ancient Romans, for instance, regarded the individual and the family—the true units of society—as mere integrants, mere segments, mere fractions of the State; and their theory has never lost its hold upon the European mind. According to that theory the individual and the family had no center of gravity of their own; they did not revolve on their own axis; their only center of attraction was the State, in which all their movements originated. In the light of that theory the

State was the creator, not the creature of society. It is to this doctrine, that we must ascribe the origin of the prejudice still so inveterate, that the State is of necessity the artificial founder and producer of every thing—of industry and material prosperity no less than morality, religion and intelligence. Modern thought has reversed these positions of the State and society; it has begun to perceive that the State emerges from and is upheld by society, and is therefore subservient to its ends. The true office of the State is simply to disembarrass the free interaction of the constituents of society; to secure justice and peace; to guard against excess and disorder. It is to keep the road clear for the footsteps of society, not to show the way; to regulate its movements, not to inaugurate them; to secure co-operation and harmony between the social elements, not to generate these elements or their laws of affinity. In most cases the State operates as a set of checks and hindrances, although it is not universally true, that those governments are best which govern least, and although Carlyle's derisive formula: "*anarchy plus the street constable*" is not an exhaustive definition. But it is strictly true, that the State can discover no truth, that it can kindle no light, that it can create no force, that it can induce no energy. The attribution to the State of the faculty to produce social energy is as absurd an error as the old delusion, that a machine could add to the quantity of its motive force.

I have said enough on this head to enable me with confidence to add: *the State can not teach religious truth and can not inculcate morality as such.* How, indeed, should the State be in a condition to teach religious truth? Where is the organ, where are the instrumentalities for its discovery? Can the State convoke an œcumenical council to decide between the disputants now assembled in this Court? To whom shall the State apply when it wishes to ascertain the fundamental, universal, neutral, achromatic truth, which, according to the claim of my friends, it must teach the children in the public schools? To your Honors? to me? tc my friends on the other side? I suspect, that if we were to address the old question: "*Quid est veritas?*" to my friend Mr. Ramsay, or to my friend Mr. Sage, or to my friend Mr. King, or to that distinguished theological taxidermist, the Pontifex Maximus of minimal religion, who, of late, has been presaging the destinies of our republic from an inspection of the visceral contents of his exenterated Christianity, the Reverend Mayo, the answer would come back to us in the old anagram of the letters composing the words of the question: "*Vir qui adest*"—that each respondent to the inquiry (the exuvial Pontifex standing forth in his most authoritative attitude) would hold himself and his opinions up as the standard of truth. Where will the State find the true measure for so many standards in this age of the unlimited differentiation of belief? By what rule of maxima and mimima will it determine the least or greatest quantum of religion which it can safely administer to Christian and Jew alike?

It is by no means a consequence of what I have tried to exhibit that the State and society are wholly independent of each other, and that the integrity and stability of the one does not presuppose the health of the other. Analogies are always treacherous, otherwise I might compare the State to the osseous system in the animal organism. There is no doubt that the bony structure would decay and become carious if the digestive and respiratory organs were not in the normal discharge of their functions; but will you conclude that therefore the osseous frame must digest or breathe?

I beg your Honors' pardon for having wearied you with this discussion, which has taken a wider range, than any of us perhaps anticipated. Allow me to add a single word to remove an apprehension which appears to be seriously entertained by my friends on the other side. In defending the action of the School Board it is not my design (as it is not the design of any member of the Board with whom I have had the opportunity to confer) to destroy the Common Schools, the people's colleges in Cincinnati, but it is my aim to save and sustain them. It has been charged that some of our citizens, who now advocate the exclusion of the Bible from the Common Schools, are intent upon a sinister ulterior purpose; that the real object of their agitation is the distribution of the school fund among the religious sects and denominations. Permit me to say that, whenever such a purpose is developed, my feeble voice will be lifted in the courts, and before the people, to thwart and defeat it. But I want to remove the only fulcrum upon which the lever to be used in dismantling the edifice of our public education can rest.

I want to be able to speak the truth then, as now, in assuring my Catholic fellow-citizens: "Your complaints are groundless; the schools are open to all, and there is nothing done or taught in them at which the most conscientious Catholic can take offense; no sectarian flag floats over the school-house, and no spirit enters there but that of peace and good will toward all men and creeds." I want to bring the children of Protestants, Catholics, Jews,—yea, of unbelievers,—together in the common school-room; and I think I can be answerable for the promise I now make to my friend, Mr. Ramsay, that none of the consequences he so eloquently laments will follow. We propose to pave the road from each church and synagogue, and from each dwelling, to the school-house, and the same roads will lead from the school-house back again to the synagogue and church. We do not mean to interfere with any faith or conviction; we do not intend to throw down the spire of any cathedral; we do not desire to seal up any holy book, or to blot out any letter that stands written within it; we do not wish to extinguish the most flickering lamp that sheds its light into the human soul, or to drown the feeblest voice which speaks the words of religious truth. The spires will point to heaven, the unmuffled church bells will speak of God, as before; the "free Bible" will have free sway, but in a *free State*, in free churches or religious schools, by the side of free secular schools. And I hope my friend will not regard it as a calamity if the son of a Presbyterian or Methodist, after his intercourse with the child of a Jew, Catholic, or unbeliever, should turn to the Scriptures with the feeling that the truth is broader than the leaves of any book; that it is brighter than black ink on brown paper; that its voice is more melodious than even the sound of a church bell; and that the human conscience may afford light for the reading of lessons of duty, which are not written in the alphabets of a Biblical code, translated into any of the varieties of human speech.

Argument of George Hoadly,

For the Board of Education.

If Your Honors Please—When this case was reserved for hearing in general term and it was agreed that the argument should proceed this day, it was suggested by a member of the Court that among the questions to be now considered would be that of the legal existence of the Board of Education of the city of Cincinnati. My friend who opened the argument for the plaintiffs has omitted to refer to this point. I do not choose to follow him, but purpose to begin my part of the discussion with its consideration, for the suggestion came from the Court, and may be renewed where we can not reply. How frequently and often how properly are cases here decided upon grounds not discussed by counsel.

I do not care to spend much time upon the proposition that there is an estoppel against the plaintiffs who have sued the Board as a lawfully constituted body, precluding them from denying its official existence. I have in my hand the pamphlet reprint of the decision of the Supreme Court in the case of *The State of Ohio* against *The Cincinnati Gas Light and Coke Company*, the report of which will appear in the 18th Ohio State Reports, in which it was held that even in *quo warranto* against a corporation, its corporate existence can not be questioned or denied, if the writ be directed against it by its corporate title. In such cases the question becomes one of forfeiture, not of corporate existence. The citation of this case is all that is needed to prove that the official character of the Board of Education can not here be denied. If a plaintiff suing a corporation, if the State seeking to forfeit a charter for abuse or non-use, may not say, "Here is no corporation," neither may those who seek to enjoin the action of corporate officers deny their title to such offices. The remedy is in *quo warranto.*

Nor do I care to inquire whether the effect would not be decisive against the injunction. Yet, surely, if my clients are not lawfully clothed with the powers which the law appears to confer upon the Board of Education of Cincinnati, there would seem to be no necessity for this remedy.

It is suggested that the act of 1853, which creates the Board, is unconstitutional, because it is a special law conferring corporate powers. I am aware that the first section of that act does, in terms, confer upon the corporate authorities of the city of Cincinnati, by name, certain powers and duties with reference to the matter of education of children within the city. But, your Honors, though put in this form, the work of education is, as Judge Stallo justly observed, no part of the proper corporate action of the city. It is the office of the State, not of municipalities, and when a city or village acts, it acts as the representative of the State. The powers of education and school government are not conferred upon councils, the ordinary legislative assemblies of municipal corporations, but upon separate boards. Upon no other principle can the levy and distribution of the State school fund be justified. Upon no other principle can that otherwise oppressive system of taxing by the rule of wealth, and distributing by the rule of numbers, be justified. I do not know how it now is, but years ago, when Mr. King was president of the School Board, the matter was investigated, and it was found that more than seventy thousand dollars were annually collected within the limits of this county, and expended in counties like Van Wert, Paulding, and the like, where the number of children within the school ages was greater, relatively to the taxable value of property, than here. This is done because Ohio acts as a State, being, in matters of education, a unit, collecting in all counties on the basis of wealth; expending in all counties on the basis of numbers needing education; a system just, if the principle be admitted, but unconstitutional and unjust if education be a corporate function.

Nor do I purpose to do more than merely allude to the suggestion that even if the function in question be corporate in its character, it is not "conferred" by the act of 1853, but had been previously granted, and was there only defined, explained and systematized. For, in studying the case in my office, I began by admitting to myself the unconstitutionality of the act of 1853, and I soon discovered that this result, apparently so portentous, is productive of no effect upon the existence or powers of the Board, of no effect whatever, not the least, and does, at most, only require it to act by another name. I admit that, in this event, the proper title of the Board is, "The Board of Trustees and Visitors of Common Schools." No other change in the legal positions and relations of the parties follows from the discovery that the act of 1853 is a "special law conferring corporate powers," forbidden by the Constitution of Ohio.

If this law, be no law, there still stands upon the statute book a law differing from it in no material respect, not repealed by this law, the ancient law of 1834—a law which was, if not written, at least urged and prompted by a man now in his grave, who was himself of that "peculiar style of irreligion" that has been spoken of—a man who would not permit his own daughters to enter the school of which they were members until after the conclusion of the morning exercises. I state the fact upon the authority of his widow. Your Honors need not be told that I refer to the author of the common school system of Ohio, the lamented Nathan Guilford.

The act of 1853 does not purport to repeal the act of 1834. Your Honors will find the repealing clause of the act of 1853 upon the 779th page of Disney's *Laws and Ordinances*, edition of 1866. It does not refer to the act of 1834.

And why? Refer to the first section of the municipal corporation law of May 3, 1852. You find that it repeals "all acts now in force for the organization or government of any such municipal corporations." (Disney, edition of 1866, p. 62.) And such was the character of the act of 1834. It was the charter of Cincinnati. This first section of the law of 1852, then, repealed it. But not altogether. For by the 109th section of the act of 1852 (Disney, edition of 1866, p. 108), it was provided that "all special acts in relation to any municipal corporation, repealed by the first section of this act, shall notwithstanding, so far as the same affects the particular police regulations, or local affairs of any municipal corporation in matters not inconsistent with this act, be and remain in force, as by-laws and ordinances of the particular municipal corporation until altered or repealed by the proper authority thereof."

It will not be pretended that the provisions as to schools contained in the act of 1834 are inconsistent with any provision of the act of 1852. Hence they are saved from the force of the repeal, and still govern the subject, if the act of 1853 be laid aside. And in the case of *Blanchard* v. *Bissell*, 11 Ohio State, 96, it is expressly decided that the act of May 3, 1852, did not abrogate the school systems then existing, nor repeal the special laws creating them in the several towns and cities of the State. And the 67th section of the general school law of the State (2 Swan & C. 1365), expressly withdraws from the grasp and scope of that act all schools established by special laws theretofore passed, which special laws, it provides, shall not thereby be "repealed, changed or modified in any respect." The Supreme Court, in *Blanchard* v. *Bissell*, say that, "The Legislature manifestly intended all special and local school laws to be left untouched, both by the towns and cities act of 1852, and by the general school law of 1853."

The provisions, then, of the act of 1834 remained as the law of the schools of Cincinnati, until the substitution of the act of 1853. If this substitution be invalid, the act of 1834 remains.

And now, as to the powers conferred by these two statutes, let us compare by reading them together. From the ninth section of the act of 1853 (Disney, edition of 1866, p. 775), I read as follows:

"That the said trustees and visitors shall have the superintendence of all the schools in said city, organized and established under this act, and from time to time shall make such regulations for the *government* and *instruction* of the children therein, *as to them shall appear proper and expedient.* * * * * * * * * * * *—and generally, do and perform all matters and things pertaining to the duties of their said office, which may be necessary and proper to promote the *education*, *morals* and *good conduct* of the children instructed in said schools.

Sec. 10. "That the said trustees and visitors, for the purpose of better organizing and classifying the schools under their supervision, shall have power to establish and maintain, out of any fund under their control, such grades of schools other than those already provided for, as may to them seem necessary and expedient, for the above-named purposes, and are hereby authorized to cause to be taught therein such other studies, in addition to those taught in their district schools, and under such regulations as said trustees and visitors may, from time to time, prescribe; *provided*, however, that said funds shall not be appropriated toward the establishment and maintenance of such other grades of schools so as in any way to impair the efficiency and permanency of the common district schools in said city."

* * * * *

SEC. 12. "That the common schools in the several districts of the city (and all other grades of schools authorized or established, and maintained in whole or in part from the school fund of said city), shall, at all times, be *equally free and accessible to all white children*, *not less than six years of age*, *who may reside in said city*, and subject only to *such regulations* for their admission, *government* and *instruction as the trustees and visitors may*, *from time to time*, *provide*."

* * * * * * * * * *

SEC. 14. "There shall be a board of examiners, composed of seven members, and at the expiration of the respective terms of those now in office the said Board of Trustees and Visitors shall appoint, for the term of three years, suitable persons, residents and citizens of said city, of competent *learning* and *abilities*, as examiners of said schools and of the qualifications of teachers thereof, which examiners, when organized by the election of a president, shall constitute and be denominated "The Board of Examiners of Common Schools in Cincinnati," and all vacancies which may occur in said board shall be filled by said trustees and visitors. It shall be the duty of said board of examiners to meet at least once in every month, examine the *qualifications*, *competency and moral character* of all persons desirous of becoming teachers and instructors in said schools, *as well with reference to their methods of instruction and mode of government*, *as literary attainments*; and any four members of said board shall have power to grant certificates thereof to such persons as in their opinion shall be entitled to receive the same, and no person shall be employed and paid directly or indirectly as teacher or instructor in any of said schools until he or she shall have obtained from said board of examiners a certificate of qualifications as to his or her *competency* or *moral character*."

By the act of May 4, 1868 (Disney's *Laws and Ordinances*, edition of 1869, p. 163), the title of the "Board of Trustees and

Visitors of Common Schools" was changed to "Board of Education."

Refer now, if you please, to the act of 1834, which may be found in volume 32 of Ohio Local Laws, p. 256, *et seq.*:

"SEC. 31. That for the purpose of more effectually supporting common schools in said city, and to secure the benefits and blessings of an education to all the children therein, it shall be the duty of said city council annually to levy or cause to be levied and collected a tax of one mill on the dollar, in addition to such tax as may be levied by or under the authority of the State for that purpose, upon all the property in said city, valued and appraised, and liable and subject to taxation for State and county purposes. * * * * * *Provided*, That said schools in the several districts of said city shall at all times *be equally free and accessible to all children not less than six years old who may reside therein, and subject only to such regulations for their government and instruction as the trustees hereinafter mentioned may from time to time prescribe.* * * * *

"SEC. 32. That the qualified voters of each ward in said city annually shall elect one [afterwards increased to two] judicious and competent person, having the qualifications of a councilman for such ward, as a trustee and visitor of common schools in said city, which trustees and visitors, elected as aforesaid, shall constitute and be denominated "The Board of Trustees and Visitors of Common Schools in Cincinnati,' who shall hold their office for one year, and until their successors shall be chosen and qualified, and fill all vacancies which may occur in their own body during the time for which they shall be elected; *they shall have the general superintendence of all the common schools in said city, and from time to time make such regulations for the government and instruction of the children therein as to them shall appear proper and expedient;* they shall appoint and employ the teachers and instructors for the same, and visit each and every such school as often as once in every month; they shall cause at least one school to be kept in each ward for the term of six months in each year, between the fifteenth day of March and the fifteenth day of October, by some competent female teacher, for the instruction of children under twelve years of age *in reading, spelling, writing, and arithmetic.* * * * * * * * * And generally do and perform all other matters and things pertaining to the duties of their said office, which may be necessary and proper to be done to promote the education and morals of the children instructed in said schools, or which may be required of them by the ordinances of said city, not inconsistent with the provisions of this act.

"SEC. 34. * * That it shall be the duty of the city council to appoint seven persons, residents and citizens of said city, of competent learning and abilities as examiners and inspectors of said schools, and the qualifications of the teachers thereof, which examiners and inspectors shall constitute and be denominated 'The Board of Examiners and Inspectors of Common Schools in Cincinnati,' who shall hold their office for the term of three years; and the vacancies which may occur in said board shall be filled for the time being by the city council. It shall be the duty of said Board of Examiners and Inspectors to examine the qualifications, competency, and *moral* character of all persons desirous of becoming teachers and instructors in said schools, or any of them, four of whom can grant certificates thereof to such as, in their opinion, may be entitled to receive the same. They shall, from time to time, and as often as they may deem proper, strictly examine all said schools, the discipline and course of instruction in each, the conduct of the several instructors and teachers therein, and the progress of improvement of the students and pupils thereof; and shall make report of all their proceedings and of all matters pertaining to the duties of their said office, as often as once in three months, to the city council, and also to the board of trustees and visitors, such alterations and improvements in the government, discipline, and instruction of said schools, and in the administration of the affairs of the same, as in their judgment will more effectually advance the cause of *education and good morals therein*, and promote the objects contemplated by this act."

Much is in these laws, your Honors, of education, of discipline, of morals; something even of reading, spelling, writing, and arithmetic is stated; not one word of the transcendently important topics of religion, piety, worship! Marvelous is it that for schools which, as we are now told, can not, under the Constitution, lawfully open their doors unless to begin with Bible reading and singing hymns, the law should be silent and entirely oblivious of the necessity for this most necessary requirement.

Such being the Constitution and declared powers of the Board, what is now, by this petition for injunction, required of it? Is this a fair case for injunction? Is it not rather an attempt to give to this writ the force of a *mandamus?*

Understand me: I make no technical objection. I wish to be understood as meeting my friend, Mr. Ramsey, as fairly as he offered to meet me. I do not object that the Court is deprived of jurisdiction by reason of the fact that the remedy is not by injunction in such cases. I do not wish to be understood as objecting that, if your Honors should be of the opinion that there is here a case fora court of law, it should be presented by *mandamus* to the Supreme Court, and the injunction is not the remedy. I do not wish to be understood as making that objection. I wish distinctly to be understood as waiving that as an objection to this proceeding. But I do wish to proceed to discuss this precise proposition for the purpose of submitting to your Honors the question what it is that is propounded to this Court by this bill of complaint, for the purpose of submitting to your Honors a further argument, that this Court is appealed to here not for the purpose of restraining anybody, not for the purpose of prohibiting anything, but that you may in the form of an injunction, establish and enforce a rule, a rule of worship and religious instruction, by this Court to be constructed out of some supposed relation of the State to Christianity, or to religion, which rule this Court must, *ex necessitate rei*, define, specify, limit, and, therefore, your Honors are in the singular position in this case, in my judgment, of being appealed to here as infallible custodians of truth, who can commit no error, from whom is to proceed for the government of the schools of this city a rule which shall specify and determine what truths are to be taught as truths of religion hereafter in Cincinnati, and what shall be the future formula or ritual of religious worship to be observed therein. This is just what is asked of your Honors. You are thus to be constituted into an ecumenical council, or into a trinity of popes. What is it that has been done that remains to be undone? What is it that your Honors can restrain? Are your Honors to restrain, by your solemn writ of injunction, Mr. Hurlbut from running, from his office, outside the building and telling these teachers what every one of them has long since known, that there is a standing rule of the School Board requiring them to perform certain acts as conditions upon which they hold their offices. The old rule is repealed. Your Honors are asked to make a new rule.

The injunction of the Code (sec. 237; 2 S. & C. 1012), "is a command to *refrain* from a particular act." "The writ of *mandamus* (Code, sec. 569; 2 S. & C. 1124), may be issued to any inferior tribunal, corporation, *board* or person, to compel the *performance* of an act, which the law especially enjoins as a duty resulting from an office, trust or station."

The School Board have passed two resolutions:

"*Resolved*, That religious instruction and the reading of religious books, including the Holy Bible, are prohibited in the Common Schools of Cincinnati, it being the true object and intent of this rule to allow the children of the parents of all sects and opinions in matters of faith and worship, to enjoy alike the benefit of the common school fund.

"*Resolved*, That so much of the regulations on the course of study and text-books in the intermediate and district schools (p. 213, Annual Report), as reads as follows: 'The opening exercises in every department shall commence by reading a portion of the Bible by or under the direction of the teacher, and appropriate singing by the pupils,' be repealed."

An injunction is a command to refrain from a particular act. From what act? From the act of promulgating this rule; from the act of telling that such a rule has been passed? Is that what has been enjoined in this case? On the contrary, the work of the School Board was accomplished when they adjourned that night. The rule was promulgated by its passage. It is the duty of every teacher to obey it. It is clear that when the Board repeals a rule, that rule is destroyed. When the Board enacts a new rule, that rule is a law of the schools, unless the passage of that rule be an abuse of the powers granted to the Board; and that is the final and last question that will be discussed in this case.

Judge Storer. Suppose they resolved that the English language should not be taught there.

Hoadly. I will come to that. My impression is that there would be no remedy then, if such a case should occur. The proper forum for the decision of such questions is once a year, at the annual election. Might they not omit German?

The Code does not provide for a mandatory injunction as an interlocutory order. As a measure of *final* relief the mandatory injunction was not abolished by the Code, as was decided in the Street Railroad case, involving the question of street railroad fares. There is no interlocutory mandatory injunction. On the contrary the injunction of the Code is a command to refrain from doing a particular act. How small is this case! How trifling is the case which we are here arguing, if this is all which is to be considered, whether Mr. Hurlbut shall be restrained from going to the school teachers and telling them that a rule has been passed. How absurd the controversy seems in that light. But that is not the true light.

Your Honors are appealed to, not to restrain Mr. Hurlbut, but you are appealed to, to compel the School Board to reinstate the ancient rule, or to make a new rule for them. If this proceeding has any sense or meaning at all, that is its sense and meaning. And in that sense I propose to discuss this case. Every teacher knows that this rule is already promulgated, and that a teacher obeys or disobeys it upon his own responsibility. How can the Board be restrained from enforcing the rule? How is the Board to enforce the rule save by punishing the teachers who disobey its mandates? How is the ancient rule to be restored save by mandate from this Court compelling its restoration? And, therefore, I say that while I here waive the objection of form, while I here concede that if your Honors should be of the opinion with me that the proper mode of proceeding, if any mode of proceeding there be, is by *mandamus*, I am willing that the power shall be exerted here by injunction, if your Honors can find any mode of applying such remedy to the case. The thing that is asked here is a mandate, a command which is to compel the School Board to restore the ancient rule (or adopt a new rule), to worship God reverently at the opening of each morning's exercises by the reading of His Holy Word, and by the singing of appropriate hymns and psalms, and by such form of religious instruction as this Court may define as necessary for the work which the School Board is required to do. That is what this Court is asked to do here.

Before passing to the consideration of the question whether this is in its nature a subject, under the Constitution of the State of Ohio, over which this Court can have no control, over which the School Board have a discretion to exercise precisely in the mode they have exercised it, I desire to call your Honors' attention to the large language with which powers have been vested in the School Board by the law of 1834 and the law of 1853. Section 9, of the law of 1853, provides that they "shall make such regulations, from time to time, for the government and instruction of the children therein, as to them shall appear proper and expedient."

To them, not to this Court, shall appear proper and expedient. The 32d section of the act of 1834 contains the same language. Your Honors are aware that that which is confided to the discretion of a corporation is not a subject of revision by a court sitting in equity, and the same is true of official boards. The discretion of an official board may be abused, but if the abuse be in a matter lawful, if the abuse is a matter of misjudgment merely, and not a matter of fraud, it has been decided in innumerable cases that courts of equity will not interfere.

It has never been denied that in a matter confided to corporate discretion—this is but a board exercising corporate functions, or exercising powers delegated by the State—I say that in a matter confided to the discretion of a board, an appeal can not be made from the board to a court of equity. Could an appeal be made to this Court should the study of arithmetic be abolished? Judge Stallo has alluded, and your Honor has playfully responded, to a suggestion founded upon the teachings of Charles Darwin—teachings which originated with as true a disciple of science as lives at the present day—which have been gladly taken up by a thousand others, and are indorsed by some of the greatest names in science to-day, and among them I may name Sir Charles Lyell—I say, if your Honors please, erroneous as in your judgment that doctrine may be, if the School Board of this city should inculcate it as true, would there be an appeal to your Honors to correct the error? I doubt it. This tribunal is not created for such purposes. Or, your Honors, if the opposite theory be true, if the catastrophe theory of creation which Professor Agassiz, in the introduction of his larger work, *The Natural History of the United States*, has so zealously espoused, be true.

If that theory be true, the theory of special creation at particular epochs by the fiat of the Almighty; if that theory be false, or be true, is there a power in this Court to require the use or omission of the text-book? My friends have referred to McGuffey's Readers. There is a series of books largely introduced into the schools of this country—I mean the readers of Marcius Willson—the Fifth Reader of which is almost wholly occupied by essays of a scientific character. Supposing that these readers should be adopted in our schools, as they are already adopted in many of the schools in the West, probably to an equal extent with McGuffey's Readers--supposing that the Willson Readers should supplant the McGuffey Readers in our schools, and it should be found that in some particular spot lurked a heresy, could an appeal be made to this Court to extirpate it?

I ask, would it be proper for a tax-payer of Cincinnati to wait upon my friend, Mr. Walker, the city solicitor, and demand that he should proceed by injunction against a book that contains a scientific heresy? Where is the end of appeals to this Court? Has this Court the schools of Cincinnati in its custody, bearing the same relation that the lord chancellor does to the property of a lunatic, or to the person of a lunatic, or of an infant? Are your Honors the custodians of these schools, sitting here to hear appeals from the Board of Education, upon questions upon which that Board may not only be wrong, but dangerously wrong? Are not all these questions finally committed to the chosen agents of the people, the delegates from their several wards, sitting in convocation as the Board of Education?

During the war I was called on, as a member of the Board of Education of the suburban village in which I reside, to examine a history of the United States, which it was proposed to introduce into our schools, and which was then, and, I presume, is yet, the text-book in the schools of the city. I found that in treating of the conduct of Massachusetts during the war of 1812, this writer laid down as undoubted principles of law that the Federal government have no right to order the militia of a State beyond its borders, and no right to fill its armies by compulsion—in other words, by draft.

Your Honors, this was in the darker days of the war, and here was what I regarded as poison—most deadly poison. No wonder that I reported against this history, and that we adhered to our former text-book, patriotic Lossing. But, could an appeal have been taken to your Honors, and the reading and study of that work been enjoined?

Another instance: There are two great schools of morals—the Utilitarian and the Intuitional—one teaching that morality is founded upon expediency: the other finding its basis in conscience,

9

in innate ideas, in intuitions. For one, I am profoundly convinced of the truth of the theory of Intuitional morals, and believe that the school of Paley and Bentham is no school of morals at all, but of immorals. Could the city solicitor, under the law giving him power to restrain by injunction abuses of corporate power—could I as a tax-payer, in case of his refusal, be permitted under the same law to refer this question to this Court? If not,—if no error in teaching and no omission to teach the true doctrine in matters of science, constitutional law, or morals, can be thus brought here,—how comes the revision of the action of the Board upon the subject of religion to be within your Honors' powers?

For errors of this kind there is, in my judgment, no safe, no final arbiter, but the result of free public discussion.

Suppose your Honors go on and decide that the Bible either shall or shall not be read in the schools. Will your Honors' decision end the question? Will an appeal to the Supreme Court of the State of Ohio end the question? Can any court pronounce upon such a question a final decision? Is there not at once taken an appeal to the people? Is not the decision a signal for renewed agitation? Is there any decision of this question short of the ascertainment of the truth, after lengthened debate, by the people themselves? There is but one way to settle such a question. It is settled when an enlightened public opinion reaches the point of settled convictions—when the community are satisfied that the just result has been attained. Then, and then only, agitation will cease. This will not be reached in an hour nor a day. It may require years of examination, of conflict. It can hardly be the result of a single election. And if so, it is not a subject as to which this Court are called upon to prescribe rules.

But again, your Honors: If religious instruction may be given in the schools, and this Court may enforce the duty by the process of injunction, then surely it can not be denied that by the same means you may provide that such instruction be correct. Surely, then, if the children may be taught that he only who "believeth and is baptized shall be saved," your Honors must, at the instance of my Baptist brother, who is to follow me, define the meaning of the original Greek, and restrain the teacher from reading its English translation, except in the words "plunge into" or "immerse;" or at the instance of Brother King, enforce as true the regenerative effect of sprinkling. Your Honors will next, on motion of a Universalist plaintiff, investigate the meaning of Gehenna and Hades, and determine whether they were places of post-mortal retribution. Your Honors will resolve the problems of free grace and limited atonement; will decide the points left unsettled by the trial of Dr. Beecher; will trace and establish the value of apostolic succession and Archbishop Parker's consecration. There is this advantage in the reference to this Court: if the world at large accept your decisions, at once disappear a thousand shades of night, a thousand casuistries, and glorious harmony is the result. But will it accept? And as for the week-day schools, even they will be "like a little heaven below." For your Honors are three in number, and can not divide equally and leave any question in doubt. You are sure to have a majority one way or the other. Unerring certainty is what our children are entitled to, and what, according to this theory, you can and must furnish.

Why, if your Honors please, recurring again to the question which I discussed a few moments ago as to the nature of this proceeding—this proceeding means that no school can be opened in Ohio under the Constitution of the State, constitutionally opened, without the reading of the Holy Bible and appropriate singing. It means that no school can constitutionally exist in the State of Ohio without religious instruction. It means that the public must be taxed, even if the public do not desire to be taxed, for religious instruction. It means a great deal more than that, if your Honors please, as I shall presently show, for, if religious instruction be once entered upon, it means that the whole truth shall be taught in the schools. It means that no modicum, no mean or small amount, shall be taught, but that the whole counsels of God shall be given through the agencies of the public schools supported by popular taxation, to the children of the parents who sent them thither. There is no result short of that.

It is not possible that there can be a limit drawn by this Court short of that which shall include all principles of truth. All religious truth must be taught, such as is fit to be expounded considering the age, considering the circumstances and the relations of the children.

To recur, if the Court please, to the question of the propriety of an appeal to this Court by a dissatisfied scholar—using "scholar" not in the sense of "pupil"—a dissatisfied citizen, who found that in some of the text-books used under the authority of the School Board, there was either error of law, or heretical doctrine in point of principle, other than religious principle or error of science. I had supposed that such application would be greeted with derision, and that the answer would at once be made that the tribunal from whom relief was sought was not a tribunal constituted for the purpose of granting relief in such cause.

The only distinction that can be made between the misuse of the powers of the School Board in matters of history, of constitutional law or of science, and in matters of religion, grows out of the higher importance of matters of religion as compared with matters of important secular knowledge. And this is precisely the ground upon which those who have burned to death have justified themselves for burning heretics. It is precisely the ground upon which *autos-da-fe* were justified in Spain,—that it was of more consequence that the souls of the people of Spain should be saved from hell or from sin than that the lives of a few men should be spared for repentance. It was on the idea that religious error is an error of such transcendent consequences, involving in the case of a human soul an eternity of perdition, according to the ordinary belief—it was upon this idea (an idea that eternal, unending welfare or woe depends upon errors of doctrine, depends upon correctness of instruction) that men have, by all denominations that have had power, been destroyed and persecuted.

Now, your Honors, the view to which I shall address myself, and attempt to persuade your Honors in some one of the various applications I shall make of it, that I am correct, is this: That if the State of Ohio undertakes to teach religion at all, she has no right to undertake to teach less than all religious truth; that if the State of Ohio is to be set up and constituted a teacher of religious truth at all, it is for the reason just suggested, of the transcendent importance of religious truth as compared with other truths; and, therefore, she has no right to withhold from any child within her borders all that is necessary for the salvation of that child from perdition. It is alleged in this petition, and not denied in the answer, that there are children in Cincinnati whose only access to religious truth is through our public schools. Is it not of infinite importance that the religious teaching they receive be true, and be complete?

It is not without purpose on our part that this allegation has been met by an explicit admission, for it is not only true, but its truth involves consequences to this case, and to the proper decision of this case, from which we can not shrink. If the State of Ohio, as is thus alleged and admitted, has the care of numbers of little children without parental care, without religious instruction in Sabbath schools, or elsewhere, and if the State of Ohio has it within the various offices she subserves toward those little children to teach them in religious truth, then it is the solemn duty of the State of Ohio to teach them all religious truth.

The State of Ohio has no right to keep from any one of those children, "the least of those little ones," any truth essential to the welfare of that child's soul. So far must we go if we are going on this road at all. Either the State of Ohio has no charge of the care of that child's soul whatever, or it has all the charge; all the charge that is not committed to others; all charge that is necessary for the protection of that child in the endless vista of time to which the soul of that child must look. What a weight of responsibility is upon the minds and consciences of those who hold that the State is justified in teaching religious truth at all, but withhold from these children sufficient instruction in religion for their salvation. What excuse to such will it be to say in the great day: "we gave them a daily reading of Scripture, and occasional passages of the Bible in McGuffey's Readers?"

The fact of the ignorance of such children is disgraceful, not to the State, but to the Church, to those who can and may instruct these children outside the public schools, and who ought to do it.

Coming to the question what the acts forbidden by these resolutions of the School Board are, I find them to be divided into these classes: First. The reading of the Holy Bible, with appropriate singing; and, Second. Religious instruction and the reading of religious books.

What does the reading of the Holy Bible, with appropriate singing, mean? As I understand it, it is an act of worship, precisely that; an act of Protestant worship. Is it anything else? Does it instruct the child other than incidentally? There are many hymns, which are, no doubt, sung in our schools which contain much theological instruction, whether true or false. I have one in my mind which contains the doctrine of justification by faith in its first lines, the hymn beginning, "Just as I am."

Almost all hymns are written, not for the purpose of expressing with poetic fervor or a playful fancy, but for the purpose of teaching in rhyme a dogma. At least such, with the imperfect poetic sense I have, I have found to be the contents of most of the hymn-books I have had occasion to examine. And the singing of hymns is held by one of our denominations to be an offense in itself. The reading of the Holy Bible, with appropriate singing, is an act of worship, and only incidentally can it be otherwise. It no doubt teaches to the child that the Holy Bible is a work *sui generis*, to be read only with a sense of awe and reverent devotion; that is to say, if it is properly read by the teacher.

I have been told that it is often carelessly and irreverently read, and that in a very large portion of our schools, including all the German schools, the rule has been, for a great many years, entirely obsolete. But so far as this exercise conveys instruction, it is only incidentally, collaterally. The main purpose and object is to perform an act of worship. If your Honors are familiar with "The Cotter's Saturday Night" of Burns, you will find that this, with the reverent prayer, constituted the family worship of that cottage, so beautifully celebrated in those lines. Does the omission of the prayer leave the reading of the Scriptures, and the singing of the hymn, any the less an act of worship? Is prayer that which makes the exercise an act of worship? Not at all.

I am aware that one, who, as Wendell Phillips once said, "lives by venturing a bold theory to-day, and spending to-morrow in taking it back, finding that he has been

'Dropping buckets into empty wells,
And growing old in drawing nothing out,'

who assures us that it is not cowardice, but want of candles and a liturgy, that makes him useless," who has set himself up as a sort of Unitarian bell-wether, and runs before the advancing flocks crying, "Suspense of faith!—no pasture in this direction," has proclaimed that the Bible in the schools is a sort of Protestant symbol, like the flag on Fort Sumter, not to be withdrawn without firing the nation's heart, the lowering of which is an insult, to be wiped out in blood. An emblem, it may be, of the supremacy of Protestantism, his Protestantism, whatever that may be. This is the man who, at Boston, once told the Unitarian left wing, the radicals, transcendentalists, infidels, or whatever you please to call us, that by our labors the Holy Ghost had visited the Unitarian churches!

But whether considered as a Protestant flag, or as an act of worship, or as religious instruction, the exercise is out of place unless the community be unanimous in uniting in the worship, or in admitting Protestant views, or in recognizing the schools as appropriate places for religious instruction.

Religious instruction is forbidden by these resolutions; and the reading of religious books. Right here I wish to examine what seems to be a very far-fetched suggestion, that McGuffey's Readers, and other books, will be cast out of the schools thereby. Not so, your Honors. McGuffey's Readers are not religious books. The religious matter in books of reading and secular instruction, is not religious instruction.

Forbidding religious instruction and the reading of religious books is certainly not intended to forbid teaching children to read, although the matter read may be in its character religious. The gentlemen forget the explanation that is put upon this in the same resolution—"the object of this resolution being to enable all to enjoy the school alike, without preference to any sect." It means, therefore, that teaching religion, and the reading of books of religion, shall be forbidden in the schools as part of the school services. But this, by no means, as I understand it, prevents, or was intended to prevent, the reading of ordinary books that are now used. Aye, more, I do not understand this to prevent the reading of passages of the Bible which occur in the ordinary books of reading, if they occur as part of the ordinary exercises of the day. But I do suppose that it was intended to prohibit, to carry out a prohibition which the School Board supposed was in the Constitution, the teaching of religious truth as part of the instruction given to the children by the State of Ohio, that the reading of the Bible as an act of worship is expressly forbidden by the very letter of the Constitution of the State of Ohio.

"No person shall be compelled to maintain any form of worship against his consent," says the Constitution of Ohio, and to take the money of a Jew or a Catholic, and employ it in hiring men to perform acts of Protestant worship, is as direct an invasion of the Constitution of Ohio as it is possible to imagine. Gentlemen can not get rid of the objection that way. If the act is not an act of worship, I desire them to tell me what it is. Why is the morning hour selected, the beginning of the day, and with appropriate singing, a passage read from the Bible, except that the day may be dedicated by the worship of Almighty God?

I admit that if this school be not supported by the money of the State; if the money of the Catholic or the Jew, or the unbeliever, do not contribute to the employment of the teacher, there can be devised by a pious teacher of a Protestant select school no more appropriate mode of commencing the day than in the way thus indicated. But the objection to this is, that while proper as a form of worship for a sincere Protestant to pass through as an introduction to the services of the day, it is, in a school, intended to be open to the children of parents of all creeds, necessarily forbidden by the Constitution of the State for the very reason that it is worship.

There can be no question but that the Supreme Court of Ohio have so declared, that their expressed opinion leads to this result; there is no escape from this conclusion but in a confusion of legal terms, by attributing to that which was a legitimate reason for the decision, lying right in the logical pathway of the Court, the force of an *obiter dictum*, because there happened to be other reasons stated by the Court.

I shall not follow my friend Mr. Ramsey into the history of the colonies, or of other States. We live in Ohio, and the example of no other commonwealth, bond or free, ancient or modern, defines the meaning of our system. But I wonder that among the historical incidents to prove the authority of the King James' Bible in the United States, he did not cite from Benedict Arnold's justification of his treason, those passages in which that Protestant villain stated as an apology for his baseness the growing tendency to Popery of those whom he had deserted.

But to return to Ohio. Our Supreme Court have told us to look to the *syllabus* of a reported case for the statements upon which the court agree. And in *Bloom* v. *Richards*, 2 Ohio State, 387, the Court unanimously agreed to these principles which I read from the *syllabus*:

"Christianity is a part of the common law of England, but under the provisions of our Constitution neither Christianity nor any other system of religion is a part of the law of this State.

"We have no union of Church and State, nor has our government ever been vested with authority to enforce anv religious observance, simply because it is religious."

The case involved the validity of a contract for the sale of land, made on Sunday. The argument was, that Christianity is part of the common law of Ohio, and that the sacred character of the first day of the week, sometimes called the Christian Sabbath, is secured by Christianity. Had this argument been sustained, the contract in question must have been pronounced against. It was not sustained, and the contract was therefore enforced.

It is true that the Court do not confine themselves to a denial that Christianity is part of our system, but proceed also in the same *syllabus* to deny that if that were so, the consequence claimed would follow. But the gentlemen who represent the plaintiffs are no more authorized to argue that the passages I have quoted from the *syllabus* are *obiter dicta* for that reason than, in another case, others would have the right to claim that the other propositions of the case are excluded from being authority by these, and, therefore, that they also are *obiter*. This mode of arguing destroys the value of every decision for which more than one reason is given. One is unnecessary, because the other would suffice; therefore each is unauthorized, and mere *obiter!*

But *Bloom* v. *Richards* is not the only case in Ohio, in which the highest tribunal known to our system has pronounced upon the subject. The same learned judge (Thurman), who delivered judgment in that case, also represented the Court in *McGatrick* v.

Wason, 4 Ohio State, 571. It was a case involving an examination again of the basis in our laws for the observance of Sunday rest. The Court changed during the two years interval between the 2d and 4th volumes, by the retirement of Judges Caldwell and Corwin, and the substitution of Judges Swan and Kennon. But the Court were again unanimous, and their views are expressed by Judge Thurman in these golden words: "For as was also said in that case (*Bloom* v. *Richards*), *no power is possessed by the Legislature over things spiritual, but only over things temporal; no power to enforce the performance of religious duties, simply because they are religious—but only within the limits of the Constitution, to maintain justice and promote the public welfare.*"

In these words lies the only safeguard that these gentlemen have against the worship of the Virgin Mary in our schools—just exactly that and no other. May not the Catholics, should they ever secure a majority and the Board is to teach religion, teach it as they believe it? For two years while I was a member of the School Board in the village of Woodburn, we had a most excellent Catholic lady at the head of our primary school. I ask your Honors what was to prohibit that young lady from opening the services of the school by the appropriate singing of a Catholic hymn. I ask your Honors what was to prevent that lady, under such a rule, from opening her school from day to day by select passages—such passages as would bear with force in favor of her views? Is it forgotten that the Catholic Church does not recognize this book as the Holy Bible? Are the Deutero-canonical books excluded from the use of a community, in which one-third of the people are Roman Catholics? Among these, are the only books of the then ancient literature of the Hebrews, clearly teaching the immortality of the soul; among them is the book of the Wisdom of Solomon, containing those wonderful verses (chap. 3):

1. "But the souls of the righteous are in the hands of God, and there shall no torment touch them.

2. "In the sight of the unwise they seemed to die, and their departure is taken for misery,

3. "And their going from us to be utter destruction; but they are in peace."

Judge Storer. You forget the verses in Job, "I know that my Redeemer liveth," etc.

Hoadly. Not so, your Honor. Consult any hand-book of Scriptural explanation, and you will find that Job refers to the avenger of the Jewish law, and has been construed to mean the promise of future life only by misunderstanding and mistranslation. So says Dr. Barnes in his notes on Job.

Judge Storer. I know. And Kitto also, but others take a different view.

Hoadly. Had this young lady of whom I have spoken seen fit to read from Maccabees those words (2 Maccabees, 12th chap. v. 44, 45), inculcating prayer for the dead, upon which the Catholic Church relies, how would the parents of Protestant children attending her school have relished the news of such an act of worship? And yet she would have been as sincere, as true to her faith in so doing as those are, who upon the opposite side of the case, insist that King James' version shall be daily read in our schools.

If you will reflect on what religion is, in its largest or its narrowest sense, you will see how impossible it is to construct a scheme of public instruction upon any other plan, than that which Judge Thurman enunciates. The bill in this case alleges that for forty years the elementary truths of religion have been taught in the public schools of Cincinnati. And what are the elementary truths of religion? Is there one single one on which all Protestant sects—let alone Catholics—can unite, save the single principle of allegiance to a personal Deity? Is there any other? Why, the moment you take a step further and undertake to define the Deity, the moment you undertake to introduce the Savior into the Godhead, the moment you undertake to touch the doctrine of the Trinity, you are met at once by such unfortunate persons as constitute the sects called Arians, called Unitarians, called Hicksite Quakers—by numbers of Spiritualists, all, or the most of whom, or at least many of them, or for the sake of argument, I will suppose one of them is as sincere and as justly entitled to the protection of the State in his religious opinions as are the great majority who enforce the rule.

Suppose you go further. The moment you touch religion

in the Catholic sense, you come upon the fundamental, the elementary principle of religion—namely, the existence of the Church as a divinely commissioned body, into whose hands Christ has given the keys of heaven and hell; to whom he has intrusted the sacred duty of interpreting Holy Writ. Certainly there can be no truth of religion, save the existence of God, of a more elementary and necessary character than this; and yet into what school can such a proposition be introduced without offending every parent, every tax-payer, save and except the Catholics and a few High Church Episcopalians; into what school can the doctrine of justification by faith be introduced and taught, either by the singing of a hymn or otherwise, without trampling upon the most sacred convictions of large bodies, not of Catholics merely, but of worshiping Protestants? The whole body of Swedenborgians has been taught by its founder the doctrine of no justification without sanctification—justification not by faith alone. The entire Unitarian body, if they agree in anything, agree in the idea that salvation is not salvation from punishment, but from sin. All denominations that believe in retribution hereafter, but retribution having an end, are disbelievers in the doctrine of justification by faith.

Turn to the sanctions of religion; surely, no truths are more necessary to be known by our children than the consequences of error. Shall the children of Universalist parents be taught eternal damnation, or, the children of parents who believe in an eternity of woe as the punishment of sin, be taught Universalism? Where are we to stop if the State undertakes religious instruction? No, your Honors, the true place to stop is to stop by not beginning. The place to instruct in religion is the family; the father to instruct his children. The place to instruct in religion is the church—the pastor to instruct the parents. The places to instruct in religion are the ragged schools. Let our philanthropists gather these little children from the highways and the byways, and teach them in industrial schools, in Sunday schools. Why should it not be entirely committed to these benevolent gentlemen, and why should those who sincerely disbelieve in any of the fundamental truths of the Christian religion be compelled to pay taxes towards the instruction of their children in these truths?

I have characterized the reading of the Bible as it is practiced in our schools as an act of worship. In my opinion, it is just that. But suppose I am wrong, and that it is not worship, what is it?

One of our newspapers (the *Times*) has, for weeks, been proclaiming that the Bible can not be read as a religious, but that it must be read as a moral instructor. But my friends upon the opposite side are too wary to put themselves upon that ground. For the School Board do not purpose to forbid all teaching of morals in the schools. And their right to say what text book of morals shall be read, and when read, can not be impugned. No, your Honors, if the Discourses of Epictetus, or Wayland's Moral Science were here in question; if from them, and not the Bible, passages had been read as a daily introduction to the labors of the day, the plaintiffs and their counsel would not be here. It is because the Bible is a book of religion that they are here. It is because it is used in worship that they are here.

If the Bible is not thus read as an act of worship, it must be by way of religious instruction. There is no middle ground. This position leads to this consequence to the case: It renders it perfectly legitimate to deny the authenticity of the Bible, or of any book or passage in it; legitimate to impeach its credibility as history; its truth as dogma. It would have been a perfectly good legal defense here to-day to have pleaded that the book is unworthy of credence, and therefore unfit to be taught to children. It is far from our purpose to do this. We assert none of these things, but that we might properly aver them, and thus render an authoritative exposition by this Court of the truth of the Bible, or the value and genuineness of particular passages, can not, as a legal proposition, be controverted. The conclusion I seek to draw from this argument, is to show that the subject is not one for the jurisdiction of a court of law. Upon such questions, no court can pronounce an authoritative judgment. They are relegated to the forum of individual intelligence and conscience, where the man is alone with God. But such questions have been, and are honestly made, and might be made by answer to this petition.

My friends say the book which they propose to use is the established version—perhaps they do not use that language—the

King James' version of the Bible. I have said enough, perhaps, already, upon the subject of the differences that exist between the denominations with regard to this work; that the Catholics admit into it what they call the Deutero-canonical books, what we call the Apocrypha; that the Jews reject the entire New Testament that there are large differences of opinion among scholars as to the value and authority of other books, we all know.

Martin Luther characterized the Epistle of James as an epistle of straw, and he left connected with his translation of the Apocalypse this injunction, (that that translation should never be published, except accompanied by his express disclaimer of belief in its inspiration—an injunction which, it need not be said, has been more honored in the breach than in the observance.)

So, too, other books have been attacked. Isaiah is divided, by some scholars, into Isaiah and the Pseudo Isaiah; Daniel is postponed to the age of Antiochus Epiphanes, and thus becomes a prophesy after the event; Second Peter is claimed to indicate, by internal evidence, a post-apostolic origin.

Indeed, in these modern times it has been found that a man could fill the office of bishop of the English church and yet entertain the most heretical views—if they be heretical—in regard to the authority and value of the five books commonly reputed as Moses'; and it has been found possible for a gentleman to occupy the position of Professor of Greek in Oxford University, and yet entertain the opinion that this work was to be treated in all respects as other human works are treated in respect of criticism, of discussion, of debate. I refer, of course, to the last essay of the work called *Essays and Reviews*, by Professor Jowett.

Ferdinand Christian Baur, the theologian of Tübingen, followed by the non-conformist divine, Dr. Samuel Davidson, the most learned English scholar of the day in this branch of research, proclaims the Gospel of John a work written after the middle of the second century, and for a dogmatic purpose.

These are questions among scholars, it may be truly said. But when you find in a community like this a very large number of persons who are taught by their pastors that the Apocrypha is a sacred work, and when you find in this community a very large number of persons who are taught by their pastors that the New

Testament is not a sacred work, then it becomes a matter of grave moment, whether to the children of the one class the Apocrypha shall be rejected, and to the children of the other class the New Testament shall be read.

And again, your Honors, there are large differences of opinion as to the genuineness of particular passages. For instance, the 7th and 8th verses of 1st John, chapter 5.

Judge Storer. They are conceded to be spurious—an interpolation of a later age.

Hoadly. Yes, your Honors; a product of the Arian controversy. But there are others. I have heard the remark made with reference to this case, that the question is whether the little children of our schools might not learn the Lord's Prayer. Why, there is no more doubtful passage in the Bible than the ascription clause of the Lord's Prayer. It is not contained in the three most ancient manuscripts. Baron Tauchnitz has thought it a worthy tribute to his calling to make his one thousandth volume a rescension by Tischendorf of the New Testament on the basis of these manuscripts. One of them is wanting in that portion of Matthew, but the others, the Sinaiatic and Vatican codices close the prayer in Greek with the words which, since the age of St. Jerome, the Catholic Church has rendered into the sonorous Latin, "*Sed libera nos a malo, Amen*"—"But deliver us from evil, Amen."

So, too, the same manuscripts end the 16th chapter of Mark, with the 8th verse, as Eusebius and St. Jerome tell us nearly all the trustworthy copies of their time did.

Also, the account of the woman taken in adultery has been disputed. And many other minor passages, especially such as bear on the Arian and Athanasian controversy.

Understand my purpose. Many of these things are of little importance. Some of the disputed books and passages have, however, an independent value of their own, irrespective of whether they belong in the canon or not, and whether they are the authentic words of the authors to whom King James' version attributes them.

But I cite them to show the nature of the questions that become legitimate the moment it is decided that this Court may require religious instruction to be provided by the Board. These, and many other problems, for example, the large one of Inspiration, its nature and extent, at once call for solution, first by the Board, and then by the Court. I refer to them to show how incompatible it is with the duties which the law imposes upon the Board for even that tribunal to consider such matters; how unlike your Honors' proper judicial duty the consideration of such topics becomes. And yet, if a member of the School Board may object to a text book of geography or history, and ask his associates to banish it from the schools because of errors, as he certainly and properly may; he may, *a fortiori*; indeed, if true to his conscience, he must object to that which, in the Bible, he deems an interpolation or a mistranslation. If the Bible is read by way of religious instruction, this consequence certainly follows.

But it is said that the Bible, the whole Bible of the King James' version, should be read, as published by the American Bible Society. But that society, unfortunately, has not been uniformly consistent. I have before me three Bibles of their publishing; editions, viz: of 1858, 1859 and 1868. They differ in the headings or synopses of the contents of the chapters. How extensive these differences are I know not. I see, however, that the Bibles of 1858–9 describe the contents of Solomon's Song quite differently from the Bible of 1868. The headings of the chapters of the former treat it as a love poem, a song of the bride and bridegroom. The latter, like the earlier Bibles, describe it as a religious work, a song of Christ's love for the Church. The history of these revisions is known to your Honors. Some enlightened gentlemen having control in the American Bible Society revised the headings which had aforetime been received, and caused them to speak the language of truth and correct description. There came a reaction, under the influence of which the ancient headings were restored. This occurred five or six years ago. I have not here one of the earlier copies, but the editions of 1858–9 are the revision, and of 1868 the product of the reaction.

My friends talk about the Bible "without note or comment." Are these headings note or comment? Are they read or omitted? Are they put into the pupils' hands in the schools? If they are, then the discussion of their value is legitimate, and, indeed, in the School Board, necessary, unless that Board, recognizing its duty to furnish religious instruction, leaves the accuracy of the contents of the text books of such instruction to chance or the dictation of others. Necessary, too, here, if your Honors undertake to compel the Board to furnish religious instruction, unless you, too, leave to chance or the judgment of others whether that instruction shall be true or false, complete or incomplete, thorough or superficial.

My friend, Mr. Ramsey, will bear with me if I say that beneath the eloquence and piety of his powerful and manly argument, to which I concede the no small praise that it shrank not from its own logic, cruel though, as in my judgment, the consequences it involve are, I heard the cold, harsh undertone of persecution. I do not believe he would consciously offend even the feelings of an opponent. Yet, whether he is aware of it or not, his speech was a plea for persecution—an argument to compel offense to conscience. Neither you nor I, your Honors, are responsible that this question is here. Some of us have felt that the time had not yet arrived for successful agitation. But the question is here. The agitation has come. It is a question of conscience. Its present condition is the result of an honest attempt to bring the fifteen thousand children of the Catholic schools into the district schools, to secure to them and to their parents that share in the benefits provided, to which their participation in the burdens imposed by the State entitles them. That attempt failed, but it led to this agitation, to these resolutions of the Board. And now, your Honors, comes the Catholic body, one-third of our entire population, and protest against the imposition of taxes upon them to pay for the reading of the Protestant Bible. Now comes the Israelite, three of whose Rabbis, Drs. Lilienthal, Wise and Goldhammer, have preached in support of the School Board, and says he ought not to be taxed to support the system of reading the New Testament. My Hicksite Quaker friend tells me his conscience is offended. My own pastor and his flock, without a creed, but not without an honest purpose to serve the truth and live manly, if not godly, lives, are taxed to support a view of the Bible which we do not entertain, for to us the Bible is not a talisman, but a help, of which we are to understand, appreciate, believe, and, if you please, disbelieve so much as our reason requires. Other unbelievers come; they whom Mr. Ramsey regards as having no rights, and they claim liberty of conscience. What is persecution? If, by law, to take the life is persecution, is it not more so to force the conscience. If to burn the child, to consume its mortal part, for believing as its parent taught it, would be persecution, how much less so is it to seize the immortal part of the little one and distort it—to do this in the name of the State, which has no capacity of infallible truth? How can the parent, the Catholic, Jew, Quaker, Unitarian, or unbelieving parent—avoid the sense of wrong, cruel wrong, when told: "Your child has the choice to disbelieve what you hold as God's most sacred truth or lose the blessings of an education. If he receives knowledge, he must reject your faith. If he adheres to your faith, he must give up the hope of knowledge."

But my friends may say the Bible without note or comment, and the singing of hymns is not making war upon Catholics, Jews, Unitarians and Hicksites; is not teaching their children to shun their fathers' faith. Aye, but it is. Even the reading of the Bible without note or comment by unanointed lips is an offense to the Catholic, and he has the same right to his belief that you have to yours, and holds it as sincerely. Is the teaching of the New Testament no just offense, when done by law or force, to the child of the Jew? And the Unbeliever—even the Atheist—has he no rights that a Christian is bound to respect?

I wish to read from the State trials a single case, which shows what are the consequences of holding that the State may teach religious truth.

I read from Cobbett's *State Trials* vol. 8, p. 526, from the trial of George Busby, for high treason, at Derby assizes, in the thirty-third year of the reign of King Charles the Second, of pious memory, defender of the faith, etc., A. D. 1681. First, let me read the indictment:

"Then the Clerk of Arraignments proceeded to arraign the prisoner.

"*Clerk*—George Busby, hold up thy hand (which he did): Thou standest indicted by the name of George Busby, late of West Hallam in the county of Derby, clerk, for that thou, being a subject of our sovereign lord the king that now is, and being likewise born within this kingdom of England, was made and ordained a priest by the authority derived and pretended from the See of Rome, after the feast of the Nativity of St. John Baptist, in the first year of the reign of our lady Elizabeth, late queen of England, etc., and before the 16th day of March, in the thirty-third year of the reign of our sovereign lord Charles the Second, of England, France and Ireland king, defender of the faith, etc., the laws and statutes of this kingdom of England little weighing, nor the punishments in the same contained not at all regarding; with force and arms, etc., at the parish of West Hallam aforesaid, in the county of Derby aforesaid, being within this kingdom of England, voluntarily, freely and treasonably, on the 16th day of March, in the thirty-third year of the reign aforesaid, hath been and remained, contrary to the form of the statute in that case made and provided; and against the peace of our sovereign lord the king, his crown and dignity."

From the statement of the prosecuting counsel on opening to the jury, I quote the following description of Busby's offense:

"Gentlemen, you hear the prisoner is indicted upon a statute made in the 27th Elizabeth, which makes it treason for any subject born to take orders from the See of Rome, and afterwards to remain in England; which law I conceive was not only made for the security of the government, but also in favour of the lay papists themselves; for though several statutes were made to keep them within the bounds of their allegiance, and to secure the government from their villainous designs; yet it was experimentally found true, that no dangers or penalties whatsoever could deter or hinder them from plotting against the state, in order to bring us back again to the slavery of Rome, whilst those juggling managers of their consciences were suffered to come amongst us; and therefore I may well call this statute, upon which the prisoner stands indicted, an act of charity to the common papists; for it was made to prevent the dangers they would otherwise run themselves into, as well as the nation."

On page 550, I find that the prisoner was found guilty, and thus sentenced:

"Then Mr. Baron Street passed sentence:

"That you the prisoner, now at the bar, be conveyed hence to the place from whence you came, and that you be conveyed thence on a hurdle to the place of execution; where you are to be hanged by the neck; that you be cut down alive, that your privy members be cut off, your bowels be taken out and burnt in your view; that your head be severed from your body; that your body be divided into four quarters; which are to be disposed of at the king's pleasure: and God of His infinite mercy have mercy upon your soul."

That is a specimen of what Protestants have done to Catholics. I was brought up on Fox's *Book of Martrs*, but I can find nothing in that book more barbaric than that. I charge neither Protestant nor Catholic with more than that they did not live in advance of the times. The logic of persecution can not be contravened. Admit the major and the minor premise, admit the duty of the State to teach religion, and the writ *de heretico comburendo* follows as a matter of course. There is but one escape, and that is by denying the authority of the State on this question. Then you have saved the citizen, the State and religion.

In the State in which I was born, there was until 1819 a church establishment supported by taxes. I refer to the Orthodox Congregational Church:—to the "standing order," as it was called, of Connecticut. In that year, the Democrats (Republicans, they then called themselves) and the Episcopalians coalesced, and under the battle cry of "toleration," with Oliver Wolcott, who had been a member of General Washington's cabinet, as their candidate for governor, overthrew the Federalists, and abolished the standing order. Dr. Lyman Beecher was then the pastor of the Congregational Church at Litchfield, and his autobiography gives a most interesting account of the revolution in the politics of the State. The apprehensions of evil of the clergy, among them, of good Dr. Beecher, were very lively. A flood-tide of immorality and wickedness would sweep the State. What actually followed? Why, sir, the honest old doctor records in the same book that he dates, from the day the Congregational Church was disestablished in that State, the growth of the greatest revival of religion that Connecticut ever knew.

Therefore I say that the total severance of Church and State is better for religion, and I believe the history of the United States proves it. Here, in proportion as we have dissolved the bonds of the Church and State, has religion increased. And it is because, I believe, that this thing, be it little or great, is the last bond that binds the State of Ohio to any ecclesiastical establishment, and because I believe it to be the bond which binds it to a Protestant ecclesiastical establishment, that I oppose it; not that the Protestant is any worse than the Catholic Church; I do not know that I should say that, but because any bond binding the State and Church is an evil to all concerned. And yet were it not a measure of real religious progress, I should take the same view I do. Unbelievers are not to be treated as having no rights. What, are the various forms of disbelief of the current religions, to make men outcasts, beyond the pale of the protection of the law? God forbid that were I as orthodox as my brothers Ramsey or Matthews, I should forget that these men have the same rights I have. God forbid that I should forget that to some of these men mankind is under the greatest obligations. That Benedict Spinoza, of pure and spotless life, who sacrificed himself to poverty in order to do what he believed to be a great work for man, the father of a philosophy which is now current all over the world, should be treated as an outcast; that Hume and Humboldt should be treated as outcasts! God forbid that I should ever lend my voice for any such purpose!

When Theodore Parker, that prophet of God to New England, lay dying, literally worn out by his labors for the emancipation of the human mind, and the relief of the destitute and perishing, wicked Christians publicly prayed in Boston that a "hook might be put in his jaws," but the tears of William and Ellen Craft, and many another whom he had helped from bondage, are shed on his grave; and his great collection of books, given to Boston to be a part of her public library, renders sacred the memory of this unbeliever wherever knowledge is valued. Unbelievers! I heard your Honor, the presiding judge, in language which did you and the object of your eulogy equal honor, introduce Ralph Waldo Emerson to a Cincinnati audience. The loftiest philosophy of this age, this man has written. No word of his will ever bring a blush to the cheek of young or old. No word of his, but is a trumpet blast, loudly calling to a better life. Alike in poetry and philosophy, the first name our literature can present, is of this so-called Infidel.

But we are told upon the other side that there is no morality without religion, and that morality dates from the Bible, and, therefore, we must have the Bible read in our public schools. When was this idea invented? When did this novel proposition emerge from the brains of men? All honor to the Bible; but morals existed before the Bible. Aye, morals existed before the world. Right and wrong bind the throne of the Almighty just as much as they bind the hearts of men.

Let me read from Cudworth *on Eternal and Immutable Morality*, a book published after his death, edited by a bishop of the English church. Let Mr. Ramsey say, as he did of Hume, that Cudworth loaded a blunderbuss, and not daring to fire in his lifetime, left the discharge to after generations. So be it, but its report is pertinent to this case:

"The distinction of right from wrong," says Cudworth, "is discerned by reason, and as soon as these words are defined, it becomes evident that it would be a contradiction in terms to affirm that any power, human or divine, could change their nature, or, in other words, make the same acts to be just and unjust at the same time."

And the golden-mouthed Chrysostom teaches the same truth:

"Another point," says St. John Chrysostom (*The Statues, Hom.* 12), "which is also demonstrative of God's providence is, that when God formed man He implanted within him from the beginning a natural law. And what, then, was this natural law? He gave utterance to conscience within us, and made the knowledge of good things, and of those which were the contrary, to be self-taught. They say that there is no self-evident law placed in our consciences, and that God hath not implanted this in our nature. But if so, whence is it, I ask, that legislators have written those laws concerning marriages, murders, trusts, of not encroaching on one another, and a thousand other things? Did such persons, perchance, learn them from their elders, and they from those that were before them, and these again from those beyond? From whom did those learn who were the first originators and first enactors of those laws? It is evident that it was from conscience; for they can not say that they held communication with Moses, or that they heard the prophets. How could they, when they were Gentiles? But it is evident, from the very law which God placed in man when he formed him, that from the beginning laws were laid down."

Have the gentlemen forgotten the great schools of Ethics, which arose before Christ? and that from one of the stoic poets (Cleanthes), St. Paul quoted upon Mars Hill, "For we also are his offspring."

Sir James Mackintosh thus speaks of the controversy between the Stoic and Epicurean systems, in his Dissertation on Ethics, *Encyclopedia Brittanica*, vol. i, p. 321.

"If any conclusion may be hazarded from this trial of systems, the greatest which history has recorded, we must not refuse our decided though not undistinguishing preference to that noble school which preserved great souls untainted at the court of dissolute and ferocious tyrants; which exalted the slave of one of Nero's courtiers to be a moral teacher of aftertimes, which for the first, and hitherto for the only time, breathed philosophy and justice into those rules of law which govern the ordinary concerns of every man; and which above all, has contributed, by the examples of Marcus Porcius Cato, and of Marcus Aurelius Antoninus, to raise the dignity of our species, to keep alive a more ardent love of virtue, and a more awful sense of duty throughout all generations."

Yes, your Honors, Epictetus, the slave, who never, so far as we know, heard of the Bible, is the moral teacher of mankind, and Marcus Aurelius, the emperor, in whose reign Christians were persecuted as Atheists, is the example, by which "a more ardent love of virtue, and a more awful sense of duty is kept alive throughout all generations."

Not many days since, I read a book written by a clergyman, Mr. Farrar, called *Seekers after God*, to prove that the great Stoics, Epictetus, Seneca, Marcus Aurelius, were not far from the Kingdom of Heaven, so closely do their teachings ally themselves to those of Jesus Christ.

Marcus Aurelius, the emperor: where, your Honors, in the rolls which preserve the names of Christian kings, will you find his equal? With all its triumphs, Christianity has never produced such a monarch. From the camp among the Quadi, from the clash of arms and the midst of warlike deeds, Marcus Aurelius Antoninus thus speaks to this case, to this Court: "From my brother Severus," says he (*Meditations*, book 1), "I learned to love my kin, and to love truth, and to love justice;" * * * "and from him I received *the idea of a polity in which there is the same law for all, a polity administered with regard to equal rights and equal freedom of speech, and the idea of a kingly government which respects most of all the freedom of the governed.*"

Morality unknown before the Bible! How happens it then that Pagan Rome possessed laws evincing a higher moral sense than that of the common law of Ohio to-day, with the Bible forty years read in the schools? Witness the law of implied warranty in sales of chattels and the doctrine of *caveat emptor.**

---

*Cicero, *de Officiis*, lib. 3, secs. 12–17, puts the case of a merchant of Alexandria, arriving at Rhodes in a time of scarcity, with a cargo of corn, having passed other vessels with corn on the way. May he lawfully sell, concealing the fact of their expected arrival? Pagan Cicero answers in the negative. Christian John Marshall in the affirmative. *Laidlaw* v. *Organ*, 2 Wheat. 178.

"It is a little singular," says Chancellor Kent (2 *Commentaries*, 10th ed., p. 491, note *a*), "that some of the best ethical writers under the Christian dispensation, should complain of the moral lessons of Cicero as being too austere in their texture and too sublime in speculation, for actual use. There is not, indeed a passage in all Greek and Roman antiquity equal, in moral dignity and grandeur, to that in which Cicero lays it down as a fixed principle that we ought to do nothing that is avaricious, nothing that is dishonest, nothing that is lascivious, even though we could escape the observation of gods and men." (*De Officiis*, 38.)

In the closing argument for the plaintiffs, to which I have no opportunity of reply, exception was taken to my estimate of the character of Marcus Aurelius. I leave that to the candid student of history. It is not an open question. If the discussion shall induce a single reader to become familiar with the *Meditations*, or as Mr. Long, in his translation, calls them, the *Thoughts*, of this great man, it will have repaid me for my share in the labor of this debate. I have no fears but that, notwithstanding my friend's criticism, there will ever shine benignly upon the historical student, what Mr. Longfellow calls.

"The clemency of Antonine,
Aurelius' countenance divine,
Firm, gentle, still."

Your Honors, the Bible itself disputes the statement. What says St. Paul (Romans, 2d chapter, verses 14 and 15)? "For when the Gentiles, which have not the law, do by nature the things contained in the law, those having not the law are a law unto themselves; which shew the work of the law written in their hearts, their conscience also bearing witness, and their thoughts the meanwhile accusing, or else excusing, one another."

In the human conscience, since it was created, has been written the law of morals, long antedating this book. In saying this, I cast no reproach upon the Bible; God forbid that I should do

---

The question how far he was personally concerned in the persecution of Christians, and the death of Polycarp, I have not space to enter upon. I do not claim for the character of Marcus Aurelius perfection—only superiority to any Christian monarch. One thing must be admitted; when their turn to persecute came, the Christians took it.

Exception was also taken, not to my comparison of the civil with the common law in respect of moral dignity, but because it characterized the Roman law as Pagan. In this question I have a professional interest, and am unwilling to leave the claim of credit to Christians for the superior morality of the Roman law, unanswered. The fact is, that the *Corpus Juris Civilis* received its present *form*, in the sixth century, from the Christian emperor, Justinian, or rather from Tribonian, and other lawyers, working by his orders, but in substance it is the product of an earlier and Pagan age. Law is history crystalized, No *deus ex machina* has ever appeared to dictate it. Justinian was no such magician. Like the common law, the Roman law is a growth, not a manufacture. Justinian and Tribonian lived, not at Rome, but in Constantinople. The compilations of law under Justinian's orders were made between A. D. 528 and 535, and it was not until 554 that this emperor reconquered Italy. Dr. Irving (*Introduction to the Study of Civil Law*, p. 23), says: "The chief splendor of the Roman lawyers is to be traced from the reign of Augustus to that of Alexander Severus—and the last name of great celebrity is that of Herennius Modestinus. With this pupil of Ulpian, the oracles of the civilians became mute; the succeeding lawyers are only known as compilers or expounders; and although the law was long afterward taught at Rome, Constantinople and Berytus, we can not, in those declining annals, discover any vestiges of ancient genius." Savigny (*History of the Roman Law*, Cathcart's translation, vol. i, p. 13), speaking of the work done under Justinian's orders, says: "Original genius was, indeed, denied to this age,

so! I am here to say that moral philosophy antedates the Bible. It is found, not in the arbitrary will of an arbitrary Deity, but in the just will of a righteous Deity, who could not have created wrong to be right, and right wrong, omnipotent though he be.

Why, your Honors, my friends have unconsciously reproduced the old heresies of the Nominalists, William of Ockham and John Gerson, who taught what Sir James Mackintosh calls "that most pernicious of moral heresies, which represents morality to be founded on will," the arbitrary will of God. Fortunate, very fortunate, was it for the cause of practical morality that both the church and the schools espoused the opinions of St. Thomas Aquinas: "Goodness he regarded as the moving principle of the Divine Government; justice as a modification of goodness, and with all his zeal to magnify the sovereignty of God, he yet taught, that though God always wills what is just, *nothing is just solely because He wills it.*" And with a wise forecast, the sweep of whose

---

and the law-sources to be consulted by Justinian's compilators belonged to a foreign" (*i. e.* Roman, not Byzantine), "and cultivated people, and were not to be found in the original literature of the Eastern empire." Judge L. S. Cushing (*Introduction to the Study of Roman Law*, p. 86), speaking of the growth of the law at Rome, says: "Out of the jurisprudence which was thus formed around the fragments of the great Roman jurists, preserved in the compilations of Justinian, have been extracted in modern times much of the material for the French and other codes of positive law."

The *Corpus Juris Civilis* consists: First, Of the Code, which is a compilation from the edicts and rescripts of the emperors, Pagan and Christian, from Hadrian to Justinian, and from the codes of two private lawyers, Gregorius and Hermogenianus, and the Emperor Theodosius II, themselves compilations from earlier sources. Secondly, Of the more important work, the Digest or Pandects, which is a general digest of legal science, in fifty books, from the writings of those lawyers who enjoyed the highest authority in the forum. "The work," says Dr. Irving, p. 53, "contains a very copious collection of legal principles and legal discussions, exhibiting one of the most remarkable specimens of ancient genius and ancient wisdom." In it are extracts from the great lawyers of Pagan Rome to the following numbers, viz: From Ulpian, 2461; Paulus, 2087; Papinian, 596; Pomponius, 588; Gaius, 536; Julian, 457.

vision embraced the dangers of interference by the civil power with things spiritual, foreseeing cases like this in hand, St. Thomas Aquinas "allowed to the church a control only over spiritual concerns, and recognized the supremacy of the civil power in all temporal affairs."

I accused my friends of pleading for persecution. Any invasion of the rights of another, done of purpose, is persecution. Any invasion of the rights of others, by large bodies, is none the less persecution; and when these rights are rights of conscience, it is persecution, and the men who suffer from it feel it as persecution the moment their attention is addressed to it. The moment that a Jew becomes aware that his taxes are appropriated to a form of worship alien to his faith, and which teaches its falsehood, he is persecuted, and it is only a question of time and humanity whether those who persecute him shall be persuaded to persecute him more.

Thirdly, The Institutes, which are a mere revision of the institutes of the Pagan lawyer Gaius or Caius. Fourthly, The *Novellæ*, or New Constitutions, viz: changes made by Justinian after the publication of the Code, Digest and Institutes. Judge Cushing (p. 109), says: "The merit of accomplishing a great and useful work must be ascribed to Justinian. But he can not be regarded as the originator of the plan upon which his reforms were effected. For his Code, he had before him as models, the Gregorian, Hermogenian and Theodosian; for the Digest, the great jurists had already furnished him with examples in the various works of the same kind executed on a more limited plan, and especially the works of Julian on the edict; and for his Institutes, he not only borrowed the plan, but actually appropriated, as he himself states, the work itself, of Gaius."

Of the eminent jurists of Heathen Rome, the first in authority was Papinian, who was *advocatus fisci*, or as we should perhaps say, solicitor of the treasury, of the Emperor Marcus Aurelius. Near him in rank was Ulpian. I can not close this note without quoting from Wendell Phillips' oration called "Idols," the following passage: "Rome points to a colossal figure, and says: 'That is Papinian, who, when the Emperor Caracalla murdered his own brother, and ordered the lawyer to defend the deed, went cheerfully to death, rather than sully his life with the atrocious plea; and that is Ulpian, who, aiding his prince to put the army below the law, was massacred at the foot of a weak but virtuous throne.'"

Christian brethren, who think all morality derived from the Bible which one of us would have done and suffered as Papinian did?

The Constitution of the State of Ohio saves him, or the Catholic, or the Protestant, from any other kind of persecution, but if we admit, as a principle, that the State has concern with things spiritual, then we have only to wait till some one of the large religious bodies, believing that the State has concern with things spiritual, is willing to exercise that concern, and we have—I know not what. We may have the infallibility of the Pope or of Ecumenical Councils taught in our schools, and the linking together of Church and State. Perhaps at the next meeting to revise the Constitution of the State of Ohio, in 1871, we shall have something of that kind. It is true that Thomas Jefferson brought about the adoption of the first amendment to the Constitution of the United States, which provides that Congress shall pass no law creating an established religion. Mr. Jefferson came home from France full of resentment because no Bill of Rights had been adopted, full of the feeling of the necessity of such provisions; full, also, of the idea of State rights, and he aided those who wished for amendments, and the very first amendment they procured begins: "*Congress* shall make no law respecting an establishment of religion, or prohibiting the free exercise thereof." This does not prevent, was not designed to prevent, the *States* from creating church establishments.

As I said before, Church and State were allied in Connecticut until 1819. What is there to forbid a church establishment in Ohio, but the provisions of our *State* Constitution, which can be changed in another year? Nothing can prevent it if the majority will it. Nothing will restrain that majority but the growth of the idea in the public mind that the State has nothing to do with things spiritual. And when that idea is once so worked into every Catholic and Protestant mind by the practices and habits and usages of years, and by the happy life that all faiths will lead under it, then we will be safe. I am told that in the city of New York the Catholics have acquired a majority, and the consequence is they are voting large amounts of the people's money for the support of Catholic institutions; and in the *Catholic World* it is upheld on the ground that it was done long before by the Protestants, when they were in power. What is to save our schools from control of this kind? Will constitutional provisions do it? They are at the mercy of the people. Nothing will do it but the belief in the minds of the American people that the State has no concern with things spiritual, and when they do believe that, there is no danger.

There is no safety in this country except in an enlightened public opinion, based on individual intelligence. When we have that, we have all we ever can get.

What will my friend, whose opening argument so forcibly represented the plaintiffs' desire that religion shall be taught in the schools, with appropriate singing, say, when *Stabat Mater Dolorosa*, or some other Catholic hymn, shall be chanted there. What will he say when his children report to him that the public school-rooms are decorated with images of Saints; that *Ave Marias*, instead of Bible readings, usher in the day; that among the things taught to his little ones is the corporeal assumption of the Virgin Mary—which, we are told, is about to be discovered as a fact in history in the coming Ecumenical Council? He would characterize it by the same name that I am using—persecution. If a majority of our community should become Israelites, and should banish the New Testament and use the Old, and in Hebrew, and the children of my friend, untaught in Hebrew, be compelled to listen to it, would he not call that persecution?

The disciples of Emanuel Swedenborg are another body who read this book in a different way from the larger denominations; who read it as it were, "between the lines," who discover in it things that the eye of man had not seen, nor the ear of man heard, until Swedenborg had attained the age of fifty years, and was illuminated with Divine light. Suppose the Swedenborgians should obtain the control of our schools, and not believing that the Church has no concern with things temporal, or the State with things spiritual, teach Swedenborgianism, instruct the children of Unitarians that Jesus Christ is God the Father, or proclaim to believers in Calvinism what Swedenborg saw, or says he saw, viz: John Calvin in perdition.

What would my friend Matthews and his co-religionists say to instruction of that kind in the public schools? They would call it persecution. Comte has left behind him a philosophy called "Positivism," which prevails largely in England and to some extent in this country. He left behind him a religious denomination which consists in worshiping collective humanity. In other words, which teaches that Deity comes to consciousness only in man. God is life, and God is consciousness, only in man, and in the men who have gone before us. They aggregated are God, and are to be worshiped. Comte left behind him a liturgy for his church. I should like toknow how my friends would like to have that liturgy expounded in our public schools?

There is but one safe course consistent with the progress of right and religion, and that is, total abstinence from interference by the State. I may be an Atheist, a Pantheist, a Positivist, a Theist, or a Deist, or any other of the various sects of unbelievers; I am responsible to God, and not to this Court, or any human tribunal, and the State of Ohio can not call me to account. It can not touch a dollar of my money, or trample upon my conscience. That is just as sacred as that of the most devout believer, and the most devout believer has no right, no safety, except in establishing my principle. Having established a principle that he may intrude upon that which is mine, he sets me an example which will be very apt to lead me to intrude upon that which is his. Abraham Lincoln once wrote that he who wishes to be free himself must be content to allow others to be free also. True and wise words, whether applied to chattel slavery, or to spiritual bondage.

The ages in which the Calvinist persecuted the Armenian, the Catholic the Calvinist, the Episcopalian the Catholic, and the French Catholics the Huguenots, have passed away, and given place to a time more favorable to religion, just in proportion as it is more free.

Your Honors: I have cause to lament my inadequacy to the theme; none whatever to regret the inadequacy of the theme itself. It is a cause wherein great benefactors of mankind have been proud to participate. Shall I feel otherwise than honored to be allowed to lift up my voice, however feebly, in its behalf?

My friend, of whose political philosophy Thomas Jefferson is the author, reproached that great man's memory yesterday because of his religious views. Jefferson, who so fully entered into the spirit of the founder of Christianity, that he copied into a manuscript volume, for his own private use, all the ethical precepts of

Jesus, left to be engraved upon his tomb this epitaph, enumerating what he regarded as his three principal services to mankind:

> "Here lies buried
> THOMAS JEFFERSON,
> Author of the Declaration of Independence;
> Of the Statute of Virginia for Religious Freedom;
> And father of the University of Virginia."

Freedom of the State! freedom of the soul! freedom of education! Just what we here contend for.

Give us deliverance from all bonds binding Church to State, or State to Church:—total abstinence by the civil officer from interference in things spiritual; and you have secured all help that can be had in your coming contest with those who shall contend for the exclusive control of the schools by denominations. You secure the principle which shall prevent intrusion upon liberty of conscience, and you obey the precept of the Constitution of the State of Ohio as expounded by the highest tribunal.

I have one more proposition to make. The Constitution of Ohio provides "that no religious or other sect or sects shall ever have any exclusive right to or control of any part of the school funds of this State." What is it that is here claimed but the exclusive control of the school fund for Evangelical Protestants? And we are coolly told that the Catholics are trying to get control of the schools by men who have already secured it for themselves.

My friend, the Hicksite Quaker, comes to me and says: "My conscience is offended. I am practically excluded, or compelled to submit to persecution in the enjoyment of the right to the public schools for my children." My friend, the Catholic, says: "I am practically excluded, because my church has taught me that the interpretation of the Scriptures is committed to a class of men who are ordained, and whose ordination is regarded as a sacrament, and here it is read by unanointed lips. I am excluded from the public schools, or am compelled to submit to persecution as a condition of enjoyment." My friends, the Israelites, whose three Rabbis here have expounded this subject from the pulpit, come to me and say: "We are practically excluded from the benefits of this system, unless we submit to persecution as a condition of enjoying it, for our children are exposed to the danger of being taught that which their parents do not believe as a condition of being taught secular knowledge." Judge Stallo and I come with our pastor and complain that the Bible, which we hold to be a most sacred, aye, a religious duty to study by the light of reason, is used as a sort of fetish, and we are compelled to permit our children to listen to that paganism or withdraw them from the schools.

Where does this leave the schools, but practically in the control of the remaining sects? No wonder they are willing to contend for the continuance of this control they have usurped. Having made the schools nurseries, propaganda of their faith, they seek so to continue them. But in the effort, what becomes of the Constitution of the State, which says that "no religious or other sect or sects shall ever have any exclusive right to or control of any part of the school funds of this State?"

Reference is made in the petition to the ordinance of 1787, as if in it were to be found some excuse for this attempt made by the plaintiffs to discourage the education of the children of Catholics, Israelites and Heretics. But even if that ordinance would bear such construction, it is only necessary to refer your Honors to the case of *Strader et al.* v. *Graham*, 10 Howard, 82, in which it was decided by the Supreme Court of the United States that the ordinance of 1787 was superseded by the Constitution of the United States; that any force it had after that time was derived from the legislation of Congress, which in time was superseded by the admission of the several new States, with constitutions of their own forming.

As I said before, my own inadequacy is great, but the cause is not inadequate. It can not be that he who to-day, in Ohio, pleads for the severance of Church and State, can be wrong. He who, with Judge Thurman and the Supreme Court, contends that the State has no authority in things spiritual, must be right. Upon this rock are our spiritual liberties founded. Here will we, in the spirit and the words of Luther, "take our stand. We can not do otherwise. So help us God."

NOTE TO THE CASE OF GEORGE BUSBY, *page* 000.—For the form of the writ *de heretico comburendo*, as executed by Protestants upon Protestants, see the cases of Bartholemew Legatt and Edward Wightman, burned to death in 1612, for heresy, being Arians and deniers of the Trinity reported in 2 Cobbett's State Trials, page 727.

Argument of George R. Sage,

Counsel for Plaintiffs

May it Please Your Honors—The plaintiffs allege that they bring their action on behalf of themselves and many others, citizens and tax-payers of the city of Cincinnati, the defendants, that they represent the views and opinions, not only of themselves, but of many others, also citizens and tax-payers of the city of Cincinnati. The truth of these allegations is admitted. The questions involved in the action are of a public and highly important character, and involve principles and rights justly held dear by us all. It is proper that the discussion be conducted with decorum and dignity, that it be based upon the facts and the law, and that we be not carried beyond either by individual prejudices or opinions.

Your Honors suggested, at the opening of the argument, that it would be proper for us to inquire what religion is meant by the declaration, in the Constitution, that "religion is essential to good government." To that question I propose, first, to address myself, and I claim that the religion referred to is that religion which is founded in a belief in the Being, Attributes and Providence of Almighty God, and in the Holy Bible, as the revelation of His will to mankind. The expression of gratitude to God in the preamble of the Constitution, and the declaration of the right of all men to worship Him according to the dictates of their own consciences, seem to me to put this proposition beyond doubt or cavil. But there are one or two facts outside the Constitution itself which remove all question upon this point. The first of these is, that there is no other religion known any where on earth which can be observed in all its requirements within the State of Ohio without conflict with the statute law, and that which has been the statute law from the beginning. The Hindoo mother, in the fervor of her religious enthusiasm, can not sacrifice her babe without being guilty of infanticide, nor can she plead the rights of conscience against the penalty of the law. The Mohammedan can not here put into practice his religious belief, nor the Mormon, with regard to polygamy, without being subject to indictment and punishment. Even the Atheist may not blaspheme the name of God, or of Jesus Christ, or of the Holy Ghost, whatever may be his opinions, without coming within the prohibitions provided by the statute. On the other hand, compliance with the teachings and requirements of the Christian religion is all that is necessary to make a perfect citizen. Whatever makes a man a good Christian, makes him a good citizen; and this, because the government is founded upon and is consistent with Christianity in all its departments and laws. This recognition of religion and of God necessarily implies the recognition of the Holy Bible, because from no other source can a knowledge of the being and attributes of God or the truths of religion be derived.

My friends have referred to the traditions upon which the Jews depend, and from which the Catholic derives a portion of his faith. If they intend to intimate that the Jew or the Catholic makes tradition superior to the Bible they are in error. There is no religious tenet held by any intelligent, conscientious Catholic, nor by any intelligent and conscientious Jew, for which he is not ready to refer to the Bible for authority and proof; that is the foundation, and the traditions come in merely as aids or supports in their opinion of that which is taught in the book itself. The Bible being the exposition, therefore, of revealed truth, is the foundation of religion.

There can be no religion without the Bible. The Bible is essential to religion, and religion is essential to good government, and both are, therefore, under the protection and fostering care of the government. This constitutional recognition of religion is a recognition of its truth and divine origin. It is impossible to suppose that the government, having in its fundamental law declared religion to be essential, can at the same time, admit that it may be false or of human origin, or any thing else than it purports to be. It follows as a legal proposition that the truth and inspiration of the Holy Scriptures, and the divinity of the religion which they teach are not to be questioned in a court of justice.

For all purposes of the State and of justice, the presumption in favor of the truth of the Bible, and of the religion of the Bible, is conclusive. Upon this proposition the decision by the Supreme Court of the United States, in the case of *Vidal et al.* v. *Girard's Executors*, 2 Howard's Reports, is exactly in point. I read from page 198:

"It is also said, and said truly, that the Christian religion is a part of the common law of Pennsylvania. But this proposition is to be received with its appropriate qualifications, and in connection with the Bill of Rights of that State, as found in its Constitution of government. The Constitution of 1790 (and the like provision will, in substance, be found in the Constitution of 1776, and in the existing Constitution of 1838), expressly declares 'that all men have a natural and indefeasible right to worship Almighty God according to the dictates of their own consciences; no man can of right be compelled to attend, erect, or support any place of worship, or to maintain any ministry against his consent; no human authority can, in any case whatever, control or interfere with the rights of conscience; and no preference shall ever be given by law to any religious establishments or modes of worship.' Language more comprehensive for the complete protection of every variety of religious opinion could scarcely be used; and it must have been intended to extend equally to all sects, whether they believed in Christianity or not, and whether they were Jews or Infidels. So that we are compelled to admit that, although Christianity be a part of the common law of the State, yet it is so in this qualified sense, that its divine origin and truth are admitted, and therefore it is not to be maliciously and openly reviled and blasphemed against to the annoyance of believers, or the injury of the public. Such was the doctrine of the Supreme Court of Pennsylvania in *Updegraff* v. *The Commonwealth*, 11 Serg. & Rawle, 394."

The Court will observe that the provisions of the Bill of Rights of the State of Pennsylvania are no stronger or more explicit than those of our own Bill of Rights, and we have, in addition, the emphatic declaration that religion is essential to good government. The Court will also observe that the recognition of the truth and divinity of the Christian religion is regarded by the highest judicial authority of the land, as entirely consistent with the complete protection of every variety of religious opinion, and perfect liberty to all who believe and all who disbelieve in Christianity.

This recognition of Christianity—and I wish to say that I use that term in a very broad sense, as meaning the religion of the Bible, not in any limited or narrow sense—this recognition of Christianity or the religion of the Bible, results from propositions which are at the foundation of and necessary to the constitution and stability of society.

De Quincey says: "As is the god of any nation, such will be that nation. God, however falsely conceived of by man, even though splintered into fragments by Polytheism, or disfigured by the darkest mythologies, is still the greatest of all objects offered to human contemplation." No nation exists in our time, no nation has existed in times past, without a religion, and that religion the basis of its distinctive national character. We have all heard of the wise man, quoted by Fletcher, of Saltoun, to the effect "that if he was permitted to make all the ballads he need not care who should make the laws of a nation." Much more true is it that if you be informed what is the religion of a nation, you can with certainty describe the general character of its laws and institutions.

Religion is, always has been, and always will be, the great conservative element of national life. It can not be otherwise. Show me a people without religion and I will show you a people without government, without laws, without civilization, without national life. Take away all religion, and you leave only barbarism. Now, upon this proposition, that religion stamps the civilization and the character of the nation, I wish to read from an authority which may, perhaps be recognized as such by some of my friends. I mean Edward Everett, in his address before the Massachusetts Bible Society, on the 27th day of May, 1850. It is to be found in vol. ii, p. 664, of his works:

"There is another consideration of a practical nature which I should be glad to offer to the meeting, if I have not exceeded my allowance of time. We all have pretty strong, and, as I think, just impressions of the superiority of Christendom over Mohammedan, Hindoo and Pagan countries. Our civilization, I know, is still very imperfect, impaired by many a vice which disgraces our Christian nurture—by many a woe which

> 'Appears a spot upon a vestal's robe,
> The worse for what it soils.'

But when we compare the condition of things in Christendom with that which prevails in the countries just named, we find that all the evils which exist among us prevail there to a greater degree, while they are subject to innumerable others, so dreadful as to make us almost ready to think it were better for the mass of the people, humanely speaking, if they had never been born. Well, now, Mr. Chairman, what maketh us to differ? I know of no final and sufficient cause but the different character of Christianity, and the religions which prevail in Turkey, Persia, India, China, and the other semi-civilized or barbarous countries, and this difference, so far as I know, is accurately reflected in their sacred books respectively. I mean, sir, that the Bible stands to the Koran and the Vedas in the same relation as that in which Christianity stands to Mohammedanism, or Brahamism, or Buddhism, or Christendom to Turkey, Hindostan, or China."

I shall not attempt to follow my learned friends on the other side, who have preceded me, through the mazes of learning which they have threaded in their arguments. I do not propose to discuss the truth of the Bible or the Christian religion as a theological proposition. I lay it down, and I think I have established that, as a legal proposition, both are true for all purposes of the State and of this case. But I will say that if the gentlemen on the other side, will, all of them, agree upon any proposition against the authority, or the authenticity of the Holy Scriptures, or upon any proposition of morals not derived from the Scriptures, to be preferred thereto, or substituted therefor, I will engage that my colleague, Mr. King, will give to either proposition such attention as may be necessary for the purposes of this case; but if they can not so agree we shall be content to leave them to the fate of a house divided against itself.

It is a great mistake to suppose that our National or State Government is indifferent to or divorced from religion. Every government depends for its support upon main strength or upon the consent of the governed. No government of strength, not even a despotism, can safely come in conflict with the religion of its people. This proposition has been so well understood that it has been the universal practice of such governments to adopt the prevailing religion, and make it an ally of the State. No government which depends upon the will of the people can, by any possibility, disregard or oppose the religion of the people. Especially is this true of a representative government such as ours. The morals of the people are derived from and depend upon their religion. The sense of right and wrong of the people is a religious sense. Their sense of duty to the State is derived from and subordinate to their sense of duty to their religion. And this moral, this religious sense of the people is, and always will be, reflected in the legislative, in the judicial and in the executive departments of the government.

Hence it is that the violation of the Christian Sabbath is forbidden by law—hence blasphemy against God, Jesus Christ or the Holy Ghost is made a statutory offense, and the requirements and prohibitions of religion touching the dealings of man with his fellow man are adopted by legislation or enforced by the courts as a part of our system of jurisprudence. Thus the commandments of the Decalogue which relate to the duty of man to man are reflected in the statute laws of Ohio. The whole doctrine of charities, as administered by the courts of equity, is an emanation from the Christian religion, and was unknown throughout all the world till the first dawn of Christianity; and the same is true as to our reformatory and benevolent institutions. Even the Golden Rule is reflected in that maxim of equity: "He who seeks equity must do equity." The inauguration of our Executive is always preceded by religious exercises. The sessions of our legislative assemblies are opened with prayer. Every year the people are called upon by the highest authority of the State, seconding the proclamation of the Executive of the nation, to render thanksgiving to Almighty God for the blessings and prosperity they have enjoyed; and when famine, pestilence or war afflicts the nation, the people are called upon to humble themselves in fasting and prayer. And when we turn to the Constitution itself, we find the solemn declaration that religion is essential to good government; a declaration so emphatically true that if Christianity were stricken from our Constitution and laws, its sanction and influence withdrawn from the affairs of the State, hopeless anarchy and confusion would result. Thus we see that Christianity has formed the State in its own image, and yet we are told upon authority of the dictum of a judge of the Supreme Court of Ohio that Christianity is no part of the law of the State. I do not propose to discuss that proposition at length. That has been assigned to my colleague, who will close the argument for the plaintiffs. But I wish merely to say that I recognize the decision in the case of *Bloom* v. *Richards* as sound law. The proposition that Christianity is no part of the law of the State, so far as it was applicable to that case, I recognize as exactly correct; but in so far as Judge Thurman has gone beyond that, and undertaken to dispose of Christianity, or put it away from the State, his decision is entitled to no more regard, and is no more authority, than what is called the Dred Scott decision. We do not claim that Christianity is part of the law of the State of Ohio, as it may be said to be part of the common law of England. We call no one into court to answer for any infraction of the precepts of the Bible unless we find a statutory provision, or a recognized provision of law which meets the case. But what we claim is that the influence, sanction and authority of religion are recognized by the State; that religion is recognized by the Constitution itself as the bond of society, the basis upon which our institutions rest, and essential to good government and the safety of the State.

But the Constitution declares that religion is essential to good government, and in the same sentence requires the establishment of common schools. Waiving, for the present, the question whether this proposition is connected with the establishment of schools, what is its meaning, and what its application? It is not an abstract proposition. Our constitutions are not so made up. Every proposition, every sentence, has its meaning, its import and its force, and a practical bearing in connection with the affairs of the State. It does not mean simply that religious worship and the rights of conscience shall be protected, for there are in the same section of the Bill of Rights ample and specific guarantees for both, and those guarantees are, moreover, for the citizen, while the proposition that religion is essential to good government is for the State. It does not mean that it is necessary that there should be an established church, for that is expressly forbidden; nor does it mean that any form of religious belief shall be forced upon the citizen; for the right of all men to worship Almighty God according to the dictates of their own consciences is declared to be a natural and indefeasible right.

We may perhaps derive some light upon this subject by considering that not merely religion, but religion, morality and knowledge, are, by the terms of the Constitution, declared to be essential to good government. As to knowledge, we understand that it is essential that it be generally diffused among the citizens. We have the same understanding as to morality. Can we then come to any other understanding as to religion? The provision of the Constitution that religion is essential to good government, properly interpreted, is then an announcement that it is necessary to the welfare of the State that religion shall pervade society—that it be recognized, and its influence felt by the citizens. That this is the true meaning of the provision is apparent from the consideration already adverted to, that our laws are in harmony with religion, and derive their greatest power and efficacy from the religious sentiment. There is nothing enjoined by law which is not in accordance with and sanctioned by the teachings of religion. There could be no law framed by the legislative authority of the State of Ohio in conflict with the religious sentiment that could stand or be enforced for one day. Suppose, for instance, the General Assembly should this winter enact that the work upon the roads throughout the State should next spring be done upon the Sundays of a certain month. Of what force would be such a law?

Mr. Matthews. Do you mean that it would be unconstitutional?

Mr. Sage. Certainly I do.

Judge Storer. I hope that point will be argued.

Mr. Sage. It would be in direct conflict with the propositions I have stated. It would be a palpable violation of the duty imposed by the Constitution upon the General Assembly, "to pass suitable laws to protect every religious denomination in the peaceable enjoyment of its mode of worship." It would be a flagrant outrage upon the right of conscience guaranteed by the Constitution, to undertake by legislative enactment to force the citizen, on the day set apart as holy by his religion, from that worship to common labor. It would not only be unconstitutional, but it would be suicidal, for the State thus to attack religion.

We have no morality which is not enjoined by religion. We have no rule of conduct prescribed by law touching the dealings of man toward his fellow man, or by the State, which is not to be found more explicitly and more forcibly commanded by the Divine Author of that religion. And as the true strength of the Government is its reliance upon the intelligence, patriotism and moral sense of the citizens, it is indispensable that religion, which is the basis of that virtue, patriotism and morality, should be encouraged, and its elementary truths made known to the people.

It is only in Christian nations that what we understand by the majesty of the law is recognized and felt in the administration of justice and the conduct of public affairs, and no where upon earth is that majesty so exemplified as in these United States of America. It is Christianity which gives to the law that power and majesty which enables the General Government to enforce its requirements, to collect its revenues and to administer its affairs in this great State of Ohio, without the presence or aid of a single soldier in arms. It is Christianity and the influence of Christianity which gives to the State Government a power, limited and measured only by the aggregate strength of the people, and which enables it by the aid of its executive and ministerial officers to preserve order, protect life and property, and regulate society, without even the semblance of military power. It is Christianity that renders this service vital and effective, and for the reason that the religious sentiment is the prevailing sentiment, and the basis of the morality of the State, on which basis alone moral habits can safely be trusted, and the Government be secure. It is, therefore, the duty of every good citizen, as a citizen, whether he be or not a believer in Christianity, to give it his countenance and support as the strong arm and main reliance of the State. The conscience of Christianity is more potent as a police agent than the standing army which enforces the will of the most powerful despot. Upon this subject the words of Daniel Webster, in his oration at Plymouth on the settlement of New England, are significant and pertinent:

"Lastly, our ancestors established this system of government on morality and religious sentiment. Moral habits, they believe, can not safely be trusted to any other foundation than religious principles, nor any government be secure which is not supported by moral habits. Living under the heavenly light of revelation, they hoped to find all the social dispositions, all the duties which men owe to each other and to society, enforced and performed. Whatever makes men good citizens makes them good Christians."

I refer also to the case of *Lindenmuller* v. *The People*, 33 Barbour's Supreme Court Reports, N. Y., 548; a case upon an indictment for an alleged violation of the Christian Sabbath. The Court decided that "Christianity is not the legal religion of the State as established by law," but that the provisions and recitals of the Constitution, which are the same in effect as those of the Constitution of Ohio, "very clearly recognize some of the fundamental principles of the Christian religion, and are certainly very far from ignoring God as the Supreme Ruler and Judge of the Universe, and the Christian religion as the religion of the people, embodying the common faith of the community with its ministers and ordinances, existing without the aid of, or political connection with, the State, but as intimately connected with a good government, and the only sure basis of sound morals." Again: "The public peace and public welfare are greatly dependent upon the protection of the religion of the country, and the preventing or punishing of offenses against it, and acts wantonly committed subversive of it. The claim of the defense, carried to its necessary sequence, is, that the Bible and religion, with all its ordinances, including the Sabbath, are as effectually abolished as they were in France during the Revolution, and so effectually abolished that duties may not be enforced as duties to the State, because they have been heretofore associated with acts of religious worship, or connected with religious duties."

So in the case of *The People* v. *Ruggles*, 8 Johnson's Reports, 291, Chief Justice Kent says that to revile the religion professed by almost the whole community is an abuse of the right of religious opinion and free discussion secured by the Constitution, and that the Constitution does not secure the same regard to the religion of Mahomet, or of the Grand Lama, as to that of our Savior, for the plain reason that we are a Christian people, and the morality of the country is deeply engrafted upon Christianity.

So, too, in the debates in the Constitutional Convention of New York, in 1821, such men as Chancellor Kent, Chief Justice Spencer, Rufus King, and Martin Van Buren, agreed that the Christian religion was engrafted upon the law, and entitled to protection as the basis of our morals and the strength of our Government.

The same principles were announced by the Supreme Court of Pennsylvania, in *Updegraff* v. *The Commonwealth*, 11 Serg. & Rawle, 394; and in Massachusetts, in *The Commonwealth* v. *Kneeland*, 20 Pickering, 206; in Arkansas, in *Show* v. *The State*, 5 Eng. 259; and in Delaware, in the case of *The State* v. *Chandler*, 2 Harrington, 553.

But there is another principle which is fundamental and vital to our system of government, and of the first importance to the purity and influence of religion. It is that the conscience of the citizen shall be as free as if the government were not in existence. It is a mockery to talk of the liberty of men whose consciences are in fetters. There is no slavery more abject than the slavery of opinion or conscience. Liberty, without liberty of soul, is liberty stripped of all that makes it valuable—it is a cheat and a delusion. To make a man free, the whole man, soul, mind and body must be free, and whatever is in conflict with this proposition is in conflict with everything dear to the true citizen and the true Christian. Mr. Webster, in the oration to which reference has already been made, says: "The love of religious liberty is a stronger sentiment, when fully excited, than an attachment to civil and political freedom. That freedom, which the conscience demands, and which men feel bound by their hope of salvation to contend for, can hardly fail to be attained. Conscience in the cause of religion and the worship of the Deity prepares the mind to act and to suffer beyond most other causes. It sometimes gives an impulse so irresistible that no fetters of power or of opinion can withstand it. History instructs us that this love of religious liberty—a compound sentiment in the breast of man, made up of the clearest sense of right, and the highest conviction of duty—is able to look the sternest despotism in the face, and, with means apparently most inadequate, to shake principalities and powers."

These propositions, in all their force, are recognized by our Constitution, and the liberty of conscience referred to is the right of every man, woman and child, of every creed, or of no creed, of every condition and station, and of every birth, native or foreign. And this right is a natural and indefeasible right. It can not, under any circumstances, be abridged, or nullified; the whole power of the State can not interfere with it, nor can the State make any movement, directly or indirectly, in conflict with it, under any pretext or for any purpose. And although religion is declared to be, and is, essential to good government, the State can not foster or encourage religion by any means which in the least violate the right of any individual conscience. On the other hand, whatever the State can do in this regard without violating that right, it not only may do, but is bound to do—not for the advancement or benefit of religion, but for its own safety and welfare—and every Board of Education, and every officer of the State, is under the same imperative obligation.

This brings us exactly to the point to be discussed, and upon which this case turns.

The General Assembly has, in accordance with the requirements of the Constitution, established a system of public instruction, which is intended for all the youth of the State. In fact, the system does furnish the educational instruction, and the only instruction of that character which the great body of the youth of the State receive. A State school fund, consisting of a sum produced by an annual levy and assessment on the grand list of the taxable property of the State is provided for, to be annually distributed to the several counties, exclusively for the support of common schools, in proportion to the number of youth between the ages of five and twenty-one years, as ascertained by an enumeration to be annually taken as provided by law, and local taxation in addition may be imposed by authority of the local boards of education. The system is a public, not a private system. It is for the benefit of the State, not merely for the benefit of the youth, for whom instruction is provided; nor for the relief, or benefit, or assistance of their parents. Accordingly, the State holds every man subject to taxation in proportion to his property, without reference to whether he himself have or have not children to be benefited by the education for which he pays. We regard the system "as a wise and liberal system of police, by which property and life, and the peace of society are secured."

Counsel for the defendants content themselves with a much more narrow and limited view. They speak of the school system as if it were a private system, and as if the citizen paid taxes for the education of his own children and for his and their benefit. Do they not know that from the city of Cincinnati and county of Hamilton sixty thousand dollars of school money raised by taxation go to Columbus and are thence distributed to other and less populous counties? Have they stopped to consider that we pay taxes every year in this city and county for the education of children in remote portions of the State? Do those who are so conscientiously exercised about religious instruction as to insist that their taxes shall not be applied in support of such instruction, flatter themselves that they will escape that result by the enforcement of the miserable resolutions put through the Board of Education, while the Bible is left in the schools of the rural districts? Let them not deceive themselves, the money they pay into the treasury goes all over the State. The common school system is not administered upon any such narrow, contracted view as that upon which the whole argument for the defense rests. There are citizens paying taxes for the support of the public schools whose children were educated in those schools, while they were paying taxes twenty, thirty, forty years ago. Yet they are not exempt, because the schools are for the benefit of the State, and not merely for the benefit of those who have children to be educated.

It is evident then that such instruction as will tend to secure life, property and the peace of society,—such instruction as will fit the youth in the schools to be good and useful citizens, should be provided. In this connection let it be borne in mind that in the petition it is alleged, that of the children educated in the schools, large numbers receive no religious instruction or knowledge of the Holy Bible except that communicated to them in the schools, and that such instruction is indispensable to fit such children to be good citizens of the State of Ohio and of the United States. Both allegations are admitted to be true by the defendants. Upon these admissions it follows that it is the duty of the Board of Education to provide such religious instruction as is necessary to qualify the children in the schools for the positions they are to occupy in the State as citizens. Up to the point of interference with the right of conscience the duty is imperative and can not be escaped.

But here we are met by an appeal to the discretion of the Board of Education. It is claimed that that discretion is unlimited, and that the Court has no jurisdiction over it. The power of the Board, it is said, is supreme, and there is no remedy but to wait for the expiration of the official terms of the members and then appeal to the people to elect better men to fill their places—in other words, the claim is that the policy of the public schools is subject solely to the shifting surges of popular opinion as represented by the Board. But the discretion of the Board is not unlimited. The members of the Board are trustees of the schools. Their discretion must be exercised in furtherance of the objects of their trust. The Court will not suffer it to be mischievously or ruinously exercised. (Hill on Trustees, 482; *De Mànneville* v. *Crompton*, 1 V. & B. 354–9; Lewin on Trusts, 538, and cases cited.) Suppose the Board were composed of savans, who should, in their wisdom, undertake to prohibit all instruction in the schools except in the Sanscrit language, could not the Court interfere? Unquestionably, for the reason that the action of the Board would be utterly subversive of the objects for which the schools were established. Suppose they should order that in a ward of the city having a majority of children of German parents and a minority of American, that instruction should be exclusively in the German language, would the Court permit that? Certainly not, for that would be in conflict with the idea, essential to the safety and welfare of the State, that we are, and are to be a homogeneous people. Let us come a little nearer. Would the Court permit the Board to carry into effect a rule excluding all teachings of morality from the schools, even if there were in the statute no clause requiring instruction in morality?

Is it not absurd to maintain that the Court would be powerless to prevent so gross an abuse of discretion by the Board? Is it not an insult to common sense to assert that there is no judicial power to stop even the most flagrant violation of duty by the Board, however detrimental to the schools or the public, notwithstanding the statute of its creation clearly makes the Board a department of the corporate authority of the city, and the municipal code expressly authorizes the Court to restrain the abuse by the city of its corporate powers, and that too, upon the application of any of the tax-payers? And now, keeping in view the declaration of the Constitution that religion is essential to good government, and that the framers of the Constitution made that the first reason for requiring the establishment of schools, is it within the discretion, is it within the power of the Board, to prohibit all religious instruction in the schools? That is what they have undertaken. The prohibition is without qualification or exception. It is absolute and imperative. It sweeps away everything, it leaves nothing. The rule is as broad and exclusive as language can make it. It can not be frittered away by the explanation or construction of counsel. Whatever religion means in the Constitution, it means in the rule. Counsel can not by any subtlety of sophistry or skill in evasion make the religion of the Constitution as broad as the universe, and the religion of the rule as narrow as the gauge of their argument. Their ingenuity is marvelous, but it is futile. The rule needs no explanation. It explains itself. They can not escape its meaning. They are here to defend it, not to attack it by denying its true and only construction.

"Religious instruction, and the reading of religious books, including the Holy Bible," is the phrase of the prohibition. There is no foundation for the plea that that means only the Bible. It means all that religion means, and it can not be made to mean any less. The Constitution says religion is essential to good government—therefore schools and the means of instruction shall be encouraged—the Board admits that religion is essential to good government, and, therefore, it shall be thrust out of the schools. Is this outrageous abuse of power to find refuge in the technicality of discretion? Can even the General Assembly appeal to its discretion to avoid judicial condemnation of its unconstitutional acts? No, if your Honors please, the discretion of the Board gives them no authority to prohibit instruction in any thing which the Constitution, in connection with the establishment of schools, declares to be essential to good government. Was it competent for the General Assembly, when it enacted the school law, to prohibit all religious instruction in the schools? Will any one of the counsel for the defense, in the face of the Constitution, commit himself to that proposition? Will they commit themselves to the proposition that the School Board, the creature of the General Assembly, can do what the General Assembly itself, under the restraint of the Constitution, can not do? If not, let them abandon this plea of discretion and meet us on the merits. Let them demonstrate if they can that no religious instruction is possible without a violation of the constitutional right of conscience.

But there is another answer to this plea of discretion. Trustees invested with a discretionary power are not bound to assign their reasons for the way in which they exercise it; yet, if they do state their reasons, and it thereby appears that they were laboring under an error, the Court will set aside the conclusion to which they come upon false premises. (Lewin on Trusts, 543; *Re Beloved Wilkes Charity*, 3 Mac. & Gor. 440.) In *Regina* v. *The Bailiffs of Ipswich*, 2 Ld. Raymond's Reports, 1240, on mandamus to restore a party whom the corporation had discharged from the office of recorder, Holt said: "That if he had been an officer *ad libitum*, the corporation ought to have returned that and relied upon it, and it would have been a good return; but they could not take advantage of that when they had returned the cause, if the cause were not sufficient." The Board has answered, setting up the reasons for its action, and every member of the Board who voted for the resolutions, has joined in the answer. We have upon their own statement all the grounds of the exercise of the pretended discretion of the Board. They are stated fully and circumstantially. We know exactly what prompted the passage of the resolutions. The Board and the majority have appealed from their discretion to their reasons. They have put the grounds of their action before the Court, and have thereby made it competent for the Court to pass judgment upon them. They have submitted themselves to the jurisdiction of the Court, and it is now too late for them to invoke their discretion as against that jurisdiction. The

Court may look into the reasons assigned, and if it find them derogatory to the Constitution or to Christianity, it may set them aside and annul the rule itself. But it is not a question of discretion. It is a question of power. If the Board has the power to do what it has attempted, there is the end of the case. If it has exceeded its power, the Court can interfere by its prohibitory writ. The rule is stated with great clearness in Story's Equity Jurisprudence, sec. 955, *a*:

"The question has been made, how far a court of equity has jurisdiction to interfere in cases of public functionaries who are exercising special public trusts or functions. As to this, the established doctrine now is, that so long as those functionaries strictly confine themselves within the exercise of those duties which are confided to them by the law, this Court will not interfere. The Court will not interfere to see whether any alteration or regulation which they may direct is good or bad; but, if they are departing from that power which the law has vested in them, if they are assuming to themselves a power over property which the law does not give to them, this Court no longer considers them as acting under authority of their commission, but treats them, whether they be a corporation or individuals, merely as persons dealing with property without legal authority."

To the same effect are the cases of *Frewin* v. *Lewis*, 4 Mylne & Craig, 254; *Freeman* v. *School Directors*, 37 Penn. State, 385; *Clark* v. *The Board of Directors*, 24 Iowa, 266. In *Dummer* v. *The Corporation of Chittenham*, 14 Vesey, 245, Lord Eldon sustained a bill against a corporation and its members, trustees for a charity, for a discovery and injunction against a resolution depriving the complainant of his office of school-master, although the corporation had the power of nominating the master, and of dismissing him at their will and pleasure. It was held that the Court could entertain a bill against the trustees as individuals to obtain a discovery whether through their means, so manifested, there was such an abuse of the discretion vested in the corporation, as trustees, as the Court would reform. In *Robinson* v. *Chartered Bank*, 1 Equity Cases, L. R. S. 32, Sir J. Romilly, M. R., held that the court of directors must exercise its power reasonably, and would be controlled by a court of equity. In *Weston's case*, 6 Equity Cases,

238, it was held that the discretion of the directors of a company was not arbitrary, but must be exercised in a just and reasonable manner. In *Davis* v. *The Mayor, etc., of the City of New York*, 1 Duer, 451, where there was an injunction restraining the mayor, aldermen and commonalty of the city, from making a grant by resolution to certain parties to construct a street railway on Broadway, the Court, said p. 498: "A court of equity will not interfere to control the exercise of a discretionary power where the discretion is legally and honestly exercised, and it has no reason to believe the fact is otherwise, but will interfere whenever it has grounds for believing that its interference is necessary to prevent abuse, injustice, or oppression, the violation of a trust, or the consummation of a fraud. It will interfere—and it is bound to interfere—whenever it has reason to believe that those in whom the discretion is vested are prepared illegally, wantonly, or corruptly, to trample upon rights and sacrifice interests, which they are specially bound to watch over and protect." This case was affirmed by the Court of Appeals, 5 Selden, 263, and is exactly in point both as to the kind of remedy and its application.

But we are met with another objection. It is insisted that the writ of injunction is not the proper remedy,—that the rule of the Board, the enforcement of which we pray to have enjoined, became operative by and upon its passage, and that in any event the repeal of the rule providing for reading a portion of the Bible by the teachers, and appropriate singing by the pupils at the opening exercises of the schools, can not be affected by the judgment of the Court because it is an accomplished fact.

The answer to these objections is easy. The petition alleges, and the answer of the Board, and of the clerk of the Board, admits, that the rule we seek to have enjoined has not been promulgated to the teachers, nor put in operation in the schools, but is yet in the hands of the clerk, through whom alone it can be officially promulgated. Moreover, we pray that upon final hearing, the rule complained of be adjudged null and void. The rules of the Board make new rules operative only when officially communicated by the clerk to the teachers, which has not been done in this instance; the writ of injunction is therefore the proper remedy. If the injunction be made perpetual the new rule never will be operative. Thus we are brought back to the question of the power of the Board. In addition to the authorities already cited, and in answer to the suggestion that a writ of *quo warranto* should have been applied for, the Court is referred to the case of *Bradley* v. *Commissioners et al.*, 2 Humphrey's Reports, 428, where it was held that "even where the writ of *quo warranto* is the common law mode of redressing certain grievances, a court of chancery will interfere upon the principle of *quia timet*, and use its process of injunction for the prevention of great and irreparable mischief." Then, too, it is objected that the writ must be refused unless the Court is prepared to say judicially just what and how much religious instruction shall be imparted in the schools, or in other words, unless we would be entitled to the mandatory writ to compel the Board to provide specific religious instruction, we can not have the prohibitory writ against its exclusion. But this is only a new statement of an old, erroneous and exploded notion. It was formerly laid down that when the positive part of an agreement could not be enforced by the Court, it would not enforce the negative by injunction. (*Kemble* v. *Kean*, 6 Sim. 333.) But it is now clearly established by the recent case of *Lumley* v. *Wagner*, (1 De G., M. & G. 604,) that where there is an agreement in part positive and in part negative, and the positive part is such as the Court might be unable to enforce specifically, it may yet interfere in respect of the negative part by means of injunction. The authorities are collected in Fry on Specific Performance, secs. 555, 556, 557.

Again, it was claimed by Judge Stallo that the act of the Board is legislative, and therefore beyond the reach of the Court. Even if legislative, it is void if in excess of the power of the Board. But if it be a legislative act, there is no sort of authority for it, because the Constitution expressly limits the legislative power to the General Assembly, and the General Assembly can not delegate that power to any other body or to the people. (*C., W. & Z. R. R. Co.* v. *The Commissioners of Clinton Co.*, 1 Ohio State Rep. 77.) From all points of view we see that the question upon which the case rests is whether the Board had the right and the power to pass and enforce the resolutions of the first of November.

The Constitution declaring that religion, morality, and knowledge, are essential to good government, and making that declaration the foundation and reason for requiring the General Assembly to pass suitable laws to encourage schools and the means of instruction, and the schools established accordingly being public and not private—for the benefit of the State and not for the benefit of individuals—the Board is under an obligation, imposed by the Constitution itself, to provide instruction in each one of the great essentials above named, unless it can be shown that such instruction can not be given without violating some constitutional right of the citizens of the State.

The only right with which it is claimed instruction in religion comes in conflict, is the right of conscience. The justification of the prohibition of all religious instruction must be found, if at all, in an insuperable and controlling objection, and that objection can rest only upon the liberty of conscience guaranteed by the Constitution. If the defendants can not plant themselves immovably there, they have no standing anywhere—no excuse—no justification. If there be any religious instruction which can be imparted in the schools without interfering with the rights of conscience, that instruction the Board must provide. To omit to provide instruction in what the State has declared to be essential to good government, and in what every member of the Board admits to be indispensable to fit the children of the schools to be good citizens, would be a palpable and gross violation of duty. To prohibit absolutely and imperatively such instruction would be to strike a blow at the great object for which the schools were established; a blow which, if it should reach its mark, would let out the life-blood of the whole system of public instruction.

Thus the great question is whether religious instruction can be imparted in the public schools without interfering with the rights of conscience. My friends on the other side admit that if it can the Board has no right to exclude it, and we admit if it can not it must go out.

Now, up to this time we have had very few definitions. My friends on the other side were for two days generalizing upon the propositions involved in this case. No one undertook to define the meaning of the expression of the Constitution, that religion is essential to good government. No one undertook to define the rights of conscience. It seemed to be assumed that the right of conscience was so indefinite, so general, so elastic, as to be whatever any citizen might choose to claim. I maintain that this right of conscience is a legal right. It is a constitutional right. It is not a whim. It is not a caprice. It is not what every citizen may choose to assert. It is something capable of ascertainment from the Constitution and the history and practice of the Government. It is that, and it is nothing more. The citizen can not establish for himself any new rights, any rights which are not recognized by the Constitution or by the State. A very good illustration of this proposition was stated by Lord Brougham, in a speech made in the House of Commons. He supposed the case of a member of the Society of Friends, who should come into a court of justice and say that his conscience not only precluded him from taking an oath, but because he had strong feelings on the subject of capital punishment, also prevented him from giving evidence which might affect the life of an individual. The answer which would be given to such a person would be this: "Sir, you have no right to have a conscience on such a subject at all; the Legislature is the only judge of the necessity of taking away a man's life, and your notion of jurisprudence must not stand in the way of justice."

Now, my friends have referred to Roger Williams, and very justly, as the founder of religious liberty. I know it is sometimes claimed that the liberty of conscience which was proclaimed in Maryland was prior to the time of Roger Williams, and that the Catholic colony in Maryland is entitled to the honor of establishing religious liberty in this country.

But we all know that that was a very qualified liberty. Any one is curious enough to refer to those old laws will find that whoever should either blaspheme or deny the Trinity, or any of the persons of the Godhead, was punishable with death. And whoever should revile or deny any of the Evangelists, or the Virgin Mary, should, for the first offense, be subject to a fine of five pounds; or, in default of payment, thirty-nine lashes, in the discretion of the lord proprietor of the province. For the second offense, ten pounds, or the same alternative. For the third offense, forfeiture of all property, and banishment from the colony forever; a sort of liberty which the Board of Cincinnati, the majority of them, would not much relish.

Roger Williams, in a letter which he addressed to the town of Providence, in January, 1654 (Arnold's *History of Rhode Island*, vol. 1, p. 254), gives an illustration of the right of conscience, which is as clear and masterly as anything since written.

"There goes many a ship to sea, with many hundred souls in one ship, whose weal and woe is common, and is a true picture of a commonwealth, or a human combination or society. It hath fallen out, sometimes, that both Papists and Protestants, Jews and Turks, may be embarked in one ship; upon which supposal I affirm that all the liberty of conscience that ever I pleaded for turns upon these two hinges; that none of the Papists, Protestants, Jews, or Turks, be forced to come to the ship's prayers or worship, nor compelled from their own particular prayers or worship, if they practice any. I further add that I never denied that, notwithstanding this liberty, the commander of the ship ought to command the ship's course; yea, and also command that justice, peace, and sobriety be kept and practiced, both among the seamen and all the passengers. If any of the seamen refuse to perform their service, or passengers to pay their freight; if any refuse to help in person or purse toward the common charges or defenses; if any refuse to obey the common laws and orders of the ship concerning their common peace or preservation; if any shall mutiny and rise up against their commanders and officers; if any should preach or write that there ought to be no commanders or officers, because all are equal in Christ; therefore no masters nor officers, no laws nor orders, no corrections nor punishments; I say I never denied but in such cases, whatever is pretended, the commander or commanders may judge, resist, compel, and punish, such transgressors, according to their deserts and merits."

My friends say that because there are Jews or Turks on board the ship there shall be no prayers or worship. Their proposition makes every man the master of the ship, and leaves it to be driven hither and thither in mid ocean, without chart or course or direction, and subject to the control of whoever chooses to mutiny against the existing order of affairs.

Mr. Matthews. It is you who are making the mutiny here.

Mr. Sage. We will see about that. The proposition we are making here is precisely in accordance with the doctrine stated by Roger Williams in this letter, and I shall undertake to prove that the gentlemen for the defense, instead of proclaiming the doctrine of liberty, are putting forward old dogmas of despotism, as though they had not long ago been exploded and recorded as a warning for the benefit of all who desire the welfare of religion or of the State.

Right here let us consider, very briefly, what conscience is and what is its office. It is said, generally, that it is the moral sense, or the faculty, power or principle within us which decides on the lawfulness or unlawfulness of our actions and affections, and instantly approves or condemns them. I understand that we derive our ideas of right and wrong from the combined action of the intellectual and moral faculties. Consequently those ideas depend greatly upon education. One child may be taught to believe that to speak an untruth under any circumstances is wrong; another that falsehood is right in certain cases. The conscience of the first child would censure where the conscience of the second would be silent or even approve. Yet conscience is the same in both cases. Conscience is not information; it is not prejudice; nor is it will. It is the executive faculty of the moral nature. It is that faculty which prompts us to do what we believe to be right, and restrains us from doing what we believe to be wrong. Liberty of conscience is liberty to obey the promptings of conscience. It is liberty to know all the facts and principles necessary to enable conscience to act intelligently and rightly. Upon this proposition I desire to read from the argument of Mr. Binney for the defense in the *Girard will case*, an extract or two so well conceived and happily expressed as to be well worthy the attention of the Court. Speaking of one of the provisions of Mr. Girard's will, he said:

"Again, he especially desires that by every proper means a pure attachment to the sacred rights of conscience shall be formed and fostered in their minds. What notion of the rights of conscience are they to obtain without being instructed in the nature and office of conscience? Are they not to be taught what conscience is, and whose voice it speaks, and that it is the great demonstrative proof, irrefragable, and universal, of the being of God? Are they not to learn that it is the faculty by which men judge of their own actions by comparing them with the law of God, as it remains perhaps faintly written on their hearts, but stands distinctly revealed in His word? And can they be instructed in its rights without being informed that this law is so much more obligatory than any law of man, that the duty of obeying the law of God is the foundation of all the rights of conscience; that conscience is in fine the expositor of the will of God?"

And further, speaking of the duty of the teachers under the will:

"May they not, must they not, enlighten the faculty in their pupils, improve its discriminating power, exercise them in reflecting on the moral character of their actions, on the character of their Creator and Redeemer, and in referring themselves ultimately to the supreme law derived from Revelation? Beyond all doubt, he does leave it to them without restraint, without a word or syllable to turn them from the path they shall think best. Beyond doubt it is their duty to walk in that path; and they can not take any path that leads to a right notion of conscience, that will not lead to the belief of a Supreme Judge and Sovereign, of whom conscience is the deputed governor in the human heart, and also to the desire of learning and obeying His will, whether inscribed on the heart itself or revealed in His word."

The very first right of conscience, that right upon which liberty of conscience altogether depends, is the right to be informed. That was always the proclamation of liberty. It was always a dogma of despotism that but one view should be communicated to the individual; that no religious tenet should be made known to the child or to the citizen, but that which was in accordance with the established religion of the State. It was against precisely that proposition that the founders of the Republic set up the standard of liberty of conscience, and established the provisions of our American Constitution. It was always the proposition of despotism that whatever the State did not approve should be concealed, and no knowledge of it be had. It was always the teaching of liberty that whether the fact were approved or disapproved, it was the right of the citizen to know that fact, and to apply his own judgment to it.

Judge Storer. It is a question whether the conscience had better not be left out of the discussion on both sides; whether the word conscience is not confined to the worship of Almighty God; whether a man has to exercise conscience, as he calls it, in doing wrong; and when he is arrested for a crime, excuse himself on the ground that he conscientiously believed he had a right to do what he did. Supposing there is a God, and he is Almighty, every man has a right to worship Him in his own form according to his own conscience.

Mr. Sage. There is a case in point in Cushing's Reports, vol. 2. The question was whether the exclusion of an Atheist from the witness stand, was a violation of the constitutional protection of the right of conscience. The Court said in their opinion, the constitutional provision had no reference to Atheists and to their competency as witnesses. It was intended to prevent persecution by punishing any one for his religious opinions, however erroneous they might be. But an Atheist is without any religion, true or false. The disbelief in the existence of any God, is not a religious, but an anti-religious sentiment.

Judge Storer. I can give an illustration of that which shows how liberal courts are in these matters. About eight months ago, a very respectable looking man appeared in that very witness box. When he was called upon to testify, he said he could not take the oath, and said he wanted to be excused, as he did not believe there was a God. I said, "Do you believe that you exist, yourself?" He said he did. Said I, "Why do you believe so?" He said, "Because I am conscious of my existence." I then said, "Who gave you that consciousness?" He thought a moment, and said, "I will be sworn."

Mr. Sage. Whatever may be the law upon that subject, I concede that the Constitution guarantees to the Atheist that there shall be no discrimination against him on account of his Atheism.

This right of conscience is no right to close up the mind against fact. That is despotism. That is not liberty. Liberty gives no right to the parent to say to his child, "You shall have no instruction in religious teachings, except what I choose to convey to you." That is the very pillar of religious despotism. It is the basis of all those persecutions to which my friend referred in his opening argument for the defense. They belong together and go together, and neither is the true doctrine of American laws or American constitutions. It seems to me that my friends clothe liberty in the black blood-stained garments of despotism, and the utterances which they give forth in her name come to us as the echoes of those old decrees of intolerance, which were followed by the rack, the faggot and the sword. I appeal from them. I appeal to the gentlemen who do not agree with me in regard to religion, that in putting forward these arguments they are putting forward propositions most dangerous and destructive of the principles of liberty. But for the translation of the Bible into the vernacular, none of us would be here to-day discussing these questions. Seal that book, proscribe it, or put it under the ban, and you put an end to our safety. But for the fact that the Bible is, and always has been, in our national life, recognized as the book of revealed truth, this republic would never have had an existence. You may take all the Korans, the Vedas, and all the treatises on morality, many of which have been so eloquently referred to by counsel for defendants, and put them in one pile and burn them, and with that burning destroy every remembrance of their teachings, and you will not affect society one whit. But take away that other Book which has stood through all times, which is the Book of to-day, the Book of a thousand years ago, and the Book of all time to come, take that away and all remembrance of its teachings and truths, and there will be nothing left upon which we may depend for our safety. And so far as you sanction the proposition that part of the community has the right to banish that Book from the public schools and the public places, to prevent its truths from being known, just so far do you establish a proposition of despotism. The provisions of the Constitution bear very significantly upon this point. The Constitution declares that religion is essential to good government, and that is given as the first reason for the establishment of schools. There is another and separate provision that no religious sect shall have exclusive control of the school fund. Why? In addition to the reasons already given, if the State give a portion of the fund to one sect or church, it will take its own children and bring them up in its own religion, and close their minds against all other religious instruction. The State would thereby lend its aid to build up a column of despotism. Ideas of intolerance in the minds of the children would be the necessary outgrowth of exclusively sectarian instruction—ideas, dangerous to the State and destructive of the liberties of the people. Hence, it is the true policy of the State that the Bible, which contains the elementary truths of religion, shall be read in the public schools, that all the children in the land, our future citizens, may know what it contains—and that those truths be made known to them, as the Almighty has revealed them, and not merely as interpreted by any sect or creed. It was the idea of the framers of the Constitution that the Bible should be free, and that all its truths should be free; that the children in the schools should be kept from the narrowing influence of one set of ideas; and from the notion that only one version of those truths should be received or tolerated. It was not the intention of the framers of the Constitution to encourage schools, to be conducted at the public expense, in which sectarian tenets alone should be taught.

And here I venture to anticipate the answer to these propositions, that the policy we advocate will produce the result we deprecate—that we are strengthening the Catholic parochial schools—whereas, if the policy of the Board be carried into operation those schools will be abandoned. Let not my friends cherish that delusion. Let them rather recall certain significant facts touching the relation of the Catholic Church to the public schools of Cincinnati. From the year 1829 to the year 1842, the Bible without note or comment was read in the schools, no one objecting. There were then no Catholic parochial schools. The Bishop of the Catholic Church—he who is now Archbishop—was for some time a member of the Board of Examiners, and active in support of the schools. In 1842 the first intimation of an objection was made. It was not to the reading of the Bible, but that Catholic children were required to read the "Protestant Bible and Testament." The Board promptly and unanimously conceded every thing suggested by the objection. From that time until the year 1852 no further objection was made. The Bible was read and the schools prospered. In 1852 the next move was made. Almost simultaneously a similar movement in the interest of the Catholic Church was made throughout the whole country. It is said that this was in accordance with the action of a secret conclave of the authorities of that church held in the city of Baltimore. Whether such was the fact is not material. A Catholic member of the Board, in the interest of the Catholic Church, presented a series of resolutions, admitting the necessity of reading the Bible in the schools, and authorizing the introduction of the translation approved by the Catholics and that approved by the Jews, and their use by those preferring them. The Board, upon assurances that its action would be satisfactory, enacted a rule granting all that the resolutions called for. The next year the Catholic parochial schools were established, and the whole power of the Catholic Church was arrayed against the public schools. The Board, in its annual report for that year, announced that they were "constrained to infer that no union of action or system is intended or desired by the assailants of the public schools upon any terms but such as are incompatible with the principles and usages which thus far have sustained the free schools of this country."

Now, my friends tell us if we will only consent to exclude the Bible and all religious instruction from the schools, the Catholic children will come into them, and the Catholic schools be broken up. How do they know? Upon what authority do they make this statement? Have they any higher authority than the Archbishop? Here is his official communication to the Board, September 18, 1869:

"The entire government of public schools in which Catholic youth are educated can not be given over to the civil power.

"We, as Catholics, can not approve of that system of education for youth which is apart from instruction in the Catholic faith and the teaching of the Church.

"If the School Board can offer anything in conformity with these principles, as has been done in England, France, Canada, Prussia, and other countries where the rights of conscience in the matter of education have been fully recognized, I am prepared to give it respectful consideration.

"JOHN B. PURCELL, Archbishop of Cincinnati."

This explicit avowal of the policy of the Catholic Church should be regarded as definite and conclusive, unless my friends can produce some higher and overruling authority. What is the true construction of his invitation to the Board to offer something in conformity with the principles of the Catholic Church, may be easily learned by consulting the columns of its official organs.

Now, the right to liberty of conscience is not only a right to be informed, but it is a natural right. It is so declared in the Constitution. It is the birth-right of every American citizen. It is an individual right. It is a right which attaches as soon as moral consciousness dawns upon the individual. It is a right for time—a right for eternity—a right to know the truth and the whole truth, and to believe and practice what God and conscience dictate. The child, when it comes to its teacher for instruction in truth and duty, with that yearning for truth and the source of truth, which the child more than any other living creature feels, has a right to be informed of the ultimate source and authority of the teachings conveyed, and no school board has the right or power to seal the teacher's lips, or require him to withhold that divine revelation which is the source of all truth.

Suppose a child of Protestant parents should intelligently and conscientiously decide to espouse the faith of the Catholic Church, and the parents should undertake, by coercion, to control the child. Suppose they should undertake to set up their parental authority against the child's conscience, and restrain it by force from following out its religious convictions. Will my friends undertake to deny that the child might not by its next friend come into Court and be released from that coercion and restraint? Would the Court require anything more or less to justify its interference, than to ascertain whether the child had arrived at such a degree of intelligence as to understand what it was proposing to do? Where do my friends find it written in American law, that the parent or the Church is absolute keeper of the conscience of the child? I do not mean to deny the right of parental control. I yield all that can be claimed under the law of God or man in that respect, but I do say that my friends can not refer me to any law which makes the parent master of the conscience of the child. It is not liberty of conscience that these men who are opposing the Bible in the schools desire. What they are seeking for is the establishment of an order of things which will enable them to so fix in the mind of their children, and so fasten upon their convictions views and tenets that they will be proof against all other teachings; to so imbue them with their own prejudices and sectarian dogmas, before they have opportunity to receive any other instruction, that liberty of conscience will never come into play with them. And all this they propose in the name of liberty and not of despotism.

But the Constitution itself defines the right of conscience. First we have the declaration that "all men have a natural and indefeasible right to worship God according to the dictates of their own conscience." This right the majority of the School Board propose to secure to the children in the schools, by withholding from them all knowledge of even the existence of God, much less that He has revealed His will to mankind, or that He is to be worshiped in any manner. How effectual would be the policy of the Board; in what heathenish darkness it would leave large numbers of the children in the schools, appears from the petition and answer. Wonderfully careful of conscience are the members of the Board who voted for the resolutions, but very slight examination reveals that their concern is for the conscience of Atheism, of bigotry and intolerance; not the conscience of the citizen desiring those things which are for the welfare of the State and the safety of society.

Following the general declaration of the right of conscience, come the constitutional specifications: "No person shall be compelled to attend, erect, or support any place of worship, or maintain any form of worship, against his consent, and no preference shall be given by law to any religious society, nor shall any interference with the rights of conscience be permitted." Now I wish my friends had at least attempted to make it appear that the communication to the children in the schools, of the elemental truths of religion, of those truths without a knowledge of which the worship of Almighty God is impossible, is in conflict with any one of these constitutional provisions. To furnish the mind with the material upon which conscience is to act, and then leave the individual free to follow the dictates of conscience, seems to be more in accord with liberty of conscience, than to prohibit all instruction and allow conscience nothing to play upon.

But even upon the construction of the rights of conscience claimed by the counsel for the defendants, the rule which the Board attempted to repeal was much more in accordance with the rights of conscience of the patrons of the schools than the rule proposed.

The old rule provided for the accommodation of every one. The pupils might read the version of the Bible preferred by their parents or guardians. In the second district there is a majority of Catholic scholars in one of the schools, and under the old rule the public reading of the Bible was from the Douay version.

Mr. King. And is so now.

Mr. Sage. I may add that during the administration of my friend, Mr. King, as President of the School Board, complaints were made by some Protestant parents, but the rule was impartially observed, and the Douay Bible continued to be read, and is read to this day in that school. I do not speak of the Douay version as the Catholic Bible, nor the King James version as the Protestant Bible. My friends upon the other side lay great stress upon these designations, but I beg to remind them that the light of Protestantism broke forth in the sixteenth century, and filled all Europe, not from the King James version, but from the old Vulgate, translated by Jerome at the request and under the patronage of Pope Damascus in the fourth century. If the Catholic Church or the Protestant Church depended solely upon the difference of versions, their duration would be short indeed.

There was another provision which, added to the choice of versions, made the old regulations of the Board complete for the protection of the rights of all. That provision was the resolution of 1842—never repealed—authorizing and directing teachers to excuse children altogether from the religious teachings of the schools upon the request of their parents and guardians. Under the old administration of affairs, then, the Catholic or Jew could have the version of the Scriptures of his choice read to his children, or he could have them altogether excused from any religious teaching, and the same privilege was extended to the Infidel and Atheist. At the same time provision was made for conveying the elemental principles of religion to the children of those not objecting, and to those who would otherwise be entirely destitute of all knowledge of religion and of the Holy Bible. Whose right of conscience was offended by that rule? Who had any right to complain? Was not my friend, Judge Stallo, carried a little beyond the facts in the heat of his argument, when he talked about "cramming the Bible down the throats of the children of Catholics or Jews," as one of the legitimate consequences of the old rule?

Now what has the Board attempted to do? Because some patrons of the school objected to having their children read the Bible, the majority decided that not merely should their children be excused, but the Bible should be excluded altogether from the schools, and all religious instruction prohibited; this, too, notwithstanding the protest of more than ten thousand citizens and patrons of the schools sent up to the Board, and the action of the majority would, as appears by their own admission, solemnly made in their answer in this case, leave large numbers of children without instruction indispensable to make them good citizens of the State and of the nation. No more flagrant abuse of power or discretion was ever attempted by any public body. No act so entirely in accordance with the old teachings of despotism was ever before even heard of in the history of the Board. And this was attempted in the name of liberty and conscience, and counsel come here and complain to us of persecution, and talk of Church and State and of an establishment of religion.

From the windows of the chamber in which the resolutions were passed, the members of the Board could have seen—no buildings intervening—first, the stately cathedral of the Catholic Church, its foundation laid, its walls built, its spire finished and capped with the cross before the year 1852, before the Catholic schools were established, and during the time when the Bible was read to the Catholic children in the schools. Next, the Jewish temple, the sanctuary of those who cling to that religion given by God to the people of Israel upon Sinai, and who hold to the tradition of thousands of years ago. Across the street, and in full view, is the house of worship of the Radical Unitarian church, whose minister—a member of the Board, and one of the defendants—was one of the leaders of the party in favor of the prohibitory resolutions, where certainly the broadest latitude is allowed, where, I may say, every member is permitted to form his own opinions of the teachings and requirements of Christianity and religion. Next beyond, they could have seen the church of the Scotch Covenanters, who adhere to the sturdy Protestant faith of their fathers, and every Sunday sing the Psalms of David in

Rouse's version. Just beyond, and a little further to the north, they could have seen the foundations for the church of Campbellite Baptists. They could have seen five churches representing five different creeds as diverse as any upon the face of the earth. If this is the natural fruit of the intolerance of the School Board of Cincinnati hitherto, let it be continued a quarter of a century longer, and we shall find all denominations, and all sects represented by buildings all around that square.

A moment's thought would have reminded them that the Catholic Church had then greater vitality and vigor in the city of Cincinnati than in the city of Rome. A moment's consideration would have brought to their minds that the Jews had in Cincinnati two costly and magnificent temples, not surpassed in any city in Christendom, and that many of their number have been advanced by the voluntary action of their fellow citizens to high positions of trust and honor. Had they been disposed to look at facts, it was within their knowledge that every Protestant sect was represented in the city by churches, active and prosperous, and that those opposed to all religion were by no means restrained in their views or utterances.

What trifling, what mockery, in the light of these facts, to talk of the suppression of religious freedom by the continuation of a rule of the schools which has been observed for forty years! What an insult to common sense to pretend that an observance which has borne such fruit must be set aside because of its intolerance!

But we have already seen that the true construction of the Constitution makes it necessary that the Board should be able to state imperative reasons to justify its total prohibition of religious instruction in the schools. The answer assigns the reasons, and I propose now to examine them, in connection with those presented in argument by the counsel for the defense who have preceded me.

First, is the old objection founded upon the differences of belief. The Jew, the Catholic and the unbeliever are put forward. It is insisted that the elemental truths of religion can not be taught without running into sectarianism. Here again counsel find it convenient to dispense with definitions and deal in general assertions. That which is sectarian pertains to some doctrine peculiar to a sect.

13

The elemental truths of religion are common to all sects professing the religion recognized by the Constitution. Only upon the hypothesis that all religion is sectarian—that religion and sectarianism are synonymous—can sectarianism be pleaded as a sufficient reason for the absolute and unqualified prohibition of all religious instruction in the schools. But the proposition is absurd. It has no foundation in theology, nor in law. The Constitution itself recognizes religion and provides against sectarianism in the affairs of the State. If there is nothing but sectarianism in religion, then the recognition of religion by the State, the administration of oaths or even the mention of the name of God is sectarian, and in conflict with the doctrines of American liberty—in one word, Amercan liberty is the liberty of Atheism, and religion is to be spoken of by the citizen only privately and in tones so low that they may not come to the ear of the State. This is the liberty of conscience to which the School Board of Cincinnati invites her citizens, and for which it would banish from the schools instruction admitted to be indispensable to fit the pupils for the duties of citizenship.

It is said that even the reading of the Holy Bible, without note or comment, is sectarian. Will my friends tell me what sect will be benefited by such reading? If they will demonstrate that the Bible teaches unmistakably the peculiar doctrines of any one sect, they will thereby demolish all other sects, and the very name sectarian, in its religious acceptation, will become obsolete. If they will point to one passage or text of the Bible and prove beyond controversy that it teaches sectarian doctrine, we will abandon this case. If they can make it appear that the Bible is nothing more than a manual of sectarianism they can establish for infidelity all that it has ever claimed against its authority or divinity.

Right here I wish to refer the Court again to the case of *Vidal et al.* v. *Girard's Executors*, and I will read from page 200 of 2 Howard's Reports:

"Why may not the Bible, and especially the New Testament, without note or comment, be read and taught as a divine revelation in the college; its general precepts expounded, its evidences explained and its glorious principles of morality inculcated?

What is there to prevent a work, not sectarian, upon the general evidences of Christianity, from being read and taught in the college by lay teachers? Certainly there is nothing in the will that proscribes such studies. Above all the testator positively enjoins 'that all the instructors and teachers in the college shall take pains to instill into the minds of the scholars the purest principles of morality, so that on their entrance into active life they may, from inclination and habit, evince benevolence towards their fellow creatures, and a love of truth, sobriety and industry, adopting at the same time such religious tenets as their matured reason may enable them to prefer.' Now, it may well be asked, what is there in all this, which is positively enjoined, inconsistent with the spirit or truths of Christianity? Are not these truths all taught by Christianity, although it teaches much more? Where can the purest principles of morality be learned so clearly or so perfectly as from the New Testament? Where are benevolence, the love of truth, sobriety and industry so powerfully and irresistibly inculcated as in the sacred volume? The testator has not said how these great principles are to be taught, or by whom, except it be by laymen, nor what books are to be used to explain or enforce them. All that we can gather from his language is, that he desired to exclude sectarians and sectarianism from the college, leaving the instructors and officers free to teach the purest morality, the love of truth, sobriety and industry, by all appropriate means; and, of course, including the best, the surest and the most impressive."

The decision of the Court, it is stated was, in this case, unanimous. I cite it, reminding your Honors that the Chief Justice was a devout Catholic, to show that the Bible, without note or comment, is recognized by the highest court of the land as the purest and best source of morality as well as of religion, and as a book not sectarian in its character or teachings.

Mr. Webster, in his argument upon the hearing of that case, had something to say in answer to those objections to the religious instruction of youth which rest on the differences of sects. My friends for the defense seemed to be conscious that he would be quoted against them, and they saw fit to insinuate that Mr. Webster was speaking as a lawyer for a fee. Well, that is not the only case in which lawyers have received retainers before coming into court, and I merely suggest that it is not quite safe for my friends to claim that the fee answers the argument. In one case somewhat celebrated, Mr. Webster intimated to counsel who took exception to his appearance for the Commonwealth, that it would be quite as well to content themselves with answering his argument so far as they were able instead of carping at his presence.

I will now read two or three paragraphs from Mr. Webster's argument.

Judge Storer. That argument was published by a committee of citizens of Washington and circulated as a tract.

Mr. Sage. Yes, sir; and if your Honor please, there was prefixed to that publication the following extract from the works of Plato:

"*Socrates.* If, then, you wish public measures to be right and noble, *virtue* must be given by you to the citizens.

"*Alcibiades.* How could any one deny that?

"*Socrates. Virtue*, therefore, is that which is to be first possessed, both by you and by every other person who would have direction and care, not only for himself and things dear to himself but for the State and things dear to the State.

"*Alcibiades.* You speak truly.

"*Socrates.* To act justly and wisely (both you and the State), YOU MUST ACT ACCORDING TO THE WILL OF GOD.

"*Alcibiades.* It is so."

I will read from page 158, vol. vi, *Webster's Works:*

"I now come to the consideration of the second part of this clause in the will, that is to say, the reasons assigned by Mr. Girard for making these restrictions with regard to the ministers of religion; and I say that these are much more derogatory to Christianity than the main provision itself, excluding them. He says that there are such a multitude of sects and such diversity of opinion, that he will exclude all religion and all its ministers, in order to keep the minds of the children free from clashing controversies. Now, does not this tend to subvert all belief in the utility of teaching the Christian religion to youth at all? Certainly, it is a broad and bold denial of such utility. To say that the evil resulting to youth from the differences of sects and creeds overbalances all the benefits which the best education can give them, what is this but to say that the branches of the tree of religious knowledge are so twisted, and twined, and commingled, and all run so much into and over each other, that there is therefore no remedy but to lay the axe at the root of the tree itself? It means that, and nothing less. Now, if there be any thing more derogatory to the

Christian religion than this, I should like to know what it is. In all this we see the attack upon religion itself, made on its ministers, its institutions, and its diversities. And that is the objection urged by all the lower and more vulgar schools of infidelity throughout the world. In all these schools, called schools of rationalism in Germany, socialism in England, and by various other names in various countries which they infest, this is the universal cant. The first step of all these philosophical moralists and regenerators of the human race is to attack the agency through which religion and Christianity are administered to man. But in this there is nothing new or original. We find the same mode of attack and remark in Paine's *Age of Reason.* At page 336 he says: 'The Brahmin, the follower of Zoroaster, the Jew, the Mahometan, the Church of Rome, the Greek Church, the Protestant Church, split into several hundred contradictory sectaries, preaching, in some instances, damnation against each other, all cry out 'Our holy religion!''

"We find the same view in Volney's *Ruins of Empires.* Mr. Volney arrays in a sort of semicircle the different and conflicting religions of the world. 'And first,' says he, 'surrounded by a group in various fantastic dresses, that confused mixture of violet, red, white, black and speckled garments, with heads shaved, with tonsures, or with short hairs, with red hats, square bonnets, pointed mitres, or long beards, is the standard of the Roman pontiff. On his right you see the Greek pontiff, and on the left are the standards of two recent chiefs (Luther and Calvin), who, shaking off a yoke that had become tyrannical, had raised altar against altar in their reform, and wrested half of Europe from the Pope. Behind these are the subaltern sects, subdivided from the principal division. The Nestorians, Eutychians, Jacobites, Iconoclasts, Anabaptists, Presbyterians, Wickliffites, Osiandrians, Manicheans, Pietists, Adamites, the Contemplatives, the Quakers, the Weepers, and a hundred others, all of distinct parties, persecuting when strong, tolerant when weak, hating each other in the name of the God of peace, forming such an exclusive heaven in a religion of universal charity, damning each other to pains without end in a future state, and realizing in this world the imaginary hell of the other.'

"Can it be doubted for an instant that sentiments like these are derogatory to the Christian religion? And yet on grounds and reasons *exactly these*, not *like* these, but EXACTLY these, Mr. Girard founds his excuse for excluding Christianity and its ministers from his school. He is a tame copyist, and has only raised marble walls to perpetuate and disseminate the principles of Paine and of Volney."

So also from page 161:

"But this objection to the multitude and differences of sects is but the old story, the old infidel argument. It is notorious that there are certain great religious truths which are admitted and believed by all Christians. All believe in the existence of a God. All believe in the immortality of the soul. All believe in the responsibility, in another world, for our conduct in this. All believe in the divine authority of the New Testament. Dr. Paley says that a single word from the New Testament shuts up the mouth of human questioning, and excludes all human reasoning. And can not all these great truths be taught to children without their minds being perplexed with clashing doctrines and sectarian controversies? Most certainly they can.

"And to compare secular with religious matters, what would become of the organization of society, what would become of man as a social being, in connection with the social system, if we applied this mode of reasoning to him in his social relations? We have a constitutional government, about the powers, and limitations, and uses of which there is a vast amount of differences of belief. Your Honors have a body of laws, now before you, in relation to which differences of opinion, almost innumerable, are daily spread before the courts; in all these we see clashing doctrines and opinions advanced daily, to as great an extent as in the religious world.

"Apply the reasoning advanced by Mr. Girard to human institutions, and you will tear them all up by the root; as you would inevitably tear all divine institutions up by the root, if such reasoning is to prevail."

I will read one more paragraph, from page 163:

"The truth is, that those who really value Christianity, and believe in its importance, not only to the spiritual welfare of man, but to the safety and prosperity of human society, rejoice that in its revelations and its teachings there is so much which mounts above controversy, and stands on universal acknowledgment. While many things about it are disputed or are dark, they still plainly see its foundation, and its main pillars; and they behold in it a sacred structure, rising up to the heavens. They wish its general principles, and all its great truths, to be spread over the whole earth. But those who do not value Christianity, nor believe in its importance to society or individuals, cavil about sects and schisms, and ring monotonous changes upon the shallow and so often refuted objections founded on alleged variety of discordant creeds and clashing doctrines."

Then my friends insist—one of them that the reading of the Bible in the schools is perfunctory, a "dog-trot" exercise—the other, that it is an act of worship, on a level, as to right, with the worship of the Virgin Mary. If the reading were only the formal, lifeless ceremony described by Judge Stallo, why did not the Board yield to the protest of the thousand citizens against the resolutions? Then, if it be, as suggested by Judge Hoadly, an act of worship—a Protestant exercise, exactly as the worship of the Virgin is a Catholic exercise, why was he willing that selections from the Bible to be found in McGuffey's Readers should be read in the schools? Has he authority for maintaining that one portion of the Bible is less sacred than another? Or does it make a difference that a chapter is read not from the Bible itself, but from a book to which it has been transferred?

But the Board assign as another reason for the total prohibition of religious instruction, that there are citizens taxed for the support of the schools who are of various sects and opinions, and who believe that the reading of the Holy Bible without note or comment is not beneficial to the children in the schools, and not only not beneficial, but hurtful. And the Board, and the majority who voted for the resolutions, plead that the reading of the version commonly used, "in the presence and hearing of Roman Catholic children is regarded by the members of the Roman Catholic Church as contrary to their rights of conscience." Now to what conclusion did the majority of the Board come upon these objections? Let us concede, for the sake of the argument, that these objectors have in keeping the consciences of their children. Here is a tax-payer who says, "I do not believe in religion or in the Bible, and I do not wish my children to learn anything not in accordance with my belief." Then comes a sectarian—a Catholic, if you please—and says, "My church is the only infallible teacher and interpreter of the Bible. I will not consent that my child hear anything but the teachings of my church." Here is the Constitution, with the declaration that religion is essential to good government, and that is announced as the first reason for the establishment of common schools. Here is the solemn admission of the Board, and of every member of the Board, that religious instruction is indispensable to fit the children attending the schools to be good citizens, and the further admission that the schools furnish the only religious instruction imparted to many of those children. Does the Board propose to those who object, to excuse their children from attendance upon the religious instruction given in the schools? Does it offer to give to those parents who desire it, sole charge of the religious instruction of their children, and yet adopt some plan to convey the elemental truths of religion to the minds and hearts of those children who would else remain in total darkness? Does it give the slightest heed to the ten thousand tax-payers who sent in their protest against the exclusion of the Bible and the prohibition of all religious instruction? Not at all. Not one of these things did the Board even attempt; but in the face of the constitutional provision, and with the full knowledge that they were thereby withholding from large numbers of children instruction indispensable to fit them to go forth from the schools to their places as citizens, the Board deliberately enacted a total prohibition, not of the Bible alone, but of all religious instruction. If this were done to appease the conscience of the Catholic, the Jew, or the unbeliever, will counsel explain to us by what right any one, or all of these classes can assume control of the consciences of those who do not agree with them? By what warrant is their conscience to be made superior to the Constitution? The Constitution recognizes religion and the Bible. Why is not the Constitution entitled to as high regard from the School Board as the consciences of those who repudiate religion and the Bible, or those who recognize only one sect or church? It hurts the consciences of these tax-payers, does it, to have the elemental truths of religion taught in the schools—not to their children, but to those children who would otherwise be totally ignorant of that knowledge which all admit to be indispensable for their welfare and the welfare of the State? If this be the plea, it is the conscience of intolerance that is hurt. It is the old plea of the despot, when he sent martyrs to the stake for the sake of his conscience. The difference is in degree, not in kind.

But this argument assumes that the parent has an absolute right to control the education—intellectual, moral and religious—of his children, and that a sect may dictate to the State the course of public education. Both propositions are unsound. The State has a paramount interest in the children who are soon to control its affairs, and has, moreover, the right to insist that what the law has defined as indispensable for the education of those children, shall be taught them. Neither parent nor church has any right to interpose private or sectarian objections. The State has a right to educate them, and to educate them in every thing necessary to make them good citizens. I refer your Honors to a case reported in 4th Wharton. This was a case where a child had been taken from his parents and placed in a House of Refuge, for reformation. There was no conviction, nor charge of crime—simply a showing of incorrigibility. The father sued out a writ of habeas corpus. Upon the hearing, the Court said (I read from page 11):

"It is to be remembered that the public has a paramount interest in the virtue and knowledge of its members, and that of strict right the business of education belongs to it. That parents are ordinarily intrusted with it, is because it can seldom be put in better hands; but where they are incompetent or corrupt, what is there to prevent the public from withdrawing their faculties, held, as they obviously are, at its sufferance? The right of parental control is a natural, but not an inalienable one. It is not excepted by the Declaration of Rights out of the subjects of ordinary legislation; and it consequently remains subject to the ordinary legislative power, which, if wantonly or inconveniently used, would soon be constitutionally restricted, but the competency of which, as the government is constituted, can not be doubted.

I refer also to Story's Equity, sec. 1341:

"The jurisdiction of the Court of Chancery extends to the care of the person of the infant, so far as necessary for his protection and education; and as to the care of the property of the infant, for its due management and preservation, and proper application for his maintenance. It is upon the former ground, principally, that is to say, for the due protection and education of the infant, that the Court interferes with the ordinary rights of parents, as guardians by nature, or by nurture, in regard to the custody and care of their children. For although, in general, parents are intrusted with the custody of the persons and the education of their children, yet this is done upon the natural presumption that the children will be properly taken care of, and will be brought up with a due education in literature, and morals, and religion; and that they will be treated with kindness and affection. But whenever this presumption is removed; whenever, for example, it is found that a father is guilty of gross ill treatment or cruelty towards his infant children, or that he is in constant habits of drunkenness and blasphemy, or low and gross debauchery; or that he professes atheistical or irreligious principles; or that his domestic associations are such as tend to the corruption and contamination of his children; or that he otherwise acts in a manner injurious to the morals or interests of his children; in every such case the Court of Chancery will interfere, and deprive him of the custody of his children, and appoint a suitable person to act as guardian, and to take care of them, and to superintend their education."

See cases cited in support of every proposition stated in the text. Also Tyler on Infancy and Coverture, p. 243, where the authorities are collected.

In the light of these authorities it is easy to see how narrow is the ground upon which the Board and the counsel for the Board undertake to stand. Here is a grand system of public instruction for the public welfare—for the benefit, yes, for the safety, of the State, made to bend to the prejudices of those who seek to engraft upon it ideas not of liberty, nor of American growth, but of intolerance, and of foreign growth—ideas which, followed to their practical results, drove our forefathers from the Old World to establish in the New, the freedom we enjoy.

Then it was objected by counsel that reading the Bible without note or comment would not answer the purpose, for the reason that the sacred text would be unintelligible to children, without appropriate explanations. The argument is, that there is not enough religious instruction in the schools, the conclusion is that, therefore, there should be none at all. We were referred to the doctrines of election and predestination, of justification by faith, or works, to Calvinism and Armenianism, and the metaphysics of theology, and the subtleties of belief were put before the Court to illustrate the difficulties to which the reading of the sacred text would introduce the children. But that was all a fancy sketch The uniform testimony of those in charge of the schools in years past,—and back to their first establishment—is that the reading of the Bible has been in the highest degree beneficial. Children to whom the Bible is read without note or comment, take in the plain obvious meaning of those simple, yet sublime teachings upon which all religion and religious sentiment rest. The Christian religion is the only religion ever known on earth, so simple as to be within the comprehension of the child lisping its prayer at its mother's knee, and at the same time so grand and sublime as to more than fill the greatest intellect God has vouchsafed to man.

Another objection is that the Bible is not the basis of morality,—that morality is older than the Bible. It is said that morality was before the world,—before time,—that it is eternal. This I will admit. Of course morality is as eternal as truth itself. But we are told of precepts, of teachings of morality, which it is claimed are older than the Bible, and of moralists whose teachings are as pure as the teachings of the Bible. Suppose I admit all this. Suppose I admit all that they claim for those teachings. Let them answer me this: Why is it that the Bible has a power which is to-day represented by the civilization and intelligence of the world; while all those other teachings of morality, pure though they may have been, have fallen dead from the lips or pens of their authors? Who, of the masses, reads the letters of Seneca or the moral teachings of Plato, or Socrates, or Confucius? Who is controlled by them? Who knows or cares anything about them? There never has been a system of morality that had any power behind it to give it success and efficacy among the nations of the earth, excepting that embraced in the teachings of the Holy Bible. The morality of the Bible is the morality of the Constitution. Religion first, morality second, and knowledge third, are declared to be essential to good government, and therefore schools and the means of instruction are to be encouraged. Are we to suppose that the State having recognized a religion which embraces all the pure morality ever taught, intended to recognize another morality than the morality of that religion? Of what use to the State is religion if the morality it teaches is to be discarded and effete heathen systems to be introduced in its stead? No, it is all idle to talk of those old systems of morality. They have been dead and buried for ages. But the morality of Christianity lives and grows, and gathers force, and it will continue to grow until it fills the whole earth. It is true, as my friend, Judge Stallo, said, "that the truths of Christianity were uttered for the first time among a people despised by the nations, and in subjection to the Romans,"—by one who had not where to lay his head,—to a little band of fishermen, the humblest of those among whom they lived. It is true, moreover, that He who proclaimed those truths was condemned and crucified as a malefactor, and that his disciples forsook him and fled. It is furthermore true, that the religion He taught has been assailed by persecution, by corruption, and by power; and that notwithstanding all, it has spread and grown until it controls not only the religious but the civil institutions of the civilized world, and all that is pure in morals, all that is true in religion, all that is stable in human affairs, we owe to its influence.

As the voyager sails along the coast at night, he may see lights as bright and clear as the port light, far away in the distance. But if he observe those lights carefully, he will discover that they are not constant. They appear and disappear. They shine and are obscured. They shine again, and again there is darkness. If he inquire of the helmsman he will learn that those are flash lights which indicate the rocks and reefs, upon which, if the ship be headed for them, she would certainly be destroyed and all on board lost. But the light away ahead, clear and steady,—which upon first view appears to be the same as the flash lights,—but which never disappears or varies, is the port light, and if the helmsman head the ship for that light he will bring her to her moorings and the passengers to their homes in safety.

Now this illustrates precisely the difference between human institutions of morality and the morality of the Bible. The morality of the Bible beams upon us with the heavenly light of inspiration. It is a morality that leads up to heaven, the home we all hope to reach at last.

In answer to the proposition that morality is independent of religion, I wish to refer again to the argument of Mr. Webster in the *Girard will case*. I read from page 152, vol. vi, *Webster's Works:*

"In the next place, this scheme of education is derogatory to Christianity, because it proceeds upon the presumption that the Christian religion is not the only true foundation, or any necessary foundation, of morals. The ground taken is, that religion is not necessary to morality; that benevolence may be insured by habit, and that all the virtues may flourish, and be safely left to the chance of flourishing, without touching the waters of the living spring of religious responsibility. With him who thinks thus, what can be the value of the Christian revelation? So the Christian world has not thought; for by that Christian world, throughout its broadcast extent, it has been, and is, held as a fundamental truth, that religion is the only solid basis of morals, and that moral instruction not resting on this basis is only a building upon sand. And at what age of the Christian era have those who professed to teach the Christian religion, or to believe in its authority and importance, not insisted on the absolute necessity of inculcating its principles and its precepts upon the minds of the young? In what age, by what sect, where, when, by whom, has religious truth been excluded from the education of youth? Nowhere; never. Everywhere, and at all times, it has been, and is, regarded as essential. It is of the essence, the vitality, of useful instruction."

The next objection is, that if we teach religion at all in the schools, we are bound to teach all that is necessary for the salvation of the souls of children, and that therefore teaching the Scriptures without note or comment is not in accordance with the full measure of our obligations; and that if we undertake to teach what is sufficient for the salvation of the children, we at once interfere with the conscience of those all about us.

Now if my friend, Judge Hoadly, had stopped to consider for what purpose religious education is to be communicated in the schools, he would never have put forward this proposition so ingeniously and prominently argued.

If the object were the spiritual welfare of the children, then I admit the proposition as he states it. But as I said before, the proposition that religion is essential to good government, is for the benefit of the State, and it ought to be construed in that light. The State does not contemplate instruction in religion, for the spiritual welfare of the children. That is not the object. The great object is to give to the children a knowledge of the truths upon which all religion is based, so that they shall be possessed of the truths which furnish the highest sanction and strongest authority to the law of the State. What is necessary for that is the measure of instruction to be given. All the religious sects—Protestants, Catholics and Jews—acknowledge the religious truths upon which the State depends. And those are the truths which are to be taught in the schools, and those only are necessary. The State has no concern for—has nothing to do with—the spiritual welfare of the citizens. It deals with temporal affairs and temporal relations alone. Thus perjury which is committed to the injury of the State or of a fellow-citizen, is punished as a crime, but if it go not to that extent, the State pays no heed to it. Now comes a citizen,—of what sect or belief is not material,—and says: "I instruct my children, or cause them to be instructed by the teachers of my faith, in all that the State requires. I further instruct them in the peculiar tenets of my religion." By the rules which have been in force for twenty-five years, the State, through the Board of Education, excuses those children from the religious teachings of the schools. That is quite as much as the parents have the right to ask. The State can not afford to omit in the training of children who depend solely on the schools for their education, that religious instruction which is necessary to good citizenship, to satisfy parents of other children, who do not believe that which the State has authoritatively declared, or do not wish to have any religious teachings conveyed, excepting those embraced in their particular faith.

It is not for the Court to prescribe the measure of instruction to be given. That may be in the discretion of the Board. What we complain of is the total prohibition. The Board may exercise its discretion within bounds, but total prohibition is beyond all bounds.

Now I know what answer my friend, who is to follow me, will make to all this. He will insist that it is the duty of the Church to communicate this instruction, but not the duty of the State. But it is the plain duty of the State, in the public schools, to communicate instruction upon all subjects which are essential to the welfare of the State, and to make the pupils good citizens.

It is alleged in the petition that there are many children who receive no instruction in religion or the Bible, except that imparted in the schools; and that is admitted in the answer. Now, it is of no consequence what may be the duties of the Church, we are here to look at facts. The claims of society are not to be postponed or made subject to the duties or failures of any church, or any sect.

No church, no sect, can go out into the highways and byways, and force children into its Sunday school or house of worship. It is demanded by the Constitution, and it is indispensable to the State that these should have the elementary truths of Christianity communicated to them in the schools, to fit them to be good citizens. It is the duty of the State, its imperative duty, to communicate that instruction.

The next proposition is that the State has no right to impart religious instruction, under any circumstances; that the State has no right to look to anything but the temporal welfare, interests and relations of its citizens; that all things spiritual devolve upon the spiritual authorities—that is to say, upon the Church; and that the State never will be wholly and entirely free until she shall be wholly and entirely divorced from religion.

Then why, will my friends explain, did the framers of the Constitution place the recognition of religion as essential to good government, in the same sentence with the provision for the establishment of schools? We are not in a convention to decide upon what should of right be the organic law. We are discussing questions depending upon a Constitution already framed and operative, and by that Constitution, and every provision of it, we are bound.

Now I wish to call attention to some facts in the administration of the affairs of the State, which I can not reconcile with the proposition that the State has no right to provide for instruction in religion under any circumstances. There are a thousand convicts in the State penitentiary. A large proportion of them—more than half—when placed in that institution were precisely in the condition to which the School Board of Cincinnati would reduce the children in the schools, so far as it has power—that is to say, entirely without religious instruction or knowledge. The State employs a chaplain at the public expense. He conducts devotional services every day, in presence of all the prisoners. On the Sabbath religious meetings are held and the prisoners are gathered in classes and receive Sabbath school instruction. Why is all this? Obviously because the State recognizes the fact that religious teachings and devotional exercises are the most powerful agencies that can be brought to bear for the reformation of those who have been proven to be unfit to be at large. Is there anything wrong in this? The right of conscience is indefeasible. It can not be rendered null or void. The Constitution protects it at all times and under all circumstances. It applies to all alike, and you can take it away from none. The convicted murderer, being conducted to the gallows, can claim it, and the State can not deprive him of it. The same logic which banishes religion from the schools, banishes it from the prison. Are we then to be compelled, upon objection being made, to exclude the teachings of religion from the prison? If so, will it be safe to set at liberty any one confined in punishment of crime? Would not the rigor of imprisonment, without the humanizing and softening influences of religious instruction make the subject of it only more dangerous to society?

Take a case nearer home. We have in this city a House of Refuge for the care and reformation of children. It is supported by taxation. The law empowers the authorities to remove from the custody of parent or guardian, upon proof that he is incapable or unwilling to exercise the proper care or discipline, a child who is incorrigible or vicious, and commit him to the guardianship of the directors. So, also, a child may be committed where it is shown that he is in danger of being brought up to lead an idle and immoral life, or that the father does not provide for his support, or is an habitual drunkard. The law makes no provision in regard to religious instruction, but it provides that the rules for the management of the institution shall be operative upon their adoption by the directors with the concurrence of the mayor of Cincinnati, and of the Superior Court. The existing rules were adopted in 1860, when the court was composed of Judges Storer, Spencer, and my friend, Judge Hoadly, and they were approved by the full bench. I have here an official copy. They require the Standing Committee to "cause the pulpit to be filled every Sabbath in the absence of the chaplain, or in case of vacancy." It is made the duty of the Committee on Schools and Library, to "provide Sabbath school instruction." The Committee on Indentures are to "procure suitable places for inmates worthy of release, in families of good moral character, and such as may be expected rightly to educate and care for the reformation and religious training of their apprentices." "They shall give a Bible and letter of advice relative to his or her course of life, to each inmate when apprenticed." The Superintendent "shall be regarded as occupying the place of a father of the family, and by an exemplary Christian life, and a kind and patient inculcation of moral and religious principles—the surest elements of success—endeavor to teach the youth to govern themselves." The Matron is required to explain to the female inmates "the unhappy results attending a wicked and profligate life, and endeavor to unfold to them the blessings of a moral and religious life."

Now I would like to ask my friend Judge Hoadly, and I appeal from him as an attorney, to himself as a judge—by what authority, or upon what principle, the court approved the system of religious instruction in use at the House of Refuge, if the State has no right to impart religious instruction under any circumstances? If it be unconstitutional to teach in the schools what the Constitution declares to be essential to good government, is it not equally so in the House of Refuge? Is not the right of conscience the same in both cases? Does the law which takes from an incompetent or unworthy parent, the custody of a vicious or incorrigible child, deprive him also of his constitutional rights? Or must we concede that the State has secured to its citizens the right to put all things at risk, and make the reformation of those who are vicious or criminal, impracticable, if not impossible? And if it be constitutional and politic to teach the elemental truths of religion for the reformation of children in the House of Refuge, can it be unconstitutional or impolitic to teach the same truths to children in the schools, and thereby keep them out of the House of Refuge?

Publicists have always given it as one of the chief reasons for the establishment of schools, that they are one of the great agents for the prevention of crime. It is better to use prevention than to apply punishment, or wait until reformatory measures become necessary.

The State Reform School, like the House of Refuge, is devoted to the reformation not only of youth who are criminal, but those who are incorrigible, or who, by reason of defect in their education at home, are unfit to be at large. A child may be taken from his parents and placed in that school without their consent, and without being charged or found guilty of any crime. Attempts have been made to question this power. The question was raised in Pennsylvania, in 1838, and the Supreme Court decided that society had a paramount interest in the child; that the parent was merely the guardian, and that his guardianship was limited, and subject to the higher claim of society The State Reform School contains some three hundred boys. Religious instruction is imparted about as in the House of Refuge. My friend, Judge Matthews, visited that institution last summer, and upon his return gave an account of the services on the Sabbath, which was published in the city papers. The Sabbath school lesson was in the Gospel of Matthew. The exercises at the chapel were opened by singing hymns from a Sabbath school book of music. The boys all joined in the singing. Then all, with bowed heads, united audibly and with great solemnity, in repeating the Lord's Prayer. In the course of the exercises, one of the "elder brothers" delivered an expository discourse to the school, based upon the morning lesson, which it was said would compare favorably with the sermons usually delivered from the sacred desk. That young preacher had received all his education, both intellectual and religious, in that institution. He was brought there originally as a vagrant and criminal. His only means of subsistence, had been petty larceny. He could neither read nor write. He knew nothing except how to lie and to steal. Under the discipline and influence of the Reform School, he learned how to work and to study, and was fitted for the work of a teacher of the institution, and to be a useful member of society. He was one of seven of the "elder brothers" in charge of "families" in the school, all of whom were, like him, indebted to the influences of the school for all their education. Now, what would that school be worth without the aid of religion? Yet if it be unconstitutional to teach the elemental truths of religion in the common schools, it is unconstitutional to teach them in the Reform School., As the boys in the Reform School have the same rights of conscience as others, and as their parents, from whom they may have been taken for reformation, have all the rights of parents of children in the common schools of Cincinnati, upon what construction of the Constitution, are we to say that religious instruction shall be imparted in one case and not in the other? By what rule, or with what consistency shall it be withheld from those children whose minds are yet free, and open, whose hearts are yet pure, and who are prepared to receive its truths and derive from them their best influences, and thereby be saved from the necessity of reformatory measures, at the public expense?

At its last session, the General Assembly made provision for a reformatory school for girls, and by express enactment, for the religious instruction of those who should become inmates. My friend, Judge Matthews, is one of the directors of that institution. I have here a copy of the by-laws and regulations, drafted, as I am informed, by him. Religious instruction is enjoined—"daily religous instruction and prayers in the school, and regular devotional services on the Sabbath." "A Bible and a letter of advice," are to be given to each inmate when indentured, and when discharged from the institution. Now, would it be safe to dispense with religion—to prohibit all religious instruction, and exclude the Bible from these reformatory institutions? I make these references with the kindest feeling. I am perfectly satisfied that every one of the counsel in this case speaks from his earnest convictions. I arraign no one for inconsistency. I know that no one has any higher regard than my friend who is to follow me, for everything which those who believe in religion hold sacred. What I wish to show is, that their propositions are unsound, their conclusions wrong, and that the policy they advocate, if pursued to its logical results, will prove most dangerous and destructive. We must look to the good of society, to the welfare of the State, and no construction of the Constitution is correct or safe which can not be applied to all cases, and under all circumstances. It appears to me, that my friends have held up before them, and magnified the ill-considered complaints of a few short-sighted objectors, until they have completely shut out from their view the great interests of the State involved—interests which they themselves have seen and recognized when their minds were free, and their vision unobscured. It appears to me that by the same principle upon which instruction in the elemental truths of religion is to be given in reformatory institutions, it is to be given in the common schools. One great purpose of the schools is the prevention of crime and depravity, and that is in part what the Constitution means when it declares that religion is essential to good government, and makes the declaration a reason for the establishment of schools.

There is nothing in all this which tends to the establishment of a church by the State. The Constitution of the United States contains a specific provision against an establishment of religion by Congress. Notwithstanding that provision, the Government has from the first appointed chaplains for the army and navy, and maintained them at the public expense. In 1853, petitions were presented to Congress for the abolition of the office of chaplain wherever it existed. These petitions were referred to the Judiciary Committees. Mr. Meacham, from the Committee of the House, made a report on the 21st of March, 1854. Senator Badger reported to the Senate.

It was claimed that the appointment of chaplains was a violation of the liberty of conscience, that it was bringing the Church into connection with the State, that it was an establishment of religion. Mr. Meacham said in his report:

"What is an establishment of religion? It must have a creed defining what a man must believe; it must have rites and ordinances, which believers must observe; it must have ministers of defined qualifications to teach the doctrines and administer the rites; it must have texts for the submissive and penalties for the non-conformist. There never was an established religion without all these. * * * Had the people during the Revolution had a suspicion of any attempt to wage war against Christianity, that Revolution would have been strangled in its cradle. At the time of the adoption of the Constitution and the amendments, the universal sentiment was that Christianity should be encouraged, not any one sect. Any attempt to level and discard all religion would have been received with universal indignation. * * * But we beg leave to rescue ourselves from the imputation of asserting that religion is not needed to the safety of civil society. It must be considered as the foundation on which the whole structure rests. Laws will not have permanence or power without the sanction of religious sentiment—without a firm belief that there is a Power above us that will reward our virtues and punish our sins. In this age there can be no substitute for Christianity; that in its general principles is the great conservative element on which we must rely for the purity and permanence of free institutions. That was the religion of the founders of the republic, and they expected it to remain the religion of their descendants. There is a great and very prevalent error on this subject, in the opinion that those who organized this government did not legislate on religion. They did legislate on it by making it free to all, 'to the Jew and the Greek, the learned and unlearned.' The error has arisen from the belief that there is no legislation unless in permissive or restricting enactments. But making a thing free is as truly a part of legislation as confining it by limitations; and what the Government has made free it is bound to keep free."

Senator Badger, in his report, used the following language:

"Our fathers were true lovers of liberty, and utterly opposed to any constraint upon the rights of conscience. They intended, by this amendment, to prohibit an 'establishment of religion,' such as the English Church presented, or any thing like it. But they had no fear or jealousy of religion itself; nor did they wish to see us an irreligious people; they did not intend to prohibit a just expression of religious devotion by the legislators of the nation, even in their public character as legislators; they did not intend to send our armies and navies forth to do battle for their country without any national recognition of that God on whom success or failure depends; they did not intend to spread over all the public authorities and the whole public action of the nation the dread and revolting spectacle of atheistical apathy. Not so had the battles of the Revolution been fought and the deliberations of the Revolutionary Congress been conducted. On the contrary, all had been done with a continual appeal to the Supreme Ruler of the world, and an habitual reliance upon His protection of the righteous cause which they commended to His care."

Again, the United States Government has at different times granted subsidies to various religious denominations for the support of missionaries to teach the Christian religion among the Indian tribes. Not because the Government wished to advance the particular church employing those missionaries, or the cause of religion, but because it is a fact recognized by the legislation of the country, by all the history of the country, that religion is one of the main, one of the indispensable elements of civilization. And in a treaty with the Potawatomies and other tribes the Government expressly reserved for the use of the Catholic Church—and it did perfectly right in doing so—one-half of three sections of land, set apart for educational purposes under its control. Thus the Government has acted upon the theory that it is proper for the State to make use of religion as a civilizing agent, and a means of preserving social order.

I have now considered all the reasons offered by the Board and by counsel in support of the resolutions of which we complain. They all rest upon propositions which have never been recognized nor acted upon by the Government in any period of its history. They assume that liberty of conscience gives to every citizen the right to demand that long cherished institutions shall be recast whenever he chooses to complain. Upon the claim that the reading of the Bible, as a general exercise in the schools, was not expedient, the Board determined, what? Not to make some other provision, which, while it would leave no possible ground of complaint to any one, would furnish instruction in religion to those who otherwise would be in total ignorance, but it at once resolved to exclude the Bible altogether, and prohibit all religious instruction. The declaration that religion morality and knowledge are essential to good government, was carried into the Constitution from the ordinance of '87, where it was connected with the requirement, and with that only, that schools and the means of education should forever be encouraged. That provision of the ordinance was, moreover, one of the articles of compact between the original States, and the people and States in the territory out of which the State of Ohio was carved, and it was forever to remain unalterable, unless by common consent. We are therefore under the highest obligation faithfully to respect and observe the requirement. It has hitherto been so respected and observed with the happiest results. Our schools have come to be a pride and glory to the State. Freedom, civil and religious, is the boon of every citizen. The School Board of Cincinnati has aimed the first blow—and it is a deadly blow—at a vital principle of the school system, without right, without reason, without justification. We are told that the rule of 1842, which provided that scholars, whose parents objected, could be excused from the opening exercise, has been obsolete some twenty years. If so, it was competent for the Board to revive it, and if a general exercise in the morning was not expedient, that was no reason for abolishing all religious instruction. This cause has been argued as if nothing were involved but the reading of the Bible. Counsel have not touched the first resolution, which prohibits all religious instruction. Keeping in view the admission in the pleadings that religious instruction is indispensable to make children good citizens, and that that is one object for which schools are established, the members of the Board had no right to pass to that extreme. It was their duty, if in their discretion they found that the general exercise was not expedient, to adopt some other expedient, which would furnish religious instruction in the schools for those children who they admit were there and would not otherwise receive it.

We do not pretend to say that the Board, in the exercise of its discretion, could not change the order of the opening exercise; nor that the plaintiffs have the right to come into court and claim that the Bible shall be read or used in a particular way. But we do claim that whereas the framers of the Constitution have given as the very first reason for the establishment of schools that religion is essential to good government, it is directly against the Constitution—against the policy of the Government—for the School Board to decree that all religious instruction shall be prohibited in the schools.

The Board could have done another thing. If the members were not willing that passages, which were not suitable, in their opinion, should be read to the children, they could have adopted a plan adopted in more than one Sabbath school in this city. They could have announced a programme of Scripture reading for the year, and in the whole year have had passages read that would not touch any proposition to which any member of any sect would have any right to object. But the Board has not resorted to any of these expedients. It has proceeded on the hypothesis that it had the right to sweep away the whole system of religious instruction and place the schools in antagonism with the policy of the State.

But this case has its practical bearings, affecting the life, liberty and property of citizens. We have a system of oaths founded on a religious belief of some sort. The proper administration of justice, the ascertainment and enforcement of legal rights, depend very largely upon the binding sense of obligation to the Supreme

Being in the mind of the witness called to testify, and of the jury sworn to pass its verdict upon the testimony. It is true we apply no religious test to the witness or juror; the Constitution forbids that; but the framers of that instrument were careful to add that that provision should not be construed to dispense with oaths or affirmations. Exclude all religious instruction from the education of the child, and what sense of obligation will the man derive from the oath? Discard the Bible, prohibit all knowledge of religion, and what value could be attached to an appeal to a Being of whom the witness had no knowledge? How is it possible to administer the laws without relying upon the religion the School Board has attempted to prohibit, the Bible they have attempted to exclude?

Less than five years since, within thirty miles of this city, a wholesale midnight murder was committed. A more horrible crime was never perpetrated in the State of Ohio. A feeble old man and three children—one a babe upon its mother's arm—were the victims. The mother herself was felled to the floor and left for dead. One only of the household escaped unharmed, and she a child of seven years. She was the only witness of the fact of the murder. Without her evidence conviction was impossible. When the murderer was brought to trial and that child placed on the stand as a witness, instantly came the objection that she was too young to testify. Now what is the rule of law in such a case? The judge shall ascertain whether the child has acquired such a sense of moral accountability to a Superior Being as to feel the binding obligation of an oath. That is the test of competency. The judge came down from the bench and took his seat beside the child. She had never been a witness. There was a startled expression when she was asked if she had taken an oath, but she knew if she should state an untruth she would be punished, and she said that "God would be angry with her." "My child, where did you learn that?" inquired the judge. "At school, and from my mother," was the answer. There were tears in many eyes in the crowded court-room when the oath was administered, and not one who heard her but believed every word of her testimony. The murderer was convicted and executed.

There is now confined in the penitentiary at Columbus a man who, years ago, in a drunken frenzy, stamped out the life of his wife. He was convicted by the testimony of a child, the only witness, and that child was competent as a witness by reason of the religious instruction she had received in the common schools. An assassin might dispatch his victim in the presence of half a dozen children educated under the scheme proposed by the Cincinnati School Board and not one of them would be qualified to testify.

Other illustrations will suggest themselves to your Honors. I have stated enough to show that there is something more at stake than questions of sects and creeds. Richard Lovell Edgeworth—induced by a noted French infidel—educated a son, from his third to his eighth year, according to the scheme proposed by the Cincinnati School Board. He sums up the result in a single sentence: "He had all the virtues of a child bred in the hut of a savage, and all the knowledge of things which could well be acquired at an early age by a boy bred in civilized society."

For forty years the Bible has been read and the elemental truths of religion have been taught in the common schools of Cincinnati. In those schools have been educated thousands upon thousands of our best citizens, of all classes of opinion and belief. No single instance of interference with any right of conscience in all that time has been shown. The reasons pleaded by the Board for its departure from the action and policy of all its predecessors, and all the arguments of counsel, are met and answered by the forty years' history of the schools, and the answer is complete and conclusive.

We are not here to advocate the cause of religion, but of the State, and of the citizens. We are not here to speak for or against any creed or sect, but for the interests of society, the protection and security of life, liberty and property. The religion of the Bible is the safeguard of all these. No free government now exists in the world unless where Christianity is acknowledged and is the religion of the country. We ask that in this great city, with its immense influence for good or evil, the children who are growing up to occupy the places we must soon vacate, shall not be deprived of that instruction in religion by the schools which all admit is necessary to keep them from the ways of vice and crime, and make them useful and valuable members of society.

I leave the case with the Court. The questions with which we are dealing have exercised in an unwonted degree the public mind, as they have touched feelings and principles which every good citizen holds most dear and sacred. Whatever may be the result, I have only to say for my clients, my colleagues and myself, that we have placed the case before a tribunal appointed and competent to judge of the law, and to decide what are the legal and constitutional rights of the parties, and by the decision we expect, cheerfully, and as good citizens, to abide.

ERRATUM.—On page 158, ninth and tenth line from the top of the page, for "Whatever makes men good citizens makes them good Christians," *read*, "Whatever makes men good Christians makes them good citizens."

Argument of Stanley Matthews,

For the Board of Education.

MAY IT PLEASE YOUR HONORS—It would cost me a very painful physical effort to appear to-day in any case ; it has cost me a very difficult and painful mental effort to appear in this. It is easy to swim with the tide, to go with the current, to follow in the wake of the multitude. To do things that are popular is not hard. But to stand by a man's individual moral convictions, in opposition not to enemies, but to friends, tries a man. If your Honors please, it tries me. Except, the loss of dear children, this is the most painful experience of my life—to be told that I am an enemy of religion, that I am an opponent of the Bible, that I have lost in this community my Christian character, and that my children and my grandchildren will reproach my memory for this day's work. For all that, and more, has not been whispered merely through the crowds, but has been told me to my face. If your Honors please, I would be silent to-day, if I dared, but I have no choice.

Believing, as I do, that an appeal is being made to this Court to wrest the law to an illegal end, as a lover of my profession, I am under a professional obligation to withstand it. Believing, as I do, that doctrines the most dangerous and mischievous to the value and safety of our glorious system of public schools are being preached and promulgated, doctrines that are equally as dangerous and mischievous to civil order and the safety and peace of the State, as a citizen, I feel under still higher obligations to oppose them. Believing, as I do, that this suit and the principles on which it is maintained, and can only be maintained, cause a book, that I believe to be of no human origin—to contain the very words of God

—to be made the subject legitimately of public criticism in a court of justice, and only next spring to be bandied about as a foot-ball between political parties, and a religion which it is the greatest honor and pride of my life to be able to-day to stand in public and confess, to be made the watchword of contending factions in the State; believing that both that book and that religion are thus discredited, as a lover of the one, and as a disciple of the other, my responsibility to God and my conscience will not allow me to do anything else than to speak.

If your Honors please, this very discussion which now for two or three days has been prolonged in this house, the arguments which have been made, the topics which have been discussed, the themes which have been broached—and all in my judgment entirely relevant and germane to the question—I say the very nature of this discussion *prima facie* establishes that these gentlemen have no business to be in Court. Why, if your Honors please, whatever the characters, individually of the three distinguished gentlemen whom I see before me, sitting as the administrators of the law, may be, though they may be deeply versed in all spiritual knowledge and profound in theology, yet your Honors do not sit there as doctors of divinity, but as doctors of the laws. And now, then, to find instead of Coke and Blackstone, and Kent, and other writers upon the science and system and rules of jurisprudence being cited and quoted to your Honors as decisive of the various views of counsel upon the mooted questions of law, what do we have? The question whether or not the Bible is a book of Divine authority; the question whether the version of King James is a true translation; the views which the Protestant evangelical denominations hold in regard to its infallible authority as the only rule of faith and practice; the opinions of the Council of Trent, and other general councils and pontiffs of the Roman Catholic Church, as to how far it contains the revealed will of God, and whence it derives its authority and title to be so regarded, and all these questions—questions of exegesis, questions of interpretation, questions of church authority, questions of inspiration—what have they to do here, and who here is competent to decide them? The very fact that this litigation necessarily draws in question opinions of this character, demonstrates, in my judgment as a lawyer, that the case has been wrongly conceived. And this, is not all. I have already alluded to the ulterior results; they are not dimly and vaguely shadowed forth.

These questions, the question of supremacy in politics between the contending churches and rival sects is the legitimate fruit of a controversy based on these grounds. And now I say, that unless all my ideas of religion are utterly perverted, unless all my opinions concerning politics, possible politics under our institutions, are wrong at the base, this state of things is wrong. It ought not to be. Legitimately it can not be. For, if the equitable, benign and impartial principles we have all been taught to understand as lying at the foundations of our civil policy in the State of Ohio mean anything, they mean that there is no room in the controversies of political parties for differences of religious belief.

Now, it is of vital importance to the proper determination of this case that we should come back to the question—the previous question—that we should understand it; that we should understand it precisely, not vaguely; that we should understand it exactly, marking its boundaries and its differences from all other questions, so that we may see precisely where we are, and what we have to decide.

It appears, if your Honors please, that the School Board, as it is called, the Board of Education of the common schools of this city, on a certain occasion, at a regular meeting, passed two resolutions, which I will read:

"*Resolved*, That religious instruction and the reading of religious books, including the Holy Bible, are prohibited in the common schools of Cincinnati, it being the true object and intent of this rule to allow the children of parents of all sects and opinions, in matters of faith and worship, to enjoy alike the benefit of the common school fund.

"*Resolved*, That so much of the regulations on the course of study and text books in the Intermediate and District Schools (page 213, Annual Report) as reads as follows: 'The opening exercises in every department shall commence by reading a portion of the Bible by or under the direction of the teacher, and appropriate singing by the pupils,' be repealed."

It is admitted, that prior to the passage of these resolutions, there never has been in the common schools of Cincinnati any formal instruction in religion other than that conveyed by the reading of the Bible and the singing connected with it at the opening exercises.

Mr. King. We admit no such thing.

Mr. Matthews. Then it must be admitted, if that is not correct, that there is to be, and to continue to be, notwithstanding these resolutions, the same amount, the same kind, the same degree of religious instruction in the schools as there was before.

Mr. King. Provided the resolution is enjoined, yes.

Mr. Matthews. No sir, if they are enforced. For, if your Honors please, the only possible difference between the conduct of the schools under these resolutions, and under the existing resolutions prior to the passage of these, is simply in dispensing with the formal reading of the Bible, and singing at the opening exercises of the schools. It is not pointed out in the pleadings or in the evidence—it can not be, for it does not exist, that there ever was, and I repeat what I said before, any formal instruction in religion in the common schools of Cincinnati other than that which was repealed by this second resolution. If there was, what was it ? Let us know.

Mr. King. It is in the evidence, judge.

Mr. Matthews. Well, what is it ? Do you mean McGuffey's Readers ?

Mr. King. Yes sir. [Laughter.]

Mr. Matthews. Well, now, is it possible ? [Renewed laughter.] In the first place I deny that the reading of lessons in McGuffey's series of Readers is formal instruction in religion. In the second place, I say if it is, it will continue in spite of anything in these resolutions.

Mr. King. Then you give up the case, as I understand it.

Mr. Matthews. Brother King, you will have your time.

Is it fair, if your Honors please, is it candid, is it squarely meeting the issue, to say that the extracts, contained in the text books in the schools, introduced for the purpose of improving the elocution, or the spelling, or the rhetoric, or the logic, or the arithmetic, or the geography of the pupils, is formal instruction in religion ?

Now, why can't we meet this question like fearless and courageous men? Everybody knows in reading these resolutions precisely what is meant. It has been stated that if there be in any of McGuffey's Readers an extract from the New or Old Testament, placed there as a reading exercise, although the motive of the author in selecting it may have been on account of the beauty and excellence of the sentiment which it inculcates, nevertheless it does not stand there to be the text of instruction in religion, for it does not come in the shape of a message from Heaven. When the Bible is read in the morning as a part of the opening exercises of the school, when singing accompanies it, that, is instruction in religion, because it is an act of worship, because the exercises are devotional, because the necessary implication is that you are listening to the inspired and revealed will of God. But when the class takes up the Fifth Reader and reads the fifth chapter of Matthew—and I don't think any better reading could be found—it is done, if your Honors please, not as the words that fell from the second person in the Godhead, when incarnate on earth, but as a beautiful specimen of English composition—fit to be the subject of the reading of a class—and stands, so far as that exercise is concerned, on the same footing precisely as a soliloquy from Hamlet, or the address of Macbeth to the air drawn dagger.

Now, that is precisely what these resolutions mean, and it is a perversion of their manifest meaning when it is charged that the necessary logical consequence of enforcing them is to eviscerate the text books in use in the schools, and every sentiment implying the existence of God or our dependence upon Him. That is my understanding of it, that the precise effect of the adoption of these resolutions upon the character and the conduct of the common schools in this city, is simply this and no more; that, whereas, prior to their passage, the morning exercises in those schools embraced the reading of the Bible and appropriate singing; after their passage these two things are dispensed with. That is the length and the breadth, the heighth and the depth of the offense of the School Board, of which they stand here to-day charged.

And, if your Honors please, in full view of the possible misrepresentations that may be made of what I am about to say, I nevertheless do say that I consider that the controversy which has, in the language of the gentlemen upon the other side, so excited the feelings of this community, is a controversy, as I understand it, on the side of the complainants in this case, about a very small matter in comparison with the evils and the wrongs which, in my judgment, the continuance of the system necessarily entails upon those who object to it. Is there any body, who says that he can not conscientiously send his child to a school which is not opened by the teacher with a selection from the Bible and the singing of a hymn? Is there any such person whose conscience is such that it is a violation of his sense of right, of his obligation to duty, that he can not send a child to a school to learn reading, writing, arithmetic, geometry, algebra, Latin, Greek, or any of the branches of ethics, humanities, sciences, arts, which may be or have been taught in any of the common schools of the State of Ohio, unless the day is first dedicated and solemnized by this or a similar act of worship? I know of none.

Again, is there any gentleman in this community who believes that the reading of the Bible and the singing of a hymn, as prescribed by the rules in force previous to the passage of this repeal, as it is read and as it is sung, has ever produced any appreciable good? Does he believe that the manner in which that exercise is performed, the manner in which it always will be performed, under such circumstances, is a reverent and beneficial act of devotion?

Now, perhaps I am going too far. Certainly I do not mean to limit the power of God or of His Spirit, nor the force of His truth, nor the omnipresence of His grace; but we are looking at this case, if your Honors please, humanly, and I will say at least deliberately this, that the little good which we may imagine in particular and individual and isolated cases has taken place is not to be weighed for an instant, with the violation of the conscience of a single, though the poorest and the meanest, citizen of the State.

And another thing. The good that may be done in that way is not to be proportioned for an instant with the evil that is done by this schism in society, which is produced by even the appearance of a predominating supremacy on the part of one sect of Christians.

In my judgment, the contest is not about religious education at all. It is about denominational supremacy, the right to be higher, to be better, to be more powerful than your neighbor; the right to say to one: "You are nothing but an unbelieving Jew," and to another, "You are the slave of a Roman bishop," and to both, "What rights of conscience that a Protestant need to respect have you?"

I do not, indeed, doubt that the majority of those whose views I am opposing, are actuated by sincere motives and an honest desire to do what seems to them to be right, and believe that their course is necessary to preserve the honor of religion, respect for the Bible and the best interest of the State. It is natural enough that they should feel with some sensitiveness the rudeness of an unexpected shock to their prejudices, hardened into habits by the practice of many years, and that they should resist and resent what they regard as an attack upon religion and an insult to a book they believe to be divine, without inquiring whether, without regard to the motives of individuals or the reasons which governed them, the action of the School Board, considered in its legal aspects and relations, is not just, reasonable and right. I am, nevertheless, constrained by my convictions, deliberately to repeat, that it seems to me that the real source of the public feeling against the action of the school authorities, is not so much a regard for the substance of religious education as solicitude for the name of Protestant supremacy. The sting consists in having to haul down the Protestant flag without thinking whether they had any business to be flaunting it in their neighbors' faces.

I do not make that charge without proposing to myself the duty of maintaining it by proof. I find it, if your Honors please, in the arguments of both the gentlemen on the other side, for that argument reduced to its ultimate result is neither more nor less than simply this: That not only by the Constitution of the State of Ohio, but by a law more fundamental and supreme than it, Protestant Christianity is the established religion of this State, and the disclaimers of the gentlemen on the other side, the opposition that they respectively express to a union between Church and State, is simply the gilding of the bitter pill.

We are told that if the people of Ohio were assembled to-day in their sovereign majesty by their delegates, in a convention, to frame for themselves a new Constitution, that they could not enact a law which would prevent the reading of the Bible in the common schools, because Protestant Christianity is founded deep, below even the sovereign reach of the supreme power in the State. That is my understanding of the proposition.

Your Honors have heard references, by both of my colleagues, to the article of the Rev. Dr. Bellows—a name appropriate—which I trust to be able to make appear to your Honors to be but sound and fury, signifying nothing. And yet, it is the argument, it is the proposition, it is the law of this case, as claimed by the gentlemen on the other side. The article was published with approval in one of our daily city papers, and no doubt was swallowed by the orthodox Protestant piety of the whole community as an authoritative exhibition of the law of the land.

Mr. Matthews here read the article referred to—one of considerable length, published recently in the Liberal Christian—*in which, after vigorously defending Christian education and the use of the Bible in the schools denouncing the attempt to expel the Bible as a Catholic movement, and claiming that this is a Protestant country, the writer says:*

"We can not concede the equal rights of Catholics with Protestants to regulate our educational system any more than we could allow monarchists to become senators and representatives. They must swear allegiance to the unmonarchial principle of the Constitution to be eligible to office. But the Catholics are denying and seeking to overthrow the political supremacy of the Protestant ideas originally imbedded in our public law. They are contending against the original recognition of the Bible—on which every President and every high officer swears his official oath of allegiance to the Constitution—to be a national book, and at the bottom of our system. And it is a weak and illogical hesitation to refuse to hold the true historic ground and to maintain the original supremacy of the Protestant idea, which is now weakening and imperiling the national fidelity to its public school system, and the national claim that the Bible is the fundamental stone in the temple of American liberty.

"If the Roman Catholics are not content with perfect toleration; if they look for the countenance and support of the American people as having an equal claim with the Protestant founders of our institutions to regulate its fundamental methods of public education, they are reckoning without their host, and will surely come to grief. They are arousing an opposition such as American slavery, in another form, aroused only after thirty years of smoldering indignation and wrath, but which finally broke out into overwhelming ruin for its insidious and fatal system. We warn our Roman Catholic fellow-citizens of what is in store for them if they continue to press their claim to break up our national system of public schools. They will sooner or later bring on a civil war, in which they and their churches will be swept, as by a whirlwind, from the land. All the liberty they can rightly ask they enjoy. But they ask, in another form, the liberty which Utah claims—she wishes to enjoy polygamy and to have the right to teach it under the American flag. We deny the right, and shall extinguish it in her ruins if she raises a finger to maintain it."

There is not a word in this extract that was not substantially in Mr. Ramsey's argument. The whole of it, from beginning to end, as was the argument of the gentleman who has just concluded, was an argument to prove that the adherents of the Roman Catholic Church in this State have not an equal right with the Protestants in the management of the public schools, and can not have, because it is unconstitutional.

The Court at this point adjourned until the following morning.

If your Honors please, I really don't know whether yesterday afternoon I said any thing offensive to my friends upon the other side. If I did, it was not done purposely, and I beg leave, publicly, if so, to apologize for it and to retract it. There are no gentlemen at the bar or elsewhere, for whom I have a deeper or more sincere respect, for them personally and for their opinions, and it would grieve me very much if in the heat of argument I should be betrayed into anything that might justly be considered as offensive to their feelings or to their opinions. I understood my friend Mr. Ramsey to take exception to my version of his proposition, which is that Christianity is the law of the land in such a sense as that it is more binding than the Constitution of the State of Ohio. I do not suppose that Mr. Ramsey has ever formally promulgated that proposition, or that he has recognized it consciously in his own mind; yet, nevertheless, that is my version of his proposition. Why, if your Honors please, if I remember rightly, in the opening of his speech at Pike's Opera Hall, the commencement of this suit and of this controversy, he laid the foundation of his argument in the dedication of the continent by its first discoverer to Christianity, and he might have added to the Pope of Rome. He and his colleagues enlarged upon the fact that all the early governments of the colonies were based upon the recognition of the binding obligation of the same law; that the Declaration of Independence was also a recognition of the same fact, and that the Federal Constitution was itself based implicitly and necessarily upon the existence of the same state of things. Now, if this be so, if Christianity is a system of law binding on the citizens, as being a command from the supreme civil power that is as extensive as our national institutions, lying at the base of them all, federal and national, then of course the conclusion follows that the people of Ohio, as such, have no right to repeal or abrogate it; and that, consequently, as being a part of that universal frame of government in which they form but a part, they can have nothing in their Constitution which denies it or is inconsistent with it. But it was not my purpose to insist upon any thing as deducible from that view. It is sufficient for the purposes of my argument to allow the gentlemen to stand upon the narrower ground, if they prefer it, that Christianity, as a system of law, is recognized and made valid and binding in the State of Ohio by the supreme civil power that exercises jurisdiction here.

Now, in the first place, it would be very strange if this were so. It is not probable that it should be so *a priori*: on the contrary the *prima facie* case is greatly against it. In this State, not to enlarge the boundaries of our view any further, though the same remark is true of all the States, we had supposed that we had founded and were living under the benign sway of republican institutions, of a free commonwealth, of a state of society and a political organization growing out of it based upon the absolute impossibility of denying the fundamental truth, that in the presence of the law, and of all the institutions of the law, and of the law-making power, and the source of law, every citizen, without respect to religion, race, color, condition, or any of the accidents of human life, was absolutely and perfectly equal. I admit that there has been up to this time only an approximation to the model, to the ideal. We have not yet arrived at the full fruition and realization of that dream, but we are approaching it; we have nearly arrived at it. The adoption of the Fifteenth Amendment to the Federal Constitution will bring into the full realization of the fundamental law the proposition that all citizens are absolutely, in all respects, equal before the law, in civil rights, in religious rights, in all the rights that spring from the possession of human life—in every thing which makes a man, a man. And in a commonwealth of that kind, based upon that model, even supposing that it had not entirely realized it, but was, nevertheless, nearly approximating to the realization of it, as much so at least as is marked in those fundamental propositions contained in the Bill of Rights—I say it would be extremely improbable to find in the Constitution of such a State the proposition that any particular creed or form of religion, no matter how numerously believed in, was not only established, but even preferred by law.

I desire, in this connection, to read some very vigorous remarks of a very celebrated man—a man who was the supporter of an aristocratic form of government and a religious establishment, but who, nevertheless, made his fame by the advocacy of free principles of government—Henry Brougham. In the third volume of his work on *Political Philosophy*, page 125, in the chapter devoted to the discussion of religious establishments, he says:

"But there is one establishment which appears incompatible with the existence of a democracy, or at least compatible only under restrictions hardly reconcilable with its healthful growth, and that is a system of religious instruction endowed and patronized by law, with a preference given to its teachers over the teachers of all other forms of belief—in other words, a religious establishment."

That is his definition of a religious establishment. "Wherever there is a system of religious instruction, endowed and patronized by law, with a preference given to it by the State over all other systems, and a preference given to its teachers over the teachers of all other forms of belief." That is his definition of a religious establishment.

He continues:

"Where all the people are equal, and no privileged order is recognized, it seems impossible to give a preference by law to the teachers of one class of believers, however numerous these may be compared with all other classes of believers. In matters of a temporal kind men may differ widely, some approving one doctrine and some another. But were the State to appoint teachers of one of these disputed systems of science, or of morals, or of legislation, and give them an endowment withheld from the teachers of other systems, no material injury would be done to the feelings or the comfort of any class, and the Government would be perfectly justified in preferring the teachers of a system tending to support the peculiar policy of the State. It is otherwise with respect to religious instruction. The happiness of men and their most anxious feelings are so deeply interested in their religious tenets that any preference given by the State to the teachings of religious doctrines which they sincerely believe to be erroneous, proves excessively galling to them, and the same persons who could well bear to pay taxes which should go to the propagation of a physical or even of a moral theory, deemed by them to be erroneous, would feel seriously aggrieved in paying their contributions toward propagating a religious doctrine which they believed to be false. Not to mention that although a government may have some legitimate interest in the dissemination of moral or political opinions favorable to the policy of the Constitution, no government can have any but an unlawful sinister object in view by seeking the support of any system of religion, or forming a political alliance with its professors."

Words of weight and words of wisdom; a demonstration, if your Honors please, not only that the form, but that the spirit of republican institutions casts out and ejects as an extraneous, and foreign, and ruinous element in its civilization, any preference by law to one set of religious opinions, to one system of religious teachings over another.

Judge Storer. Just here there is a difficulty in my mind. I would be most fully in accord with you if there was an attempt to establish any dogmatic teaching or any sectarian doctrine; but the question is here whether the introduction of the Holy Scriptures tends to establish sectarianism.

Mr. Matthews. I will proceed out of the line of my argument right here to answer your Honor. I do say that the reading of the Holy Bible in the manner repealed by this resolution, is the teaching of a dogma in religion, held by only a portion of the religious community, objected to by a large part of the others, and that it is in a just, true and sober sense—as to all who either reject it, in whole or in part, as a divinely inspired and infallible book, and as to all others, who admitting that to be its character, nevertheless deny that it can properly be understood without the interpreting aid of external authority, as to unbelievers, Jews and Roman Catholics—a merely sectarian book. Now, if your Honors please, the community is divided, you may say, in a general way, as a matter of fact, of which your Honors can take judicial notice, and to which your Honors' notice is addressed specially by the answer in this case, into at least three main divisions of positive religious belief, throwing out of view all those who have merely a negative position, sometimes called Nullifidians—believers in nothing, if you choose, except what they see, and hear, and feel. But I propose to confine myself now only to that division of the community as to their positive religious belief; and I will include under one name all Protestant Christians, including every variety of faith, every sect and denomination, from those who take a merely humanitarian view of the person and the work of our divine Savior up to those who believe that he was the incarnate God, and embracing every possible shade and variation of religious belief, which, although they may appear small and minute, yet are so great in their estimation as that they are erected into matters of conscientious difference. So that, if your Honors please, my friend who immediately preceded me, if I understand his religious convictions rightly, is forbidden by his conscience to sit at the same communion table with me, because he has been immersed, as the form of baptism, and I have not. And another will not admit me into the membership of his communion or sit with me at the same table of our common Lord, because I will insist on singing human compositions, just as these Sabbath school hymns that are forbidden in these resolutions in the common schools. They may perhaps not deny me every quality of a Christian; they may possibly believe that I may be ultimately saved and go to Heaven, but they reserve for themselves the first places at the Lord's table, and only allow me to come to the second.

Here are all these varieties of belief. The gentlemen say, What is conscience? It may be a very small matter, in their estimation, applied to other people—a very small matter not to be taken notice of; and one gentleman quotes the legal maxim, "*De minimis non curat lex*," in reference to the supposed conscience of an infidel.

But this will not do. We may call the eccentricities of conscience, vagaries, if we please; but in matters of religious concern we have no right to disregard or despise them, no matter how trivial and absurd we may conceive them to be. In the days of the early Christian martyrs, the Roman lictors and soldiers despised and ridiculed the fanaticism that refused the trifling conformity of a pinch of incense upon the altar, erected to the Cæsar that arrogated to himself the title and honor of "divine," or of a heathen statue. History is filled with the record of bloody sacrifices which holy men who feared God rather than men, have not withheld, on account of what seemed to cruel persecutors but trifling observances and concessions. And especially the history of the Protestant divisions in religion, is the record of the fearlessness with which men, in the exercise of the rights of conscience, have not hesitated to fill the world with their schisms, upon what to others appear to be the merest and most insignificant forms; so that they have seemed to worship iconoclasm rather than what seemed to them to be forbidden images. A posture, a gesture, the sign of a cross, the bowing of the head, a genuflexion, the sprinkling of a few drops of water, a few words said over a wafer, a picture, a lighted candle, a vestment, whether words shall be said or sung, whether choristers shall be dressed in surplices, whether there shall be a black gown, or a white gown, or no gown at all, whether prayer shall be read or said, whether a psalm shall be chanted, or if read, whether by minister alone or minister and people responsively, or whether a hymn not composed by inspiration may be sung, whether the music shall be led by a precentor or accompanied by an instrument, and if an instrument whether it shall be viol or organ, whether a sermon may be read, or shall be committed to memory and spoken without manuscript, or preached without verbal preparation; these and perhaps a hundred other like things, of no greater import, not to speak of the numberless variances of opinion upon matters confessedly not essential to religious conduct and character, have nevertheless been regarded by religious men as sufficient in conscience to justify a breach of the unity of the Church; and it is notorious, that the heat of contention between sects, divided upon points of faith or order, has been in proportion to the narrowness of the line that has divided them.

Conscience, if your Honors please, is a tender thing, and tenderly to be regarded; and in the same proportion in which a man treasures his own moral integrity, sets up the light of conscience within him as the glory of God shining in him to discover to him the truth, so ought he to regard the conscience of every other man, and apply the cardinal maxim of Christian life and practice, "Whatsoever ye would that men should do unto you, do ye even so unto them."

Now here is the Christian community. Then there are a large number of the citizens of this community who are not Christians at all, and yet are devout religionists. They are the descendants of the men who crucified Christ; and yet, as old Sir Thomas Browne says, in the book to which your Honor referred the other day, we ought not to bear malice against them for that, for how often since have we, who profess His name, crucified Him, too!

> Quousque patiere, bone Jesu!
> Judæi te semel, ego sœpius crucifixi;
> Illi in Asia, ego in Britannica,
> Gallia, Germania;
> Bone Jesu, miserere mei, et Judæorum.

But here they are in this community, devout worshipers of the only living and true God, according to their conscientious convictions, and I will say, if your Honors please, in all respects capable of performing every duty of the civil state (and equally entitled to, not toleration—I hate that word, there is no such thing known in this country as toleration—but civil and religious equality, equality because it is right, and a right.) Then there is another sect of religionists, and they are Christians. They are the Roman Catholics. I know the Protestant prejudices against the Roman Catholic hierachy and the Roman Catholic system of faith, and the Roman Catholic Church. I know, too, from a reading of that history, a part of which has been reproduced in argument upon this occasion, that the Roman Catholic Church has too well deserved that bitter memory at the hands of those whom it persecuted. But it is not to be denied that the victims of persecution, with singular inconsistency, have not always omitted the opportunity, when power was in their hands, to inflict upon their oppressors the same measure of persecution, as if the wrong consisted not in the principle, but only in the person.

Now, if your Honors please, I try to stand impartial and neutral in this argument between these three sets of men. I am bound to look upon them all as citizens, all as entitled to every right, to every privilege that I claim for myself. And, further, if your Honors please, I do in my heart entertain the charity of believing that they are just as honest and just as sincere in their religious convictions as I am. I will say further, that from the study which I have made, as time and opportunity have been given me, of the doctrinal basis of the Roman Catholic faith, I am bound to say that it is not an ignorant superstition, but a scheme of well constructed logic, which he is a bold man who says he can easily answer. Give them one proposition, concede to them one single premise, and the whole of their faith follows most legitimately and logically, and that is the fundamental doctrine, the doctrine of what the church is, what it was intended to be, by whom it was founded, by whom it has been perpetuated, being the casket which contains, to-day, shining as brightly as before the ages, the ever living, actually present body of God teaching and training men for life here and life hereafter. Convince me, out of the lids of that book, which I recognize as absolute and infallible authority upon the point, that Jesus Christ, when on earth, founded such a visible organization for such purposes, and continues present with it by his spirit, and I bow before it as I do before my Maker, and I believe everything that it teaches, no matter what it is.

Now, if your Honors please, that is the doctrine of the

Roman Catholic Church; that is the doctrine that is believed in by the Roman Catholic people; believed in sincerely, conscientiously, under their responsibilities, as they understand them, to answer at the bar of Almighty God, in the day of judgment, according to the light which they have received, in their own reason and their own conscience; for you must bear in mind that the process by which a Roman Catholic attains his faith is the same by which your Honors do. We seem to make a difference, in that respect, as if the Roman Catholic believed in his church in some other way, by some other organs than those which a Protestant uses when he comes to his convictions. Why, if your Honors please, there is no compulsion about it; it is a voluntary matter; they believe or not, as they choose; there is no external power which forces them to believe. They believe because they are taught; they believe because they are so educated; they believe because they have been trained up in it; just as we believe in the Protestant form of religion, because our fathers and our grandfathers and our grandfather's fathers were Protestants. They think they have sufficient reason for their belief; it may be an insufficient reason, but that don't make any difference to you and me; it is their reason, and that is enough. Now, they have—at any rate so far as the impersonal spirit of jurisprudence is concerned, so far as the presiding genius of the civil law is affected with jurisdiction; so far as, your Honors, the embodiment of that artificial reason which consists in the collective wisdom of the State, can take any notice—civil rights and religious rights, equal to yours and mine. Here are these three great divisions of men and of opinions and of religious faith and worship, all standing before you to-day upon a platform of absolute and perfect equality.

And now, then, to answer your Honor's question. Your Honor said that if you could be made to believe that the reading of King James' translation of the Holy Scriptures was the teachings of a religious dogma, and that it was a sectarian practice, your Honor would pronounce in this case for the defendants.

Judge Storer. Certainly I should.

Mr. Matthews. Now, then, your Honor, if the Roman Catholic Church teaches that the reading of King James' version by or to its members—if the Roman Catholic father or mother believes that the reading of any version of the Holy Bible, without note or comment, and especially in the hands of an unanointed man, is necessarily the source of pernicious spiritual evil—ah, your Honor shakes your head, I don't ask whether that be true, but whether the Catholic Church teaches it?

Mr. King. Then it becomes an establishment.

Mr. Matthews. Certainly; it is an establishment inside that church.

Mr. King. No; the whole country, you say.

Mr. Matthews. No, I say this—the gentleman shall not escape—that if the Roman Catholic Church holds that dogma it has a legal, civil right to hold it, and the law and the State in all its departments and regulations, is bound to recognize the existence of it, as a right, to respect it as such, and in no wise to interfere with its exercise. To do so, is to violate a right of conscience.

Judge Storer. Suppose the Bible were removed from these schools, have not learned clergymen whom I esteem said, and has not the Archbishop, who is my personal friend, and a man of whose Christianity I have no doubt, said, that these schools never would be places, without the Bible, such as Catholic children could attend?

Mr. Matthews. Your Honor has asked a second question before I have got through with the answer to the first. I will come to that by and by, remarking for the present simply that the Archbishop is no party to this record. I ask your Honor the question if the Roman Catholic Church has not the civil right to teach, as a religious dogma, that the reading of the Scriptures is a heresy and a sin? I say they have. They have just as good a right to do that as the Protestant denominations have to shout, in the language of Chillingworth, "The Bible, the Bible is the religion of Protestants." If it be, then it is a sectarian book, according to the confession of their own mouths. Now, I say that is what the Church does teach—the Catholic Church—and I read but a sentence or two from an acknowledged exponent of their views, and a most able and candid writer. I read from the work of John Adam Moehler on *Symbolism*, in which he is arguing the question of the divine foundation by our Lord and Master of a visible organization which should contain His body and His spirit for all time upon the earth. He says :

"On the other hand, the authority of the Church is the medium of all which in the Christian religion resteth on authority, and is authority ; that is to say, the Christian religion itself ; so that Christ himself is only in so far an authority as the Church is an authority."

Further on, he says :

"If the Church be not an authority representing Christ, then all again relapses into darkness, uncertainty, doubt, distraction, unbelief and superstition ; revelation becomes null and void, fails of its real purpose, and must henceforth be ever called in question and finally denied."

The Church, the Church alone, is the depository of the truth of God. It is not in the Bible except so far as the Church interprets and reveals it to her children, and whoever else, with unhallowed and unsanctified hands and lips, attempts to teach any truth out of that book can never be certain that what he teaches is the truth, and is liable to teach only error. "The faith existing in the Church, from the beginning throughout all ages, is the infallible standard to determine the true sense of Scripture." * * * "This accordingly is the doctrine of Catholics. Those will obtain the knowledge full and entire of the Christian religion, only in connection with its essential form, which is the Church."

Judge Storer. Therefore we laymen have no right to say a word.

Mr. Matthews. Exactly. Now that is the doctrine of the Church—the Catholic Church—and I maintain the proposition, if your Honor please, that that church has just as great and high a civil right to teach that doctrine and to enforce it upon its members by its spiritual jurisdiction as your Honor's church has to teach the doctrine of justification by faith ; and that that right is held by that church, by all its adherents, by the fathers and mothers of its children just as sacredly, with just as high a sense of its entire importance to the future salvation of their souls, as that some in your Honor's church believe it to be essential to the purity of the Christian religion that there should be two lighted candles burning on the altar.

Now, if your Honors please, what will you do with the Jew, of whom it was said once by a Jew whose authority your Honor recognizes: "What advantage it is to be a Jew? Much every way, but chiefly because to him were committed the oracles of God." Your Honor has lectured in Jewish Sabbath schools.

Judge Storer. Certainly, and I would do it again, and in Catholic schools if they would let me.

Mr. Matthews. And, therefore, your Honor recognizes not only civilly but religiously that, as far as they go, they are on the right road.

Judge Storer. They have the Bible.

Mr. Matthews. They have a part of it, if your Honor pleases, but the remainder of it to the Jews is sacrilege, and blasphemy against God.

Judge Storer. Not quite as far as that, because my friend, Dr. Lilienthal, gave me a Syriac Testament, a while ago, and said that was the language in which the Savior spoke.

Mr. Matthews. Dr. Lilienthal did not live in the day (taking up a copy of the Bible) "when the chief priests therefore and officers saw him, they cried out, saying Crucify him, crucify him. Pilate sayeth unto them, Take ye him and crucify him, for I find no fault in him. The Jews answered him, We have a law and by our law he ought to die, because he made himself the Son of God."

So the record of this divine life and death and resurrection is something more to the Jew than an ordinary history: it is a blasphemy, sacrilege. And yet, your Honor would, by law, compel the reading of that book, of that record of the sayings and doings of that life, of the manner of that death, of that resurrection, to the children of Jewish parents, or else forbid them to come into the common schools that belong to them as they do to your Honor and to us all, equally, or at least tax them equally for the support of schools, in which, by law, their religion and the religion of their fathers is taught to be false, and that they themselves are unbelievers and rejecters of God.

But it is asked by some, who by asking it betray their want of comprehension of the real question: Have Protestants no rights? Can not the majority of the community insist upon their consciences? Must the rights of minorities alone be consulted? Are we to be ruled by Catholics, or Jews, or Infidels?

The answer is obvious and easy. Protestants have no rights, as such, which do not at the same time and to the same extent, belong to Catholics as such, to Jews and Infidels too. Protestants have a civil right to enjoy their own belief, to worship in their own way, to read the Bible and to teach it as part of their religion, but they have no right in this respect to any preference from the State, or any of its institutions; they have no right to insist upon Protestant practices at public expense, or in public buildings, or to turn public schools into seminaries for the dissemination of Protestant ideas. They can claim nothing on the score of conscience, which they can not concede equally to all others. It is not a question of majorities or minorities; for if the conscience of the majority is to be the standard, then there is no such thing as right of conscience at all. It is against the predominance and power of majorities, that the rights of conscience are protected, and have need to be.

If it be said that the Protestant conscience requires that the Bible be read by and to Protestant children, and it is a denial of a right of conscience to forbid it, waiving at present the obvious and conclusive answer that no such right of conscience can require that the State shall provide out of the common taxes for its gratification, it is enough to say, that Catholics then, too, have the same right to have their children taught religion according to their views—not out of the Douay Bible, if they do not consider that sufficient, but by catechism and in the celebration of the mass, if they choose to insist—that Jews have the same right to have their religion taught in the common schools, not from the English version of the Old Testament, but according to the practice of their synagogues—and Infidels have the same right to have their children taught Deism, or Pantheism, or Positivism. And then we should see a state of things, such as is described in the following extract from the *London Spectator*:

"In the colony of Victoria a grant of £50,000 a year has hitherto been made 'in aid' of religion, but it is now to be gradually withdrawn, decreasing £10,000 every year until it is extinguished. The cause of the change of feeling on the subject is not a little curious. The grant is to all denominations, and even the Jews after a severe fight, got some; but then came the Chinese and put in their claim, and the Australians could not stand paying for joss-houses. It never seems to have occurred to them that to tax Chinamen to support churches was just as unfair as to tax Christians for the support of joss-houses. To refuse help to all alike is easy statesmanship, but we do not see why it is more righteous than to give it to all alike. Buddhism is not a creed clearly inimical to civilization."

"Easy statesmanship" in such a case, is certainly the best and wisest.

If your Honors please, I do not know how often it may be necessary for me to disclaim that I am not a Roman Catholic and that I am not a Jew. [Laughter.] I am a Calvinistic Protestant. I believe in the doctrines of election and predestination. I believe that the Saints don't fall from grace, and I hope my friends who have fears of me will take comfort for that.

Judge Storer. It is a very comfortable doctrine. [Renewed laughter.]

Mr. Matthews. But if your Honors please, aside from all badinage and jesting, which are, perhaps, not exactly appropriate to the place and the occasion, do let me say, for I conceive it to be a privilege to say it, that I believe that this book, which I hold in my hands, is a sacred book in the highest sense of the term. I believe that it is the word of the living God, as essential to our spiritual nourishment and life as the bread that we eat, and the water that we drink to quench our thirst is, for our bodies. It records the history of the most marvelous appearance that ever occurred in human history—the advent in Judea of the man Christ Jesus, the promised Messiah of old, whom Moses wrote about, and of whom Moses was a feeble type; whom Joshua predicted when he led the hosts to take possession of the happy land and prefigured; whom all the prophets foretold, and the Psalmist sung, and the people sighed for, throughout all the weary ages of their captivity and bondage; who appeared in the light and brightness of the heathen civilization of the Augustan age; who spake as never man spake;

who healed the diseases of the people; who opened their eyes; who caused the dumb to speak, the blind to see, the deaf to hear, and preached the Gospel to the poor; who was persecuted because he was the living representative of divine and absolute truth, and who was lifted up upon the cross charged with blasphemy untruly, but slain upon the baser charge of treason to the Roman Cæsar, while in the very act of declaring that his "kingdom was not of this world;" lifted up, to be sure, by the hands of men, of ignorant men, for whom and for whose forgiveness he prayed, "because they knew not what they did;" lifted up by their hands, but in pursuance of a covenant that he had made in eternity with His Father that it should thus come to pass, because without the shedding of blood there was to be no remission of sin; lifted up in order that he might draw all men unto himself, that whosoever looked upon him might be healed of the poison of original sin and live. "Behold the Lamb of God which taketh away the sins of the world!" That, if your Honors please, is my *credo.* If I am asked how I prove it, I enter into no disputation or doubtful argument. I simply say that his divinity shone into my heart, and proved itself by its self-evidence. I have not three witnesses only, if your Honors please, above. I have five—five witnesses in heaven to-day, that are calling to me to come to them. I would not give up, I would not abate a jot or a tittle of my belief in that book, and in the God that it reveals, and the salvation that it offers for all that this world can give. And yet, if your Honors please, in the spirit of my Divine Master, I do not want to compel any man. If he can not believe—oh! it is his misfortune, not less than his fault, and not to be visited upon him as a penalty by any human judgment. It is not to be the ground of exclusion from civil rights; it is not to bar him from any privilege. It is even, if your Honors please, to protect him from the finger of scorn being pointed and slowly moved at him as if he were out of the pale of divine charity. Oh, no; it was to the lost that the Savior came, to seek them as well as to save them; and I know no other way, I know no better way, to recommend the truth of that book to those who can not receive it, but to live like him whose teaching is to be just, to be good, to be kind, to be charitable, to receive them all into the arms of my human sympathy, and

16

to say to them, "Sacred as I believe that truth to be, just so sacred is your right to judge it."

Now, what can the law do—the civil law—in the presence of eternity and of these eternal truths, and of these distinctions and differences, and human weaknesses and disabilities? Can the law rudely step in and say, because a majority of people profess faith in that, that therefore you shall be daily confronted with what you do not and can not receive? For—and that is the gist of the thing—the reading of the Holy Scriptures as the appropriate commencement of the morning daily exercises of the public school is the teaching of the religious dogma that they are the inspired Word of God; and if it was not so held by the Protestant members of this community, there would be no such lawsuit here to-day as there is. If it was the writings of Epictetus, of Seneca, or of Pliny, or moral philosophy, or anything of human composition and origin only, that taught the purest and the highest morality, nobody would be found to pay the expense of filing this bill to compel its daily reading. It is because that exercise is intended, and valued only as it is intended to teach the Christian doctrine as to the scheme of salvation offered by Christ, and the Protestant doctrine, that the book without note or comment is the infallible rule of faith and practice.

And therefore I say, in answer to your Honors' inquiry, that the practice sought to be perpetuated by the power of the civil arm in this suit, is a practice which teaches a religious dogma, and that in a sectarian sense; and I say that it is so indisputable, it is so self-evident—it is written upon every countenance in this room—that nothing else than that could account for the extraordinary interest taken in this trial and the efforts which are made to secure the interposition of this Court.

Your Honor asked me another question which I said I would answer, and although it takes me completely out from the line of my argument, I will answer it now.

Judge Storer. It is well always to have a compass.

Mr. Matthews. It is still better, if your Honor please, to have a rudder, and neither compass nor helm may do any good without ballast. Your Honor has said that the Archbishop of Cincinnati will not permit children of his communion to attend these schools, if the Bible is excluded. Then your Honor's interrogatory is *cui bono?* I will answer that. I know that the teaching and the doctrine of the Roman Catholic Archbishop, as well as of the Roman Pontiff and all the Roman hierarchy upon the subject of the necessity of combining religious instruction with secular education is exactly that advocated by my friends on the other side. It is neither larger nor smaller, and the object of the Archbishop, it may very possibly be, is, by a flank movement, first to secularize the schools so far as the Catholic participation in the movement is concerned, and then to strike a bargain with the former President of the School Board and his allies, holding them consistently to their present doctrine. "Now," he says, "you say that religious instruction must necessarily *ex vi termini* go hand in hand with grammar, and arithmetic, and geography, and conic sections. So say I, so says Mother Church, and so says good Father Pius the Ninth. Now, then, what is to be done? Why, combine our forces in an alliance to divide the school funds among the several denominations *pro rata.*"

And to that proposition and against it I stand here, I stand everywhere, always opposed, with all the strength of my body and my mind. And yet, while I make that declaration, I am bound in all fairness and in candor to the Archbishop to say this: that if his doctrine and that of my learned friends upon the other side who coincide with him as enunciated in this case, is the truth; if the schools can not be secularized, if religious instruction must accompany secular instruction, if it is impossible to teach the children of the State reading, writing, arithmetic, geography, grammar, history of the United States, and all the elements of a common school English education, without combining with it religious instruction, then I say the Archbishop's position is the fair one, and ought to be accepted. Common decency forbids the mere majority to grab the whole treasure of the State and turn it into its own coffers. A mere sense of common justice, the justice that reigns by right of nature, even in the heathen breast, ought at least to govern the Christian conscience so far as to allow others to participate in this partnership of wrong. And I do not hesitate to say that whenever it is authoritatively declared by the highest tribunals of this State, and sanctioned by the popular sovereignty, that common school education can not be given without religious instruction combined, then the principle of equality absolutely requires a division of the school fund among the religious denominations. But I will make the fight on the ground where I now stand. So much for the Archbishop and the hierarchy.

I propose now to turn my attention for a few moments to the Catholic people, to the Catholic citizens of Cincinnati, to the individual men and women, to the voters; and it is a great mistake, if your Honors please, to suppose because a man is a Catholic that, therefore, he don't think; some of them don't think; some Protestants don't think; not thinking is not an attribute of either religion. Whenever we establish the doctrine in this State that the Protestant Bible shall not be used as a means of proselyting their children from their fathers' faith under the rule of the State in the people's colleges, by secularizing those schools, then the archbishops and the priests may call upon them to contribute to the support of their parish schools; but it will be like calling "spirits from the vasty deep." They will call in vain. No longer will priests be able to say to the Catholic conscientious father and mother, "Don't send your children to those schools, because the poison of Protestantism will be inhaled into their lungs in every breath that they draw." They can not say that. If they do, the people will say to the priest, "Father, you are mistaken; our children are unmolested; they are not being pointed to as other than the rest; they are all on an equality; this is a kind, equal, paternal system; it knows no distinctions between religious opinions and religious sects; it takes my money, and it takes the money of the rich and the poor alike, whether they have children or not, and puts it into a common fund for their common benefit; now, having contributed my proportionate share of the public burden, I intend to enjoy for my children my proportionate share of the public privilege, and I will send my children to the district school, and I will not contribute to your parish school." The day that your Honors decree the dismissal of this petition you write upon these walls the destruction of every denominational Catholic parish school in the city of Cincinnati, with the consent of their constituents, with their approbation and to their great relief. It was dangerous for the gentlemen on the other side to remind me of this. What is it? It is a confession that the public schools of Cincinnati, as they have been heretofore conducted, do not command the public confidence—not the confidence merely of priests and the Cincinnati Archbishop, but the confidence of the constituency, the confidence of the people, the confidence of the mass whose taxes are wrung from them to support these schools. How are you going to win that confidence back? In the same way that the Mother Government undertook to conciliate the Colonies—by fire and sword, by opposition and vexation, and grinding down with precedents of arbitrary law, and talking of the supremacy of Protestantism? Is that the way? No; but by bringing them back to a sense of our intention to do right, by doing justice to them.

There is one practical test to which this matter can be brought, that, if it would only be honestly applied by every one within the sound of my voice, I think would settle this controversy without another word, and that is this: Suppose this was a Catholic community and the Protestants were in the minority, and suppose that the Catholics had established a system of common schools in which they had declared that religion, morality and knowledge being essential to good government, therefore the General Assembly should pass laws for the purpose of protecting every religious denomination in the enjoyment of its own mode of public worship, and also for the encouragement of schools and the means of education; and that, therefore, they had created a large fund, taken partly out of my pocket and partly out of yours, and of the remainder of the citizens, for the establishment of a magnificent system of schools, and had said: "But inasmuch as our Constitution requires that religion shall be the handmaid of government, therefore we must incorporate religious instruction into those schools, and we know no religion except that which Mother Church teaches, and we know no hands to teach it except those whom God has appointed, and whom His representative and vicegerent upon earth has anointed with the holy oil of His approbation for that purpose. Now, therefore, we shall declare by a constitutional rule, which shall be so firmly fixed in the social institutions of the country that nothing can change it, that every morning the exercises of the day shall be commenced by the solemn worship of

Almighty God in the only way in which He can acceptably be approached, namely—in the sacrifice of the Mass."

Suppose your children were brought to that school and were taught and were made, by a rule of that school, at the name of Christ, to bow the head in adoration, and to cross themselves with the sign of the cross, how would your Honors like it?

Or suppose the Catholic majority should prove themselves extremely liberal and say—we do not propose to violate your rights of conscience, and if you, who are Protestants, Jews and Infidels, do not desire your children to be taught religious truth as we understand it, and to be present at the religious services in these public schools, they shall be excused from attendance, for we are willing to grant you perfect toleration, and more than this you can not ask, or if you do, we can not grant, for our consciences require this much, and we, too, have rights. Would not the Protestant answer be ready—we are not only not willing that our children shall be exposed to the dangerous influences of your religious practices and examples, but also, we are not willing to be taxed to support you in the education of your own children, in what we conceive to be religious error, destructive to their eternal interests. If you are willing to take the responsibility, do so, but we can not share it with you. Teach them what you please at home or in your church, but not your religion in schools that belong to us as much as to you.

Now, I understand the answer to this. It is that the proposition is not that; it is only the reading of the Protestant Bible. If your Honors please, the reading of the Bible is just as offensive to the Catholic's conscience as participation in the sacrifice of the Mass is to a devout Protestant, every whit; and they are the judges of their own conscience, and not you. Why, if the very thing that has been done for twenty-five years in reference to the Roman Catholic population of this city had, in a reversed state of things, been attempted upon a like number of Protestants, there would have been just what Mr. Bellows invites, because the Protestants are a fighting people. Their religion was born and baptized in blood, and they will die rather than surrender the right of private judgment on questions between themselves and God. All I ask is—being a Protestant—that we make manifest the value of our Protestantism to those we seek to convert, by showing what it can do for a man by making him magnanimous, and liberal, and great. Oh, what a solemn mission it is to which your Honors are called—to vindicate the truth of the religion you privately profess by showing how equal, how just it is!

And now, having wandered from the direct line of my argument, for the purpose of answering some questions that your Honor has asked, I propose, with what strength I have left, to argue one or two propositions. The basis of this suit necessarily consists—and that is the essence of it—in the denial of the existence in the Board of Education of all discretion over the course of study in these schools. I use that phrase deliberately because it is broad. It is not a mere question of the reading of the Bible. It is a question of the particular arithmetic that may be used; it is a question of the particular geography; a question of the particular reader, because if religion and morality are essential to good government, and if Protestant Christianity is the fundamental law included in that word "religion," all my friends on the other side will have to do to obtain any further injunctions, after they have got the precedent of this, is to file a bill and allege that in a certain book introduced into the text books of the common schools with the authority of the Board of Education, there are some one or more articles or paragraphs which, in the opinion of the petitioners, are contrary to the Christian religion, and if they can get your Honors to agree with them in their interpretation of Christian doctrine on that subject, your Honors are bound to expurgate the book. And there is no limit to the interference. There is no other limit than a possible limit—and there is none—to the variety, the infinite variety, of opinion on questions of religion and morality; and we might have the strange spectacle of one sect of Protestants seeking to get an injunction against one book, and another against another book, until every sect had its injunction, and no boy had any education. The object of the common schools, as I understand it, is to furnish education to the boys, and not injunctions to the sects.

The reliance of the gentlemen is upon the seventh section of the Bill of Rights, wherein it is recited, by way of preamble, that "religion, morality and knowledge, being essential to good government," etc. That is the expression, you may say, first of the framers of the Constitution, and then of the people who adopted it, and they put it into that clause of that section by way of preamble, introductory, however, of the commencement of a duty to which they think that principle leads. Now, that is a duty on the General Assembly. "It shall be the duty of the General Assembly"—not the duty of the School Board, not the duty of the Superior Court of Cincinnati—to do what? "To pass suitable laws." Now, suppose the General Assembly don't do it; and they may refuse to do it in two ways. In the first place they may refuse to pass any laws at all—and that would be a violation of it—or, in the next place, if they passed laws, they might not, in the opinion of the complainants, be "suitable laws." Now, in case they do not pass any laws at all, what is to be done? I wonder if my friends would apply for a *mandamus* from a court, directed to the General Assembly, requiring them to proceed in the execution of their duty, enjoined not only by the Constitution of the State, but by that other constitution of society, namely, the Christian scheme of religion, to pass laws to protect every religious denomination in the peaceable enjoyment of its own mode of worship, and to encourage schools.

Suppose that the General Assembly did pass laws, who is the judge of their suitableness? It is not necessary for me to argue that question. There would be no sense in my arguing it to a court that required an argument upon it, and I might therefore as well spare the time. The General Assembly must be the sole and exclusive judges of the suitableness of the laws the Constitution enjoins upon them to pass.

Now, then, they have passed laws, and they are suitable in the language and meaning of the Constitution, and those laws confide to the Board of Education in the city of Cincinnati absolute and unrestricted and unlimited discretion over the whole curriculum of school exercises and school education. The General Assembly have done it in pursuance to the Constitution. The fact that they have done it is conclusive that it was the suitable thing to do; and now, after the exercise of a discretion confided to them by the Constitution, they are called in question, and your Honors are required to revise and reverse that exercise of discretion. Where do you get the authority? Not from the General Assembly, not from the Constitution. Now, it may have been wise or unwise, viewed from our individual standpoint, for the General Assembly to have intrusted any such discretion to any such body; but that is nothing with which we have anything to do. And, that, if your Honors please, disposes of that part of the argument of my friend Mr. Sage in reference to Judge Hoadly and myself in connection with the House of Refuge and the State Industrial and Reform School for boys and girls. Whatever may be the law with regard to them, there is no pretense that in any law passed in reference to the conduct of the common schools, there is anything less than an unlimited discretion on the part of the Board of Education. Now will your Honors take something up out of the briefs of the gentlemen and put it into the statute? Will your Honors pick up something found floating loose in the community because it happens to be the passing public opinion, and put it into the Constitution? I was about to ask the question in a form that I fear might be considered offensive. I was going to ask—but I will not—will your Honors usurp the functions of the School Board?

Now, I understand that it is beyond question, that in all the laws passed on the subject of schools by the General Assembly, there is nothing that requires any religious instruction whatever—the reading of the Bible, the singing of hymns, or the use of any book of religion. If the General Assembly has not enjoined it, if the General Assembly has not required it, if it has submitted the entire discretion over every question to the School Board, who, in the discharge of the duties of a good citizenship, shall dare say nay? Now, is not that true, and is it not conclusive? Why, let us look at it—admitting now everything else that has been said—that religion, in the language of the Constitution, means the Christianity of the Bible, and that instruction in it is essential to good government; yet, nevertheless, if the General Assembly have become derelict in their duty, and have not passed suitable laws making a perfect system of education, can you supplement their folly with your Honors' wisdom or the wisdom of the gentlemen?

Now, *lex ita scripta est*—"what is writ is writ;" and there it is, and it is the command of the lawful superior to your Honors, and to me, and to these gentlemen. The School Board are the legal and intrusted guardians of the school interests, and whatever they choose to do, or whatever they choose to omit in reference to the manner of conducting the exercises of the school, the subjects of instruction, the extent to which that instruction shall be carried, the manner in which it shall be imparted and the persons by whom it shall be given, the times, places—every circumstance of that character is absolutely at their disposal. And if it is not done to the satisfaction of the community, all the community have to do is to blame themselves, for they are the people who appointed these Trustees. All they have to do is to vacate their places when the legal expiration of their term arrives, and select new and better men. There is the remedy—a plain one—better, more satisfying, every way, than an injunction.

Take my friend Mr. Ramsey's definition of education, quoted from Horace Mann. I agree to it. What does it define a complete and perfect education to be? Why, first the development of the life and vigor of the physical frame into the full proportions of manhood and womanhood; next, the development and strengthening and invigorating of the intellectual faculties; next, last, and not least, the improvement and culture of all the moral sentiments and affections.

Now the School Board omits a gymnasium, gymnastic exercises, calisthenics, dumb-bells, these performances by girls and boys for the purpose of developing their muscular power, of enabling them to strike the right attitude, to maintain the proper and graceful gait—and that, bye-the-bye, is a part of religion in the estimation of some, for I have been told by a clergyman of the High Church that he knows a Presbyterian woman when she walks up the aisle, for she always walks upon her heels, whereas your High Church ladies have been taught to trip the light fantastic toe. [Laughter.]

Suppose the School Board, being composed of a body of dried up and withered old fellows that have always been intent on black letter, or in poring over works of alchemy and distorting mind and body, as is charged against my friend, Judge Stallo, in recondite research after the truths of nature, have acquired a bad opinion of anything like muscular Christianity, and do not care about the body, holding that it is the soul that is to be expanded into the ethereal—that the body is nothing—that it is dust, and shall return to dust—and, therefore, they will not have any calisthenics, will not allow the girls to grow and expand and become vigorous, nor allow the boys to play base ball; and, perhaps, a little restraint in that might do the rising generation some good.

Now, then, Mr. Ramsey comes in, or rather the president of the "Red Stockings," who is a member of the bar, and gets out an injunction against the School Board, on the ground that this course they are pursuing will dwarf the bodies of the children—"*mens sana in corpore sano*" being the foundation, without which education, either moral or intellectual, is of no value. I do not know of any authority on the point that a bad state of health is advantageous to knowledge or light of any kind, except as contained in a couplet, I think, of Shenstone—

> "The soul's dark cottage, battered and decayed,
> Lets in new light through chinks that Time has made."

But ordinarily, so far as youth is concerned, physical education is just as necessary to good citizenship as intellectual and religious—as that religious education that the counsel on the other side say is limited by the necessities of the State. Now, then, the School Board passes a resolution not permitting the youths to have gymnastics, or to "skin the cat" [laughter], or to practice any of the exercises proper for that age; why not apply for an injunction?

Judge Storer. The boys would take that liberty at any rate.

Mr. Matthews. But they might get whipped for it. My illustration, however, was to enforce the idea that in this matter the Legislature of the State and the Constitution of the State have remitted the entire discretion and control of this whole subject to the School Board, and I shall not take the time of your Honors to cite an authority to show that the lawful exercise of a legal discretion can not be controlled by a court of law, however unwisely it may have been exercised. But then, it is said, there is something behind the Constitution—that there is a necessary implication in the use of the word "religion" in the Bill of Rights, that the reading of the Bible is indispensable in the schools.

Now, I dispute that proposition. I dispute the proposition that the word "religion," in the Constitution, means even the Christian religion. I am very far from thinking it means the Protestant religion. I think, to go no farther, it is evident it does not mean any form of religion that may be professed by one and dissented from by another, because the very same section of the Bill of Rights is full of declarations of absolute neutrality on the part of the State, and therefore when it uses the word religion it does not use it even in the sense understood by Mr. Sage, when he calls it a "broad Christianity"—a Christianity which I confess I do not understand. But the word as employed in the Constitution simply means those indestructible principles of right that are written by the finger of God, even on the fallen nature of man, and revealed to him by the light of his conscience, and of which, so far as its moral precepts are concerned, the Bible is only the republication. For if that book inculcated a single moral precept to which there was not an answering voice in human nature, it would be just like speaking in an unknown tongue. The Decalogue is older than Moses. It is as old as man, and was transferred unto him by God, in whose image he was made, and, however perverted and ruined by transgression, either inherited or committed, that transcript of God's image remains there indelible, indestructible. It makes man a moral being, and without it society would be impossible, government impossible and schools worse than a farce. Now, then, when the Constitution of the State of Ohio says religion and morality and knowledge are essential to government, it simply means that the instinctive sense of right and wrong should be brought out by exercise and developed. The only religion that it considers vital to the preservation of the State is that religion which is written on human nature. I do not deny that the State has to do with religion. It has a good deal to do with it. It has the right, and it is its duty to recognize the fact that man is a moral being, and therefore recognizes himself as under a responsibility to do right; and that is the very foundation of society, and it is the foundation of government, because government, being the aggregation by voluntary consent of the heads of families, is instituted by man for the purpose of doing justice—that is, of seeing that justice is done, of exercising its compulsory power, so as to compel the performance by man of the duties required in society, to render, in the language of civil law, every man his own—*suum cuique tribuere.* The origin of society is the family, and the man is the head of the family and its natural representative, and that is the way we get rid of female suffrage.

> " This is a very good world that we live in,
> To lend and to spend, and to give in,
> But to beg and to borrow, and to get a man's own,
> It is the worst world that ever was known."

And to improve it in that latter particular, governments were instituted, and justice can not be known except as it is developed from the intuitive instincts of men, especially that which teaches the distinction between right and wrong.

And, if your Honors please, whatever does belong to a man, that he has by virtue of being a man in society, and not under government. He had it before government was. It was his. That is the meaning of it. He does not hold it by any sub-infeudation; he holds it by direct homage and allegiance to the owner and the Lord of all. Moreover, whatever was his, just that same belonged to everybody else. On the natural plane, at least, God has not any favorites. Whatever in point of right He gave to you, He gave to me; and inasmuch as you and I might dispute, we agreed upon a common arbiter, and that is government that settles the boundary between your right and mine. It makes no difference how small a right it is. If it is only a little piece of a right, our law says an action for damages shall lie for its breach, because the law presumes damage from the denial even of that right. If it is only so small a matter as the conscience of a Jew or an Infidel, it is his, and can not be taken away.

My friends on the other side said they were asking light on this question, as to what, and how absolute and universal are the rights of conscience. I hold in my hand a book written by Isaac Taylor, one of the most thorough masters of English style.

Judge Storer. And one of the most learned.

Mr. Matthews. And I will add one of the most devout Christians, and a Presbyterian. It is an *Essay on Ultimate Civilization.*

He undertakes to shadow forth what shall be the condition of society when all the social functions are brought to their highest altitude and perfection, and that social equilibrium is attained which opens the way for the indefinite and unobstructed progress of the individual man; and in laying down the propositions that are fundamental to that ultimate, best, highest civilization, he says:

"The rights of man, as man, must be understood in a sense that can admit of no single exception; for to allege an exception is the same thing as to deny the principle. We reject, therefore, with scorn, any profession of respect to the principle which, in fact, comes to us clogged and contradicted by a petition for an exception."

He says again:

"The rights of man must everywhere all the world over be recognized and respected, and religiously watched over and courageously defended; and that to do this is the audible call of God now addressed to the British people."

He says again:

"We have just now said, in relation to the rights of man, that they are universal and *unexceptive;* or, if not so, then they are none at all. To profess the principle and then to plead for an exception—let the plea be what it may—is to deny the principle and it is to utter a treason against humanity. The same is true, and it is true with an emphasis, in relation to those rights which are at once the surest guarantee of every other, and the most precious of all—namely, the Rights of Conscience. We say *Rights;* for although they are *one*, they yet include what must be carefully specified in detail, as a caution against all contradictions and against any infringement.

"Besides:—Liberty is no liberty, in any sense if at all it be bandaged. These restraints, which attach to social life for the safety of all alike are none in the feeling of the right-minded. But the bandaging of men in respect of their religious convictions and professions and conduct is a restraint which is useless more than any other; for danger on this ground does not come, if it be not created; and it is prejudicial more than any other; because religious liberty, in its amplitude and when it is enjoyed by many, does by itself, render despotisms impossible.

"The Rights of Conscience not understood, or if they be misunderstood by a government—then the civilization of such a people is—a glittering barbarism; it is nothing better."

And he shows that this sacred protection of the rights of conscience, although it encourages and develops differences of religious opinion, does by that very act, multiply and invigorate the forces that supply energy to social progress. He says:

"Everybody among ourselves has at length come to understand, or at least passively to assent to, this simple and most momentous truth—that religious differences, when inflamed by intolerance, become active causes of social confusion—tending toward national disintegration; this has been signally exemplified in the past history of Spain and of France. It is a truth not so generally understood among ourselves—or it is not so cordially admitted—that the absolutely unrestricted development and the fixed conservation of religious differences, is a principal and indeed an indispensable condition of social advancement and of the progress of a people toward a state of equipoise without stagnation. Religious differences well defined, firmly maintained and fully developed, and in such a condition that they are not merely *elements*, but are *energies* within the social mass, when duly attempered, stand, if not *foremost*, quite *prominent* among the forces that are carrying us forward toward a higher civilization."

Most noble and tolerant political philosophy! and exactly expresses and justifies that wise secularism of our constitutions of government, which but serves the cause of religion, by preserving its spirit and its freedom, in all its forms and growths, by absolute neutrality.

And applying these principles to the subject of popular education, the same writer says:

"Something should be said concerning popular education, and to all men of ordinary intelligence and unsectarian feeling, the obstructions thrown in the way of popular education are causes at once of great irritation, amazement and humiliation also. How is it that many estimable men, benevolent, but narrow in understanding and rigid in temper, would rather see millions die in starvation than help to distribute loaves not baked in their oven and not crossed with their mark."

Yet that observation and protest are made in the face of a system of education in England just as tender of the rights of conscience as the conscience clause my friends rely on in this case. A conscience clause—that is what it is called there; properly there because they have a legally established religion; properly so there, because there it is toleration, and not equality; properly there, because although they claim to be a free government, and to have abolished all the remnants of barbaric persecution, yet, after all, it is only toleration. They permit it. It is indulgence on the part of the State. And yet they have there a conscience clause. Here we have a conscience clause with which, we are told, we ought to be satisfied. We ought to be, if Protestantism is established as a law of the State, because we can get nothing else. But if we are all on an equality, there can be no conscience clause, for that implies an exception—it must be a rule universal in its application, providing equally for all. It does not merely permit it—it does not merely consent that a child may come by permission of the parent and be excused by way of exception from the operation of a general rule. No; it says every child shall have just the same right there as every other. There shall be no conscience clause but that, because there can be no question of conscience—that is legally.

Now, I ask attention to the educational system in England, as existing at the time of that indignant protest of Isaac Taylor. I read from a new and able book on the *Parliamentary Government of England*, by Alpheus Todd (vol. 2, p. 646.) He says:

"Another educational question, which has given rise to much controversy, has grown out of what is termed the conscience clause. This is a regulation (not yet embodied in any formal minute) which was first framed by the Educational Office about the year 1860, and which has since been made generally, though not invariably, applicable to grants on behalf of schools. It is as follows: 'The managers of the school shall be bound to make such orders as shall provide for admitting to the benefits of the school the children of parents not in communion with the Church of England, as by law established, but such orders shall be confined to the exemption of such children, if their parents desire it, from attendance at public worship, and from instruction in the doctrines and formularies of the said church, and shall not otherwise interfere with the religious teaching of the scholars.'

"The practical effect of this clause is to allow parents who do not wish their children to be taught any particular doctrine, to withdraw them from the schools at the time religious instruction is given. At first this clause was strenuously opposed by the clergy of the Established Church, who deprecated the withdrawal of any children from their own oversight and pastoral care, and who feared that even this concession to Dissenters would tend to destroy the denominational character of the schools, and lead to all religious teaching therein being done away with."

Just the same provision as these gentlemen are seeking to impose on these public schools. They include everything which they call a "broad Christianity;" everything, I suppose, from Bellows up [laughter]; but if any children whose parents desire that they may be excused from attending the service prescribed by law as only preparatory to the opening of school every day, they can retire.

Your Honors are aware that all the liberal minded men in England have banded together under a party name called "Voluntaryism," both in regard to religion and education, one of the great exponents of their principles, Dr. Ralph Wardlaw, declaring that the province of the State in matters of religion was that it has no province at all.

Now, that is the English system, which gives, in deference to the rights of conscience, the right on the part of children of Dissenters to withdraw from the schools at those times.

But even that is considered offensive and justly so. And to remedy the inequality, the Duke of Marlborough, Lord President of the Council in Mr. D'Israeli's administration, last year, introduced into the House of Lords, the project of a law, of which the chief features were dispensing with the condition requiring all schools aided by the State to be in connection with some religious denomination, and that payments should be made for results obtained in regard to secular teaching alone, providing, nevertheless, that denominational schools might continue to receive State aid, provided, that when required by the circumstances of the particular case "*conscience clauses*" for the protection of the rights of children of other denominations attending the school, should be duly inserted in their trust deeds. And to avoid misapprehension it was proposed to insert in the schedules of this bill, the management clauses of the Church of England, the Wesleyan, the Congregational, the Roman Catholic, the Jewish, and other denominational schools, as used by these religious bodies; but if a purely secular school presents its scholars for examination, the State would not refuse to examine and pay for the results of their teaching.

But upon the argument made by counsel for the plaintiffs in this case, if I understand it, and if carried to its logical results, we can not constitutionally afford to be so liberal, even as is proposed in England where they have an Established Church. For if religion be here, under our Constitution the care of the State, to a certain extent as claimed, and that religion means the religion of the Bible—a broad Christianity—so that the State is bound by its fundamental law to provide education in that religion as a necessary part of the instruction to be given in the public schools, then it can not permit exceptions to be made, even upon the plea of conscience—for the exception destroys in this case, not proves the rule—and the State may, yea, if the argument be sound, must by the terms of its Constitution, step in between father and child, and educate the child in opposition to its father's faith. And to justify this interference, we are told that parents neglect their duty, and that a child has rights of conscience as against its father!

I protest against the doctrine. Its application would be a monstrous tyranny. Its idea is Pagan, not Christian.

It was upon just such a pretense that the Pope of Rome stole a Jewish child from its parents, on the plea that it was the right of the child and for the good of his soul; that it was the duty of a Christian State to provide for all the children of its peoole a Christian education.*

---

*Since the close of the argument in this case, I have received from an anonymous but evidently intelligent, and I think sincere correspondent, a letter criticising this view of the *Mortara case*. As an illustration of my argument, and for the sake of the explanation, I make the following extract:

"I was very much pained, however, when I heard escaping from your lips one grievous misstatement, which was no doubt owing to the excitement of the moment, and not considering of the merits of the case. I mean the reference you made to the *Mortara Case* which you characterized as the Pope having stolen a Jewish child. Bear with me whilst I give you an unbiased statement of the case.

"There is a law in the Roman States forbidding Jewish families keep-

In opposition to this doctrine, listen to some noble, true, and eloquent utterances, from the gifted Father Hyacinthe, entitled by his present anomalous position, to be regarded, if not as authority, at least, with respect, both by Protestant and Catholic, and to the sympathy of the liberal minded of every creed. In a discourse on civil society and Christianity, a translation of which has recently been published, I find the following:

"One of the acutest and exactest thinkers of our day, whom I desire to mention by name, on account of the obligation I am under to him, in my own studies, the illustrious Abbé Rosmini-Sorbati—a genuine Italian to the very marrow of his bones, and at the same time a very Catholic to the core of his heart—has helped me to the best conception of civil society. According to him civil society has for its object not—like the family in its natural order, or the church in its supernatural order—the *substance* of rights, but simply the *modality* of rights. It does not create rights. Man exists before the State, with all those essential and inalienable rights which he holds directly from God, by virtue of reason and moral liberty. The family, also, exists before the State with rights equally essential, equally inalienable, exercised in its bosom by the human person raised to his fullest dignity and felicity. It is not for the State to create these rights which are antecedent to it, and

---

ing Christian servants. The chief rationale of this law is to protect the Jewish household and to prevent the arising of conflicts between them and the authorities. The Mortara family held a Christian servant contrary to law, and made itself thereby liable to its penalties. It happened, that one of their children, the boy in question, fell dangerously ill and his life was despaired of. The servant, firmly believing that baptism is necessary to salvation, and thinking the infant dying, felt bound in conscience to give the needed assistance for its eternal welfare, and administered private baptism, thereby making the child a Christian. The boy unexpectedly recovered. The servant for some years concealed her action, but finally feeling uneasy about it, made the fact known to the authorities, and the Government, being Christian, not of a broad Christianity, which you have well said is a broad humbug, felt in duty bound to provide for that child a Christian education, to which it had acquired a strict right by the fact of its baptism. This it would manifestly not have received in the bosom of its family, and hence it was removed to a public institution, where the parents were free to visit it, and where it was educated at the

which come, I am bold to say, from a higher source; it is only for the State not to destroy them, nor to encroach upon them. Its mission extends no farther than to protect them and to establish over them the sway of what the English in their noble language call the 'Queen's peace' what Saint Paul bids us ask for when we pray for kings and all that are in authority, 'that we may lead a quiet and peaceable life in all godliness and honesty.' The mission of the State consists then, in fixing the *modality* of rights, that is, in regulating the best way in which the reciprocal duties of individuals and families should be exercised in order to help, rather than hinder each other in their common development. It consists further, in protecting by force the right and interests which belong to it, from every unjust and violent attack, whether from within or from without. Such are the natural frontiers of civil society and domestic society—the family and the State—frontiers far more important for the peace and liberty of the world than those of the Pyranees, the Alps, or the Rhine! On these frontiers I pause, and salute that scepter which requires nothing but righteousness, produces nothing but peace; the oppressor of none, the liberator of all. I salute the sword of which Saint Peter declares that the king bears it not in vain. Next to righteousness I know nothing more sacred than force, when force is not the assassin of right, but its champion."

---

expense of the State. We all know what a fearful storm of hatred and angry passions was at that time raised against Rome for this action, and how, by false representation, the intervention of various European governments was obtained to remonstrate in the name of Christianity against the Christian education of a Christian child; but Rome stood firm to its recognized duty and protected through good and evil report, the divine right of that child to a Christian education, acquired by the fact of its baptism.

"Considering all this, ought we not rather admire the courage and fortitude of Rome in thus shielding the rights of this child, even in the face of all the clamor and invectives of a misguided public opinion, and does it not sound harsh to hear such an action styled by an honored and learned lawyer, in the sacred precincts of a court of justice, "the Pope stole a child?" Why, dear Judge, if the Pope has a penchant for the child stealing business, I suppose he might gratify it almost daily, in the Ghetto, without much ado being made about it."

And again:

"The child belongs to its parents. I know the prejudices of my contemporaries, but I affirm none the less, in some measure, a right of property of man in man; and there can be no example of this sort of right more legitimate and noble than that of the right of the father to the child. Doubtless the *person* of every human being is essentially free and sovereign; it belongs to itself under the 'eminent domain' of God. But it is not so with its *nature*. Saving and excepting the rights of the person, we may say—we must say—that the nature of the son belongs to the father. It is flesh of his flesh and bone of his bone. The breath which inspires it is breathed from his nostrils; the vital heat which animates it is kindled from himself; and, as they were wont to say in Israel, it is his spark, his lamp which is to go shining on when he is dead, and perpetuate his name and glory in the midst of his people. The father is then, indeed, the proprietor of this sacred nature; to him alone it belongs to impress upon it its controlling momentum and direction toward the future. Consequently the school, the sanctuary of education, has its proper place beneath or near the parental roof.

"The public interest, that pagan idea so often appealed to against the rights of the individual and the family, could not give to the State a power over education which it does not possess itself. In Sparta, the Republic claimed the right of educating the children, because it regarded them as its property; and this principle was, in a greater or less degree, that of all Greek and Roman antiquity.

"The grand principle of Lycurgus, repeated in express terms by Aristotle, was, that as the children belonged to the State, they should be educated by the State, according to the views of the State."

The contrary doctrine—that it belongs primarily to the State, and not to the family, to provide for the education of children—and especially that fatal and needless extension of the principle, so as to embrace their religious instruction, is fruitful of the worst and most unhappy results, and can not fail, if carried in application to its final consequences, to subvert society itself, for it attacks it in its most vital point—the sanctity of the family relation.

May it please your Honors, the example of European systems of popular education has been cited as proof of the universal opinion of the necessity of coupling religious with secular instruction. The fact that in every country of Europe where education is made the care of the State, there is also a legally established State religion and church is sufficient to show the source of the opinion, and to turn the example into a warning. Certainly such precedent can have no authority here. All our traditional policy, all our republican principles, all our democratic ideas, all our notions of civil and religious liberty, all our political theories, all our social philosophy, habits and manners are entirely opposed to it. And yet were it otherwise, there is no European system of popular education that can be adduced as a justification of what is claimed by the plaintiffs in this case. If in Europe they do not completely secularize popular instruction, at least they treat every religious opinion and sect equally and fairly. There is not a kingdom or an empire in Europe to-day, despotic as it may be, and in which religion is established by law through a State Church, where king or emperor dares to trespass upon the rights of conscience of either Protestant, Catholic or Jew. The National Council of Education in France contains, as representatives, Catholic priests, Protestant ministers and Jewish rabbis.

Matthew Arnold, in his official report upon Continental Schools to the British Government, pp. 87–88, says:

"I have several times mentioned the *aumôniers*, or chaplains, attached to the French public schools. None of these schools, secondary or primary, are secular schools; in all of them religious instruction is given. It is given, too, in the vast majority of private schools. An hour's lesson in the week, certain exercises and prizes in connection with this lesson, and service on Sundays, are what this instruction amounts to in the secondary schools. The provisor and the chaplain regulate it between them; that of Catholic boys is under the inspection of the bishop of the diocese, or his delegate, in concert with the provisor. Protestant and Jewish boys receive the religious instruction of their own communion, regulated, *mutatis mutandis*, precisely like that of Catholic boys. The great *lycées* of Paris have Protestant and Jewish chaplains attached to them, just as they have Catholic chaplains. Where Protestants or Jews are not numerous enough for the school to have a special chaplain for them, boys of these persuasions still receive their religious instruction, from ministers of their own creed appointed to visit them, and are entirely exempted from the religious instruction of the Catholics. I can not myself see that the religious lessons (I do not, of course, speak of the services and ordinances of religion) come to very much in secondary instruction, though I must think, differing in this respect from many liberals, that they have an important and indispensable part in primary. But it is indisputable that they give rise, neither in France nor Germany, to any religious difficulty, as we say, whatever. They are regulated with absolute fairness, and there are no complaints at all of improper interference and proselytism. This, I say, is indisputable; and Protestants and Jews would testify to it as much as Catholics."

In respect to Prussia, the same writer says:

"In Protestant schools, the religious instructor is usually a layman; in Catholic, an ecclesiastic. The public schools are open to scholars of all creeds; in general, one of the two confessions, Evangelical or Catholic, greatly preponderates, and the Catholics, in especial, prefer schools of their own confession. But the State holds the balance quite fairly between them. Where the scholars of that confession which is not the established confession of the school are in considerable numbers, a special religious instructor is paid out of the school funds to come and give this religious instruction at the school. Thus, in the gymnasium at Bonn, which is Catholic, I heard a lesson on the Epistle to the Galatians (in the Greek) given to the Protestant boys of one of the higher forms, by a young Protestant minister of the town, engaged by the gymnasium for that purpose. When the scholars whose confession is in the minority are very few in number, their parents have to provide by private arrangements of their own for their children's religious instruction."

And in reference to the schools in Switzerland, Mr. Arnold says, p. 241:

"In Canton Geneva, the lay tendencies of modern democracy have so far prevailed that the pastor, or the curé, is not *ex officio* a member of the communal school committee; but all the communal schools have a dogmatic religious instruction, Catholic or Protestant. Many people in England seem to have a notion that a State system of education must of necessity be undenominational and secular. So far is this from being the case that in all the countries to which the present work relates—France, Italy, Germany and Switzerland—there is a State system of education, and that system is both denominational and religious. *Only the different denominations are not suffered to persecute one another.*"

The last sentence contains a sting that ought to bring blood to the cheeks of every one who, professing to believe it to be the duty of the State to include religious instruction in its system of public education, at the same time insists that that religious instruction shall be such that none but a Protestant can approve it, which excludes the Catholic and insults the Jew.

Now, if your Honors please, I characterized this proceeding, in the beginning, as an attempt to wrest and pervert the law, and I claim I have a professional interest to resist that attempt; and it consists not only in the solicitation held out by the other side to a usurpation by a court of law of duties imposed upon another Board, but in maintaining another proposition, and it is that in any just sense of the term applicable to the issue in this case, Christianity is a part of the law of the land. I ask your Honors' attention, in the first place, to the Bill of Rights, as I have already adverted to the provisions of the Constitution in reference to schools. In one thing I agree with the gentlemen on the other side—that that Bill of Rights is not a mere series of glittering generalities.

Your Honors, at one time, seemed to grow impatient in listening to my colleagues reciting the various acts of oppression and persecution inflicted by the Pagans on Christians, by Catholics on Protestants, by Protestants on fellow Protestants and Catholics, as if that recital of historical facts was not germane and relevant to this case. I think it was very much so, because it is in that recital, it is in those records of history, that are written the rise, the progress, the devolopment, the establishment of the principles contained in this Bill of Rights. Every martyr to civil oppression and religious persecution is a witness to the truth of these propositions. They are the landmarks which establish the boundaries of our present knowledge of political science. They are the records on which the people of Ohio have inscribed the advance made from generation to generation in the study and the practical application of political elementary truth, and every departure from them should be carefully watched, and most sedulously prevented. And yet, in spite of history, we are told by gentlemen, as I understand them, that it is a legal proposition; that the Protestant view of religion, as founded on this version of the Bible, is a part of the law of the State; and not only of this State, but of the United States, for, in maintaining the proposition they have to overrule two deliberate decisions of the Supreme Court of this State, and they seem to think they have successfully accomplished by it, by a decision of the Supreme Court of the United States.

Now I maintain, if your Honors please, that the establishment by law, which is compulsory—the thing which is sought by the invocation to this Court in the present suit—of the reading of the Bible in the public schools as a part of a system of religious instruction required to be adopted and pursued in them, is a violation of every specification of the seventh section of our Bill of Rights.

1. That provides that all men have a natural and indefeasible right to worship Almighty God according to the dictates of their own conscience.

This is a clear recognition of the principle that religion is a concern exclusively of the individual person—a matter between man and God—with which the State has no right whatever to interfere. And this includes and protects as a civil right, unbelief and disbelief—the neglect of worship and even the denial of religion. No man can be treated as an outlaw because he is an infidel.

2. It provides that no person shall be compelled to attend, erect, or support any place of worship or maintain any form of worship against his consent.

Yet this Court is asked to declare that in all our public schools, devotional and religious exercises, by the reading of the Bible and singing of religious songs, shall be daily practiced, and that as a means for the religious instruction of the pupils, constituting a form of worship in which neither Catholic, Jew, or Infidel can voluntarily unite, and yet which they are all taxed to support.

3. The Bill of Rights declares that no preference shall be given by law to any religious society; and the sixth article of the Constitution provides that no religious or other sect or sects shall ever have any exclusive right to or control of any part of the school funds of this State.

And yet we are asked to believe that at the same time our fundamental law ordains that instruction in the Christian religion is imperatively incorporated into the system of public education, and that that instruction must be committed to those Christian sects who in common recognize the Protestant version of the Bible as the only revealed will of God and the only infallible rule of faith and practice.

4. The Bill of Rights also declares that no interference with the rights of conscience shall be permitted and that no religious test shall be required as a qualification for office.

That the rule sought to be enforced in this proceeding does most seriously and materially interfere with rights of conscience I do most sincerely believe, and have endeavored to show; and that it establishes a religious test as a qualification for office, is manifest in the case of every teacher, required to read the Protestant version of the Bible, as the inspired and authoritative word of God. How can a Catholic priest, a Jew, or one who rejects the Bible as the only foundation of true religion, accept a situation as a teacher in the public schools on condition of participating in the religious exercises and instructions which it is declared are legally necessary to our public schools? Would not the peculiar religious opinions of such candidates be regarded under such a regime as an absolute disqualification?

Now what is there in the Bill of Rights that contradicts or qualifies these declarations and the conclusions which they require? Nothing else is relied upon, as the foundation of the whole argument, but the simple sentence that "religion, morality, and knowledge, however, being essential to good government"—what then? —"it shall be the duty of the General Assembly to protect every religious denomination in the peaceable enjoyment of its own mode of public worship, and to encourage schools and the means of instruction." And now let me ask—do the words "every religious denomination," include every sect of religionists, or are they confined to those Christian sects and churches that are founded on the basis of the Bible as the only infallible rule of faith and practice and the exercise of private judgment in its interpretation? Do they not include Roman Catholics? Do they not embrace Jews? Do they not include Unitarians, Socinians, Deists and Theists of every name, who choose to associate for the purpose of religious worship? There is but one answer to these questions. Every religious body and association, without respect to its name or faith, is included and all are expressly placed upon an equality as respects their civil rights, and equally entitled to the protection of the civil power in the peaceable and undisturbed exercise and enjoyment of their religious rights. With this admission, then, what becomes of the assumption that the word "religion" used in the previous and introductory part of the sentence—the reciting clause—shall be construed to mean only the prevailing religion of the people—the religion of a political majority—the religion of the first settlers—the traditionary religion of the community—the religion of Christianity—the religion of the Bible—the Protestant religion? It is utterly without foundation, and must vanish and disappear the moment you attack it with an interrogation. It will not stay long enough to be questioned.

And with that assumption, the whole ground of the argument that the Constitution ordains the Bible as a perpetual text book for religious exercises in the public schools sinks away into nothingness and the argument itself topples over.

Indeed, if there be any logic in it, at all, it proves entirely too much for the plaintiffs' case. For if religious education or instruction in religion, is a constitutional necessity in the State schools, as counsel contend—and if by the Constitution, religion is defined to be whatever any individual or association professes to hold as such—and all are on an equality under the protection of the State—then every form and description of religious tenets, opinions and doctrines must be taught alike, and as of equal claim to truth and authority, by the religious teachers appointed by the State. And this is simply a *reductio ad absurdum.*

It is sought to escape this absurdity by limiting the constitutional definition to a "broad Christianity"—meaning by that, if meaning can be attached to such a phrase—the opinions and precepts common to all Christian denominations. But this I have already shown to be a constitutional impossibility, for that instrument equally recognizes other religions besides Christianity; besides which it is an impossibility in fact as well as in law, to obtain from any resolution of the conflicts of Christian sects, any residuum of a common factor. The attempt would be hopeless.

The truth is, the plain and common sense construction of the clause is the only admissible one. It is recited that "religion, morality, and knowledge are essential to good government." For that reason the legislative body are enjoined to do two things—first, equally to protect the peaceable exercise by every religious denomination of its own peculiarities—second, to establish by law, a system of public instruction, such as to the General Assembly may seem best. There is no implication whatever, that such a system may not be purely secular—may not include only the elementary branches of an English education. There is nothing whatever to require, or even to justify the conclusion that any express instruction in religion should be given in the schools at all.

It might well be claimed that the provision should be interpreted distributively, so that religion and morality would be considered as being promoted by the protection to be given to religious assemblies and worship; and knowledge, by the establishment of schools. But without insisting on that—how can it be said, as it has been, that schools, in which instruction is confined merely to secular knowledge, are irreligious, godless, and atheistic? Is it the necessary tendency of learning to read, to write, to cipher, to promote impurity? Is the study of geography and grammar immoral? Is the growth of knowledge in history and science essentially productive of infidelity? If it be said, as it has been said, that the establishment of such a system of public instruction, is the establishment of Atheism by law, then, what escape is there from the conclusion that religious instruction as insisted upon in this case, as being required by law, is also therefore the establishment of a State religion, and that, the religion of only a portion of the community.

Let me not be misunderstood. I believe in religion, in its priceless, inestimable importance and value, both "for the life that now is, and for that which is to come"—for this world and eternity.

I believe in the religious education of children; in their careful training, from infancy to youth and manhood, by precept and example, in true and practical piety, in the fear of God, and to love their fellow men; that they should be taught to remember their Creator in the days of their youth. I believe as firmly as a man can, that they should be most watchfully and sedulously instructed, day by day, precept upon precept, line upon line, here a little and there a little, not merely in the learning of abstract morals, but in the duties of a religious life, based upon the motives, sanctions, instructions, examples, and inspirations that can only be found in the Gospel of God our Savior, and the scheme of redemption for a lost and sinful race as revealed in the person and work of the God-Man, Christ Jesus, and held forth in the instructions, and services, and means of grace, and living oracles, committed to the keeping of the church of the living God, as his kingdom on the earth.

But what I do say, and say most earnestly and with vehement protest, is, that with this branch of education the State, the civil power—through its law-making, judicial and executive administration; through its politics and its parties; through its secular agents and officers; through its boards of education and school teachers—has, rightfully, and can have, nothing whatever to do. *Procul, procul este profani!* Let no unholy hands be laid upon the sacred ark.

And now, let us recur to the proposition and claim of the opposing counsel—that Christianity is part of our common law, of our internal public law, of our fundamental public policy, in such a sense that instruction in it, by reading the Bible and otherwise, is a constitutional necessity in our system of public schools.

To this general proposition the gentlemen have cited the opinion of the Supreme Court of the United States, as delivered by Mr. Justice Story in the case of *Vidal* v. *Girard's Executors*, 2 Howard's Rep. 127, the great case upon the trusts for Girard College, and quoted certain parts of that opinion as if conclusive upon this question. It is to be remarked, however, that they were more profuse in their extracts from the unsuccessful argument of Mr. Webster in the case than liberal in reading from the judgment of the court which overruled it.

It will be remembered that the attack upon the will was made upon two grounds—as far as the present question was concerned—that the testator had prohibited religious instruction, and had forbidden Christian ministers from being instructors in his college; and the argument was precisely that relied upon by the counsel for the plaintiffs in the present case.

I will read that portion of Judge Story's opinion which disposes of these objections, pp. 200, 201:

"The objection, then, in this case, goes to this: either that the testator has totally omitted to provide for religious instruction, in his scheme of education (which, from what has already been said, is an inadmissible interpretation), or that it includes but partial and imperfect instruction in those truths. In either view can it be truly said that it contravenes the known law of the State of Pennsylvania upon the subject of charities, or is not allowable under the article of the Bill of Rights already cited? Is an omission to provide for instruction in Christianity, in any scheme of school or college education, a fatal defect, which avoids it, under the law of Pennsylvania? If the instruction provided is incomplete and imperfect, is it equally fatal? These questions are propounded because we are not aware that anything exists in the Constitution or laws of Pennsylvania, or the judicial decisions of its tribunals, which would justify us in pronouncing that such defects would be so fatal. Let us take the case of a charitable donation to teach poor orphans reading, writing, arithmetic, geography, and navigation, and excluding all other studies and instruction, would the donation be void as a charity in Pennsylvania; as being deemed derogatory to Christianity? Hitherto, it has been supposed that a charity for the instruction of the poor might be good and valid in England, even if it did not go beyond the establishment of a grammar school. And, in America, it has been thought, in the absence of any express prohibitions, that the donor might select the studies, as well as the classes of persons who were to receive his bounty, without being compelled to make religious instruction a necessary part of their studies. It has hitherto been thought sufficient if he does not require anything to be taught inconsistent with Christianity."

I leave it to the gentlemen to say why they did not bring to the notice of the Court that part of the decision.

Mr. Sage. That was not an institution to be supported by taxation.

Mr. Matthews. What difference does that make? The gentlemen claimed by that decision that Christianity was so much a part of the law of Pennsylvania, so much a part of a collegiate education, that a scheme of education which did not include it was void. Judge Story expressly decides the contrary. But Judge Story is not alone. The authorities are not contradictory. They are absolutely unanimous on that point in this country.

I find the law upon this subject, in all its aspects, stated with clearness and force by Judge Cooley, one of the justices of the Supreme Court of Michigan, in his recent and very valuable treatise on *Constitutional Limitations*, chap. 13, p. 467. I read a few extracts, commending the entire chapter to the careful perusal of the Court. He says:

"He who shall examine with care the American Constitutions will find nothing more fully or plainly expressed than the desire of their framers to preserve and perpetuate religious liberty, and to guard against the slightest approach towards inequality of civil or political rights, based upon difference of religious belief. * * *

"Those things which are not lawful under any of the American Constitutions may be stated thus:

"1. Any law respecting an establishment of religion. The Legislatures have not been left at liberty to effect a union of Church and State, or to establish preferences by law in favor of any one religious denomination or mode of worship. There is not religious liberty where any one sect is favored by the State and given advantage by law over other sects. Whatever establishes a distinction against one class or sect is, to the extent to which the distinction operates unfavorably, a persecution; and, if based on religious grounds, is religious persecution. It is not toleration which is established in our system, but religious equality.

"2. Compulsory support, by taxation or otherwise, of religious instruction. Not only is no one denomination to be favored at the expense of the rest, but all support of religious instruction must be entirely voluntary.

"3. Compulsory attendance upon religious worship. Whoever is not led by choice or a sense of duty to attend upon the ordinances of religion, is not to be compelled to do so by the State. The State will seek, so far as practicable, to enforce the obligations and duties which the citizen may owe to his fellow citizen, but those which he owes to his Maker are to be enforced by the admonitions of the conscience, and not by the penalties of human laws.'

Again, this writer says:

"It is frequently said that Christianity is a part of the law of the land. In a certain sense, and for certain purposes, this is true. * * * But the law does not attempt to enforce the precepts of Christianity on the ground of their sacred character or divine origin. Some of these precepts are universally recognized as being incapable of enforcement by human laws, notwithstanding they are of continual and universal obligation. Christianity, therefore, is not a part of the law of the land, in the sense that would entitle the courts to take notice of, and base their judgments upon it, except so far as they should find that its precepts had been incorporated in and thus become a component part of the law."

In another place, page 477, he says:

"Whatever deference the Constitution or the laws may require to be paid in some cases to the conscientious scruples or religious convictions of the majority, the general policy always is to carefully avoid any compulsion which infringes on the religious scruples of any, however little reason may seem to other persons to underlie them."

The case of the *State* v. *Chandler*, 2 Harrington's Rep. 553, was an indictment for blasphemy against the Christian religion, and involved the discussion of the question how and in what sense it could be said that Christianity was part of the law of the land. It is very elaborately and learnedly examined and explained in the opinion of the court by Justice Clayton. It declares that "the common law was, as Lord Coke expressed it in *Sir Wm. Herbert's* case, 3 Rep. 426, the preserver of the common peace of the land;" and therefore we find it punished outrages on or breaches of the peace of society, and also acts whose tendency was to disturb that peace. * * * But even in England, Christianity was never considered as a part of the common law, so far as that for a violation of its injunctions, independent of the established laws of man, and without the sanction of any positive act of Parliament made to enforce these injunctions, any man could be drawn to answer in a common law court. It was a part of the common law "so far that any person reviling, subverting or ridiculing it might be prosecuted at common law," as Lord Mansfield has declared; because, in the judgment of our English ancestors and their judicial tribunals he who reviled, subverted or ridiculed Christianity, did an act which struck at the foundation of their civil society and tended by its necessary consequences as they believed to disturb the common peace of the land of which (as Lord Coke had reported) the common law was the preserver. * * * It adapted itself to the religion of the country just so far as was necessary for the peace and safety of civil institutions; but it took cognizance of offenses against God only where, by their inevitable effects, they became offenses against man and his temporal security." * * * * * * It is true, that the maxim of the English law "that Christianity is a part of the common law" may be liable to misconstruction and has been misunderstood. It is a current phrase among the special pleaders "that the almanac is a part of the law of the land." By this it is meant that the courts will judicially notice the days of the week, month, and other things, properly belonging to an almanac, without pleading or proving them. In the same sense it is sometimes said that the *lex parliamentaria* is a part of the law of the land. So too, we apprehend, every court in a civilized country is bound to notice in the same way what is the prevailing religion of the people. *If in Delaware the people should adopt the Jewish or Mahometan religion, as they have an unquestionable right to do, if they prefer it, this Court is bound to notice it as their religion and to respect it accordingly.*" * * * *

"It (the common law) became the preserver of the peace and good order of society throughout the land, and noticed what was the religion of the people, to the end that it might preserve that peace and good order. It sustained indictments for wantonly and maliciously blaspheming God or the founder of the Christian religion, because such blasphemy tended to subvert the peace and good order which it was bound to protect. But it sustained no indictment for a mere sin against God as a common law offense where these objects of its care were not affected. It did not look to the condition of man in another world to punish and thus prepare him for it in this. That was the loathsome duty of some ecclesiastical commissioner, some fiery bigot or Star Chamber judge. While these punished blasphemy as a spiritual offense *pro salute animæ*, the common law only punished it when it tended to create a riot or break the peace in some other mode, or subvert the very foundation on which civil society rested." * * * * "We hold and have already said that the people of Delaware have a full and perfect constitutional right to change their religion as often as they see fit. They may, to-morrow, if they think it right, profess Mahometanism or Judaism, or adopt any other religious creed they please; and so far from any court having power to punish them for such an exercise of right, all their judges are bound to notice their free choice and religious preference and to protect them in the exercise of their right. Put the case then, that they repudiate the religion of their fathers and adopt Judaism; and that their legislature, in obedience to their wishes, ordains that to deride or ridicule the Jewish creed shall be blasphemy, and punishable as blasphemy is now punished. On an indictment against any man for maliciously reviling Moses in public, in the language of this defendant and publishing the Jewish religion as a villainous imposition, are we, or are we not, bound to sentence him according to the statute? Suppose the people then abjure Judaism, adopt the Koran, and profess the religion of Mahomet. If their legislature enact that to revile or ridicule the prophet shall be blasphemy, may we, or may we not, against him who shall go into their public places and with a loud voice maliciously revile and ridicule Mahomet, denounce the penalties of their statute?" * * * * "It will be seen then that in our judgment by the Constitution and laws of Delaware the Christian religion is a part of those laws; so far that blasphemy against it is punishable, *while the people prefer it as their religion and no longer.* The moment they change it and adopt any other, as they may do, the new religion becomes in the same sense, a part of the law, for their courts are bound to yield it faith and credit and respect it as their religion."

From these extracts it appears that the right to create and punish the offense of blasphemy, does not rest upon the ground of a lawful power in government, to punish what are only sins against God; nor upon the ground that Christianity is of divine origin and authority; nor that it is a part of the law of the land in any other sense, than, that being professed by the mass of the population, the law takes notice of that as a fact, in determining that an act which grossly outrages the public sense of decency, and is directly calculated to provoke a breach of the public peace and order, may be treated as an offense against civil society.

What is important and particularly to be pondered is, that in the same sense in which it is claimed that that form of Christianity which sets forth the right of private judgment exercised in the reading of the Bible without note or comment, as its creed—to-wit: Protestant Christianity—is now the law of the land, so that it has a right to control the character of religious instruction furnished to the schools of the State, in that same sense, to-morrow or next day, Judaism or Infidelity, or if that is considered too remote, then Roman Catholicism, if professed by a political majority in the community, may assert its corresponding right, and using the very arguments invented against it, not only exclude the Protestant Bible, but insist upon the adoption of Romish forms of worship, the celebration of the Mass and sacred hymns to the Virgin Mary, the election of Romish priests as teachers, and the use of text-books, inculcating the views of the Romish Church upon religion. On what ground could the Protestant then object? The religion of the majority is the law of the land. Will he say that his rights of conscience are invaded? It will be replied: Your children may retire from the regular exercises of the school and read the Protestant version in private. Does he still answer and protest: You have no right to tax us for the support of instruction in what we believe to be dangerous religious error, under political institutions which forbid all preferences by law in matters of religion. The reply is ready: So did ye unto us, when you had political power. By the same measure ye meted to us, we measure to you again. And what can the gainsayer say to that?

May it please the Court I was considering the proposition that the State, the civil power, as such, in its treatment of religion, in respect to what are called offenses against religion, did not interfere upon religious grounds, and claiming it on the decision of Judge Clayton in the case in Harrington's Reports, which showed that the statutes against blasphemy were upheld only on the ground that an infraction of them tended to produce civil disorder, tended to provoke breaches of the public peace, because it insulted the opinions and feelings of the mass of the people; and that the same principle would protect Mohammedanism, or Buddhism, or Judaism, as well as Christianity; and that the same principle lies at the foundation of what are called the Sabbath laws, the laws that are usually looked to for the purpose of protecting the Christian Sabbath from desecration. How is it? As I said the civil power does not shut its eyes to facts, it sees them. It recognizes the fact that a large body of the community acknowledge the religious duty of keeping as a sacred rest a certain day. Now, then, the State, as a mere civil regulation on its side, looking also at the physical and intellectual and moral facts of human nature, comes to the conclusion, that as a mere civil institution, it is well to have one day in seven set apart as a day of secular, not of sacred rest; and, therefore, it passes laws forbidding labor one day in the week, and for the purpose of conformity merely it selects the day which the majority of the community recognizes as a day of religious rest. But it might as well have selected any other, and the statute is supportable only on the idea of its being a civil regulation, founded on civil modes of human conduct.

Such is the express and positive judgment of the Supreme Court of this State in the case of *Bloom* v. *Richards*, 2 Ohio State Rep. 387, in which it was held that, "under the provisions of our Constitution, neither Christianity nor any other system of religion is a part of the law of this State. We have no union of Church and State, nor has our government ever been vested with authority to enforce any religious observance simply because it is religious. Of course it is no objection, but on the contrary it is a high recommendation to a legislative enactment, based upon justice or public policy, that it is found to coincide with the precepts of a pure religion; nevertheless, the power to make the law rests in the legislative control over things temporal, and not over things spiritual. The statute prohibiting common labor on the Sabbath could not stand for a moment as the law of this State if its sole foundation was the Christian duty of keeping that day holy, and its sole motive to enforce the observance of that duty. It is to be regarded as a mere municipal or police regulation, whose validity is neither strengthened nor weakened by the fact that the day of rest it enjoins is the Sabbath day."

This view of the relation of law to morality is maintained by a recent law writer, Mr. James Fitzjames Stephens, in his work on the *Criminal Law of England*, p. 90, in the following language:

"Does then the law affirm any, and if so, what system of morals to be true? The law makes no such affirmation. *It has nothing whatever to do with truth.* It is an exclusively practical system, invented and maintained for the purpose of an actually existing state of society. But though the law is entirely independent of all moral speculation, *and though the judges who administer it are and ought to be deaf to all arguments drawn from such a source*, it constantly refers to, and for particular purposes, notices, the moral sentiments which, *as a matter of fact*, are generally entertained in the nation in which it is established. Thus the rule as to privileged communications in cases of libel recognizes 'moral and social duties of imperfect obligation' as having the *legal effect* of justifying communications which might otherwise be actionable and perhaps indictable." (*Harrison* v. *Bush*, 5 Ell. & Bl. 344.) And adds, "that this is the only ground on which the punishment of blasphemy, or the administration of the law relating to libel and conspiracy can be understood."

So I have no doubt that the power of the State extends, as it is expressly declared in our Bill of Rights, to the protection of every religious community or association, in the peaceable enjoyment of their public worship; so it punishes as an aggressor a breaker of laws, a violator of the public peace, any person who disturbs religious assemblies. And I have no doubt that the civil power extends so far that where certain religious observances come in conflict with the peace and good order of society, that the State can suppress them.

As, for instance, if any body of Christians should see fit to make a practice of having public religious processions through the streets, on the day when other bodies are worshiping in public places of assembly, so as to disturb them, the civil law can forbid them without any infraction of conscientious rights, and against any objections; it being the business of the civil power to protect society in its peace and order.

But I deny the proposition that the civil power has any authority in spiritual matters, or any right to found any civil enactments upon the ground that they are breaches of the Divine law.

I would like to read a paragraph upon that point from an exceedingly able and philosophic discussion of the ground of law and civil obligations, by Charles Spencer M. Phillips, in his work on *Jurisprudence*, p. 274:

"To what extent the State is morally justified in exercising its penal jurisdiction, is a question of policy, rather than of jurisprudence. The offender himself can not complain so long as he undergoes no suffering which exceeds that inflicted by him. But it must never be forgotten that evil for evil is the limit, though not necessarily the measure, of criminal punishment. The argument that experience has shown the insufficiency of equitable retaliation to suppress a particular offense, is one which, though long used with terrible force by the men of blood who wore the English ermine in the past generation, will never be admitted by a conscientious moralist.

"Lord Campbell's anecdote of the judge who prayed that a convicted forger might receive that mercy in Heaven which the safety of the paper currency made it necessary to deny him upon earth, appears in these days no less ludicrous than shocking. But it may be feared that, in days still far from remote, the English legislature seriously reasoned in the same unscrupulous spirit. Some moralists have maintained the opinion more specious, but for that very reason, more dangerous than the plea of expediency, that the State is entitled to punish crimes, not through the medium of the natural right of retaliation belonging to every injured party, but as the earthly representative of Divine authority, and as the earthly minister of Divine justice. Those who believe that one human being is morally justified in avenging whatever he chooses to think sin in another, are clearly consistent in ascribing the same authority to the State, and to question whether anarchy or slavery is preferable is altogether one of taste. But it would be difficult to maintain that a certain number of human beings acquire, by acting in concert, a power of detecting and a right of punishing moral evil, which no individual among them singly possesses; or that they are able, by selecting a fellow-creature and styling him a king or a judge, to confer upon him a jurisdiction which God has not conferred upon them.

"It is painful to recall the arguments by which some men of unquestionable piety and ability have endeavored to support this extravagant doctrine.

"They lay down the principle that the world is God's world, and that all who inhabit it are bound by God's law, and from this they infer that human justice ought, so far as human fallibility will allow, to be a precise counterpart of God's justice. They do not advert to the obvious possibility that there may be some of God's laws which it is not His will to communicate to human administration, and which human beings would, therefore, be guilty of a sin by attempting to enforce. But the truth is that a school of moralists has lately arisen who are in the habit of justifying their own feelings by gratuitously attributing them to the Deity, and in whose writings the use of the divine name only means that the writer entertains a strong consciousness of sympathy or antipathy for which he can give no intelligent reason."

"It ought moreover to be carefully borne in mind, that by admitting the principle of inflicting punishment as a retribution for moral evil, we introduce not only a new scale of penalties, but a new list of offenses. If we punish violence or fraud not as a crime against man, but as a sin against God, how can we refuse to punish those sins against God which are not crimes against man. And if we punish whatever we think a sin, how can we blame the most besotted fanatic for punishing whatever he thinks a sin? How can we complain of the Puritan for imprisoning the unwary Sabbath breaker, or of the abbess for immuring the fugitive nun? How can we even condemn the Languedocian crusades or the Spanish Inquisition? Justification by the necessity of self-defense is a plain question of fact, but there is no atrocity of persecution which may not be defended if we once permit human passion and folly to usurp the prerogatives of perfect wisdom and perfect love."

To the same point I wish to read some extracts from Macauley's celebrated review of Gladstone's work on *Church and State*, which appeared in the *Edinburgh Review* for 1839:

"We are desirous, before we enter on the discussion of this important question, to point out clearly a distinction which, though very obvious, seems to be overlooked by many excellent people. In their opinion, to say that the ends of government are temporal and not spiritual, is tantamount to saying that the temporal welfare of man is of more importance than his spiritual welfare. But this is an entire mistake. The question is not whether spiritual interests be or be not superior in importance to temporal interests; but whether the machinery which happens at any time to be employed for the purpose of protecting certain temporal interests of a society, be necessarily such a machinery as is fitted to promote the spiritual interests of society. It is certain that without a division of duties the world could not go on. It is of very much more importance that men should have food than that they should have piano fortes. Yet it by no means follows that every piano forte maker ought to add the business of a baker to his own; for if he did so, we should have both much worse music and much worse bread. It is of much more importance that the knowledge of religious truth should be widely diffused, than that the art of sculpture should flourish among us. Yet it by no means follows that the Royal Academy ought to unite with its present functions those of the Society for promoting Christian knowledge, to distribute theological tracts, to send forth missionaries, to turn out Nollikins for being a Catholic, Bacon for being a Methodist, and Flaxman for being a Swedenborgian. For the effect of such folly would be that we should have the worst possible Academy of Arts and the worst possible Society for the promotion of Christian knowledge. The community, it is plain, would be thrown into universal confusion if it were supposed to be the duty of every association which is formed for one good object, to promote every other good object.

"As to some of the ends of civil government, all people are agreed. That it is designed to protect our persons and our property—that it is designed to compel us to satisfy our wants, not by rapine, but by industry—that it is designed to compel us to decide our differences, not by the strong hand, but by arbitration—that it is designed to direct our whole force, as that of one man, against any other society which may offer us injury—these are propositions which will hardly be disputed."

* * * * * * * * *

"We think that government, like any other contrivance of human wisdom, from the highest to the lowest, is likely to answer its main end best when it is constructed with a single view to that end. Mr. Gladstone, who loves Plato, will not quarrel with us for illustrating our proposition, after Plato's fashion, from the most familiar objects. Take cutlery, for example. A blade which is designed both to shave and carve will certainly not shave so well as a razor, or carve so well as a carving-knife. An academy of painting, which should also be a bank, would, in all probability, exhibit very bad pictures and discount very bad bills. A gas company, which should also be an infant school society, would, we apprehend, light the streets ill, and teach the children ill. On this principle, we think that government should be organized solely with a view to its main end, and that no part of its efficiency for that end should be sacrificed in order to promote any other end, however excellent."

* * * * * * * * *

"We may illustrate our view of the policy which governments ought to pursue with respect to religious instruction, by recurring to the analogy of a hospital. Religious instruction is not the main end for which a hospital is built; and to introduce into a hospital any regulations prejudicial to the health of the patients, on the plea of promoting their spiritual improvement—to send a ranting preacher to a man who has just been ordered by the physician to lie quiet and try to get a little sleep—to impose a strict observance of Lent on a convalescent who has been advised to eat heartily of nourishing food—to direct, as the bigoted Pius the Fifth actually did, that no medical assistance should be given to any person who declined spiritual attendance—would be the most extravagant folly. Yet it by no means follows that it would not be right to have a chaplain to attend the sick, and to pay such a chaplain out of the hospital funds. Whether it will be proper to have such a chaplain at all, and of what religious persuasion such a chaplain ought to be, must depend on circumstances. There may be a town in which it would be impossible to set up a good hospital without the help of people of different opinions. And religious parties may run so high that, though people of different opinions are willing to contribute to the relief of the sick, they will not concur in the choice of any one chaplain. The High Churchmen insist that, if there is a paid chaplain, he shall be a High Churchman. The Evangelicals stickle for an Evangelical. Here it would evidently be absurd and cruel to let a useful and humane design, about which all are agreed, fall to the ground, because all can not agree about something else. The governors must either appoint two chaplains, and pay them both, or they must appoint none; and every one of them must, in his individual capacity, do what he can for the purpose of providing the sick with such religious instruction and consolation as will, in his opinion, be most useful to them."

* * * * * * * * *

"Again, on our principle, no government ought to press on the people religious instruction, however sound, in such a manner as to excite among them discontents dangerous to public order. For here again no government should sacrifice its primary end, to an end intrinsically indeed of the highest importance, but still only a secondary end of government, as government."

This celebrated essay states the case of the English Church in Ireland, and the duty of a British statesman towards it, in this language.

"But, if there were, in any part of the world, a national Church regarded as heretical by four-fifths of the nation committed to his care—a Church established and maintained by the sword—a Church producing twice as many riots as conversions—a Church which, though possessing great wealth and power, and though long backed by persecuting laws, had, in the course of many generations, been found unable to propagate its doctrines, and barely able to maintain its ground—a Church so odious, that fraud and violence, when used against its clear rights of property, were generally regarded as fair play—a Church whose ministers were preaching to desolate walls, and with difficulty obtaining their lawful subsistence by the help of bayonets—such a Church, on our principles, could not, we must own, be defended. We should say that the State which allied itself with such a Church, postponed the primary end of government to the secondary; and that the consequences had been such as any sagacious observer would have predicted. Neither the primary nor the secondary end is attained. The temporal and spiritual interests of the people suffer alike. The minds of men, instead of being drawn to the Church, are alienated from the State. The magistrate, after sacrificing order, peace, union, all the interests which it is his first duty to protect, for the purpose of promoting pure religion, is forced after the experience of centuries, to admit that he has really been promoting error. The sounder the doctrines of such a Church—the more absurd and noxious the superstition by which those doctrines are opposed—the stronger are the arguments against the policy which has deprived a good cause of its natural advantages. Those who preach to rulers the duty of employing power to propagate truth would do well to remember that falsehood, though no match for truth alone, has often been found more than a match for truth and power together." * *

The man whom Macauley thus reviewed in 1839 was the man who thirty years later was borne into the chief seat of power as Prime Minister of England upon a popular decree in favor of the disestablishment of the State Church in Ireland, and who vindicated his reputation as a wise statesman by carrying that measure through Parliament—that, too, in the face of a most determined opposition from the most conservative and aristocratic influences in the House of Lords, at the sacrifice of his own reputation for consistency, rising superior to the prejudices of his previous opinions, and against the remonstrances and protests of a large body of good men throughout the three Kingdoms, who contended that the measure was a blow struck at religion itself, whose interests and rights the Prime Minister was loudly accused of betraying. But time and reflection had set Gladstone right, though it took thirty years to do it, and justified Macaulay, his celebrated critic and reviewer, who did not live to see the full fruit of his own liberal teaching: and time and reflection will set right those who complain of him: history and posterity will vindicate and magnify the fame of the great statesman, who could lead in the accomplishment of a great act of justice, notwithstanding the prejudices of his earlier convictions, and who when intrusted with the responsibility of power, was honest enough and bold enough to use it, against the bigotry of his co-religionists, but in the interest of religion itself, though in hostility to the domination of his own church.

I wish partly as a personal gratification to myself, and partly for the sound and wholesome truth conveyed in sound and wholesome words which it contains, to read to your Honors a part of the confession of the church to which I belong, on the duties and functions of the civil magistrate. The *Westminster Confession of Faith*, chapter xxiii, section 3, says:

> "Civil magistrates may not assume to themselves the administration of the word and sacraments, or the power of the keys of the kingdom of heaven, or in the least interfere in the matters of faith. Yet, as nursing fathers, it is the duty of civil magistrates to protect the church of our common Lord without giving the preference to any denomination of Christians above the rest, in such manner that all ecclesiastical persons whatever shall enjoy the full, free and unquestioned liberty of discharging every part of their sacred functions, without violence or danger. And as Jesus Christ hath appointed a regular government and discipline in His church, no law of any Commonwealth should interfere, let or hinder the due exercise thereof among the voluntary members of any denomination of Christians, according to their own profession and belief. It is the duty of civil magistrates to protect the person and good name of all their people, in such an effectual manner as that no person be suffered, either upon pretense of religion or infidelity, to offer any indignity, violence, abuse or injury to any other person whatsoever; and to take order that all religious and ecclesiastical assemblies be held without molestation or disturbance."

Thus, may it please your Honors, am I taught by my own church—a church which elsewhere in the same confession teaches that "God alone is Lord of the conscience"—and which here plainly defines and declares its own rights and the rights of the whole Christian Church, and the limits of the civil power in respect of them; and in so doing, denies to the civil magistrate any assumed right *in the administration of the word*, which means neither more nor less, than, any part or lot in instructing in religion—

denies his right, *in the least, to interfere in matters of faith*, which he attempts to exert when, by law, he decrees that a particular version or translation of the Bible shall be publicly read, as part of a system of religious worship and instruction, by and to particular persons, at stated times and places, thereby implicitly sitting in judgment upon the questions relating to its inspiration, its canonical character, the accuracy of its translation, its character and claims as the Word of God, and opening the way, if such a power is admitted, for a further claim, to expound, interpret and teach by authority its true meaning; denies his right to give the preference to any denomination of Christians above the rest, a right which is clearly exercised where the State authorities, school boards or courts of law imperatively ordain a form of religious devotion to be practiced, or a mode of religious instruction to be adopted, in the public and common schools, which the consciences of any Christian denomination prevent them from attending, supporting or countenancing; declares the right of every denomination of Christians, to exercise its discipline and government ecclesiastically, among its voluntary members, according to their own profession and belief, without let, hinderance or interference with, by the law of any commonwealth, and thus justifies, *as a civil right*, the practice and discipline of the Roman Catholic Church in withholding from its members the use of the Bible, its denial of their ecclesiastical right to judge for themselves of its meaning, and its forbidding any instruction in religion except such as it approves and appoints; a doctrine, in this particular, I will add, most seriously and grossly violated in a late case in Chicago, where a civil tribunal laid its injunction on the proceedings of an ecclesiastical court, when engaged in the administration of its discipline upon a minister of its own church, for an alleged ecclesiastical offense, and which I can not but believe was a dangerous invasion of the rights of religion by the civil power.

But this noble article of the Westminster Confession of Faith goes one step farther, in its vindication of the rights of conscience against the power of the civil magistrate. It recognises and throws the mantle of its protection, not merely over rights which it claims for those whom it regards as peculiarly its own—the confessors of its own faith—but concedes the same *to all others*, even to those who deny, not only its own confession, but the very faith itself—even infidels ; for it maintains it to be the duty of civil government equally to protect and defend all the people, both in person and good name, and so effectually, that no person be suffered to offer any indignity, violence, abuse or injury to any other person whatsoever, *either upon pretense of religion or infidelity!*

In other words it is not orthodox Presbyterianism in this country, to deny to an infidel the same civil rights that belong to a saint.

I have already referred your Honors, as have also my colleagues, to the judgment and opinion of the Supreme Court of this State in the case of *Bloom* v. *Richards*, 2 Ohio State Rep. 387, which is approved and followed in the subsequent case of *McGatrick* v. *Wason*, 4 Ohio State Rep. 566.

The gentlemen on the other side vainly seek to escape the effect of these decisions by dismissing the opinions as *obiter dicta.* There is no way of escape for them. The point to which they are cited was directly and necessarily involved in the judgment and was expressly ruled. And the authority of these cases is not merely persuasive ; it is binding and conclusive.

And the proposition they establish is very significant upon the argument I am now considering. It is that no power whatever is possessed by the legislature over things spiritual, but only over things temporal ; no power, whatever, to enforce the performance of religious duties, simply because they are religious—but only, within the limits of the Constitution, to maintain justice and promote the public welfare. Does it not strictly follow from that also that it has no power to provide by law, at public expense, for any instruction in religion ? Is not religious learning or education, more of a spiritual and less of a secular concern, than the performance of religious duties—the practice of religious precepts—the leading of a religious life ? If it be said that religious education tends to good citizenship, and therefore on that ground may be encouraged and provided for by law, is it not a sufficient answer to say that while religious education only tends in that direction, practical religion—the performance of religious duties as such, and merely as such—not only tends toward, but is the very substance of good citizenship; and yet the State is absolutely prohibited from attempting the enforcement of a religious duty as such.

But if the State is to furnish education in religion, in what I ask, shall it consist? Who shall judge and determine what is true and what false in all that claims to be religion, or even Christianity—who shall pronounce with authority of law, what is to be taught as embraced within what have been styled the fundamental or elementary truths of religion—who shall declare the amount, and kind, and degree of the knowledge to be imparted?

These are important questions, seriously propounded and deserving of respectful answer. The gentlemen on the other side, say they limit the religious instruction demanded to what they call a "broad Christianity." I have already once or twice adverted to the term. I do not know that I understand it. If I do, it is a "broad" humbug. The Christian religion is not a vain and unmeaning generality. It is a definite and positive thing. It means something or it means nothing. In my view it is a supernatural scheme of redemption—a revelation from God of His gracious purpose and plan of salvation, to a race, "dead in trespasses and sins," through the mediation and atonement of Jesus Christ, who, being God from eternity, became incarnate and by his death upon the cross became a sacrifice for sin, made expiation for it, and having risen from the grave ascended into Heaven, and there sitteth on the right hand of the Father, to make intercession for his people. The whole character and value of it as a religion consists altogether in being, as it claims to be, a supernatural plan of salvation from sin, otherwise irremediable. Strike out from the Bible the parts which disclose, reveal and teach that scheme, and the rest is insignificant. And any instruction or education in religion which does not specifically teach the facts which constitute that scheme, and which can not be stated even, except as conveying dogma, is no instruction in the Christian religion whatever—it is simply instruction in philosophy and ethics, or practical morals.

Now, I deny the authority and the ability of civil government to decide upon questions of religious truth.

The point is very cogently and conclusively argued in the case of *Andrew* v. *The N. Y. Bible and Prayer Book Society*, 4 Sandford's Superior Court Rep. pp. 180–184. The question at issue there was, whether a legacy given for the purpose of promoting the circulation of the Prayer Book of the Episcopal Church in New York could be sustained upon the ground of its being a *pious* use.

The following extract from the opinion of the Court is long, but it is exceedingly to the point, and I can not excuse myself for not reading it at length. It is as follows:

"In the present case, we go still further, and shall refer our denial of the power of our Chancellor to sustain and execute a trust similar to that which the legacy creates, to a much earlier period than the repeal of the statute of Elizabeth. The use attached to this legacy is not a charitable use, in the usual and legal sense of the term. It is strictly a *pious use*, not otherwise charitable than as the noblest office of charity is the dissemination of religious truth, but it is impossible for a court of justice to sustain a use upon this ground, unless in a country where the truths of religion have been settled and defined by law, or judges have a discretionary power to determine and declare them. If, at any period in the juridical history of this State, it has been within the power of our Court of Chancery to decree the execution of a pious use violating the general rules of law, this branch of its jurisdiction was, in our judgment, wholly abolished long before the statute of Elizabeth was repealed. It was wholly abolished when the Constitution of 1777 was adopted. Under a Constitution which extends the same protection to every religion, and to every form and sect of religion, which establishes none and gives no preference to any, there is no possible standard by which the validity of a use as pious can be determined; there are no possible means by which judges can be enabled to discriminate between such uses as tend to promote the best interest of society by spreading the knowledge and inculcating the practice of true religion, and those which can have no other effect than to foster the growth of pernicious errors, to give a dangerous permanence to the reveries of a wild fanaticism, or encourage and perpetuate the observances of a corrupt and degrading superstition. Hence, unless all uses that may be denominated pious shall be subjected to the same rule as other trusts, we shall find no escape from this alternative; either all uses for a religious purpose, whether the religion which they are intended to aid be true or false, rational or absurd, must be upheld and enforced; or the uses connected with a particular form of religion must be selected as the special and exclusive objects of favor and encouragement. If we adopt the first course, we renounce the principle upon which pious uses were first introduced, and upon which alone their defense can be rested, namely—their tendency to

benefit society by diffusing the knowledge and practice of true religion. We disregard and practically deny the eternal distinctions between truth and falsehood, and give the sanction of law to the pernicious absurdity that all religions, however contradictory in their tenets and in their precepts, have a just and equal claim, not merely to the protection, but to the favor of government, and are not simply to be tolerated, but encouraged. If we adopt the second alternative, we violate that equality between different religions and different forms and sects of religion, which the principles of our government and the provisions of our Constitution are designed to secure; we create an odious distinction in the power to dispose of their own property between different classes of our citizens; and by declaring that the religion which we favor is alone true, we establish it, in a restricted, it is true, but in a definite, sense, as the religion of the State.

"We are quite aware of the answer that has been given to this objection. Christianity, it has been asserted, is now, in a modified sense, the religion of the State. It is so, as a part of that common law which our ancestors introduced and we have retained. Christianity, therefore, furnishes the test that is desired, so that in judging of the validity of a use as pious, we have only to inquire whether it is in harmony with the doctrines that Christianity teaches. The maxim that Christianity is part and parcel of the common law has been frequently repeated by judges and text writers, but few have chosen to examine its truth or attempt to explain its meaning. We have, however, the high authority of Lord Mansfield, and of his successor, the present Chief Justice of the Queen's Bench, Lord Campbell (Campbell's *Lives of Chief Justices*, vol. 2, p. 513), for stating, as its true and only sense, that the law will not permit the essential truths of revealed religion to be ridiculed and reviled. In other words, that blasphemy is an indictable offense at common law. The truth of the maxim in this very partial and limited sense may be admitted. But if we attempt to extend its application we shall find ourselves obliged to confess that it is unmeaning or untrue. If Christianity is a municipal law, in the proper sense of the term, as it must be if a part of the common law, every person is liable to be punished by the civil power who refuses to embrace its doctrines and follow its precepts; and if it must be conceded that in this sense the maxim is untrue, it ceases to be intelligible, since a law without a sanction is an absurdity in logic and a nullity in fact.

"Let it be admitted, however, that Christianity is a part of the common law, in any sense of the maxim which those who assert its truth may choose to attribute to it. The only effect of the admission is to create new difficulties quite as impossible to overcome as

those that have already been stated. How, we would then ask, in judging of the validity of a use as pious, are we to apply the test which Christianity is said to furnish? It will not be pretended that the common law has supplied us with any definition of Christianity. Yet, without a judicial knowledge of what Christianity is, how is it possible to determine whether a particular use, alleged to be pious, is or is not consistent with the truths which Christianity reveals? No religious use has been or can be created that does not imply the existence and truth of some particular religious doctrine, and hence, when we affirm the validity of a use as pious, we necessarily affirm the truth of the doctrine upon which it is founded. In a country where a definite form of Christianity is the religion established by law, the difficulty to which we refer is not felt, since the doctrines of the established church then supply the criterion which is sought; but with us it can readily be shown that the difficulty is not merely real and serious, but insurmountable.

"Let us suppose that a Roman Catholic had devised his whole estate, real and personal, to trustees and their heirs in trust, to apply the income forever, one half to the purchase of indulgences for the benefit of such as might seek them, and the other moiety to the payment of daily masses for the safety of his soul, and that the validity of this devise were the question now to be determined. In England, such uses are held to be void as superstitious, but the statute by which they are declared so we havere pealed, and some other rule or principle must be found to govern our decision. The uses, it is manifest, imply the existence and truth of certain important doctrines. They imply that our Savior has delegated to the Pope, as his vicar upon earth, the absolute and unconditional power of pardoning sin. They imply the existence of a purgatory, and the duty and efficacy of prayers for the dead. Such is the necessary import of the uses, upon the validity of which, guided by the light of Christianity, we are required to pronounce. Shall we, by sustaining them as pious, declare that the doctrines which they imply belong to the class of truths which the New Testament reveals; or shall we, by rejecting them as superstitious, condemn as false and corrupt the ancient faith which so large a class of our citizens avow and follow? Are these questions over which we, as judges, whatever we may privately think, have any jurisdiction? Are they questions which any court of justice in this State, at any time since the formation of our present government, could rightfully entertain and decide? Such are the questions that must be considered and decided, if uses inconsistent with the general rule of law are to be sustained as pious, and the proper test of their legality as such, is their correspondence with the true doctrines of Christianity.

"For ourselves, if the case that we have supposed were now before us we should not hesitate in pronouncing our judgment, abstaining from any remarks upon the nature and tendency of the uses, neither admitting them to be pious nor condemning them as superstitious. We should hold the devise to be entirely void, as repugnant to those wise and salutary rules of law which forbid the citizen to withdraw his property, beyond a limited period, from that free circulation which the interests of commerce and the healthful action and permanence of our republican institutions alike demand; and if this would be a proper decision in the case supposed, it is manifest that the same judgment ought to be pronounced in every case where a trust which involves a perpetuity is sought to be maintained upon the sole ground of its piety. We may be disposed to regret that a perpetual trust for the distribution of that sublime manual of true devotion, perhaps the noblest of human compositions, the Book of Common Prayer, can not be sustained; but the regret must cease, when we reflect that it can only be sustained upon a principle that would render just as valid a similar trust for the circulation of the monstrous fables of the Talmud, or the gross impostures of the Koran."

There is no escape, that I see, out of the difficulty. If the State is bound to provide religious education it has the right and the power to determine in what religious education consists, and to say what shall be taught as religious truth and what shall be rejected as religious error. A writer in behalf of the theory of religious education by the State, writing in England, and quoted in the appendix to the work of the late Dr. Bannermann, of Edinburgh, on the *Church of Christ* (vol. 2, p. 359), meets the difficulty in this way. He says:

"It is usual with those who take the extreme views adopted by Dr. Wardlaw to lay stress on the question: Who is to determine what is to be taught for religious truth to the community? There is, no doubt, a difficulty here; but it is one which surely has been immensely exaggerated, both theoretically and practically. In this country, the omniscience of Parliament is as much a principle of government as its omnipotence—in the modified sense, of course, in which alone such language can be used of any human institution. We proceed continually on the assumption that there is nothing on which Parliament may not arrive at full and accurate knowledge. On all questions of science, of art, of business, of diplomacy, of warfare; on questions of medicine and metallurgy, of engineering and education, of manufacture and painting—on every subject, in short, that concerns the welfare of the community, Parliament is continually called to pronounce decisions involving the assumption of all but infallible capacity for determining the truth. It will not be easy to show why a body, in whose powers of ascertaining truth in all other departments of knowledge the community implictly confides, should be pronounced helplessly incompetent in the department of theological truth. It is no doubt possible that Parliament may err in the opinions it may authorize to be taught to the people; but the probability of this is not so great as to render it incompetent for Parliament to make the attempt, and if liberty be left to all who choose to dissent from the opinions taught by the Government teachers, every freedom seems to be secured to the community which, on grounds of general policy, can be required."

Here we have the "conscience clause" again, as the grand cure-all of all schemes of religious establishment, as if the conscience of a Roman Catholic, or a Jew, or an Infidel, was not as much violated by being compelled to assist in supporting by taxation what they deem to be religious error, as by being compelled to listen to it! And yet it is gravely argued and believed that because the Protestant Christians are a majority of this community, they not only have the right, but their conscience requires it of them as a duty, to take the common fund, contributed alike by all of every creed, Protestant, Catholic, Jew and Infidel, and use it for instructing their own children exclusively in their own religion, saving the consciences of their neighbors by telling them if they can not consent to that kind of religious education for their children they can either go without or provide it elsewhere at their own expense!

But what extraordinary reasoning is that in the extract that I have just read! That Parliament, that the Ohio Legislature, civil government, because it is and must be considered, from the necessity of the case, competent to deal with secular matters—subjects of natural knowledge—for dealing with which it was expressly organized, and for which it exists as the only agency provided, or that can be provided, therefore it must also be considered as competent to deal with spiritual matters—subjects of supernatural knowledge—divine things—for dealing with which it was not organized and has no faculty, and for which there exists another agency expressly designed to meet this want, and claiming as its exclusive prerogative, conferred by a divine commission, to do so. The infallibility in religion of the civil State, of its political parties in their conventions and platforms—how much better is that than the infallibility of the Pope, or of general councils?

In other words, having fallen back from the doctrine of the infallibility of the Pope, this Scotch Presbyterian writer has fallen upon the infallibility of Parliament, and authorized the civil power, the Legislature of the State, to decide with all the infallible power of the Ecumenical Council upon the doctrines of religion. Why, that is not modern doctrine. That is simply the ancient doctrine of old Hobbes, who illustrates the whole argument of his book in his frontispiece, by painting the picture of that monster called the Leviathan, holding in one hand the sword; in the other, the crozier. "*Non est potestas, super terram, quæ comparetur ei.*" Job, 41; 24. And describing that commonwealth which is invested with this power, both civil and spiritual, he says:

"This done, the multitude so united in one person is called a commonwealth; in Latin, *civitas*. This is the generation of that great Leviathan, or rather, to speak more reverently, of that mortal god, to which we owe, under the Immortal God, our peace and defense. For, by this authority, given him by every particular man in the Commonwealth, he hath the use of so much power and strength conferred on him that by terror thereof he is enabled to perform the wills of them all, to peace at home and mutual aid against their enemies abroad. And in him consisteth the essence of the Commonwealth, which, to define it, is one person, of whose acts a great multitude, by mutual covenants one with another, have made themselves every one the author, to the end that he may use the strength and means of them all, as he shall think expedient, for their peace and common defense."

I will also read his views on a Christian commonwealth:

"From this consideration of the right politic, and ecclesiastic in Christian sovereigns, it is evident they have all manner of power over their subjects that can be given to man for the government of men's external actions, both in policy and religion; and may make such laws as themselves judge fittest for the government of their own subjects, both as they are the Commonwealth, and as they are the Church; for both State and Church are the same men."

It is substantially the same doctrine which is often inculcated and elaborated in sonorous phrase by the judicious Hooker, maintained by Warburton, by Paley, in modern days by Arnold, reproduced in 1839 by the eloquent and accomplished scholarship of William E. Gladstone, the same doctrine, the same principle, and that is, that the State, in matters of religion, is gifted with power from on high to discern the truth.

Now, if your Honors please, the truth of religion is a matter of spiritual discernment. As the Apostle Paul has said: "But the natural man receiveth not the things of the spirit of God; for they are foolishness unto him; neither can he know them, because they are spiritually discerned." It is a matter of spiritual discernment, and I ask the question in all sobriety where, in the constitution and organization of any civil commonwealth on the earth, from the beginning to the present day, there has ever been found a body of civil legislators capable of deciding for anybody but itself, what is the truth in religion.

There is an old lesson on this subject. I find that in the trial of Jesus, as recorded in the Gospel of John, that the chief priests accused him before Pilate of blasphemy, saying, "We have a law, and by our law he ought to die, because he made himself the Son of God." Now, when Pilate had arraigned him, he said to him, "Art thou the King of the Jews?" Jesus answered him, "Sayest thou this thing of thyself, or did others tell it thee of me?" Pilate answered him: "Am I a Jew? Thine own nation and the chief priests have delivered thee unto me. What hast thou done?" Jesus answered: "My kingdom is not of this world. If my kingdom were of this world, then would my servants fight that I should not be delivered to the Jews; but now is my kingdom not from hence." Then when the Jews found that Pilate would not take jurisdiction of the case on the charge of blasphemy, on the ground that he had made himself the Son of God, and so had violated the law of the Jewish theocracy, they charged him with treason, on the ground that he was claiming to set himself up against Cæsar as king, and when they found out that Pilate sought to release him, the Jews cried out: "If thou let this man go, thou art not Cæsar's friend. Whosoever maketh himself a king, speaketh against Cæsar."

Now, in this colloquy between Pilate and our Lord on this point, as to his kingship, and the nature of his kingdom, Pilate said unto him: "Art thou a king, then?" Jesus answered: "Thou sayest that I am a king. To this end was I born, and for this cause came I into the world, that I should bear witness unto the Truth. Every one that is of the Truth heareth my voice." Pilate said unto Him: "What is Truth?" Then was the head of the civil State unable to comprehend, because unable, spiritually, to see the Truth, as it is in Jesus—the truth of religion.

Let the civil authorities now as well as then, beware, when called upon by popular clamor, whether of Pharisees or Priests, to pronounce upon religious truth, lest, in their necessary ignorance to discern it, they do not crucify the Lord of Glory afresh! And let His disciples beware, lest, in tossing the Bible and its precious truths into the arena of political controversy, they violate that injunction and warning—"*Give not that which is holy unto the dogs, neither cast ye your pearls before swine, lest they trample them under their feet, and turn again and rend you.*"

If, your Honors please, religion does not need the assistance of Pilate, and wherever religion organized in any church has sought or consented to receive any alliance with the civil power, it has corrupted her purity and shorn her of her strength, and it will be so to the end of time. It was a remark of that celebrated and philosophic observer of society in America, De Tocqueville, that the thing that first struck him, when he landed on the shores of these United States, was that in a country where all religion was divorced from every connection with the State, there was a religious earnestness settled upon every face, and religious zeal burned in every heart. And Dr. Dollinger, a Roman Catholic writer, in a work on *The Church and the Churches, or the Papacy and the Temporal Power,*" in reference to this very question of the divorce of religion from the schools, denounced it as godless and atheistic; nevertheless, most unconsciously betrayed himself into an acknowledgment that nowhere in the world does the religious spirit so pervade the whole people as it does here, where it is free from the hateful and corrupting embraces of secular power. He says:

"All churches or religious communities have, therefore, complete equal rights. Every person can join any sect he pleases, or belong to none, or found a new sect for himself. As in politics, in trade, and in all other occupations, so also in the domain of religion, the freest competition prevails and produces energetic action and elasticity of Church organism, combined, however, with an indecorous grasping at and hunting after proselytes, which favorably contrasts with the passive tranquility and stagnation of State Church bodies. For their practical skill in spreading these nets, and drawing in the masses, the Methodists appear to excel all others, but so much the more are the others obliged to concentrate their forces, keep their followers together, and endeavor to procure new proselytes. The mere prospect of being supported in case of falling into distress, brings in troops of converts. The art of getting money for religious purposes is here carefully cultivated; and for their talent in making money out of everything, and therefore also out of religion, the Americans certainly surpass all other nations. By exercising a kind of moral pressure that gives no offense, and leaves the appearance of voluntary action, they know how to incite crowds of people to bestow religious contributions—these, too, being persons who, if left to themselves, would give nothing. Their success in this way is truly extraordinary."

Judge Hoadly alluded to a circumstance in the life of Dr. Lyman Beecher, strongly illustrative of this. Up to 1819, your Honors may remember, in the State of Connecticut, the Congregational churches were supported by a tax imposed upon and paid by all citizens, and agitation was gotten up for the purpose of repealing that enactment, and the same outcry was made there then, as is made here and now, in reference to the exclusion of the Bible from the common schools; that it was an atheistic attack upon religion; and it was supposed that when that law was repealed religion would go to the dogs; that there would be no more of it; that it was a fatal attack, a deadly assault. And now hear how Dr. Beecher records his sentiments on page 452 of his autobiography:

"I remember how we all used to feel before the revolution happened. Our people thought they should be destroyed if the law should be taken away from under them. They did not think anything about God—did not seem to. And the fact is, we all felt that our children would scatter like partridges if the tax law was lost. We saw it coming. In Goshen they raised a fund. In Litchfield the people bid off the pews, and so it has been ever since. But the effect, when it did come, was just the reverse of the expectation. When the storm burst upon us, indeed, we thought we were dead for awhile. But we found we were thrown on God and on ourselves, and this created that moral coercion which makes men work. Before we had been standing on what our fathers had done, but now we were obliged to develop all our energy."

It is said there are hundreds and thousands of children in this goodly, this Christian city, that have no chance or opportunity for being educated in what my friends on the other side call "the elementary truths of Christianity," not even in a knowledge of that "broad Christianity," unless it can be given to them by a perusal every morning, by the teacher, of a few verses out of the Bible in the common schools. I say, if it be so, it is a lamentable confession of great lack and neglect of duty, not on the part of the State, but on the part of the Church, meaning by that the invisible body of true believers who are, as they believe, to create the Kingdom of Heaven upon earth.

It is said they are in the by-ways, lanes and alleys. And can they not be reached there? Can not the Church send out its ministers? or are they too busy, day after day, in their studies, preparing to dole out dogmatic theology Sunday after Sunday, to the tired ears of their wearied congregations? Can not they send out their Sunday-school teachers? Can not they send out their missionaries? Why, the command of the Savior was to go out into the streets and lanes of the city, and into the highways and hedges, and bring all in, bring them into the feast which he had prepared—this feast of fat things, of goodly things. Must we say that the Church has grown idle and lazy, and can only hobble on its crutches, and therefore that our school directors must set themselves up as teachers of religious truth? No! let the Church cease to depend upon any adventitious or external aids. Let her rely solely upon the omnipotent strength of the spirit of the Lord that is in it. Let it say to the State, hands off; it is our business, it is our duty, it is our privilege to educate the children in religion and the true knowledge of godliness. Don't let them starve on the husks of a broad Christianity. Let us give them that which is definite, and distinct and pointed,—the everlasting and saving truths of God's immortal Gospel.

Don't teach them, "Be virtuous and you shall be happy," but

"Believe on the Lord Jesus Christ and thou shalt be saved." Now, I say, and I say it with all due humility, as one not called upon to instruct, but, nevertheless, to say what is in me to say—let the Church say: Here is our field; it is white to the harvest; here is our duty; here is our mission; here is our work to evangelize, to save the lost and perishing crowd.

Let her rise up in the full measure and majesty of her innate spiritual strength—let her gird her loins for the mighty task—let her address herself with all earnestness and heroic zeal to the great but self-rewarding labors of Christian love—let her prove herself by her works of self-denying charity, to be the true Church as Jesus proved himself to the disciples of John to be the true Messiah, when He told them, "Go and show John again those things which ye do hear and see; the blind receive their sight and the lame walk, the lepers are cleansed and the deaf hear, the dead are raised up and the poor have the Gospel preached to them." Let her organize all her forces for a more determined and closer, hand-to-hand, struggle with sin and evil, of every form, and the misery and wretchedness, of which they are the cause. Let her ministers and missionaries not only proclaim from their pulpits "the unsearchable riches of Christ," but descending among the hungry multitudes, distribute to them the precious bread of life. Let them declare to the rich, and the educated, their duties, their responsibilities and their privileges, and lead them in person to the places where their work is to be done, and stimulate them by their example to do it. Let them inspire by their enthusiasm, and fire with their zeal, the indifferent and the slothful. Let them, by setting forth the beauty of holiness and the purity of "the truth as it is in Jesus," which is able to make us wise unto salvation, send the healthful and invigorating influences of our holy religion through every social relation, and glorify the business and the pleasures of our daily and secular life, by consecrating them to the glory of our Father who is Heaven. Let them turn these streams of the pure water of life, welling up in the hearts of their followers, into the dark and pestilential receptacles, where ignorance, poverty, misery and sin are gathered, and breed disorder and death. Then the great and the good, the noble and the wise, in the unity of the Spirit and the bond of peace, forgetting those things which are behind and reaching forth unto those things which are before, pressing toward the mark for the prize of the high calling of God in Christ Jesus, in one grand array will meet and wrestle against principalities, against powers, against the rulers of the darkness of this world, against spiritual wickedness in high places, and shall wrestle not in vain, for they shall be strong in the Lord and in the power of His might; clad in the whole armor of God, their loins girt about with truth, and having on the breast-plate of righteousness; their feet shod with the preparation of the gospel of peace, and above all, taking the shield of faith wherewith they shall be able to quench all the fiery darts of the wicked, the helmet of salvation and the sword of the Spirit, which is the word of God, praying always with all prayer and supplication in the Spirit. Then shall be hastened the promised time of the coming of our King when there shall be a new heaven and a new earth, wherein dwelleth righteousness—the holy city, New Jerusalem, coming down from God out of Heaven, prepared as a bride adorned for her husband, the tabernacle of God with men, where He will dwell with them and they shall be His people, and God himself shall be with them and be their God.

But let them remember that to advance this glorious consummation the Church must throw away the sword of civil authority which some of her too eager and impetuous sons would put into her hands; that the Kingdom of her Lord is not of this world; that she must render unto Cæsar the things that are Cæsar's, and unto God the things that are God's; that she must not permit any unholy dalliance with the solicitations of worldly power or advantage, but keep herself unspotted from the world; that her dominion is over the minds and hearts of men, and her victory achieved with spiritual weapons alone, by appeals to their reason, to their conscience, to the highest and best in their ruined nature, to be restored by the power, not of human laws, but of the Spirit of God; and that in proportion as she becomes conscious of her origin and destiny, of the divine and immortal life she bears in her bosom, hid with Christ in God, and grows into the recognition of her mission and place in the work and history of the world and of eternity, she will dissolve all ties that bind her to secular influences and the natural sphere of human interests and actions, and establish herself firmly upon the seat of her spiritual throne, whence shall silently but most potently issue streams of truth and goodness, wisdom and love, faith and charity, into all the channels of human thought and activity, to restore upon earth the Paradise of God.

I have not, may it please your Honors, strength to continue. There is a world of things that crowd upon me to say, but I must forbear; but I can not close and take my leave of this case without saying that I owe my profound and sincere acknowledgments to your Honors for the patience with which I have been treated. I know that I have needed forbearance; I have not perhaps deserved it, but your Honors know the palliations of the case. I could not say less. What I have said, I know your Honors will believe me, I have said in the fear of God, because I believed it was the truth and the right. If I have erred, if I am wrong, I can only look to Him for pardon who is willing to extend it to all who humbly seek it. But I tell your Honors my heart is in this thing. I believe it to be a matter of the most vital, of the most momentous and profound importance. Whether I be right or wrong, it calls upon your Honors, it summons you to a very high, a very difficult and a very important duty. I shall make no appeal to your Honors. Your Honors know what your duty is, and I know you will perform it.

Note.—The foregoing has been revised from the report of the argument published, at the time of its delivery, in the daily papers. It is, perhaps, not out of place, to say that it was made while suffering from physical pain, which prevented such verbal and formal preparation as the importance of the occasion demanded, and which, with other circumstances, not necessary to allude to, led to some expressions and passages which it has been thought best not to preserve in this more permanent form, and which, indeed, it would have been better not to have uttered.

In their place I have taken the liberty of supplying such additions as seemed desirable to the development of the argument; otherwise it has been my aim to preserve accurately its identity, both in spirit and form.

Argument of Rufus King,

Counsel for Plaintiffs.

This is an issue, may it please your Honors, of the first magnitude; not merely because of the intense interest it has excited in this community, but, in fact, throughout the land; an interest which, in my judgment, the gentlemen who appear for the defense are greatly mistaken when they suppose it arises simply out of sectarianism. I believe it is a real, heartfelt, conscientious conviction, as strong, as deep, as abiding and as righteous as the feeling of either of my friends on the other side, that a great institution in this country is really at stake in this issue. But the question is one of importance and interest to your Honors, not so much upon this ground as it is as a matter of law; and that is the ground upon which the case is to be decided.

Now, the part I have to take in this case has been made somewhat peculiar. In the ordinary course of proceeding, the whole argument on both sides being before your Honors, it is my duty to reply to my friends who preceded me in the defense, and having done that it would be my duty to take my seat.

But the counsel for the defense, not only the gentleman who preceded me, but all of them, have gone into a line of argument which, according to my opinion of the issue, is so remote, so foreign, so wide of the point which your Honors have to decide, that if I undertake to follow the argument which the Court have now so patiently, for four days, listened to, I should have to lose sight of all the consideration upon which my clients came into this Court.

If this were a debating society, or a meeting at Pike's Hall, or, which I wish were the case, if your Honors were sitting here as a constitutional convention, I admit that the arguments of my friends on the other side were able; they were rich in learning, and I was glad that they came up to certain points that one of your Honors suggested and desired to be brought out, to show that the profession was not unlearned in matters of such importance.

But, taking the main points upon which the gentlemen have spent their force in the defense of the School Board in this case, what have they to do with the question which is now before your Honors?

The people of Ohio, in convention assembled, have adopted as part of their fundamental laws, and not simply of their fundamental laws, but they have seen fit to frame and set it in their Bill of Rights, the law of laws, which precedes government, underlying and controlling all laws, and supplying your Honors with the motives upon which to interpret laws, a provision which this Court is called upon to interpret and apply to the action of the School Board in this defense. I will not repeat Mr. Webster's remark as to taking our bearings, but I read the concluding paragraph of section 7 of the Bill of Rights prefixed to our Constitution:

"Religion, morality and knowledge, however, being essential to good government, it shall be the duty of the General Assembly to pass suitable laws to protect every religious denomination in the peaceable enjoyment of its own mode of public worship, and to encourage schools and the means of instruction."

And right upon that, by superposition, apply these resolutions, adopted by the School Board of Cincinnati, November 1, 1869:

"*Resolved*, That religious instruction, and the reading of religious books, including the Holy Bible, are prohibited in the common schools of Cincinnati, it being the true object and intent of this rule to allow the children of the parents of all sects and opinions, in matters of faith and worship, to enjoy alike the benefit of the common school fund.

"*Resolved*, That so much of the regulations on the course of study and text books in the intermediate and district schools (p. 213, Annual Report,) as reads as follows: 'The opening exercises in every department shall commence by reading a portion of the Bible by or under the direction of the teacher, and appropriate singing of the pupils,' be repealed."

It is not denied that those schools are established under that Constitution. There, then, is the issue which it was very easy to approach if the gentlemen wanted to. The almost general concurrence of the three counsel in not approaching that question was not fortuitous; it was not by catastrophe, but it was by design. And may I be permitted to ask what is the legal and reasonable inference, what must have been the design in carefully avoiding the discussion of this issue? The learned counsel who closed the case for the defense, after a most impressive allusion to his difficult and peculiar position (in which he has my profound sympathy), proceeded to administer a rebuke to somebody for having converted this court of law into an arena of theological, doctrinal and religious—or perhaps it might have been better to say irreligious—discussion; and there, again, in so far as the rebuke applied to his colleagues, I sympathize with the gentleman; for having listened with the most profound attention to his two colleagues who preceded him in the discussion, I was really at a loss to know where the case was drifting, and where we were to end.

We seemed to have cut loose from those rules which we generally go by here, and the affair seemed to have resolved itself into a revision of the Constitution. The gentleman who preceded me thereupon called for the previous question, and he read the resolutions adopted by the School Board, but straightway following the example of his two colleagues, he forgot the question, which I have just presented to the Court and which I believe to be the true issue in the case. But then he was pleased not to forget, in turning off into those intricate regions into which the defense has wandered, to turn upon the plaintiffs whom we have the honor—and I may add, if it please the Court, nothing but the honor—to represent in this case, and rebuke them in tones somewhat angry and loud for making this sacred book—I took down the words—"the football of parties; and stirring up schism in society." May it please your Honors, these are bold words, "brave words, my masters;" but did the gentleman forget who began this thing, who threw the first stone? Where did this "football" come from? And who started this schism in society? I commend the question back to his consideration.

He then went on to rebuke my clients again, that instead of leaving this matter to the people—I beg leave just here to interpose a question: how, until the Court has *decided the law*, are the people to settle the points which it has taken these profound pundits so long to bring out? If the people have to consider the whole mass of curious research which has been here presented, they will have a very steep time of it before the next Spring election. He rebuked my clients, I say, for not having left this matter to the people, and we are taunted and shamed for coming into this Court. Why, what would the gentleman have? Does he propose now to turn round and remind us of those principles which he and his colleagues have scouted for the last three days as a part of popular government; that we should practice the Christian grace of humility, and having been smitten upon one cheek, we should turn the other also? Were we to lie down and be kicked till the breath of life, and, as we believe, of government, was taken out of us?

There is an inconsistency here between the gentleman's argument and his practice. He does not hold to his own doctrine, and he has shown us a very poor example of that Christian maxim which teaches that we should take the beam out of our own eye in order that we may see the mote in our neighbor's.

The next proposition I understood my friend to lay down to the charge of my clients was, that this was a very small matter. Before his argument was concluded, he made it a very large matter, and, if I recollect, fully vindicated the plaintiffs in coming into this Court for relief. If this was a very small matter, why did not the School Board leave it alone? Why did they set this "football" in motion, and create this schism in society, when there was not a complaint to ripple the smooth surface of the summer sea, upon which the schools in this city were sailing? Precepts and practice do not go together in this case. Why was this doubling and shifting about this matter? I ask again, who began it?

I come now to a more serious matter, in which I shall have controversy with my friend who last addressed the Court on the other side, and that is in regard to this: The very first words of this resolution, the forefront of it, prohibit religious instruction. Now, it is immaterial what instruction, and whether any religious instruction, was before given in the public schools. It is enough for the purpose in this case, upon the principle of *quia timet*, which the case in the Tennessee Reports, referred to, lays down distinctly as a ground of relief, it was sufficient on this ground for these plaintiffs to come into court prospectively; even if there never had been a scrap of religious teaching in the schools, there was a violation of the Constitution threatened, which cut off our population from the benefits of the very ground-work of religion and government. It suffices for our case, that whereas the Constitution enjoins religion as a means of instruction, this resolution declares there shall be none, squarely and diametrically. It violates the Constitution *totidem verbis*, for whereas the Constitution says religion shall be taught and encouraged, the Cincinnati School Board says it shall not, and there is a square issue.

Now, the learned counsel, conscious, and pressed by this very awkward predicament into which part of his clients—for it seems they are not all of the same way of thinking—have fallen, and appearing here in direct opposition to the terms of the Constitution and the fundamental law, ingeniously, and, as I thought, very subtly, threw out the intimation that it was admitted that there had been, with the exception of reading the Bible, no religious instruction in the public schools, using what they did not find in the resotion, a substitution of the words, "formal instruction," thereby conveying to your Honors the idea that the first resolution was merely a blank cartridge, that there was nothing in it; it was a poor, harmless sort of thing, and therefore your Honors would confine your attention to the second resolution, which prohibits this reading of the Bible the first thing in the morning, and let this first resolution pass as a matter of no consequence. But the evidence pricks the air out of this bubble.

The gentleman turned and asked if we referred to McGuffey's Readers as containing religious instruction; I said yes, and, may it please the Court, McGuffey's Readers are enough for my case.

20

They were, fortunately, put in evidence, and your Honors will find marked on the blank leaves of these books the contents precisely defined of what is denominated by all dictionaries, lexicographers and religious men, religious and moral instruction; and your Honors will find it very good reading, consisting not merely of extracts from the Bible, but some most beautiful lessons of religion and morality, prepared by Mr. McGuffey, who all his life has been an instructor of youth, and perhaps one of the best in the country to compile such books. He has compiled, arranged and adorned that instruction, with strict reference to this provision of law, for laying the foundation of religious character, virtue and morality broad and deep throughout the country.

Now, just here is the point I quarrel with. Your Honors were very quietly asked to put no stress whatever upon this resolution. But, mark you, that resolution in all the breadth of those words, and certainly more comprehensive words could not have been adopted, has to go into the hands of over four hundred other judges, the teachers of the public schools in this city.

I ask you, in the sense in which any teacher of Cincinnati is authorized and enjoined to put upon the terms used in that first resolution, whether it is possible to have the name of God mentioned, much less explained, in these public schools. No, your Honors, that resolution, not only in the German schools, to which we have had two or three references here, and which I was sorry to hear, for I have a high respect for them, but in any of those schools where these teachers go, I say is a command to them that you shall not teach the name of God in your schools. For that is the foundation of all religion, even in the sense in which my friends on the other side were compelled to concede, and upon which they gave up some sort of a recognition of a God. Thus it was hoped to save this first resolution; but the argument stultifies the School Board, and will not and can not stand. The School Board, when they passed that resolution, meant something—some sort of religious instruction.

They meant to recognize some sort of religious instruction as now prevailing in the public schools. There it is, and can not be evaded. For religious instruction, the reading of religious books, including the Bible, is prohibited. But something more was intended than the Bible; for that book being merely "included," there must have been more to include it, on the axiom that the part is less than the whole. Some other religious instruction than the Bible lesson must, therefore, have been in view, to be suppressed. Now, what was it? It certainly could not have been the spelling books or the arithmetic, although I think one gentleman did argue that there was some religion even in the multiplication table. I do not think the learned counsel had in his eye the geography or history taught in the public schools, for I do not think the kingdom of heaven is laid down in the books on those subjects used in the public schools. Then it comes down to this, that either the School Board were a set of fools in passing that resolution, or they must have meant one of two other books, which are the only ones left in the list, and that is the copy-books or McGuffey's Readers, and I leave that to be decided by the gentlemen on the other side, and also by the *claqueurs* from whom I heard a little laugh the other afternoon, with regard to the McGuffey Readers, which reminded me of the distich of Pope, concerning a class—I omit the epithet—who

———"Still have an itch to deride,
And fain would be on the laughing side."

The Court has heard the answer in this action, and the defense which it sets up, and the argument, and I submit that if these resolutions, which it has been somewhere intimated are the tocsin of a new era, should prevail, and some of these—I will call them Pagans for the sake of respectable association, for it embraces Cicero and a great many respectable names—if some of this new progeny, whose instruction is to be confined to reading, writing and ciphering, should, at some future and distant time, like Macauley's New Zealander on the ruins of London, be prowling about the archives in this Court House, and should find no fragment of the record in this case remaining, save that answer and defense, I submit that they would not dream that the people of Ohio had any such law upon their books as that clause just read from the State Constitution. The true issue has not been met.

The gentlemen went off into many things unpleasant, not only because they were irrelevant, but because the purpose of them seemed to have more significance than appeared upon their face. One of my friends, for example, referred to this letter of Dr. Bellows, and the fact that Dr. Bellows held up the Bible as the flag of Protestantism; and he made use of an expression I regarded as unfortunate. "That flag," said he, "must come down." An unfortunate expression, because its association with General Dix's orders upon a certain occasion about pulling down the flag might have occurred to his hearers, and therefore it was better not to have been brought into this connection. Then, again, there was a little repertory of scandal in regard to Franklin, Madison, Washington, old Dr. Johnson, and a great many other good men.

If the abuse of a thing is to be the argument for its abolition, I suppose we shall have to abolish the freedom of the press; for though certain firms among booksellers may print only fifty copies of a certain sort of thing, still copies exist in some repositories here and there.

Here, too, was this matter of the first lesson of the day in the public schools, which I venture to say that no man who has witnessed it, who was ever present at the opening at one of these schools, and saw these children, fifty up to sometimes as many as three hundred, assembled in a single room, all hushed, silent and reduced to the most perfect order, and in the most fervent manner, either listening to the reading of the teacher, or, what is more common, joining responsively in that same exercise which my friend insisted upon so strongly in his church at Glendale—no one, I say, who has visited the public schools and listened to those exercises, could find it in his heart to quarrel. But it is here held up to reproach as an act of worship.

Reading the Bible and singing the chants, which is often done, are held up here as an act of worship, when to any man who knows anything about the matter, it is perfectly understood that the intention is, by these exercises, to bring the school into a quiet frame of mind and attention which lasts throughout the day. And I venture to say that there is hardly an exercise which the children regard with so much pleasure as that. But my friends call it perfunctory, and they call it "dog-trot"; but if they would only take up their dog-trot and go to the schools some morning, they will find this exercise to be beautiful and profitable, and such as could be ill dispensed with. The attempt to censure it as worship and illegal, is a perversion of words. Worship is adoration.

Then there is another thing which Mr. Matthews has defended as a legal and proper distinction. Whereas, your penitentiary and houses of refuge and reform schools, may have, and must have, the Bible read to them, these children of the public schools have no such legal right; and it comes down to this, that no child in Ohio, unless he becomes wholly reprobate, has the right by public authority, to have the Bible or religious instruction. That is shutting the door after the horse is stolen, with a vengeance.

There were made here some curious critical remarks in regard to the authenticity of the Gospels, but what have they to do with this case? They can not change the law. I do not pretend to be learned, and there is such a diversity of opinion in matters of that kind that I do not wish to enter into discussion, for a great deal, perhaps, as about most things, can be said for both sides. I will, therefore, say nothing, except that Dr. Davidson, whose book has been referred to here, is not good authority, and is not so recognized. If I am not mistaken, the King James version is recognized now, by all scholars of all sects, as the best translation. It may not be entirely perfect, because nothing of that kind can be.

Now, in regard to the canon of the Gospels. I think that while Mr. Stallo is correct in stating that the canon was not established until about A. D. 150, it would lead to a wrong idea to suppose that the Gospels were not generally recognized as authentic from a period within twenty years from the death of our Savior. They were not collected in the canon for perhaps one hundred years later, but their authenticity was recognized. Nevertheless, the authenticity of that book is better established at this day than any other book of ancient times.

We come now to the point so zealously pressed by the first two counsel who addressed your Honors for the defendants, the abuses of religion.

Religion, under the name of Christianity, has been held up here for four or five mortal hours and choked until it was black in the face, and for what earthly purpose? What is there which has not been abused? God knows that if the abuse of a thing is a sufficient reason to abolish it, we had better begin by abolishing the steam engine, for the abuse of it is most shocking; and it seems that all the laws of Congress can not prevent it. But who ever heard that the abuse of Christianity was an argument against it? I can not pretend to be much of a Christian. I do not belong to any church, in the strict sense of the term, but in my judgment and belief, and, I think in the judgment of any fair mind, profoundly considering the whole length, breadth, height and depth of the history of the Christian religion, the most powerful evidence of its divine character, is that it has been able to carry the whole load of the abuses and outrages that have been perpetrated in its name. There is a very pertinent story in Boccaccio in reference to this which my friends may read, if they desire.

Where, in all history, can we find another system which has stood for five hundred years against such assaults? Christianity has lived and strengthened, and is yet progressing in a manner that indicates, in another century, the whole world will rejoice in it.

I thought that just here Mr. Stallo was guilty of a little ingratitude in thus holding up the abuses of Christianity, for had it not been for the abuses of Christianity, he would not have been able to come over here from his native land and enjoy with us the liberty and happiness of the institutions of this country. We know it was the abuses of Christianity which settled that belt of territory along the Atlantic coast, and which led to these mighty institutions which we have attained. For had it not been for the grace of God in planting that little colony along the Atlantic coast, this whole land might have been living under the flag of the Bourbon or the tri-color of France.

We know that the French were here ahead of the English, and occupied this land clear up the St. Lawrence and lakes, down these Western rivers to the Gulf of Mexico, and that they held this Western country in a vise, but it was wrested from them, by the energy of William Pitt, and converted into a land of freedom, under religious instruction in free schools, and religious institutions, living under the tree of liberty, in happiness and prosperity. I hope my friend Stallo will not pluck a leaf from that tree, but let it grow, and water its roots rather than kill it.

There was a point discussed by Mr. Stallo first, and then by Mr.

Hoadly, questioning the tendency of religion to elevate society, which I thought more germane to the case, because it is a justification of our fathers for putting that word religion into our Constitution. I was surprised that my brother Matthews should concur in the point. I was surprised at my two brothers who preceded him, standing up here to deny the influence of Christianity upon modern civilization, and as its foundation.

Draw a line across the track of history just there at the death of Christ; survey both sides of that line, and what do we see? The blackness of darkness beyond it, times not fit to record; and yet if you turn this way all is bright and brighter and still brightening as you go on. My friends, I know, will refer all this to physical and material causes, and talk most learnedly with regard to the influences of exact science; but where, I ask, do the sciences come from? From that equality of the human race which Christ proclaimed and was the first to establish upon a just footing upon this earth. It came from a system of doctrine, at first extreme, but the abuse did not last long.

I may be somewhat rusty, as were my brethren, in regard to their quotations, but your Honors will recollect that the early Christians, almost immediately after the establishment of Christianity, sold their possessions and parted the proceeds among all men, according to their needs, and you will recollect that the first thing we hear of anything like an asylum for widows, was that quarrel between the Hebrews and the Greeks about administering to the widows, in which the Hebrews got the advantage, and the Greeks complained. Then there was that magnificent speech of St. Paul on Mars Hill, in which he confounded both Epicureans and Stoics. And what did he say to them? He preached that God had made of one blood all nations upon all the face of the earth. So it was that out of the Divine preaching, example and practice of Him who was more than man, came that equality before God, which was the first genuine basis of democracy in the world, which put all men upon an equality; and the result of which has been little by little to raise the lowly masses, the poor and the downcast, out of the degradation which lies beyond that time to which I have just referred, up, and up, and up, until now society has got the whole force of the human family arrayed in this advance of science and art, and material improvement, if you please, which the gentlemen are pleased to regard as self-created, but which comes out of the development of the whole human race, which the Christian religion first began

It is hard to quarrel with the Church in regard to this matter, for it must be said, for the Roman Catholic Church, that it has been the bridge of learning, and not merely a bridge, but a great instrumentality by which religion then, as now, lifted up and took its ministers out of the lowly classes of society. And it was from them all intellect, art, and science first received their start in the awakening in the Middle Ages known as the Renaissance. My brother Hoadly in disparaging the influence of Christianity upon civilization, was very unfortunate in his illustrations. He took as his model prince, of all time, that blood-thirsty tyrant, Marcus Aurelius (for there never was a bloodier-minded gentleman on the face of the earth), as Lord Byron might have said:

> ———"As mild a mannered man
> As ever swore a prayer, or cut a throat."

There was that gentleman lolling philosophically, to be sure, in Rome, and if you take Gibbons' account of his empire, it enjoyed great prosperity; but he was a bloody persecutor. He brought the venerable St. Polycarp hundreds of miles to amuse the citizens in one of their holidays—a man ninety years of age, as pious, and good a man as adorned history, and as far superior to the wretch who persecuted him as to Nena Sahib. Having compelled him to submit to three days' torture, to swear by Jupiter, or to suffer death, he cast him away to the wild beasts, to gratify the brutal populace, who having no public schools, we suppose these amusements, the *panem et circenses*, naturally had to be substituted.*

There was another thing about which my brother Hoadly was mistaken. He referred to the Roman Code. Why, who published the code but Justinian, the Christian emperor? and I undertake to say, that excepting here and there fragmentary passages, which are brought from the old age of the Roman law prior to Adrian, which by many was considered the golden period of the Roman laws, the *corpus juris civilis* is no Pagan code. But where did it come from?

* See note at close of argument.

The great majority of the edicts of the prætors, and the responsa, as well as the rescripts, found in the Roman Code were from Christian lawyers. That is to say, they were as good Christians as lawyers generally.

And now, as to one part of this subject, I think the gentlemen will surrender. I mean in regard to the influence of Christianity. I should like to ask what was the condition of woman in this world prior to that era? You can not open a history of that brilliant and intellectual people, the Greeks, where any woman of culture can be found named in any but a class whom it is not fit here to mention.

They were slaves. They were born slaves, and kept slaves; and so they are to this day in every land where Christianity does not prevail. I need need not enter into any panegyric upon women. They now speak for themselves. Then the ages of chivalry—from what did they derive their inspiration but woman thus uplifted?

And now, if it please the Court, I turn away from these considerations, so persistently argued by Messrs. Stallo and Hoadly, with this one remark—I am not sorry that they have gone into this line of argument, for it has enabled your Honors to see the animus of the resolutions. Your Honors now see what these resolutions *do not disclose on their face*, what really is the motive of the men who passed them. You have it now. You can see just what the four hundred teachers of Cincinnati are going to interpret as the light in which they, acting up to these orders from their superiors, may teach and lead your children; for here are Messrs. Stallo's and Hoadly's speeches in which Christianity is denounced from right to left, from beginning to end, as a humbug; and of such teaching we say unbelief, materialism, and sensualism are to be the result. And the people, too, will have an opportunity of seeing from these speeches what this movement really means, all this specious argument to the contrary notwithstanding, and they show beyond question the wisdom of the Constitution, and the wickedness of these resolutions.

In regard to the staple of the argument of my friends on the other side, there seems to be a concerted effort to escape the consequences of these very rash and ruinous resolutions, which the counsel feel are in violation of law, by attempting to throw upon the complainants here the wolfish charge of muddying the stream. We are oppressors, forcing the Bible down their throats! We are sectarians, they the oppressed! We are the guilty; they the injured. But, if I may be permitted now in a few words—for I can not undertake to follow my friends through the whole of their argument, away off into these foreign regions, and thus be diverted from the real issues of this case—if I may sum up what I conceive the essential fallacies running through the whole argument of the three gentlemen, it is this,—that they have been pleased to turn upon religion, as a sect; and as though religion were asking something from the State; whereas, in point of fact, it is the State here asking succor from religion. And then, again, this difficulty—and I don't wonder, after this confession of Mr. Matthews about the Holy Church, that there is but one single step to carry him over—the idea that there is no religion outside the Church. Where did he get that idea? To what sect did the Holy Jesus belong? The Bible sectarian! What sect owns the Bible? Does the gentleman mean to say that the Catholic does not regard the Bible as his book, when it is the boast of his Church that it preserved and brought it down to us?

The whole thing is a fallacy from beginning to end, and turns upon the broad palpable mistake that religion is seeking the State, when on the contrary the State is seeking religion for the good of the public, *not* for the safety of souls; and that is where my friend Matthews fell into deep error, and struggled like a strong man, as he is, in a morass. Entertaining the doctrine that he spoke of yesterday, I do not wonder at it, and his trouble must be great. But all these three gentlemen attempted to establish their defense by denouncing the Bible as Protestant and sectarian. If your Honors please, I might pass this portion of the argument. I might, for all purposes of this case, admit both propositions. Everybody ought to understand perfectly well that nobody in these schools reads King James' version, or any other Bible, unless he chooses; because the resolution of 1842, in the first place, gives him absolute exemption from any Bible whatever; and then the rule of 1852 gives him free choice, if he wants the Bible. Nobody is constrained. No conscience is touched. There is freedom for all.

I admit that there is in the answer in this case an attempt to raise a point here; but your Honors will find upon looking into the pleadings that it does not answer. The petition charges, in terms, that the rule of 1842 expressly and absolutely exempts all children whose parents desire it from hearing or reading the Bible, and that the rule is in full force. The answer is cautiously drawn; it does not come up to the requirement of the Code; it does not deny; it avoids—I will not say equivocates—by saying that as to this matter they are not informed. Now we have informed them by putting on file a transcript of that rule of 1842; and it is in the record.

But in order to show that there is no ground for the pretense that this rule is obsolete,—it may be that it never was invoked; because there never was a man bad enough to go to the school-house to tell the teacher of his children not to let them hear or read the Bible,—to show that it is not obsolete in point of fact, here are two quotations from the reports, published by law, in 1852 and 1863, proclaiming that the rule is still in force, and complaining that although the School Board have for twenty years sought to have the obnoxious passages pointed out in any of the text books, up to this day it never has been answered, for the reason that I will presently mention.

There can be nothing made therefore in this case by denouncing the Bible as Protestant, or sectarian. By the rule of 1842 you need not, if you choose, have the Bible at all. By the rule of 1852, you may have your choice, and the Mormon Bible could be read in the schools of Cincinnati if the parents desired it; but I can not speak upon that subject with authority, as I do not belong to the School Board.

As in regard to those two points, so also, all the three counsel persisted in perpetually confusing the idea of religion with mere dogma; as though there were no such thing as religion antecedent to Church, no such thing as religion pure of sectarianism.

But here the gentlemen divided a little and fought each upon his own hook. Mr. Stallo set up a man of straw, and assumed that somebody or other—it certainly was not either of the three counsel for the plaintiffs—stated that Christianity was part of the law of Ohio. I suppose that Mr. Stallo must have made that point in his argument beforehand, assuming that some one on our side would take that position, but we disclaim any such proposition as that Christianity is part of the law of Ohio, except in the sense which Chief Justice Clayton so admirably marks out in the decision which Mr. Matthews read yesterday.

I quote from 2 Harrington, 556:

"This is the true meaning of the English maxim as usually applied. It was never pretended that the common law punished the violation of every precept of Christianity. No judge of common law ever decided that he who did not to others as he would that they should do to him, which is one of the most sublime of all the precepts of that religion, or that he that did not repent and believe in Christianity, was therefore liable to a penalty or punishment at common law. Indeed, in the very speech of Lord Mansfield already referred to, which was a noble and most successful effort in behalf of the Dissenters and the great cause of religious liberty, he says there never was a single instance, from the Saxon times down to our own, in which a man was ever punished by the common law for erroneous opinions concerning rites or modes of worship. The common law of England, which is only common reason or usage, knows of no prosecution for mere opinions. For Atheism, blasphemy, and reviling the Christian religion, there have been instances of persons prosecuted and punished upon the common law, but bare non-conformity to established rites and modes (of worship) is no sin by the common law.

"The common law was, as Lord Coke expressed it in *Sir William Herbert's case*, 3 Rep. 42 *b*, 'the preserver of the common peace of the land,' and therefore we find it punished outrages on or breaches of the peace of society, and also acts whose tendency was to disturb that peace.

"The union between Church and State in England, by which the Christian religion became connected with the Government itself, induced a series of penal statutes to protect and prefer that religion as a part of Government itself. But, even in England, Christianity was never considered as a part of the common law, so far as that a violation of its injunctions, independent of the established laws of man, and without the sanction of any positive act of Parliament made to enforce those injunctions, any man could be drawn to answer in a common law court. It was a part of the common law 'so far that any person reviling, subverting or ridiculing it might be prosecuted at common law,' as Lord Mansfield has declared, because, in the judgment of our English ancestors and their judicial tribunals, he who reviled, subverted or ridiculed Christianity did an act which struck at the foundation of their civil society, and tended, by its necessary consequences, as they believed, to disturb that common peace of the land of which (as Lord Coke had reported) the common law was *the* preserver. The common law never lighted the fires of Smithfield on the one hand, nor preferred the doctrines of infidelity (which is proved by all history to be in character not less intolerant than fanaticism) on the other. It adapted itself to the religion of the country just so far as was necessary for the peace and safety of civil institutions, but it took cognizance of offenses against God only when, by their inevitable effects, they became offenses against man and his temporal security."

So much for that point. Mr. Hoadly then set up another John Doe and Richard Roe, to-wit, Church and State, for us in Ohio long since dead and buried, but I don't care about answering that. He also advanced the singular idea that if the State enters at all upon religious instruction, it must teach *all* religious truth, "the whole councils of God." This mistakes the object. He commits the palpable error of assuming that religion, morality and knowledge are sought by the Constitution not as essential to the State, but for the salvation of souls. And that is about as near as he could go to the idea of part of his clients.

Mr. Matthews took pains, in several passages of his speech, to declare and set his approval upon all the various propositions which had been made by his two colleagues, and without discrimination, as legitimate and applicable in this case. I do not know that the gentleman meant to make himself responsible for the full meaning of the words, and will therefore not hold him to it; I do not think he did. His first great proposition, concurring with his colleagues, was that the Bible is sectarian, and therefore he proposed to hold your Honor (Judge Storer) very strictly to your word, and I think your Honor conceded that if he would satisfy you that the reading of King James' version of the Scriptures is sectarian, you would decide to exclude it. And now, then, he proceeds to establish it thus: There are three great divisions of religious men, the Israelites, the Roman Catholics, and the Nullifidians—I will take the word Pagan back. He said these three and the Protestants are all equal; mark that, if you please; secondly, because that church, between whom and himself there stands now but one link to be supplied, because the Roman Catholic Church, holding it as a religious dogma—mark that again, if you please—that the reading of the Bible is a heresy and sin, and having the right so to do, he made the proposition that they had the right to lay down as a dogma that it is a heresy and sin to read, or suffer others, in the exercise of private judgment, to read the Bible; therefore the Bible is sectarian in the public schools in the sense of the Roman Catholic, and takes them under the peril of damnation, and they must protest against its being read by anybody, Roman Catholic, Protestant, Israelite, or Nullifidian. That is the doctrine.

Now, what do your Honors think of that? That is equality, with a vengeance. We all started equal, but it comes to this, that these gentlemen have a right to turn round and say you shall not read the Bible in the school-house, and by that same token all the rest of us have got to assent to the doctrine, because a Catholic will be damned if he allows you to do it. And if so, when that time comes predicted by the gentleman, when the Roman Catholics, having the majority, and controlling the schools as they please, unless we can hold them by the interposition of this court, and when the Mass shall be celebrated and the worship of the Virgin Mary shall be established in the public schools, why, as a matter of course, you will be estopped from reading the Bible at home. That is what I call a religious establishment built upon Mr. Matthews' argument; for this is exactly what it is, and you can not make anything else out of it. Every one, therefore, has a right to be educated upon a precisely similar implicit yielding of the public schools to *his dogma*, just as much as to the dogma of the Roman Catholics. The Israelite, who believes in his Talmud, or he who believes he will be damned unless we read the Book of Mormon, must have their consciences relieved likewise; and so we shall come to be like that philosopher who reads all and believes all of them, and believes they are all alike; and thus we perish in a general cataclysm of conscience. But the whole point is imaginary. And so is this difficulty which has been raised as to "private judgment." For, whatever be the rule of the Roman Catholic Church in that matter, it is undeniable that their people, in this country at least, freely have their Bible, and read it too.

The next great central proposition of Mr. Matthews' argument is this: that you shall not have religion in the public schools, because it is historically a fact that the alliance of religion and State has been fatal to both. If he means Church and State, yes; otherwise, no. One hundred years of American history holds up its hand in protestation against that argument as untrue. It can not be maintained. We stand alone,—I admit it. There has been nothing like the American common school, associating religious and moral with intellectual education, as a substitute for Church and State, in the past history of mankind. American history, I admit, stands alone. I say that this argument, no doubt the result of much thought and profound conviction, only satisfies me the more that my friend is a strong man struggling in a morass.

Then came what I was very sorry to hear; it is as hard and cold as Lycurgus. There is a passage in this answer which I desire to read to the Court again:

> "These defendants believe it to be true that a number of children that are educated in the common schools receive no religious instruction except that communicated in said schools."

What in the name of heaven is it proposed to do with these children? Why, says the gentleman, let their parents take care of them; let them go to Sunday school; just as the maid of honor, who was told the people had no bread, said to the queen, "why then don't the poor children have cake and marmalade?"

And then my friend launched out into a tirade against the clergy and churches, which I thought was very extraordinary in an elder of a Presbyterian church, and which, I believe, the General Assembly will not allow. Go to their parents—parents admitted by the answer in this cause to be utterly derelict! Why did not the gentleman say, go to the devil? The argument begs the question. It is too broad; it proves too much. If you can send these children home for their religion and morality, which is the peculiar jewel sought by the State of the public school system, why not send them back for their reading, writing and ciphering? What will become of your public school system? What becomes of your tax? Why am I bound to pay taxes for the teaching of other people's children in mere reading, writing and ciphering, when it only makes a little rascal of a boy twice as sharp as he was before, thrice the greater adept in vice and villainy, while it gives me no protection for my throat. And this is what the system means when instruction shall be divested of its morality and religion.

A little difficulty takes place just here in regard to this matter of parents. Mr. Matthews insists that my colleague, who preceded him in the argument, advanced the proposition that the State has a right to force the child away from its parents into schools, and then impose upon him the teachings of religion. What my colleague stated—for I took it down—and what we maintain, is that the State has a paramount interest in the virtue and knowledge of its members, and that prerogative belongs to it; and that the child also has a right of conscience which is superior to the right of the parent. I refer to 4 Wharton, p. 11.

I will close this matter with an inquiry. The law of this country having got rid of this terrible curse which they denounce so furiously—churches supported by the State—where, I ask, are the churches and Sunday schools to which the poor and outcast are to go? Where are the pews these people shall sit in? Where are the clothes which we know the poor man wants when he sends his children to Sunday school or church? Can Mr. Murray Shipley, and the other benevolent gentlemen who labor with him, undertake to accommodate, in their house forty-five by eighty feet, the thousands of those little outcasts who are now to pick up morals and character by charity? They will have a very large house full.

I now propose to go to the direct and only question before the Court. Has the School Board violated the law? Here arises a point about which there has been the greatest imaginable misunderstanding, not only in the argument of counsel, but out of court. It has been assumed here and everywhere that the Bible and nothing but the Bible is in controversy in this cause. *That is not the issue.* The Bible is only an incident in this controversy, and for the purposes of this case it might be conceded, though I do not concede it, I only say it might be conceded, that the School Board, in the exercise of a proper discretionary power over text books, could direct it to be omitted. But the real question here is, whether under the law of Ohio the School Board can shut out *all religious instruction*? If so, the Bible and all is engulfed, and it is immaterial whether the reading of the Bible be discussed. Nor is there any pretense on our part, as insinuated by counsel, that this

Court can dictate what text-books shall be used in the public schools. What we say is, that even admitting the School Board has discretion in directing what text-books shall be used, there still remains in this Court the broad power of saying that they shall not *exclude* text-books or instruction which the law commands. The difference between the power of commanding the School Board what they shall do, and prohibiting what they may not do, is so familiar to your Honors that it needs only to be mentioned to show the fallacy in Mr. Hoadly's argument on this point.

The true issue, as I have stated, and the question for the Court to decide is, do these resolutions violate that provision of the Constitution which I began by reading? And it is a question of law, not of theological doctrine and casuistry. The first aspect of these resolutions is that utter intolerance toward all but unbelievers, or if you please, Nullifidians, which Mr. Sage and Mr. Ramsey have both so fully depicted, that it is not necessary to say more about it. This resolution is not only intolerant, but it is in bad faith.

To see its intolerance I ask your Honors to refer back to the history of the schools of this city, established just forty years ago, and always conformed and conforming in their instruction with this injunction of the Constitution. See how they have worked. The Bible was adopted at the beginning, and held ever since to be a proper text-book of morality and of religion, if you please in the "broad" sense. The defendants knew this.

No one ever questioned the reading of the Bible in school by his neighbor's children, provided every child was excused whose parents objected. The only objection that ever was made was by Bishop, now Archbishop, Purcell, in 1842. He was then a member of the Board of School Examiners, and after the passage of the broad exemption secured by the resolution of 1842, he never complained, much less set up any such dogmas as those advanced by Mr. Matthews yesterday.

This system of schools went on, and worked so admirably, with the additional rule made in 1852, that about the years 1857–8 the Israelites of this city, who up to that time had been carrying on their own schools, keeping up a separate system, under the guidance of their own rabbis, saw no reason longer to keep up their own school system, and admitted that the public schools were good enough for them; and one of their rabbis has been an active member of the School Board up to a recent period, and never, on any occasion, has there been any objection by them or by him to this terribly obnoxious violation of the rights of conscience.

Down to the first of November last every one in this city was perfectly at liberty, because no one was or could be injured. There was a perfect equality; each had his rights, and nobody stepped upon the toes of any body else. Not a parent, Israelite or Catholic, complained to this Board, or brought a case of this kind to their notice.

But all at once a very strange coalition of twenty-two gentlemen takes place, ten of whom were Catholics; and what I can not well reconcile with my knowledge of the School Board, is how ten Catholics got into that Board so suddenly.

For the fourteen years I knew that Board there were never more than two or three gentlemen of that faith on the Board, because they did not consider it a matter of sufficient interest to them. But all at once ten of them are on the Board! What are they there for! They, with twelve other gentlemen, making twenty-two in all, nearly all of whom, I believe, are from Europe, at least a majority of them, and who in their native country had been accustomed to love one another with the love that wolves have for sheep, and treated each other with such soft dalliance as the ax and the faggot, these gentlemen are found all at once in loving embrace, and they pass these resolutions.

Now what turns out to be the secret in regard to this matter? I do not believe the person who penned this first resolution supposed any one would be for an instant deceived by this pretense, which is thrown in there, as its motive, in these words: "It being the true object and intent of this rule to allow the children of parents of all sects, in matters of faith, to enjoy alike the benefits of the school fund." Do your Honors see the coming events by the shadows which they cast before them? Mark, it is the funds these gentlemen are after for the sects! There is not a word about the State, and the desire to have good citizens; but the motive is the equality of the sects in order to have a fair share or grab at the funds, in an indirect way, to be sure.

Does this look like the free, fair, equal, and universally satisfactory state of things that was previously existing? Equality, indeed! Does it take any man a moment to see who gets the advantage by this resolution, and who loses by it? Equality! The tyrant who has accustomed himself to live upon some vile chaff, noxious to every one but himself, issues his edict that no man shall eat bread, and derisively forces it down by adding, because he desires his subjects to live upon an equality.

Thus if the Court will come to the pith of the matter, men having no belief, Nullifidians, Mr. Matthews gently calls them, and who do not want any belief, do not want any body else to have any, passed these resolutions, not for any love of equality, but because they oppose and hate and scoff at all who believe in religious instruction. And to what a condition does this reduce the public schools. Is that sectarian in the sense in which Mr. Matthews lays it down here? Oh! not at all; these men are "the Liberals!"

But besides this tyranny I think these gentlemen were acting in bad faith in this matter. We had a meeting in Pike's Hall to oppose their views, but they took snap judgment on us.

Let that pass; what I am now pointing at is that the two parties to this coalition were not acting in good faith with their constituents and the State, nor even with each other. What think you each was driving at? One part of them seeks—what? To split the Catholic church. They hope to have a division of the Catholic church in this city. I get this from the *Cincinnati Commercial*, which has been the active ally, and, I suppose, in the secrets of this party. Mr. Matthews also put it plainly yesterday, in argument, that they have got up this thing as the wedge which they are going to drive in between the Catholic clergy and their people. Heaven save the mark! What have these gentlemen been doing, that they have not read, in the history of that church for a thousand years, the efforts of far more dangerous adversaries than they—of kings and potentates—to divide and break it, all of which have disastrously failed and recoiled upon their contrivers.

The fate of my friends on the other side is perfectly clear. It will be like that of those poor Indians on the Plains we read of lately in the newspapers, who tried to head the Pacific Railroad train. Poor, unsophisticated sons of the prairie! They had heard of capturing trains—a little diversion invented during the late war—and one night, as the train was approaching, two or three hundred of these copper-colored individuals stretched a rope across the track, half of them holding on to each end. Along came the train, and in a moment the poor Indians were flying in the air, as you may suppose, in most disorderly attitudes.

Now, my friends have my best wishes, in the way Sidney Smith gave his to a friend, a colonial bishop, who was about sailing for New Zealand. He went on board the ship to comfort him and see him off, telling him what terrible man-eaters these savages were and there was nothing they liked so much as cold missionary on the side-board, and finally consoling his friend as they parted, with the hope: "My dear brother, may you disagree with the fellows that eat you." I don't want to be there, your Honors, when the train comes along, but, still, would like to see my friends, Stallo, Hoadly, and Matthews, holding the rope about the time the Roman Catholic Church comes thundering down upon this little plot. All I can wish, then, is that when tossed into the air they may fall outside of the track.

That is the object of the left wing, these twelve gentlemen, who are mainly defending this suit—a very shallow and preposterous thing for sensible men to attempt—and I think it will give Archbishop Purcell a pleasant little laugh, if your Honors allow them to try it.

But the other party in this coalition, may it please the Court, is engaged in an effort which it behooves your Honors to regard with more vital and penetrating search, because it is vastly more dangerous than this idea of splitting the Catholic Church.

It is their pious object to break up the present system of public schools, and bring about in earnest that division of the school fund among the sects which is only shadowed in these resolutions. This is their motive in this plot; and how it is to ripen and come to pass, and what probability there is that the Roman Catholic people are going to break up their system of separate schools, violate all their traditions, and transfer their children over to such schools as these will be under the auspices of these resolutions, as expounded here by learned counsel, may be judged from extracts which I shall now read from newspapers known as their leading indexes of opinion.

Three days after the passing of these resolutions, thus spoke the *Catholic Telegraph*, of this city, unquestionably good authority for all Roman Catholics:

"The first chapter in this school controversy is now closed; it ends with the triumph of law. The second chapter will open with agitation against the law itself, in the name of justice, and the the right that both Protestants and Catholics have to positive religious instruction in separate schools. If the school laws be modified to secure denominational education for all, Catholics will cheerfully pay their portion of the school fund. If this wise amendment can not be made, taxation for school purposes must cease. Now that the Bible has been excluded from the schools, if the professed Protestants have been sincere in all that they have said in its favor, they must agree with the Catholics in the second issue of this question. Consistency will make them our friends in the future."

There, your Honors, is policy; something deeper and more worthy of your apprehension than tricks to divide a Church. There is a stroke which measures the gauge of men who are earnest in believing as all Roman Catholics do, people and clergy, —and I respect them for it—that religion is inseparable from education. I do not, of course, mean religion in their sense, but religion in the sense of the great cause now at stake, and defined in the words of the Master; that religion which the State encourages and must have—the religion which the Constitution here calls for and which your Honors are bound, as ministers of that Constitution, to uphold.

I will now read another authority from the pen of a man unequalled, in some respects, by any Roman Catholic in this country—a brilliant and far-seeing writer—Mr. McMasters, of the New York *Freeman's Journal:*

"If the Catholic translation of the books of Holy Writ, which is to be found in the homes of all our better educated Catholics, were to be dissected by the ablest Catholic theologian in the land, and merely lessons to be taken from it—such as Catholic mothers read to their children, and with all the notes and comments in the popular edition, and others added, with the highest Catholic indorsement—and if these admirable Bible lessons, and these alone, were to be ruled as to be read in all the public schools, this would not diminish, in any substantial degree, the objection we Catholics have to letting Catholic children attend the public schools.

"This declaration is very sweeping, but we will prove its correctness.

"1. We will not subject our Catholic children to your teachers. You ought to know why, in a multitude of cases.

"2. We will not expose our Catholic children to association with all the children who have a right to attend the public schools. Do you not know why?

"3. The perfunctory reading of the best of Bible lessons amounts to nothing as a rule of practical morals. The practical religion of the school-room is to inculcate lessons of piety at every opportunity. Except the system be founded on fraud, the teacher in our public schools has no right to explain, even, any one of the Christian virtues. The Jew and the Infidel has a right to send his child to such a school as much as the Catholic. The teacher, according to the programme, has no right to explain to a child what is meant by 'Our Redeemer.'

"The plain and undeniable resolution of the whole question is this; the State or the city has no more right to tax me for schooling my neighbor's children than for feeding them, or clothing them, or housing them. The utmost that can be granted is, that for abandoned children the State may provide schooling, as it provides food and clothes for its paupers. I will not suffer my child to go to the poor-house for its dinner, nor to wear the clothes of the alms-house, so long as I can prevent it. And as little will I suffer the political power to dispense poor-house instruction to my child."

Here is another excellent authority among Roman Catholics—*The Tablet:*

"The School Board of Cincinnati have voted, we see from the papers, to exclude the Bible and all religious instruction from the public schools of the city. If this has been done with a view to reconciling Catholics to the common school system, its purpose will not be realized. It does not meet, or in any degree lessen, our objection to the public school system, and only proves the impracticability of that system in a mixed community of Catholics and Protestants; for it proves that the schools must, to be sustained, become thoroughly godless. But to us, godless schools are still less acceptable than sectarian schools, and we object less to the reading of King James' Bible, even in the schools, than we do to the exclusion of all religious instruction. American Protestantism of the orthodox stamp is far less evil than German infidelity.

"Since our community is composed of Catholics and Protestants, and the Government is bound to respect and protect the conscience or full religious liberty of each, it can sustain no system of schools for both to which either the Catholic or Protestant objects.

"It must, then, either leave the whole question of education, as it does religion, to the voluntary principle, or it must divide the schools, as it does in most European nations, into two classes, the one for Catholics and the other for Protestants, with the education in each under the supervision and control of its respective religious authority. Nothing less than either the one or the other will secure to Catholics their equal rights, and satisfy Catholic conscience.

"The system of common schools, as now adopted in this country, is in the main an imitation of the system decreed by the Convention which sentenced Louis XVI to the guillotine, abolished Christianity, and declared death an eternal sleep. The object of the Convention was, by a system of godless schools, to root out religion from the French mind, and to train up the French youth in absolute ignorance of, or unbelief in, any life beyond this life, and any world that transcends the senses. If we adopt and carry out the same system, our American youth must grow up thoroughly unbelieving and godless, as the order of the Cincinnati Board of Education not directly foreshadows. Catholics will do well to be on their guard against forming alliances to help them get rid of one evil by fastening on the country another, an infinitely greater evil —the very evil the forever infamous Convention sought, with devilish ingenuity, to fasten on France."

Shade of Cotton Mather! The idea that the common schools of America originated in the devilish ingenuity of Robespierre, Couthon, etc. That, indeed, is new.

But, now, I beg leave to quote a paper addressed to this Board of Education, and which applies directly to this case. It not only shows that no such dogma as that which the defendants' counsel have been imputing to the Roman Catholics is set up by them, but the folly of this idea that they will come to your "secularized schools." It will also raise, in every inquiring mind, the question why these defendants, instead of creating a "schism in society," did not pay heed to the invitation extended in the last paragraph, the meaning of which I will presently show more fully:

"The entire government of public schools in which Catholic youth are educated can not be given over to the civil power.

"We, as Catholics, can not approve of that system of education for youth which is apart from instruction in the Catholic faith and the teaching of the Church.

"If the School Board can offer anything in conformity with these principles, as has been done in England, France, Canada, Prussia, and other countries where the rights of conscience in the matter of education have been fully recognized, I am prepared to give it respectful consideration.

"JOHN B. PURCELL, Archbishop of Cincinnati.

"CINCINNATI, *September* 18, 1869."

Now, the theory of the learned counsel and their clients is, that when the Catholics come to our schools, then this split is to take place. But will they come?

No, your Honors! Roman Catholics join in applauding these resolutions, but with no idea of committing their children to such schools! Having rifled them of all which, in the conscience of the men of that faith—aye, or of any faith—makes them valuable or respectable as a system of education for the masses, they will turn from them and spurn them with contempt; they will hiss at them as an open shame; and your schools, recreant to the principles upon which your fathers planted and fostered them, will deserve the scorn and derision which will fall upon them in the sight of all righteous men. The supremacy of God has been the ever-ruling faith of this land. What the aims and traditions of Americans have heretofore been, so they will continue. Protestant, Catholic or Israelite, all will join in scouting a system which will be but a "poor-house" affair, and to which poor men will disdain to send their children.

I say there is not a true-hearted Catholic nor Israelite in this city who would not rather have his tongue plucked from its root than give his assent to the doctrine laid down here for the defense. No man of patriotism or heart, much less of sense, will agree to this idea of turning adrift these unfortunate children of vice and misery, who, it is admitted in one passage of the answer, are destitute of all religious influence but that of the schools, and yet are declared in another passage to be unworthy of citizenship without its elevating spirit.

These resolutions may be the doctrine of the fanatics of both extremes, but, thank God, it is not the doctrine of the Government and Constitution of Ohio.

Let us now inquire whether the mode in which I have shown that the equality of all creeds and the freedom of all sects were so thoroughly respected and secured in these schools by the rules of 1842 and of 1852, does not accord with Catholic conscience and Catholic laws and usages elsewhere. And here we shall get further light upon the suggestion held out by Archbishop Purcell to the defendants.

First, I turn to Catholic Ireland, certainly a "fighting people,"—as Mr. Matthews remarked of the Protestantism of America—and quite as likely as any people upon earth to revolt against any aggression upon their religious or conscientious convictions. I read, from the thirty-fourth annual report of the Commissioners of National Education in Ireland, the following outlines of the system which has been established in that country upon the principle of protecting children of all sects, united in the same school, from religious proselytism, without any sacrifice of religious and moral instruction:

"The object of the system of national education is to afford *combined* literary and moral, and *separate* religious instruction, to children of all persuasions, as far as possible, in the same schools, upon the fundamental principle that no attempt shall be made to interfere with the peculiar religious tenets of any description of religious pupils.

"It is the earnest wish of Her Majesty's Government and of the Commissioners that the clergy and laity of the different religious denominations should co-operate in conducting national schools.

"No national school-house shall be employed, at any time, even temporarily, as the stated place of worship of any religious community. No aid will be granted to a school held in any place of worship. No emblems or symbols of a denominational character shall be exhibited in the school-room during the hours of united instruction.

"Apartments are to be afforded to the children of all national schools for receiving such religious instruction as their parents or guardians approve of.

"Religious instruction must be so arranged that each school shall be open to children of all communions. No child shall receive, or be present at any religious instruction of which his parents or guardians disapprove, and the time for giving such instruction shall be so fixed that no child shall be thereby, in effect, excluded, directly or indirectly, from the other advantages which the school affords."

Such is the mode, in brief, of the Irish "national schools," established in 1833, and organized by a mixed board of Catholics and Protestants, chief among whom were Archbishop Murray, then the venerable head of the Roman Catholic clergy of Ireland, and Whately, the Archbishop of the English Church in Ireland. Out of nearly one million pupils attending these "national schools" in 1867, the Roman Catholics were in an immense majority, numbering 738,837, while only 171,236 were of the Protestant faith. So entirely are all denominations united in this great work of elementary education that only eleven per cent. of the whole number of children are attending schools exclusively Protestant or exclusively Catholic, while eighty-nine per cent. are in these mixed schools, where Protestant children are instructed in the Protestant religion without any such peril to Catholic souls as the eloquent imagination of counsel would lead us to deplore. In these schools no difficulty has been found in conducting them upon a principle, regulated by fixed rules, which inculcates religion, morality and knowledge to all, and yet tampers with the religious faith and conscience of none.

Next, to show how easily this question was adjusted in France, the nation which stands pre-eminent in Catholic Europe, and by such a statesman as M. Guizot, I beg leave to read a passage from Mr. Kay's excellent work on *The Social Condition and Education of the People.* It is long, but truly valuable:

"In 1833, M. Guizot, then Minister of Public Instruction, laid before the Chambers a great and comprehensive scheme of national education, which received their assent and was immediately put into operation throughout the whole of France.

"It was long a question of great doubt among French legislators in what manner the difficulties arising from religious differences could be overcome. The different religious parties in France were as earnest in their demands as the Church and dissenting parties in England at the present day.

"The Chambers were called upon to decide whether they would establish separate schools for all the different sects; or whether they would establish mixed schools, where no religious education should be given, and where the children of all sects should be instructed together; or whether they would allow the parishes to found their own schools, and elect teachers educated in the religious belief of the majority of the parishioners, merely requiring, as an indispensable preliminary, that the children of the minority should be allowed to avail themselves of the secular instruction given in the schools, and to leave the class-rooms when the religious instruction was given there—on condition, however, that their parents provided in some other manner for the efficient education of their children in their own religious belief.

"The Chambers felt, that to adopt the first course, would be to leave the education of many children totally unprovided for, in the cases of those communes, where there was not a sufficient number of some one sect in a commune to enable the government to establish a separate school for them; that, to adopt the second alternative, would be to leave the most deeply important part of education either wholly neglected, or at least most indifferently provided for; and that to deny the master the liberty of giving practical religious education in the school, was to deprive him of the most powerful means of improving the character of his children. They, therefore, adopted the third alternative, and resolved to place each of the normal colleges of the different departments, and each of the primary schools of the different communes, under the management of a professor or teacher, selected from the most numerous Christian sect of the department or communes in which the college or school was situated. They further determined, that the parents, who differed in their religious belief from the director of the college, or from the teacher of the school, *should have the power of requiring their children to absent themselves during the periods of religious instruction; on condition, however, that such parents provided elsewhere for the religious education of their children.*

"This liberal and excellent scheme has been undeservedly taunted with irreligion. The cries of the French Jesuits, raised from purely interested motives, have found an echo in the mouths of English Protestants, and this belief, strengthened by our laudable fear of excessive centralization, and by our national prejudices against the French, have prevented us doing justice to the magnificent efforts which they are making to educate their people, and by that means to raise their virtue and their happiness.

"The importance of the religious element in the education of the children, is put forward in great prominence by the French statutes and regulations upon the subject. In the words of the statute of April 25th, 1834, upon the elementary schools:

"'In all the divisions (of each school), the moral and religious instructions shall rank *first*. Prayers shall commence and close all the classes. Some verses of the Holy Scriptures shall be learned every day. Every Saturday, the Gospel of the following Sunday shall be recited. On the Sundays and fast days the scholars shall be conducted to divine service. The reading books, the writing copies, the discourses and exhortations of the teachers shall tend continually to penetrate the soul of the scholars, with the feelings and principles, which are the safeguards of morality, and which are proper to inspire the fear and love of God.'

"And M. Guizot, in the letters which he addressed, while Minister of Public Instruction, to each of the teachers of France, says:

"'Among the objects of instruction, there is one which demands of me particular notice; *or, rather, it is the law itself*, which, by placing it at the head of all the others, has committed it more especially to our zeal; I refer to moral and religious instruction. Your labors, in this respect, ought to be both direct and sometimes indirect.

"If by your character and your example, you have succeeded in obtaining in your school all the authority, with which I desire to see you clothed; the moral lessons which you will give, will be received with deference; they will be something more than an instruction for the minds of the pupils; they will supply the insufficiency of the primary education so incomplete, and often so vicious in the present state of our morals and our intelligence.

"Do not neglect any means of exercising this salutary influence; increase it by means of conversation with individual scholars, as well as by means of general lessons; let it be your constant thought and your constant duty.

"It is absolutely necessary, that popular instruction should not be confined to the development of the intelligence; it should embrace the whole soul; it should awaken the conscience, which ought to be elevated and strengthened according as the intelligence is developed. It suffices to tell you, sir, what importance the religious instruction ought to have in your eyes. The teachers, who will be called upon to give this instruction in the elementary schools, ought to have been well prepared for this duty, by having themselves received a sound and religious education in the normal colleges. Do not, however, satisfy yourself with the regularity of forms and appearances; it is not sufficient, that certain observances should be maintained, that certain hours should be consecrated to religious instruction; it is necessary to be able to assure ourselves of its reality and efficiency. I invite you to make known to me the exact state of religious education in your own school.'"

These are examples of what is suffered and done in Roman Catholic countries; and they serve to show how empty are these pretenses of learned counsel that the consciences of Roman Catholics are oppressed by the freer system heretofore practiced in the public schools of Cincinnati. Here are the common "national schools" of Roman Catholic States, mingling religious and secular instruction; but none of that difficulty, or peril of heresy and damnation of souls, so eloquently imagined in the name and behalf of Roman Catholics, by the gentleman who preceded me. These, and the examples of Prussia, Switzerland, and other European States, already placed before you by other counsel, show your Honors not only that these countries, one by one, have adopted the American system of public schools as a national necessity, but this, also, that none of them countenance this crude idea of secularizing education. In all of them religion, morality, and knowledge are taught in the common schools, and there is no difficulty about it.

We come back now to the words of the Constitution: "Religion, morality, and knowledge are essential"—essential for what? The salvation of the soul? the inculcation of a dogma? Not at all: no such whisper there; no Church and State; no dogma, but "essential for good government." That is the object at which this law is aiming. We are dealing with common sense now, and have not got out into this region of air where no man can define anything. If the Court please, what is religion in the sense of this Constitution? There is no theology, no dogma necessary here, no Church. But, to show the religion which the Constitution intends the schools are to teach, I go directly back to the pure words of Him who was more than man, and who has given you and me a definition that, if we can not live up to more, will suffice all the purposes of this State, and that will admit no lawyer a half a minute to quibble over. Turn to the twenty-second chapter of Matthew, thirty-fifth verse, and you will find that one of our profession, tempting the Master—

Judge Storer. Just like a lawyer.

Mr. King. Yes; but he was a pretty good man, as your Honor will presently see. He asked this question: "Tempting him and saying, 'Master, which is the great commandment in the law?' Jesus said unto him, 'Thou shalt love the Lord, thy God with all thy heart, and with all thy soul, and with all thy mind.'" (St. Mark adds to it—"and with all thy strength.") "This is the first and great commandment, and the second is like unto it. 'Thou shalt love thy neighbor as thyself.' On these two commandments hang all the law and the prophets." St. Mark's narrative adds: "And the scribe said unto Him, 'Well, Master, thou hast said the truth; for there is but one God; and there is none other but He; and to love him with all the heart, and with all the understanding, and with all the soul, and with all the strength, and to love his neighbor as himself, is more than all whole burnt offerings and sacrifices. And when Jesus saw that he answered discreetly, he said unto him: Thou art not far from the Kingdom of God."

This, if your Honors please, is the religion of the Constitution and of the public schools. It is drawn from the Bible; and just here my eye falls upon some lines, of what poet I know not, a tribute to that Book:

"How pure, how perfect are Jehovah's laws,
From them the soul its best instruction draws,
Truth, virtue, love and wisdom they impart,
Light to the eyes and rapture to the heart.
Bright is the gloomy cavern's jeweled ore,
Sweet is the roving bee's collected store;
But what can nature, what can art bestow
Like the pure words that from Jehovah flow?"

But, gentlemen on the other side, although they do not like the Bible, can not object to the dictionary. Dr. Johnson, prince of lexicographers, defines religion to be "Virtue, as founded upon reverence of God, and expectation of future rewards and punishments." Dr. Webster defines it, "as distinct from theology, religion is godliness, a real piety, in practice, consisting in the performance of all known duties to God and our fellow-men, in obedience to divine commands or from love to God and His law."

[*Mr. King also quoted Dr. Watts, Bishop South, and Richardson's and Worcester's dictionaries. He claimed that McGuffey's Readers, as would appear by the lessons marked on the fly leaves of the copies which had been placed in evidence, abounded in references to these definitions, and, from beginning to end, not only contained large and copious extracts from the Scriptures, but tended by a regular progressive series of lessons to inculcate in children precisely those two precepts of reverence to God and His attributes, and love for their neighbor, and in a manner admirably adapted to fix the interest and impress their character.*]

For a practical and compendious statement, the function of the common schools is best expressed in the Massachusetts statute—*Rev. Stat.* of 1860, p. 216, sec. 10.

"It shall be the duty of the President, professors, and tutors of the University of Cambridge, and of the several colleges, of all preceptors and teachers of academies, and of all other instructors of youth, to exert their best endeavors to impress on the minds of children and youth committed to their care and instruction, the principles of piety and justice and a sacred regard for truth; love of their country, humanity and benevolence; sobriety, industry and frugality; chastity, moderation and temperance; and those other virtues which are the ornament of human society and the basis upon which a republican constitution is founded; and it shall be the duty of such instructors to endeavor to lead their pupils, as their ages and capacities will admit, into a clear understanding of the tendency of the above-mentioned virtues to preserve and perfect a republican constitution, and secure the blessings of liberty as well as to promote their future happiness; and, also, to point out to them the evil tendency of the opposite vices."

This is the religion and morality which the Constitution seeks to inculcate through the common schools, as essential to good government; and this is the "religious instruction" which the School Board of Cincinnati seeks, by the first of these resolutions, to cut off from the people. The argument that this is not "formal instruction," and, therefore, is not prohibited by this resolution, is an evasion. The resolution does not contain the word "formal."

It prohibits any religious instruction, no matter in what form; and the Court may well suspect its sweeping terms when an artifice like this is brought to its aid.

But then, all this is denounced as "broad religion" and a "humbug." Religion, it is insisted, must be something more distinctive. One of the counsel denounces Church and State, while another insists that religion means some creed or church, and demands which of them we are going to adopt; again and again confusing all religion with theology and church. Here, too, we are confronted with the cases of *Bloom* v. *Richards*, 2 Ohio State, 387, and *McGatrick* v. *Wason*, 4 Ohio State, 566, which are cited as confidently as though they repealed the provision of the Constitution now in controversy. It is true that in those cases the proposition is laid down that Christianity is no part of the law of Ohio—a proposition which nobody controverts, for the reason sufficiently explained in the passage already quoted from, the case in 2 Harrington, 553. But this, and all that is said in those cases concerning the relation between religion and the State, is simply *obiter dictum*—irrelevant to the matter decided. No such question was involved. Both cases turned upon that section of the "Act for the prevention of certain immoral practices" which makes it penal to be engaged on Sunday at "common labor, works of necessity or charity only excepted; *provided*, nothing herein contained shall be construed to extend to those who conscientiously do observe the seventh day of the week as the Sabbath." In *Bloom* v. *Richards* it was attempted to defeat a contract for the sale of land because made on Sunday; but the Court decided that, being a single act, privately done, it was not "common labor," and no violation of the statute. In *McGatrick* v. *Wason*, a laborer who was hired to ship cargo on a vessel on Sunday, sued for his wages. It being proved that navigation was about to close, and that the master refused to take the cargo unless shipped that day, the Court decided that it was a "work of necessity," and excused by the statute. Your Honors, therefore, see that in both cases it was merely a question whether the statute applied; and that the first was determined by deciding that a single private contract on Sunday is not "common labor," and the second, that the labor was a "work of necessity." The constitutionality or obligation of the statute was not disputed. No one questioned its motive or policy. It was sufficient that the statute did not apply in either case, and that was the end of it. Hence, there was no occasion nor ground for tacking on, as an appendix, the abstract propositions printed in the syllabus of those cases, that "neither Christianity nor any other system of religion is a part of the law of this State," and that "the statute would not stand for a moment as the law of the State if its sole motive was to enforce the observance of the Christian duty of keeping that day holy." Such comments were simply wasted. They have the force merely of private opinions of the judges, but not of law. And it is extraordinary that a man of such ability as the judge who delivered the decision in both cases should have failed to catch the salient hint, so quickly taken by Judge Caldwell, dissenting in 18 Ohio, 489, and Judge Scott, in 9 Ohio State, 439, from the title and proviso of the act. He hastily overlooked the fact that the very title of the act is to prevent "immoral practices," and that the proviso exempts only those who do conscientiously observe the seventh day of the week *as the Sabbath*." Why are they exempted? Why, but because they religiously observe another "Sabbath?" Why, then, does the law of Ohio enforce the observance of Sunday? Manifestly, the motive is religious. Without a doubt, it is reverence for that day as the Christian Sabbath. Stranger still was the learned judge's oversight in failing to observe that this same "Act for the prevention of immoral practices," in another section, makes it penal to "profanely swear by the name of God, Jesus Christ, or the Holy Ghost." Here he would have found not only the motive and enforcement of a religious duty because it is Christian, but a recognition of the doctrine of the Trinity itself.

Not to dwell longer upon this point, he who would see the true doctrine, and a perfect exposition, of the relation existing by law, in this country, between religion and the State, will read that masterly decision of Chief Justice Clayton, 2 Harrington, 553. In that case the prisoner was convicted of blasphemy against Jesus Christ, and a reversal was sought upon the ground that the statute was unconstitutional, because it preferred Christianity over other modes of worship. Thus the question was raised directly and in a manner not attempted in either of the cases in the Ohio Reports. Chief Justice Clayton, in concluding his opinion, said:

"We hold these to be legal proofs of what has been and now is the religion preferred by the people of Delaware. And independent of these and other evidence existing on the statute book of the State we are bound to notice, as judges acting under the authority of the people, at all times, what is that religion which they have voluntarily preferred. We know not only from the oaths that are administered by our authority to witnesses and jurors, but from that evidence to which every man has access beyond these halls, that the religion of the people of Delaware is Christian. * * * The distinction is a sound one between a religion preferred *by law* and a religion preferred *by the people* without the coercion of law; between a legal establishment which the Constitution expressly forbids and a religious creed freely chosen by the people themselves."

The religion to be taught in the common schools, I have endeavored to show, is not sectarianism, nor theology, but the eternal, immutable, and essential principles of the Bible, the religion taught by the great head of all religion. Certainly the Constitution means something. That can not be denied; and while it is not claimed by the plaintiffs that Christianity is part of the law in that sense which counsel for defendants would fain have us to claim, yet it is just as undeniable that the "religion" which the Constitution of Ohio expressly recognizes, is Christianity. This is beyond doubt or cavil, a Christian State. That is the general and prevailing religion of the people; and the courts are bound to notice and maintain it, just as they would any general custom of the State, whenever it is called in question. That custom defines that word as used in the Constitution. It is not part of law; yet its precepts and principles enter largely into the formation of the common law as now administered here in the Court. This becomes evident if we search back to the fountains—the *origines legis.* It begins with the laws of Alfred and Edward the Confessor, which continually cite the Scriptures as their sanction; and the same practice is distinctly traceable in the days of Coke. The influence of religion appears more or less to this day not only in the decisions but in the daily practice here in our courts. A jury is not impaneled to try a case and the judge does not sit upon the bench without taking an oath before Almighty God. And this is so, not only here in Court, but it is all about us. We breathe the influence of religion unconsciously, as we breathe the air; it flows through the whole body of the community as the rich blood flows through our bodies, carrying with it the right materials of those tissues, from which the very protoplasm of society must be derived, and to which it must look for succor and regeneration. The law itself is plain; it is written down. It means something, and it is the duty of the Court to extract that meaning from it. The Court is bound to make some sense out of the law. "Religion, morality, and knowledge being essential to good government, the legislature shall pass suitable laws to encourage schools and the means of instruction." Instruction in what? Why manifestly in the three subjects which go before; the antecedents, grammatically, of the sentence. If the language had been, "reading, writing and ciphering, being essential to good government, it shall be the duty of the legislature to encourage schools and the means of instruction," the learned counsel would have had no difficulty in determining the grammatical force and intent of the words.

And now, may it please your Honors, let us briefly trace the history of this provision, and see whence it derives its origin. As it now stands in the Constitution of 1851, the text is literally thus:

"SEC. 7. [*Bill of Rights.*] All men have a natural and indefeasible right to worship Almighty God according to the dictates of their own conscience. No person shall be compelled to attend, erect, or support any place of worship, or maintain any form of worship, against his consent; and no preference shall be given, by law, to any religious society; nor shall any interference with the rights of conscience be permitted. No religious test shall be required as a qualification for office, nor shall any person be incompetent to be a witness on account of his religious belief; but nothing herein shall be construed to dispense with oaths and affirmations. Religion, morality, and knowledge, however, being essential to good government, it shall be the duty of the General Assembly to pass suitable laws to protect every religious denomination in the peaceable enjoyment of its own mode of public worship, and to encourage schools and the means of instruction."

All this except the clauses which save the incompetency of

witnesses and protect religious denominations in their own mode of worship—is derived, almost in terms, from the Constitution of 1802. In that instrument the third section of the Bill of Rights concludes in these words:

"But religion, morality and knowledge, being essentially necessary to good government and the happiness of mankind, schools and the means of instruction shall forever be encouraged by legislative provision, not inconsistent with the rights of conscience."

That, your Honors, was the clear language and sentiment of the men who founded the State. That clause shows the scope and sense of the provision as it now stands in section seven of the Bill of Rights; differing, only by adding, and inserting just here, a new security to each religious denomination of its mode of worship, an addition in no wise repealing or detracting from the original text, which distinctly denotes the schools as the means of propagating the three great essentials of good government. The Constitution of 1851 omits the qualifying clause, "not inconsistent with the rights of conscience." But nevertheless it stands by implication. We do not claim that the omission alters the great principle of equality which we defend.

But let us go back a step further, your Honors, and see where we find the true derivation of this law. Turn to that venerable charter of liberty, of which as a son of the North-west I am ever grateful and proud, "the Ordinance of 1787"—and there, firmly rooted among those special articles which it is declared shall be "articles of compact between the original States and the people and States in the said territory, and forever remain unalterable, unless by common consent," you will find this:

"ARTICLE III. Religion, morality and knowledge, being necessary to good government and the happiness of mankind, schools, and the means of education, shall forever be encouraged."

We stand here, therefore, in defense of a perpetual compact, unalterable save by common consent; and thus your Honors see why this provision in the present Bill of Rights has been so sacredly preserved and handed down to us, almost in the same words, through the two successive Constitutions of the State. It is the primordial law of the North-west. It is the testimony and covenant of the fathers. And to show your Honors whence they derived it and why it was sacred in their eyes, let me quote again from the ordinance, a record which imports absolute verity. There you will find it declared, in the preamble to the special articles of compact which I have mentioned, that, "for extending the fundamental principles of civil and religious liberty, WHICH FORM THE BASIS WHEREON THESE REPUBLICS, THEIR LAWS AND CONSTITUTIONS ARE ERECTED—to fix and establish those principles as the basis of all laws, constitutions and governments, which forever hereafter shall be formed in the said territory, etc., it is hereby ordained," etc.

There then is my authority. There you find it laid down, in words which are ineffaceable, not only as a principle "of civil and religious liberty," but as one of the principles upon which "these republics, their laws and constitutions are erected," that religion, morality and knowledge, are forever to be encouraged by schools and the means of education, as necessary to good government. There is the power by which the thirteen colonies became a great nation.

And to show that this declaration of the ordinance was no sudden or superficial idea of religious liberty, here is a resolution passed by Congress, October 12, 1778:

> "WHEREAS, true religion and good morals are the only solid foundations of public liberty and happiness;
>
> *Resolved*, That it be and it is hereby earnestly recommended to the several States to take the most effectual measures for the encouragement thereof."

Another resolution, on the 7th of March, 1778, appoints a day of fasting and prayer to God, that among other blessings "it may please Him to bless our schools and seminaries of learning, and make them *nurseries of true piety, virtue and useful knowledge.*"

Wholesome doctrine! And may it please your Honors, it comes from good judges in the matter of "civil and religious liberty." We have had copious quotations here from various European scholars and theorists, among them that extremely extreme man, Henry Brougham. But mark, I pray you, that the men who founded these republics, who knew the principles by which they triumphed, and how a small people became the great example to the nations, these men entertain none of these speculative theories of "secularizing" education—but tell you that religion and morals are the only solid foundations of liberty and happiness; and that your schools and seminaries should be "nurseries of true piety, virtue and useful knowledge."

These were statesmen, whom the world credits with tolerably intelligent and practical ideas of liberty, and of the institutions by which liberty advances. If there ever was a practical and liberal statesman, if there was a man who typifies the fair average of American opinion at that great epoch, it was Benjamin Franklin. And here is his idea of "secularizing" schools. In an *Address to the Public*, published by him, in 1789, as President of the Pennsylvania Society for promoting the abolition of slavery, and the relief of free negroes, etc., he proposes a "plan for improving the condition of the free blacks," one article of which is as follows:

> "3. A Committee of Education, who shall superintend the school instruction of the children and youth of the free blacks. They may either influence them to attend regularly the schools already established in this city, or form others with this view; they shall, in either case, provide that the pupils may receive such learning as is necessary for their future situation in life, and especially a deep impression of the most important and generally acknowledged moral and religious principles." *Franklin's Writings* (Sparks' edition), vol. 2, 513.

That gives you Dr. Franklin's view of a common school education; and I take the more pleasure in quoting it because the times seem inclined for practical men.

Just here I protest against the mistake of one of my friends on the other side, who seemed to take comfort in proclaiming that Dr. Franklin was "an arrant old heathen as ever lived;" a fashion to which gentlemen of "liberal views" are much addicted. The "old heathen" in earlier years compiled a prayer book out of the Church of England's service; but, as evidence of his fixed sentiments, here is an extract from his letter to Dr. Stiles, President of Yale College, written expressly in answer to the question:

"You desire to know something of my religion. It is the first time I have been questioned upon it. But I can not take your curiosity amiss, and shall endeavor in a few words to gratify it. Here is my creed. I believe in one God, the creator of the universe. That He governs it by His Providence. That He ought to be worshiped. That the most acceptable service we render to Him is doing good to his other children. That the soul of man is immortal, and will be treated with justice in another life respecting its conduct in this. These I take to be the fundamental points in all sound religion, and I regard them as you do in whatever sect I meet with them.

"As to Jesus of Nazareth, my opinion of whom you particularly desire, I think His system of morals and His religion, as he left them to us, the best the world ever saw or is like to see." *Franklin's Writings* (Sparks' edition), vol. 10, 422.

Then there is another letter in this same volume, page 281, supposed to have been addressed to Thomas Paine, which I beg leave to read entire, because every word of it goes directly to a point in this case:

"I have read your manuscript with some attention. By the argument it contains against a particular Providence, though you allow a general Providence, you strike at the foundations of all religion. For without the belief of a Providence, that takes cognizance of guards and guides, and may favor particular persons, there is no motive to worship a Deity, to fear his displeasure, or to pray for his protection. I will not enter into any discussion of your principles, though you seem to desire it. At present I shall only give you my opinion, that, though your reasonings are subtle, and may prevail with some readers, you will not succeed so as to change the general sentiments of mankind on that subject, and the consequence of printing this piece will be, a great deal of odium drawn upon yourself, mischief to you, and no benefit to others. He that spits against the wind, spits in his own face.

"But, were you to succeed, do you imagine any good would be done by it? You yourself may find it easy to live a virtuous life, without the assistance afforded by religion; you having a clear perception of the advantages of virtue, and the disadvantages of vice, and possessing a strength of resolution sufficient to enable you to resist common temptations. But think how great a portion of mankind consists of weak and ignorant men and women, and of inexperienced, inconsiderate youth of both sexes, who have need of the motives of religion to restrain them from vice, to support their virtue, and retain them in the practice of it till it becomes *habitual*, which is the great point for its security. And perhaps you are indebted to her originally, that is, to your religious education, for the habits of virtue upon which you now justly value yourself. You might easily display your excellent talents of reasoning upon a less hazardous subject, and thereby obtain a rank with our most distinguished authors. For among us it is not necessary, as among the Hottentots, that a youth to be raised into the company of men, should prove his manhood by beating his mother.

"I would advise you, therefore, not to attempt unchaining the tiger, but to burn this piece before it is seen by any other person; whereby you will save yourself a great deal of mortification by the enemies it may raise against you, and perhaps a good deal of regret and repentance.

"If men are so wicked *with religion*, what would they be *if without it.* I intend this letter itself as a *proof* of my friendship, and therefore add no professions to it; but subscribe simply,

Yours, B. FRANKLIN."

I have gone into the history and origin of this clause in the Constitution for the purpose, may it please your Honors, of showing that it is no new thing, but has its roots in the early history of the colonies. I claim, in short, that this idea of the public school teaching the general truths of religion and morality, is an American institution, adopted early in the history of this country in place of the rejected idea of Church and State. There is no question but that a great mistake prevailed in regard to the matter of religious liberty, at an early period, in one or two colonies. But it is equally certain that at least one hundred and fifty years ago the true doctrine on that subject was maintained throughout all the colonies, and that long before the Declaration of Independence, this thing of the public school teaching the elementary principles and precepts of religion, as the basis of the body politic, was generally understood as characteristic throughout the country. I trust that we shall one of these days get rid of the idea that this country began on the 4th of July, 1776.

Having shown where this clause came from, and that it is part of the compact which was declared to be perpetual and unalterable; having proved by the earliest records of Congress, and by the authority of a man, one of the most liberal and tolerant of statesmen, that such was the usage of the country, I therefore claim that instruction in all fundamental principles of religion and morality, as provided for in the seventh section of the Bill of Rights, was understood on all hands, at the time the Constitution of 1851 was adopted, to be an integral element of common school education, and one of the fixed institutes of this land, linked back, through the Constitution of 1802 and the Ordinance of 1787, with the period anterior to the Revolution. On that subject the language of the ordinance is unmistakable testimony.

Now, if the Court please, has it been violated? This is not only a right of the citizen, but a pillar of the State, declared such here in this Constitution, in the Bill of Rights. These resolutions do oppose and conflict with the Constitution diametrically. If the man who drew that first resolution had had it in his mind to show disregard for the law thus declared, he could not have framed his intention in better terms. It is not merely misjudgment. It is not merely an unwise exercise of discretion. I say it is in direct contempt of the Constitution. It declares that schools established expressly under that mandate shall not be the means of instruction in the matter commanded.

Now then I come to the only point in which Mr. Matthews approached the real issue. He sought, rather, to avoid it, on the two grounds, that the School Board has absolute, uncontrolable discretion, and that any religious instruction in public schools is inconsistent with freedom of conscience.

To support the first position he quoted the seventh clause of the Bill of Rights down to the words, "it shall be the duty of the General Assembly to pass suitable laws," and there he stopped. And now, said he, the legislature has passed a suitable law but in that law has not directed that religion and morality shall be taught in these schools. And then he laid down a proposition for which no authority can be found; that is to say that, therefore, the School Board under that law possesses an unlimited and absolute authority over this matter which cannot be controlled by any tribunal. Mr. Stallo took a broader position than that. He takes the extraordinary ground that the law which establishes this School Board makes it part of the high legislative power of the State of Ohio. That seems very extraordinary indeed; for when your Honors come to read that law, the act passed January 27, 1853, you will find it is provided in the very first section that this Board are constituted a part only of "the corporate authorities of the city of Cincinnati."

Mr. Matthews argues that there being nothing in this act,—the General Assembly having passed no law that requires religion to be taught—therefore, the power of the School Board, by virtue of that act, to regulate studies and text-books is indisputable. But I say there is no board in the State of Ohio of such absolute power. Much less can a mere School Board assume to have such a prerogative. It is out of the question that this "part" of the city authorities can be greater than the whole; and your Honors know that the whole power of the city, the City Council itself, has been enjoined in these Courts in cases where their discretion was as broad. If the City Council can be enjoined from supplying the city of Covington with water, as an abuse of power, why shall not this School Board be restrained, when they have not only exceeded but done violence to their trust.

But the fatal defect in the learned counsel's argument is that the General Assembly had no such power or discretion to impart. The Constitution gives the Legislature itself no choice; does not say it shall pass "suitable laws" providing whether or not religion, morality, and knowledge shall be inculcated; but commands it thus: "Religion, morality, and knowledge being essential, etc., it shall be the duty of the General Assembly to pass suitable laws *to encourage schools and the means of instruction.*" The purpose of the schools, the nature of the instruction, is not left to its judgment or control. It is fixed. The Legislature has nothing to do with it; and, therefore, as the gentleman said, and said truly, did nothing but establish the schools. If these resolutions of this local board had been passed by the Legislature itself, they would be in violation of the Constitution, and "as clearly void," as said in 1 Ohio State, 77, "as though expressly prohibited, because not fairly within the scope of its legislative authority." The School Board, even on Mr. Stallo's high ground, can not do more than the Legislature itself. There is no discretion about it, either in the Legislature or the Board. The mandate is that they shall establish schools. When that is done, then comes the Constitution into each of those schools and inscribes there upon its walls these golden words: "Dedicated by the State to instruction in religion, morality, and knowledge, as essential to good government."

That, may it please your Honors, is the plain language of the whole sentence in the Constitution, and not to be frittered away by half reading. Nor can I be wrong in supposing that you will ascertain, by exercise of the power which the law gives the Court of looking about and seeing the general customs and opinion of the people, what the religion, the prevailing religion of the people of the country is. It is religion in that clear sense, defined in words which I have quoted from the lips of the great Master; "achromatic" enough for any but the evil eye; but not the religion taught, as some of these gentlemen would have it, in sectarian schools.

What the counsel for defendants propose comes to this: they are simply claiming here that there is an unlimited discretion in this School Board which entitles them to violate the Constitution. That is exactly the sequence of maintaining these resolutions; a discretion to violate law! Who ever heard of that proposition before? There is the command planted in the Constitution, which these men swore to maintain. It declares the motive and purpose of the schools, and plainly it is in some sense to replace that which was utterly abolished by the same section of the Bill of Rights, and that was the power of an established church, spreading abroad the word of God through its ministers. It may be that Mr. Matthews regards "broad religion as a broad humbug;" but such was not the view of the men whom your Honors have to consider—the men who made this law—and is directly against the judgment of men who were as great statesmen as the world has yet seen, and well knew what the true law of liberty means. This word "religion" must here have a liberal but significant interpretation.

As to the point of jurisdiction, we say there can be no such thing as a power or discretion to violate law, either in this Board or in the Legislature. If these resolutions are not an utter "abuse of power," then the words have no sense.

We now come to the other defense, and are met by the zeal and fires of fanaticism itself. It is claimed, and counsel concentrate here all the force of their argument, that because in the first clauses of this 7th section of the Bill of Rights the right of conscience is protected, therefore that overrides the last clause, and the teaching of religion in the public schools must necessarily succumb. But that is not the way to interpret Constitutions. The two clauses must, if possible, be construed so that both shall stand. And it is easy to see how all the parts of this section are to be reconciled. The first clauses plainly relate to the protection of the individual, the last to the protection of the State. The citizen shall worship God as his own conscience dictates, and not be compelled to attend or support any church, nor shall any church have preference by law, nor any interference with the rights of conscience be permitted. Thus far the individual. Then follows the clause which, by a single word, rises above the selfish, and proclaims the safety of the community paramount to all this: "Religion, morality, and knowledge, HOWEVER," mark the word, "being essential to good government, it shall be the duty," etc. If there be any conflict, it is manifest that this is the clause which must prevail.

But I come back gratefully to the freedom of conscience. I am glad that there is a point, and we have reached it at last, at which I can join with my brethren of the other side, hand in hand. For here we are of one accord. We, too, are for the boon of a free conscience. We claim a share in that inestimable liberty. Not only that, but we claim freedom of conscience for all, exactly in these terms of the Constitution: "All men have a natural and indefeasible right," etc. I say the true doctrine,—for I will go clear through here with the gentlemen,—is that a man shall not only have freedom to believe, but that this doctrine must be carried out, so that a man may, moreover, if he must, disbelieve. The man who has that misfortune, though in my judgment the honest skeptic will rather put his hand upon his mouth and his mouth in the dust, and will keep his doubts all to himself and his God, this man, too, I say, is protected. You can not compel him to believe. Here I subscribe to the language of Lord Brougham: "The great truth has gone forth to all the ends of the earth that man shall no more render an account to man for his belief, over which he himself has no control."

No, your Honors; God's truth needs no favor. It wants no covert, no vantage point. It courts the free arena of the universe. Free inquiry, free speech, if you please, provided always that it be decent. And I say, let the zoologists and geologists and archæologists, and all these gentlemen, have their way; the Cardiff giant, if you wish. Let science stretch its line and sound its plummet; scale the firmament, out to the "bounds of flaming space, where angels tremble while they gaze;" sound the ocean's depths; penetrate earth's secrets, deep as the artesian bore can go; search out all animated nature; bring it all out, and the whole of it will but serve the more to praise and magnify Him "whose righteousness is everlasting and whose truth endureth forever." His religion needs no casemates; and if his ministers and servants know their advantage they will meet these gentlemen willingly upon their own ground, for there they can vanquish them always.

I repeat it, let there be freedom for all of us, from the highest to the lowest in faith; from the zenith of Damian's zealotry down to the nadir; down even through materialism and all extinction of hope, even to the depth of Tom Paine, at whose vile blasphemy I stop. Let conscience have a "charter free as the wind."

But no; that is not the idea of our friends on the other side. They are crying aloud here for conscience, but it is for their own, and not with the least charity for ours. There is no reciprocity, no love of their neighbor, in their philosophy. Every man is to set up himself, his conscience, regardless of others, and the result can only be a repetition of the old story of the Kilkenny cats. We shall eat each other up. But, may it please the Court, this is not conscience. This is bigotry. It is the absurdest fanaticism. Conscience lives and lets live. It is content with its own, and seeks no injury of others. That is not the doctrine that prompted these resolutions of the School Board. In this tumult let us not forget that the Constitution prohibits not only "religious," but also any "*other* sect or sects" from ever having any exclusive right to or control of any part of the school funds of this State." "Phraseology more emphatic," says Mr. Stallo, "it would be difficult to devise," and he might have added "more comprehensive." There be "other sects," it seems, than the religious. And in these resolutions we detect a combination of both sorts. But I have shown that there never was a freer field for conscience than existed previous to the sinister combination of these parties to pass these resolutions. Their pretenses are untrue. Nobody was injured. Nobody ever complained.. All was free. The trouble of these gentlemen, then, is not for free conscience. They want it all their own way, and there can be but one result to such a proposition. No court is bound to reconcile a proposition so absurd as that everybody shall be endowed with the right to put his conscience in opposition to everybody else. The man who has the least conscience is, according to this defense, to be the standard. That is what is here proposed. The sect in all this city who have the least faith are to be taken as the criterion of popular education. The theory of these resolutions is that public schools shall teach nothing that is above the level of the lowest capacity in belief; otherwise you are taxing that sect to support your creed. This, too, notwithstanding they are exempted by the rules of your schools from being present or participating in that instruction which the highest law declares is essential to good government. This blind self-worship not only sacrifices the rights and conscience of others, but foolishly demands that the State itself shall yield its first principles to their crude theories. No statesman ever gave his sanction to a government or polity founded upon this idea of total secularization, nor is it possible to sustain a system of government framed upon that principle. It is a chimera, fantastical as that other notion, that Christianity is unfavorable to a stalwart spirit of republicanism. John Hampden and Oliver Cromwell were singular examples.

There is a case of conscience put forward in the answer, but not much pressed in argument, which, if it were not indecorous, would seem like jesting. It is intimated that there are persons in this community who are deterred on conscientious grounds from "employment as teachers" on account of the reading of the Bible. But it would be vain to search for an instance, within the memory of "the oldest inhabitant," of a resignation or refusal on this self-sacrificing ground. Be that as it may, it is enough to say that such a man should seek another vocation. He is no fit teacher for children under the law of Ohio.

I claim, then, your Honors, that this section of the Constitution has a clear, consistent meaning, and interprets itself thus: that while these first clauses are a barrier against any sectarian or church imposition upon the citizen, the last just as absolutely enjoins religious culture in the schools as a necessity of *the State*, and therefore paramount. Your liberty of conscience and belief, your exemption from any church establishment, is to be found in the first terms; but the men who drafted that ordinance, in 1787, having secured these great principles, carefully added that, nevertheless, the public safety being paramount, *salus populi est suprema lex*, and religion, morality and knowledge being essential to that end, schools must forever be encouraged as the means of instruction in all three, and in neither more nor less than in the others. That provision of the ordinance, faithfully and unalterably handed down to you by the Constitution, and wounded by these defendants, now rests in the care of your Honors, as keepers of the law, and there I leave it.

But I am not willing to quit the case upon the mere fiat of the law. I am willing to show upon what I rest my faith.

Why are religion and morality, as well as knowledge, essential to government? Why was it that our fathers held to that sentiment? Because there are but two principles of power in government. The one is the virtue of the people—the power of self government—that gets all its vitality out of the Bible; the other is the power of the bayonet. And you can not govern a nation upon any but one of these two principles. For I say, in general terms, that the nation which throws away the culture and support of religious principle, throws away the only enduring security of self government for the masses, and must come, in no great lapse of time, to force. It is one thing for scholars and philosophers, sitting in their closets, to refine about this matter. Their fine-spun sentiments may do to govern Utopias; but to govern States is another thing. I speak, and your Honors are to judge, of history, of man in the mass and in action, of the forces essential to guide and control nations, not in sunshine and prosperity only, but when storms run high and the State is distracted and rent by the conflict of parties maddened with passion or interest. It is then that safety calls for stronger forces than philosophy and intellect. It must be the deep, eternal forces which curb and compel the most trying emergencies, and which belong only to religious education and faith.

I have invoked the founders of this Republic. But as

European opinion has been quoted, let me read from a speech of Count Bismarck, in the Prussian Chambers:

"Without a religious foundation, the State is only an accidental aggregate of rights; a bulwark against the king; a bulwark of all against all. Its legislation will not be regenerated out of the original foundation of eternal wisdom, but stand upon the shifting sands of vague and changeable ideas of humanity."

That is the practical statesmanship of the strong-handed and strong-headed man who now rules the destinies of Germany. But I am not afraid to go into the enemies' camp. I will venture to quote a writer who was no special admirer of Christianity, and I think has furnished some of the weapons of my adversaries; but he was compelled to make the concession to religion which I now read. I refer to Jean Jaques Rousseau, from whose *Treatise on the Social Compact*, bk. 4, ch. 8, I quote this extract:

"Now, it is of great importance to a State that every citizen should be of a religion that may inspire him with a regard for his duty; but the tenets of that religion are no farther interesting to the community than as they relate to morals and to the discharge of those obligations which the professor lies under to his fellow citizens. If we except these, the individual may profess what others he pleases without the sovereign's having any right to interfere; for, having no jurisdiction in the other world, it is nothing to the sovereign what becomes of the citizens in a future life, provided they discharge the duties incumbent on them in the present.

"There is a profession of faith, therefore, purely political; the articles of which it is in the province of the sovereign to ascertain, not precisely as articles of religion, but as the sentiments due to society, without which it is impossible to be a good citizen or faithful subject. * * * The tenets of political religion should be few and simple; they should be laid down, also, with precision, and without explication or comment. The existence of a powerful, intelligent, beneficent, prescient and provident Deity; a future state; the reward of the virtuous and the punishment of the wicked; the sacred nature of the social contract and of the laws; these should be its positive tenets. As to those of a negative kind, I would confine myself solely to one, by forbidding persecution."

There being no established church, Church and State being

abolished, the public school is the only means left by which you can penetrate and infuse the whole mass of society with the principles which these men declare to be the only safe reliance for a State—especially a republican State. Through the public school the Commonwealth easily and powerfully spreads the simple tenets of political religion, as Rousseau denominates it, and which he defines in a manner clearly adapted to our Constitution and wants. There must be a religious element in public education, or it utterly fails to supply the want. Religion affords security to government, because it holds men not by the uncertain allegiance of present interest or expediency only, but adds the constant, ever-during power of the still, small voice which controls the will and subdues the passions.

Secularized education will not do it. No nation ever obtained even civilization, much less security and happiness, upon the mere light of reason or the laws of nature, unaided by a religious faith. Even Pagan rulers courted their priesthood and consulted the oracles. But what is it we want, your Honors? It is character, national character, sterling public sentiment—the habit, the enduring, universal habit, of resisting wrong and evil; and among others let me instance that which seems to be the consuming passion of the American heart, but which this Bible teaches us is the root of all evil, the love of money. Our people, with a servility to wealth which is unaccountable in a truly republican nation, bow down and worship it as blindly as the Israelites did the golden calf. Hence, the frauds and huge defalcations, the "rings" and corruptions which we read and hear of every day. A man just from the penitentiary, the forger of millions, is followed by maudlin sympathy, as though a martyr in some great work, and that, too, by the public press. These things do not speak well for us, your Honors, and this School Board, instead of "putting down the brakes" upon the moral force of the schools, had better endeavor, by all possible help, to increase it. I beg leave to inquire what has turned up in this city of Cincinnati—what new dispensation—all at once, that encourages these gentlemen to resolve and say it is time to throw away these aids and restraints which our laws, and all experience, declare are essential to society?

[*Mr. King here called attention to the last annual report of the "Cincinnati Relief Union," and read the article, p.* 44, *on* Vice,

Pauperism and Crime in Cincinnati; Its Alarming Increase; Neglect by Parents, *etc.; and continued:*]

That, your Honors, gives you a more correct apprehension of the wants of the State than these resolutions. And to combat these evils requires stronger remedies than reading, writing and ciphering, called "secularized education." No merely intellectual education, I care not if it be the best, will serve the purpose of the State. It only sharpens the bad propensities. If you take the moral and religious instruction out of the schools, it is admitted that you have deprived them of all the resource which thousands of children have. The intellect, despite our pride and boasts, is but the poor vassal of the will. The heart and passions sway it at will; and there is the point of danger. When was the demagogue—be it your newspaper or your stump orator—ever heard to address the intellect, or play upon any key but the licentious passions and prejudices, which he well knows are sovereign?

Now, what do these gentlemen propose to substitute? What do they propose to do for these children who have no church, no spiritual guide, no resort but the school-house?

[*Mr. King quoted largely from a work on the* Necessity of Popular Education as a National Object, *by James Simpson, a Scotch author, sometime engaged in the management of schools in Scotland, and forcibly depicting the inadequacy of education of the intellect merely in schools for the people, "scarcely deserving the name." He quoted also this passage from a letter of Milton to Hartlib:*]

"The end of learning is to repair the ruin of our first parents, by regaining to know God aright, and out of that knowledge to love Him, to imitate Him, to be like Him, as we may the nearest, by possessing our souls of true virtue, which being united to the Heavenly grace of faith, make up the highest perfection."

Also, this passage from Locke's *Thoughts Concerning Education*, section 70:

"It is virtue, then, direct virtue, which is the hard and valuable part to be aimed at in education, and not a forward pertness, or any little arts of shifting. All other considerations and accomplishments should give way and be postponed to this. This is the solid and substantial good, which tutors should not only read lectures and talk of, but the labor and art of education should furnish the mind with and fasten there, and never cease till the young man had a true relish of it, and placed his strength, his glory and his pleasure in it." And in section 147, he adds: "Learning must be had, but, in the second place, as subservient only to greater qualities. Seek out somebody (as your son's tutor) that may know how discreetly to form his manners; place him in hands where you may, as much as possible, secure his innocence, cherish and nurse up the good, and gently correct and weed out any bad inclinations, and settle him in good habits. This is the main point, and *this being provided for*, *learning may be had into the bargain*."

But is this provided for in these resolutions? Do these resolutions meet this, the very spirit of the Constitution? Is this that education and care of the vicious, the idle, those elements most dangerous to society and government, the classes, if your Honors please, which the public school was first and specially instituted to reach. Nobody imagines it was needed primarily for the education of the better classes. The difficulty lies lower down, in a stratum which nothing but the public school can reach; and there, the very strongest inducement for this lowlier class to attend the public schools is the fact that they are attended by children of the better order. This attraction has been found unequalled. The highest advance that the schools of this city ever made in influence, was when our public education was put up to the point which these defendants would now destroy, when the best men in the community found it to be to their children's advantage to send them to these schools.

But I have too long wearied the patience of the Court. In all that I have said I claim that this is an American institution, this thing of the public school teaching religion along with, but distinct from, the church; that America was the first to substitute public schools as a means of instructing the people in religion as well as knowledge; that it was an American institution from the beginning; that it has been imitated by all Europe; that the verdict of all wise nations is in its favor, and that it is now proposed to be thrown away in the city of Cincinnati just as all the world has set its approval upon it.

There has been a good deal said here about zoology. I recollect seeing a poor little blind fish, taken out of the subterranean river in the Mammoth Cave; proving, as I suppose, the fact that the river must be subterranean, because it had no eyes whatever. There being no light the organ lost its purpose; it had shrunk away, and there was nothing there but a slight speck and a slight bony process where the eye might have been. And that is what it is proposed to make out of the children of this city. Educated in a medium destitute of the blessed rays of God's light, the only inspiring source of virtue, brought up purposely in blindness and darkness, with no vision to their souls, they are to be kept here groping about without knowledge of the Creator and Giver of all these things that they are reading in these books of exact science; and I suppose the best of them would be in the sad, helpless condition ascribed to Humboldt by one of the orators at the late anniversary of his birthday, who ended his oration, put the climax to it, by declaring that Humboldt died, having discovered that the universe was governed by fixed laws. Wondrous Eureka! Promethean, yea, godlike science! The great Humboldt, whose mind could glance from heaven to earth, and who penetrated all things in space, expiring with the discovery that the world was governed by fixed laws, and yet knew not, as the poorest little child in the public schools in this city, simply holding the Bible in his hands, could have told him, who was the author of those laws: "the hand that made us is divine."

Just give me the common schools of this country for two generations and I will make it even what you please. In two generations you may make a people what you will by a well regulated system of public schools; and I tell you now that there is not a more formidable phalanx in this town than the four hundred men and women who have your children under their control, and who it appears are now to be deprived of the power of teaching them anything like religion or knowledge of their Maker.

[*Mr. King, as an illustration of his proposition, pointed to Prussia, where, by means of the common school, the House of Brandenburg have taught the people to turn their hearts up to their king as their father, and have established the most solid and enduring monarchy in the world!*]

I say, in conclusion, we stand, therefore, upon the proposition that the law of Ohio—based and preserved upon this Ordinance of 1787, and upon principles of liberty which, by God's blessing, gave us independence, happiness and prosperity, and which the wisdom of our forefathers, and the success of their institutions secured—not only permits, but commands that religious and moral instruction, so it be consistent with religious conscience, shall—that is the word of the Constitution, if your Honors please, and that is your guide—shall be mingled with the teachings of the common schools, and ought to be encouraged, and not forbidden.

This, we say, is law for us, and it is law, if your Honors please, for all who come among us to dwell under that sacred tree under which we are living and prospering; and it is not right, it is not fair, it is not grateful that we should be called upon by these gentlemen from other countries, to turn our backs upon the institutions of our fathers, when we have enjoyed the fruits they now come to share with us. And, if your Honors please, I say, as those stout old English barons said upon similar occasions: "*Nolumus leges nostros mutari.*" We will stand here upon the ways of our forefathers. We believe in them, and, by the blessing of God, we will live in them and die in them.

More: I say that equality of conscience is not the intent of these resolutions. I say that the true intent and meaning has been divulged in the argument that has been made here in support of them. I beg your Honors to take heed to it, that this first resolution is to be in the hands of teachers not skilled, as my brother Matthews, in dialectics, unable like him to draw this sharp distinction between a "reading lesson" and "religious instruction," and will be executed in the literal sense of the words which you see there. I tell you that these speeches will be taken as the exegesis of those resolutions, that these speeches will be read in the public schools as the exposition by learned lawyers of what those rules mean; and I give warning that those four hundred teachers, who have to sit in judgment upon these resolutions, will have no doubt as to their meaning, and will not accept the meaning that my friend Mr. Matthews has attempted to force upon them. That is the danger, if your Honors please. Recollect who have to act upon that resolution. It is these ladies and gentlemen, unused to the quirks and quibbles of law, and who will take these rules into the schools and execute them to the letter.

Now, I say, if your Honors please, the violation of the Constitution is plain; it negatives the Constitution *in totidem verbis;* and, sitting here in chancery, holding the protective prerogative of *parens patriæ*, as representatives of the power of the State, your Honors are bound to notice and uphold this sacred injunction that schools shall be encouraged, as the means of instructing these children in religion, morality and knowledge, as the basis of the State; not only for the protection of children, which is your primary trust, but still higher for the protection of the State from abuse of its authority. I call upon your Honors, not only by virtue of this positive injunction of the Bill of Rights, but by the wisdom and tradition of our fathers, to stay these resolutions by your preventive justice. And standing here, if I may be permitted, as next friend for that class of children whom this answer demands shall be turned out without the means, which this Constitution intended they should have, of becoming good citizens, speaking, if I may, for the thousands of that class of children yet unborn, I beseech your Honors not to allow this provision of the Constitution to be trampled under foot, but sustain it, uphold it, high above all sects, and give it all its vigor and power, in order that the mischief may be suppressed and the destruction of our schools averted.

In conclusion Mr. King presented the following points of law on behalf of the plaintiffs:

1. That the common schools are established and maintained by the State, expressly as the means of instructing the people in religion, morality and knowledge, as the basis of good government. This, as an article of compact in the Ordinance of 1787, has been steadily adhered to ever since.

Ohio Bill of Rights, sec. 7.
Constitution of 1802—Bill of Rights, sec. 3.
Ordinance of 1787—3d Article of Compact.
As to Ordinance of '87, see 5 Ohio, 410; 9 Ohio, 52; 17 Ohio, 409, 425.

2. That religion and morality, as intended by this provision in the Bill of Rights, are the essential and generally received principles of religion to be derived from the Bible; and as such, will be judicially recognized and upheld by the courts.

> Story on the Constitution—Abr., sec. 986—Original, sec. 1865.
> Act to prevent Immoral Practices, secs. 1, 4.
> 1 S. & C. 447—Amended, S. & S. 289.
> *The State* v. *Chandler*, 2 Harrington, 553.
> *The People* v. *Ruggles*, 8 Johns. 291.
> *Updegraff* v. *Commonwealth*, 11 S. & R. 394.
> *Commonwealth* v. *Kneeland*, 20 Pick. 206.
> *Lindenmuller* v. *The People*, 33 Barb. 548.

3. That the Bible being the foundation and the authoritative exponent of the religion and morality so recognized by the Constitution as essential to government, ought to be held inseparable from the common school education thus enjoined—saving always the rights of those who conscientiously object to the reading or hearing of the Bible, or any particular version of it, by their children.

4. But even if the exclusion of the Bible be held to be within the discretion belonging to the defendants in the choice of textbooks, yet the prohibition of all "religious instruction" in the common schools, being a direct infraction of the terms of the Constitution, and subversive of one of the cardinal principles of the State government, the two resolutions passed by the defendants November 1, 1869, or the first, at all events, are a usurpation and wanton abuse of power, and, therefore, ought to be suppressed by the perpetual injunction of the Court.

5. The jurisdiction of the Court is complete;

First. Because the defendants are not an independent or legislative body, but are a part only of the corporate authorities of the city, by the act of January 27, 1853, Disney, 772—and subjected by that act to the control of the city council in various particulars. As such, they are, therefore, clearly within the special statutory control given to the Court by sec. 159 of the Municipal Code. 66 Ohio Laws, 175.

Second. But independent of this they are subject to the broad, general jurisdiction of the court. *Scofield* v. *Eighth School District*, 27 Conn. 499; 2 Story Eq'y Jurisp. sec. 955 *a*, and sec. 1431; 4 Mylne & Craig, 254; 37 Penn. St. 385; 2 Humphrey (Tenn.), 428; 24 Iowa, 266; 14 Vesey, 245; 1 Duer, 451; 5 Selden, 263.

The claim that they are invested with absolute discretion, by the act of January 1853, can not be maintained, because the act does not purport to confer that power. If it did, the act itself would be a nullity, because the Legislature had no such power or discretion, and could not confer it upon the defendants. 1 Ohio St. 77.

6. The Constitution, and not the Legislature, settles the question. It gives no power over this matter to the Legislature.

It declares "it shall be the duty of the General Assembly to establish schools, and means of instruction;" not that it *may* but *shall;* and not that it shall establish schools and *may* direct what shall be taught; but it imports that religion, morality, and knowledge, all, shall be taught therein. The Legislature may appoint the means by which the object shall be obtained, but could not forbid religion or morality, any more than knowledge, as a subject of instruction. All stand together.

7. If these propositions are true, it follows that these resolutions would be a violation of law, and abuse of power, even if enacted by the General Assembly: and whether regarded as a defect of power, or a wrongful exercise of power, either way it is an abuse of power, and within the control of the court. 1 Ohio St. 77.

8. The cases of *Bloom* v. *Richards*, 2 Ohio St. 387, and *McGatrick* v. *Wason*, 4 Ohio St. 566, do not apply. Neither

case involved the construction of sec. 7 of the Bill of Rights; nor can the *dicta* of judges in those reports be put in opposition to a plain mandate of the Constitution.

9. The injunction prayed by the plaintiffs is not in the nature of a mandamus. The court is not asked to compel, or command the defendants what they shall do, but to say what they *shall not do;* to forbid and prevent the enforcing of these illegal resolutions, by declaring them null and void. *Lumley* v. *Wagner*, 1 DeGex, M. & G. 604; Fry on Specific Performance, secs. 555–6–7.

NOTE TO *page* 300—MARCUS AURELIUS.—Justin Martyr was another distinguished victim of this bloody moralist. The signal martyrology of this reign, shows the imperial hand. Notwithstanding Mr. Hoadly's justificatory note, and Mr. Longfellow's poetic sanction, Aurelius was but a hypocrite in professing to "love justice," and to "respect, most of all, the freedom of the governed." I agree his character is "not an open question." Gibbon himself dismissed it by saying: "Marcus despised the Christians as a philosopher, and punished them as a sovereign." See *Fall of Rom. Emp.*, ch. 16. Dean Milman, whose review is full and fair, says, "his acts are at issue with the sentiments expressed in his grave and lofty meditations." *Hist. of Christianity*, bk. 2, ch. 7. These same Meditations praise the fidelity and manners of a Faustina.

Superior Court of Cincinnati.

John D. Minor et als., *Plaintiffs,* VERSUS *The Board of Education of the City of Cincinnati et als.,* *Defendants.*	*In General Term.* ON RESERVATION.

The Court assembled in General Term on Wednesday, February 15th, and delivered their several Opinions, as follows:

OPINION OF JUDGE HAGANS.

The record of this cause shows that it was reserved here for the opinion of this court upon all the questions which it presents. The cause was argued to us at the November Term, 1869, with great ability and learning. And, as the case presented many novel questions, with few or no precedents directly in point, it is not surprising that the argument took a very wide range, and embraced considerations that were thought then to bear more or less upon those questions. It is not criticism to say that some confusion exists in the arguments of counsel, in that they do not always carefully distinguish the wide difference between sects and sectarianism, on the one hand, and Christians and Christianity, on the other. Nor is it criticism, nor a curious fact—though it is a fact—that the arguments for the plaintiffs were mainly directed to the first of the resolutions which are the subjects of this controversy, while those for the defendants were mainly directed to the second. For, we do not understand that either of the parties to this suit, has abandoned the one or the other of the two resolutions, but rely upon both of them. And, finally, the difficulties that surround the questions involved in this cause do not seem, upon a close inspection, to be very great; certainly not so great that they may not be satisfactorily solved according to the principles of the law, and far less than the transcendent importance of the questions themselves.

I.

The first question that presents itself is upon the proposition of the plaintiffs, that this Court has power to hear this cause and grant the relief demanded. Waiving all technical objections, and casting aside mere verbiage, it is not so much a question of the jurisdiction of the Court to hear and determine the controversy, for the necessary parties, plaintiffs and defendants, and the subject-matter, are before us; but it is a question of power merely, though the power of a Court is a necessary part of its jurisdiction. Is this a case for the equitable interference of the Court?

The propriety of the exercise of this power in this cause depends upon the proposition, that it is within some one of the familiar principles of equity jurisprudence in this class of cases. If, in all other respects, there be no objection to the exercise of the power of the Court, to authorize its interference, "it must be shown," as is well stated by the plaintiffs' counsel, p. 27, "that the action of the Board of Education is illegal, either by reason of positive prohibition or the entire absence of statutory authority, or that in the exercise of power over a subject within their general control, the defendants have acted so capriciously, so wantonly, so injuriously, as to warrant the Court in holding that their action was not based upon a proper sense of duty, and that it is therefore unlawful and void. The plaintiffs must make a strong case; the right must be clear; the threatened injury great, with the entire absence of any other remedy than that which is here invoked."

To the exercise of the power of the Court in this case it is objected that the injunction of the Code (2 S. and C. 1012, sec. 237) "is a command to *refrain* from a particular act;" that immediately upon the passage of the two Resolutions of the Board in question, the old rule was repealed and the new one promulgated, and that therefore there is no act from which we can command the defendants to refrain; and that if there be reason for the exercise of any power at all, it must be either in the direction of forming a new rule for the government of the common schools, or of restoring the old one, which would be rather the office of a *mandamus.* A reference to the prayer of the petition (p. 10) will show the precise extent of the relief demanded, and that the plaintiffs ask for nothing affirmative. To this objection there are two answers. First, that it assumes that the Board had the legal power or discretion to pass the resolutions, which is the very matter to be determined; and second, that the pleadings are not framed with any such view, and even if they were, that this would not be a case to authorize a mandatory injunction as a measure of final relief.

Without stopping to discuss any other question made in this branch of the case, it will suffice to state generally, that a reference to our statutes and the authorities shows clearly that the Court not only has the power in this case of granting the relief demanded by the plaintiffs, if the case falls within any one of the principles of equity jurisprudence already stated; but that the defendants are subject to its exercise.

The State of Ohio v. *The Cin. Gas Light & Coke Co.* (to be reported in), 18 Ohio St. R.
Disney's Laws and Ordinances, 772.
66 Ohio Laws, 179; 27 Conn. 499–504.
2 Story's Equity Jursp. 955, and p. 1341.
Hill on Trustees, 482; Lewin on Trustees, 538, 543.
2 Humphreys, 428; Fry on Spec. Per. 555–6–7.
Lumly v. *Wagner*, 1 De Gex, M. & G. 604.
DeManneville v. *Crompton*, 1 V. & B. 354, 359.
Frewin v. *Lewis*, 4 Mylne & C. 254.
Freeman v. *School Directors, etc.*, 37 Penna. St. 385.
Clark v. *Board of Directors*, 24 Iowa, 266.

1 Duer, 451; 5 Selden, 451; 14 Vesey, 245.
Robinson v. *Chartered Bank*, 1 Eq. Cases, L. R. S. 32.
Weston's case, 6 Eq. Ca. 238.
Regina v. *The Bailiffs of Ipswich*, 2 Lord Raymond, 440.

We are remitted then to the consideration of the principal question underlying this case.

II.

Had the Board of Education the power to pass the resolutions complained of? Is the action prohibited? Or, if it had that power, has it been abused? These are the vital inquiries presented to us by the pleadings and proofs, and we need consider no others.

For the purpose of convenience and brevity, these questions will be considered together in their application to the case.

1. And here the plaintiffs are met at the very threshold of their complaint, by two cases decided by the Supreme Court of Ohio, viz: *Bloom* v. *Richards*, 2 Ohio State R. 387, and *McGatrick* v. *Wasson*, 4 Ohio State R. 571; in which the Court held that neither Christianity nor any other system of religion, is any part of the law of Ohio, and that our statute relating to the observance of the Sabbath "would not stand for a moment, if its sole motive was to enforce the observance of the Christian duty of keeping that day holy." Besides the alleged objection that there are *obiter dicta* in these decisions, and that the Court overlooked at least suggestive intimations in one or two previous cases, it may be sufficient here to say, that if the pleadings in the case at bar, were framed with a view of demanding *affirmative and mandatory relief*, and if the Court could grant it, those cases would be entitled to their proper weight, by which we would be bound. It is not perceived, that as this case presents itself to us, the two cases referred to, have either any force or pertinence. But more of this presently.

2. It is admitted that the common schools of Ohio, are in operation under the present Constitution, adopted in 1851. The last sentence of the seventh section of the Bill of Rights declares that:

"Religion, morality and knowledge, however, being essential to good government, *it shall be the duty of the General Assembly* to pass suitable laws, to protect every religious denomination in the peaceable enjoyment of its own mode of public worship and to encourage schools and the means of instruction."

The Legislature has nowhere defined the purposes for which our common schools were established, has not prescribed text-books as a course of study, the discipline, nor any thing else relating to the administration of the system. Now, it is claimed, that whatever the Board of Education may "choose to omit in reference to the manner of conducting the exercises of the schools, the subjects of instruction, the extent to which that instruction shall be carried, the manner in which it shall be imparted, the persons by whom it shall be given, the times, places," and text-books; that these things have been left by the Legislature absolutely at their disposal; that inasmuch as the Legislature has not required those things provided for in the old rule of the Board of Education, though it might be constitutional for the Legislature to make that requirement in pursuance of the duty enjoined in the Bill of Rights: that the Legislature, having thus left the full and unlimited discretionary power to act or not, in these respects, with the Board of Education, to whom no constitutional duty is addressed and upon whom there is none enjoined, *therefore*, to grant the relief demanded by the plaintiffs, would be to usurp the functions of the School Board! The Legislature may refuse or omit to pass "suitable laws," "to encourage schools and the means of instruction," and thus the duties imposed upon the Legislature by that important declaration of the Bill of Rights, be somehow remitted to the uncontrolled discretionary action of the School Board, subject only to the periodical elections of the members of the Board of School Trustees by the people: and that, therefore, there is no judicial power that can reach or remedy the difficulty. A novel predicament truly! While there is some truth in these propositions, there is a great deal more of error. There are two answers which dispose of the objections that stand in the way of the farther consideration of this case:—first, the Legislature has passed "suitable laws" for the establishment of common schools, in pursuance of the duty enjoined by the Bill of Rights; and, second, the propositions contain the assumption that the School Board may do, what it is claimed the Legislature can not do. The Board has unlimited discretion in the premises, it is said, without regard to the Bill of Rights, and the School Board can not be interfered with, in the exercise of a lawful discretion. Undoubtedly there is no judicial power to restrain even the erroneous judgment of the School Board, lawfully exercised. *Donahoe* v. *Richards*, 38 Maine, 379. But the argument makes the creature greater than the creator; and assumes the very question in controversy, to which thus far we are continually remitted, and by which the plaintiffs' case must stand or fall. The Constitution, and not the Legislature or the School Board, must determine this question.

3. Let us now recur to the resolutions complained of. We shall have no need of the other evidence adduced in the cause, except incidentally.

"*Resolved*, That religious instruction and the reading of religious books, including the Holy Bible, are prohibited in the common schools of Cincinnati; it being the true object and intent of this rule to allow the children of the parents of all sects and opinions in matters of faith and worship, to enjoy alike the benefit of the common school fund.

"*Resolved*, That so much of the regulations on the course of study and text-books in the Intermediate and District Schools (page 213 Annual Report), as reads as follows: 'The opening exercises in every department shall commence by reading a portion of the Bible by, or under the direction of, the teacher, and appropriate singing by the pupils,' be repealed."

The resolutions do not say the religious instruction *heretofore* given, etc., in the common schools is prohibited, though there is a strained and intricate sense in which they may be so understood. Doubtless the Board desired to avoid the appearance of saying so. But even if this were the fair construction, inasmuch, as has already been stated, as the plaintiffs do not ask affirmative and mandatory relief, and inasmuch as we could not grant that relief if they did, it does not seem to us necessary to the determination of the case to consider that view of the resolutions. Still there is a sense in which it may be proper to consider it hereafter.

Quite a wide difference among counsel arose on the argument

as to the true intent and meaning of these resolutions. Without farther calling attention to these differences of construction, it may suffice to say, that the resolutions and the differences about them, resolve themselves into *a prohibition of religious instruction and the reading of religious books, including the Holy Bible, with appropriate singing, in the common schools of Cincinnati;* or, in fewer words, *a prohibition of "religious instruction."* That is the proposition of the resolutions, and everything else in them is either an incident to, or a corollary from, it. They probably mean more; but they do mean that; and that is enough for the purposes of the case. In this the true aspect of these resolutions, it does not matter, when we come to consider the questions presented by the pleadings and proofs, whether the School Board had ever, before their passage, provided for any religious instruction in the common schools of Cincinnati, or not. We have nothing to do, as the cause is presented to us, with any rule, text-book, policy, or management of the schools, or any religious instruction, or its abuses, that may have been adopted or introduced by the School Board, prior to the passage of these resolutions; nor with their operation or consequences, however illegal, inequitable, or even disastrous, they may have been. It will be time enough to consider those things, or any of them, when presented in a proper case, which, it may not be amiss to suggest, could have been very easily done, in several forms. It seems to have been supposed by counsel, that we were to try the validity of the old rule of the School Board, mentioned in the second resolution, as to the practice which had thereby obtained in the management of the schools; and that we were, somehow, to determine whether that practice was there as a matter of right, though there should be nothing in the issues presented by the pleadings that would authorize such a determination. It can not be that we are to make a case that does not appear in the pleadings, and then decide it, either to suit the desire of counsel, or fit their arguments. If we should do so unnecessary a thing, our judgments would be mere *obiter dicta*, and of no more force or value than the opinions of any other equal number of citizens.

It will at once be seen that a very large part of the argument has wandered from, or has no pertinence to, the real question at issue. Such are the historical references to sects, and their well, and, especially, their ill-doing: and those parts of the discussion relating to the truth or falsity of the Christian religion, and the authority and canonicity of the Holy Scriptures: questions which can not be authoritatively decided in a court of justice, but which are of far less moment, than the bearing and conduct of our individual lives.

Stripped, then, of all verbiage, and analyzed to their constituents, the pleadings and proofs present the bare issue, whether religious instruction can be prohibited from the common schools of Cincinnati, by the School Board. And this issue must be judged by the Constitution of the State. And here it will be necessary to refer again to the seventh section of the Bill of Rights:

> "All men have a natural and indefeasible right to worship Almighty God according to the dictates of their own conscience. No person shall be compelled to attend, erect or support any place of worship, or maintain any form of worship, against his consent; and no preference shall be given, by law, to any religious society: nor shall any interference with the rights of conscience be permitted. No religious test shall be required as a qualification for office, nor shall any person be incompetent to be a witness on account of his religious belief; but nothing herein shall be construed to dispense with oaths and affirmations. Religion, morality, and knowledge, however, being essential to good government, it shall be the duty of the General Assembly to pass suitable laws to protect every religious denomination in the peaceable enjoyment of its own mode of public worship, and to encourage schools and the means of instruction."

The provisions of this section are all pregnant with meaning, and must be construed together. There is ample protection to those who believe in Almighty God, and to those who believe in nothing, and to those of all shades of opinion and belief between, with a guarantee of the freedom of conscience to all. There is the complete defense, with which the citizen is surrounded, and his rights, in these respects, secured beyond all hazard or conjecture. The reason of the law may be this: that the religious belief of the individual, or, if he be a nullifidian, then his no-belief, is so much a part of himself, and constitutes so important a constituent of his daily life, that it is of the highest moment, not only for his own happiness, but even for the safety of the State itself, that perfect freedom and security should be assured to him. The terrible religious persecutions and wars in Europe and elsewhere, to which such eloquent allusions were made in the argument, and which stand as a perpetual shame to, and furnish irresistible arguments against, sectarianism, as such, taught our fathers those lessons which they have embodied in the fundamental laws of all the States. It is one of the glories of our country, that we have no religious establishments: and our experience has not only demonstrated the wisdom and justice of these principles, but the success of our example is being felt all over the world.

Thus far, this section of the Bill of Rights has in view the safety, security, happiness, and freedom of the conscience of, the *individual citizen.* Then it proceeds: "Religion, morality and knowledge, however, being essential to good government, it shall be the duty of the General Assembly to pass suitable laws, to protect every religious denomination in the peaceable enjoyment of their own mode of public worship, and to encourage schools and the means of instruction." As if the framers of the Constitution had said to us, we have already guaranteed the freedom of conscience and conduct to the citizen, by negative provisions, *now*, *positively.* "Religion, morality, and knowledge, however," *notwithstandiug*, *at all events*, "being essential to good government," th greatest safety of the State and the highest freedom and happiness of the citizen, how shall these essentials be obtained and secured to it?—its subjects being made up of all sects of religious, belief, and of no belief at all, whose consciences, for which we have already provided the amplest freedom, are the tenderest part of their being, and from which, judging the future by the past, we have reasons to apprehend danger to both the safety of the state and the security of the citizen.

The constitution furnishes two answers to this question and provides two modes of reaching the declared end: "It shall be the duty of the Legislature, to have suitable laws,"

First. "To protect every religious denomination in the peaceable enjoyment of its own mode of public worship."

This provision seems to have been entirely overlooked by counsel; but it is one full of meaning in this connection. It will be observed that in the prior Constitutions of Ohio, this provision does not appear; but the framers of the present Constitution justly thought these agencies too valuable and essential to good government, to be without positive injunctions upon the Legislature to pass laws for their protection.

The spirit that actuated the framers of this provision, is perhaps, illustrated by an anecdote of John Wesley, who, in a dream, visited hell, and found members of every religious sect there, and afterward visited heaven, and found no members of any religious sect there—nobody but Christians. Here then we have an unmistakable clue to the "religion, morality and knowledge" of the Constitution, which are essential to good government. And it is an undeniable fact, that in, and as part of every form of public worship, in the pulpits and on the platforms, and in the Sabbath schools of all sects, every question of religion, morals, science, literature, art, politics, and what not, have been freely discussed and taught, and they have exerted a powerful influence on the government, and have contributed very largely to making it what it is—the boast of modern civilization. These sects have been one of the most convenient and effective conservators of the public morals and agents for the diffusion of knowledge; and thus they have been the leaven of society, and oftentimes, by the sanctions of the morality they teach, the mainstays of good government. Instances will occur to every one. This may be regarded as one reason for National and State Thanksgivings and Fast-days; and for making Christmas a legal holiday. Accordingly, there will be found in our statute books, legislation for the protection of religious denominations in the peaceable enjoyment of their own mode of public worship, as well as a variety of cognate acts, having more or less relation to the same general end. There shall be no respect to the consciences or opinions of nullifidians, or other sects of belief, by law, nor shall any rights of conscience they have, be allowed as against the "peaceable enjoyment of their own mode of public worship," by "every religious denomination," and the reason, as declared by the Constitution, is, because "religion, morality and knowledge," are essential to good government.

As another, and the last mode which the Constitution enjoins on the Legislature to provide for reaching the desired end, is enacts,

Second. "And" — mark the copulative conjunction — "to encourage schools and the means of instruction;" and according to sec. 2, art. 6, the Legislature is to "secure, by taxation or otherwise, a thorough and efficient system of common schools throughout the State."

Here, it will be observed, the words "not inconsistent with the rights of conscience," which appear at the end of a similar clause in the Constitution of 1802, are omitted; perhaps, because the rights of conscience had been abundantly guaranteed by what preceded in the present Bill of Rights, or perhaps, the omission may be significant as strengthening the construction we give this clause.

In pursuance of this duty enjoined by these clauses, the Legislature has established a system of common schools for this city, as will be seen by the various acts which were referred to in the argument. See pp. 109–112.

It is argued, that applying the same reasons and the same construction to these clauses, that we have applied to the one immediately preceding, conflicts with those other clauses in the same section relating to the freedom of the conscience. While all religious denominations may flourish and be secure under the protection afforded for the "enjoyment of their own mode of public worship," and while they get along together in tolerable harmony, or, at least, without any trouble with the State, *here* you come to the domain of conscience, into which you must not enter. And our attention is called to the closing clause of sec. 2, art. 6, of the Constitution, "but no religious or other sect or sects, shall have any exclusive right to, or control of, any part of the school funds of this State," in connection with the declaration of the closing sentences of the first resolution.

And here seemed to be the great stress of the argument, a large part of which would have been suitable in a convention engaged in revising the frame of the fundamental law: it is entitled to no force in a court whose duty it is to construe and enforce the law as it is.

It will be the most convenient to consider objections and construe these provisions together.

It is argued that the introduction of religious teaching, as such, into the common schools, is not necessary, because natural religion, or the religion of the natural heart, is quite enough to answer the purposes of the Constitution; that it is perfunctory; that it is a solemn act of religious worship; that heartburnings, jealousies and violations of tender consciences will follow; that around the conscience the Constitution has thrown its bulwarks and made it the citidal of the freedom of the individual; that it compels a support of public worship, etc., without consent and against conscience; that the exact sciences, etc., are sufficient.

Some of these are considerations of the most momentous importance, and deserve a careful judgment.

First. An obvious distinction obtains between those provisions of the Constitution which assure the protection of *the man*, and those which are purely designed for the security of the *State*. One of those radical things necessary for that security is, the homogeniety of its subjects, not in matters of faith, but as citizens. Whatever tends to break down classes, clans, or nationalities, as such, among our people, is of the highest importance, and is thoroughly in accordance with the spirit of our institutions; so that it shall be our greatest pride, not that we are Protestants, or Atheists, or Catholics, or Jews, or Mormons, or of any other, or no, faith, nor yet that we are, or have been, Germans, Irish, English, Swedes, or Chinese, but that we are American citizens. And this is the more important, as our territory has increased, and is likely to be increased. The common school, it is admitted, has a powerful tendency in that direction. Taking the children at an age when the mind is the most easily impressed, and the aims and affections the most readily molded for the purposes of the State, no wonder the framers of the Constitution, profoundly impressed with the inestimable value of these instrumentalities, should have made the completest provision for the efficiency and thoroughness of schools. With a single stroke of the pen they developed the true philosophy of our government, and put in motion those irresistible forces to secure the unity and integrity of the populations in our midst. The wide difference between the culture and the happiness of the palace and the hovel, must not be seen here, as in the old world; but all are to be entitled alike to the munificent provision, which the State makes in this direction; and our common humanity is to be elevated to the highest pitch of freedom and civilization.

Second. The State is necessary to society and had its existence by nature. It is aboriginal.

> "The State being part of society in which the ideas of right and the means to obtain and protect it are more or less clearly developed, it exists, likewise, of necessity. Man can not live without the State; it is necessary to his nature. * * * And what is this nature? the imprint of all created things stamped upon them by their Creator; the vital principle of life He laid down as the foundation of their essence and being. 'Laws,' says Harrington in his Political Aphorisms, 'are founded in nature. Nature is God.'" *Lieber's Political Ethics*, vol. 1, p. 170.

And this was Aristotle's idea. Now, Religion has exactly the same divine origin. Both the State and Religion grow out of the same element of the human soul; and they can not, therefore, be separated, or treated, one as independent of the other. Hence, we shall find that religion of some sort, was always a necessary adjunct of the State, furnishing both bonds and sanctions, as the pledges of its safety and perpetuity. And, just in proportion as those bonds and sanctions were weak, growing out of the relative purity of the religion of the people, more or less force was necessary for government. But there never was a State that existed long without the bonds and sanctions of some religion. The mistake of most governments has been, that the State has allied itself with Religion; has erected establishments with a view of producing uniformity of faith; an alliance that has been hurtful to both of the parties to it. But while the State and Religion are thus inseparably connected with each other in their origin, and necessary to each other's existence and perpetuity, their objects, spheres, means and ends are widely different.

Third: The necessary connection of Religion with the State, is so obviously set forth and asserted in that clause relating to the duty of the Legislature to pass suitable laws to protect "every religious denomination in the peaceable enjoyment of its own mode of public worship," to secure that "religion, morality, and knowledge, essential to good government," that it needs only to have the attention called to it. Now, the State taxes all citizens to administer, and enforce the legislation for the protection of public worship. That can not be justified on any other ground, than that "religion, morality, and knowledge, are essential to good government." No Legislature can deprive any religious denomination of that "protection in the peaceable enjoyment of its own mode of public worship." Nor, would it be constitutional for the Legislature, or any other body, to undertake to prohibit any religious denomination from furnishing religious instruction, by a law or ordinance, commanding it to refrain from, or to prohibit, the reading of the Bible, or any other confessedly religious book, in public worship, on the ground that somebody's conscience would be thereby violated. Again, the exemption of church property from the payment of taxes, which amounts annually to a very large sum, thereby increases the burdens thrown upon the population at large, of all sects and no sects; and is justifiable upon the principles suggested. The State, however, has nothing to do with any question as to modes of worship, or doctrines, whether orthodox or not, but with a selfish, yet paternal care, looking to its own safety and perpetuity, mainly, stretches out its protecting arm over all alike; and in just so far as common compulsory taxation is necessary to insure that protection of the laws to public worship, and to make up the exemption of church property from taxation, just in so far are we all, in a sense, technical and remote it is true, but appreciable, "supporting places of worship and maintaining forms of worship against our consent," and against conscience.

Fourth: For like reasons, the Constitution enjoins the encouragement of schools and the means of instruction, and that the system of schools shall be made thorough and efficient. While the elementary principles of religion are in the human soul, as arithmetic or any other science is in the human mind, they need development and direction for the good of the State, and the highest civilization and happiness of the subjects; and that is education, instruction. If religious development and direction, then it is "religious instruction." And it is this religious instruction which the State has declared essential to good government, and the means of it which the Legislature is to encourage, that these resolutions prohibit.

The State proposes to use both instrumentalities mentioned in the Constitution, to secure its ends—instrumentalities so closely and intimately connected, that they may never be divorced; but the one protected, and the other encouraged, by a paternal legislation. And this is strictly according to the canons of constitutional interpretation, to which it may be well here to refer.

The clause of the seventh section of the Bill of Rights, has its antecedents, and its two consequents, the latter being connected together with the copulative conjunction, showing that they are both to be used and construed with reference to the former. The very first and fundamental rule of interpretation is, that the instrument is to be construed *according to the sense of the terms and the intention of the parties*, and to gather that intention, where the words are doubtful even, light may be obtained from contemporary facts, antecedent mischiefs, from known habits, manners, and from other sources.

Construing this clause with sec. 2, art. vi, of the Constitution, another rule of interpretation is "that the natural import of a single clause, is not to be narrowed, so as to exclude implied powers resulting from its character, simply because there is another clause, which enumerates certain powers which ought otherwise be deemed implied powers within its scope. The affirmative specification does not always exclude all other implications."

"Constitutions are not designed for metaphysical or logical subtleties, for niceties of expression, for critical propriety, for elaborate shades of meaning, for philosphical acuteness, or judicial research;" but their words are to be construed in their plain, obvious, common sense, unless the context furnishes some ground to control, qualify, or enlarge them. 1 Story on the Constitution, 400, 402, 449, 451, 455; and there are numerous decisions in Ohio to the same effect.

Fifth. The connection of the State with Religion, and the relations of both to the conscience, as set forth in our Constitution, are so tersely shown in an article in *The Bibliotheca Sacra*, vol. xiii, No. 52 written by Dr. Seelye, that its adoption here needs no apology, though perhaps its expressions are not always strictly accurate:

"The authority of the State may never be subordinated to the individual conscience. The State has its own end, of highest freedom; government has its end, of securing to its subjects the enjoyment of this freedom. The State uses Religion as a means to this end; but religion itself is never an end with the State. Every thing relating to the moral and Religious life of its subjects, is of interest to the State, only so far as the State can use it for its own ends. The State has nothing to do with the inner character, and cares nothing about this, so long as the outward action pleases it. To the individual, conscience is of more importance than the State; but to the State, nothing is so important as its own supremacy. If the will of the State come in conflict with the will or the conscience of an individual, the individual may suffer martyrdom, but the State may not waver. That the safety of the public is the supreme law, is a maxim of universal application, and liberty of conscience may never interfere with the public weal.

"The real difficulty in this question lies in confounding two things radically different. The State is for time; conscience, for eternity. The State knows nothing higher than itself; conscience is responsible to God. With the State, religion is a means; with conscience, it is an end. When, therefore, these two spheres come in hostile conflict, we need not ask which should yield to the other; each must triumph on its own ground; the State, for this world; conscience, for the next; the State enforcing its own claims, and conscience adhering to the claims of God; the State using conscience as a means, and conscience triumphing in it as an end.

"Another point should here be noticed: Any argument which affirms a connection of the State with religion, and the duty of the State to maintain its religion, is very apt to be met with the objection that this might sanction any extent of religious persecution. But the objection overlooks some of the principles we have advanced, and has no force against the others. Religion is not, in any proper sense, an end of the State. The State, though having its ground in the spiritual or religious element in humanity, has no aim beyond this present life. Its relations are altogether to mankind as an organized community; and its peculiar and entire province is, to guide the working of this community according to the highest civilization and freedom. This is its true and highest end; and while it may use every thing else subordinately to this, it may use this for nothing. Religion may be employed by the State as a means to secure the end of civilization and freedom; but these latter may never be yielded to subserve any religious advancement. With the individual, religion is primary and an end; with the State, it is only secondary, and a means. To suppose that there could be any other true relation between the two, would make the State a nullity. Hence, whenever the demands of civilization and of freedom are disregarded, and the State tramples on these interests for the sake of any religious considerations, it has gone beyond its true bounds, and altogether transcended its legitimate authority. We may say that the State in such a case is wrong, not because it has sought to maintain its Religion, but because it has made this its *supreme end*, and reduced to an inferior importance what are really its highest objects of pursuit. The principles upon which we must determine the right and the wrong of a State's action, in any given instance, are not those Divine laws which are to control the spiritual life of the individual for eternity. There are temporal and earthly interests for the individual; and it is to subserve these that there is a State, a community, among men. These interests are undoubtedly secured more perfectly through the agency of some religion; and hence the proper and necessary connection of Religion with the State. But in this connection, Religion is ever the servant, never the sovereign. It is to be used to secure some end; and may never be changed by the State so as to become, itself, the end to be secured. The highest question for the State to ask is, not what does Religion demand, but what are the demands of civilization and freedom? since these cover the individual's highest temporal and earthly interests. The wrong of persecution by the State, can be demonstrated on no other grounds. It is wrong because it makes religion an end, and interferes with the highest civilization and freedom, the only true end of the State."

In a word, it is the *political value* of "religion, morality and knowledge," which the State proposes to secure for its varied purposes, and that only. And it is only on this ground that compulsory taxation for the support of common schools, and that a large portion of the moneys collected for that purpose in this county, are distributed in other counties of the State, can be justified.

In looking into the authorities, it will be found that the principles just stated have been sustained.

Cooley's Constitutional Limitations, 470, 471, 477, and the cases cited. It ought to be stated that Mr. Cooley, in his excellent work, in speaking, on page 469, of "things which are not lawful under *any* of the American Constitutions," evidently had not had his attention called to the present, or any of the preceding Constitutions, of Ohio. Otherwise, he would not have made the unqualified declaration that "compulsory support, by taxation or otherwise, of religious instruction," is not lawful.

Donahoe v. *Richards*, 38 Maine, 379, was a suit by a scholar, against the Superintending School Committee for expulsion from the town school, because she had refused to read King James' Version of the Bible. In the course of the opinion, Appleton, J., says:

"The Legislature establishes general rules for the guidance of its citizens. It does not necessarily follow that they are unconstitutional, nor that a citizen is to be legally absolved from obedience, because they may conflict with his conscientious views of religious duty or right. To allow this, would be to subordinate the State to the individual conscience. A law is not unconstitutional, because it may prohibit what a citizen may conscientiously think right, or require what he may conscientiously think wrong."

A fortiori, is this true of the organic law.

And again, on page 412, the same judge says:

"Even Mr. Jefferson, than whom a more resolute champion of liberty never lived, claims no indulgence for anything that is detrimental to society, though it springs from a religious belief or no belief at all. His position is, that civil government is instituted for civil objects, and that spiritual matters are legitimate subjects of civil cognizance no further than they may stand in the way of those objects. He denies the right of society to interfere, only when society is a party in interest, and the consequences being only between the man and his Creator. But as far as the interests of society are involved, its right to interfere on the principle of self-preservation, is not disputed, and this right is resolvable into the most absolute necessity; for were the laws dispensed with, whenever they happen to come into collision with some supposed religious obligation, government would be perpetually falling short of the exigency. There are few things, however simple, that stand indifferent in the view of all sects into which the Christian world is divided."

Sixth. Recurring to section 2, article 6, of the Constitution, already quoted, it will be apparent that the main design of the framers of the Constitution was to prevent any religious or other sect from having *exclusive right to, or control of*, any part of the school fund, which we do not understand the parties to complain of, in the constitutional sense of the words, whatever ma be they fate of this cause. It is not known that any sect or sects has had, in the past, or proposes in the future to have, such right or control. The fund shall not be controlled by any sect or sects, as such, *by any legal or legislative right*, is, obviously, the sense of the clause.

Seventh. It will now be quite apparent that *Bloom* v. *Richards* and *McGatrick* v. *Wasson* have little or no bearing on this case whatever.

Eighth. We have nothing to do with the consequences of a reasonable and proper construction of the law as we find it. In the introduction of Religion in the common schools, the conscience of any of us must be subordinated to the public good, just as we surrender some other natural rights, not only that the common good shall be subserved, but that our remaining rights shall be the better secured. "*Salus populi suprema lex*, is a maxim of universal application, and when liberty of conscience would interfere with the paramount rights of the public, it ought to be restrained." *Donahoe* v. *Richards*, 38 Maine, 412. One thing is certain; that a bad man is a dangerous man; and that the *quantum* of morality to make a man a good citizen is small, and easily comprehended by the meanest intellect is, happily for the State, true.

Ninth. Strictly speaking, we are not called upon to determine what "religion, morality and knowledge" is intended by the Constitution. It will be time enough to do that, when the School Board are properly called to account before a court for the religion and morality they may introduce in the schools, and for the manner in, and extent to, which they are inculcated. The history of schools and of the legislation respecting them, in Ohio and in other States and countries, would then be full of argument. The first Annual Report of Samuel Lewis, our first State School Superintendent, made to the Legislature, in 1838, is suggestive in this respect, as well as the uniform practice subsequently, all over the State, in relation to the management of common schools.

The Resolutions positively prohibit religious instruction, and thus cut off the instrumentality by which those essentials to good government are cultivated, and that is the only question before us.

Tenth. If we should, in any sense, worship science, or art, or the collective wisdom of all ages, or the souls of our ancestors and of posterity like Compte, or intellect like Buckle, or virtue like Bentham, or any other divinity, and make that worship the manifestation of our religious convictions, these Resolutions would prohibit instruction therein and emasculate the schools, besides doing violence to some consciences.

Eleventh. There is no complaint against the High Schools, the pupils of which read the Holy Bible, with appropriate singing, and the Greek Testament, and that too, at an age when opinions are fast crystalizing, and when, if at all, the exclusion of religious teaching is a matter of the utmost moment. Nor yet are these complaints by those children, without parents living, or who are worse than orphans—homeless, helpless, and properly the wards of the State in regard to education—that the "reading of the Bible, with appropriate singing," is either irksome or illegal.

We dismiss all other matters from special comment, brought to our attention, either in the pleadings or argument, because they either have no bearing in this view of the case, or have been disposed of heretofore.

Our common schools can not be secularized under the Constitution of Ohio. It is a serious question whether as a matter of policy merely, it would not be better that they were, rather than offend conscience. With this, however, we have now nothing to do.

But in the view of the Constitution we have taken in its application to this case, the resolutions passed by the School Board are unconstitutional and void.

III.

A remark or two seems necessary and proper with respect to other views of these Resolutions, and especially, as connected with their *effect*, other than the one in the light of which they have been discussed in this opinion. To all other legitimate views that may be said to belong to, and be involved in, the determination of this cause, it will be enough to say, without repeating what has already been said, that it appears, from a careful survey of the character and spirit of the constitutional provisions we have been examining, and of the legislation in pursuance thereof, that it must be true, for the purposes of the state, that Christianity, not in the sense of ecclesiasticism, is the prevailing Religion in the State. That is a *fact*, which seems unquestionably to be recognized in the clause providing both for the protection of religious worship, *and* the encouragement of schools, as means of instruction in religion, morality and knowledge. The framers of the Constitution felt, that the moral sense must necessarily be regulated and controlled by the religious belief: and that whatever was opposed to religious belief, estimated by a Christian standard, and taking into consideration the welfare of the State, would be, in the highest degree, opposed to the general public sense, and have a direct tendency to undermine the moral support of the laws, and corrupt the community. And in a Republic like ours, these would be fatal to it. There appears nothing in the opinions of our Supreme Court, in the cases cited, that conflicts with this idea. Some curious deductions flow from these principles—more curious than practical—such as, that, if Mahommedanism, or some other form of barbarism, were, or should happen to become, the prevailing religion in the State, an application of these principles would be shocking to the moral sense. This course of argument is set out in the cases in 38 Maine and 2 Harrington, *ubi sup.*, and others.

It is not claimed, anywhere, that the Holy Bible does not impress on the children of the common schools, the principles and duties of morality and justice, and a sacred regard to truth, love of country, humanity, universal benevolence, sobriety, industry, chastity, moderation, temperance, and all other virtues, which are the ornaments of human society; and that these principles and duties are not in entire conformity with the demands of the Constitution and the necessities of the State. Nor is it claimed, seriously, that the Bible is adverse, in any translation, to any of these virtues, as proper to be inculcated. On the contrary, its sublime morality furnishes those teachings best fitted to develop the morals, and promote the virtues, that strengthen and adorn both the social and the public life.

In any view that we can take of these resolutions, in this case, they are unconstitutional and void. And these views are sustained by the authorities and references; and they are here grouped together for convenience:

The Ordinance of 1787; 3d Article of Compact.
The Constitution of Ohio, of 1802; Bill of Rights, sec. 3.
Story on the Constitution; sec. 1865.
State v. *Chandler*, 2 Harrington, 553.
The People v. *Ruggles*, 8 Johnson, 291.
Donahoe v. *Richards*, 38 Maine, 412.
Lindenmuller v. *The People*, 33 Barb. 548.
Updegraff v. *Commonwealth*, 11 S. & R. 394.
Commonwealth v. *Kneeland*, 20 Pick. 206.
Vidal et als. v. *Girard's Ex'rs.*, 2 Howard, 198.
Shaw v. *The State*, 5 Eng. 259.
C. W. & Z. Railway Co. v. *The Comm. Clinton Co.*, 1 Ohio St. 77.
Acts to Prevent Immoral Practices, 1 S. & C. 447; amended, S. & S. 289.
The Acts relating to Reformatory, Eelemosynary and Punitive Institutions.

Finally, a thoughtful survey of our individual weakness and imperfections, will certainly teach us to cultivate a spirit of mutual forbearance and charity; and we shall be prepared the better to labor for the elevation of our race, and the spread of true civilization in the earth.

THE INJUNCTION MUST BE PERPETUAL.

OPINION OF JUDGE STORER.

A brief statement of the case submitted for our decision will more clearly present the real question in controversy between the parties :

Under the law of 1829 the common schools of Cincinnati were first organized, and from that time until the passage of the resolution by the defendants, which, it is now claimed, they had no legal authority to pass, the Holy Scriptures, without note or comment, have been in use in the schools, parts of which have been read either by the teachers or scholars as an opening exercise. In the year 1842, at a meeting of the Trustees, it being suggested, among other things, that the Catholic's children were required to read the Protestant Testament and Bible, it was resolved "that no pupil of the common schools shall be required to read the Testament or Bible, if its parents or guardian desire that it may be excused from that exercise."

This resolution was afterward discussed by the Trustees and Visitors of the school then composing the Board of Education, in 1852, when it was again determined "That the opening exercises in every department shall commence by reading a portion of the Bible, by or under the direction of the teachers, and appropriate singing by the pupils, the pupils of the common schools may read such versions of the Scriptures as their parents or guardians may prefer; provided that such preference of any version, except the one now in use, be communicated by the parents and guardians to the principal teachers, and that no notes or marginal readings be allowed in the schools, or comments made by the teachers on the text or any version that is or may be introduced."

This was the rule, and to which no exception seems to have been taken, until November, 1869, when a majority of the Board of Education passed these resolutions. First, "that religious instruction and the reading of religious books, including the Holy Bible, are prohibited in the common schools of Cincinnati, it being the true object and intent of this rule to allow the children of the parents of all sects and opinion in matters of faith and worship to enjoy alike the benefits of the common school fund." Second, that so much of the regulations in the course of study and text-books in the intermediate and district schools as reads as follows : "The opening exercise in every department shall commence by reading a portion of the Bible by or under the direction of the teachers, and appropriate singing by the pupils," be repealed.

The majority of the members justify, in their answer, their action by setting forth "that many of the citizens who were tax-payers, are much divided in opinion and practice upon matters connected with religious belief and worship, and who do not believe the writings contained in the Bible, are entitled to be considered as an authoritative declaration of religious truth; that the version now read is objected to by the Catholic Church as improperly translated, and omits certain books held by that denomination to be canonical, and the volume itself has not its sanction; and there are others who are qualified to teach in the schools, but are precluded by their conscientious convictions as to the verity of the Bible. A large minority, however, state in their answer that the resolutions were passed against their open and persistent opposition, and disclaim all connection with, or responsibility for the same.

The action of the defendants has proceeded no further than the passage of these resolutions, and we are now asked to enjoin all further proceedings that they may adopt to give them effect.

There has been no formal announcement to the teachers of the schools of the new rule, which, it will be seen, is a mere negation of the use of the Bible, singing by the children, and all religious teaching, without declaring affirmatively what books may be read, or what instruction may be given.

We are asked to interfere between these parties, and determine what are the rights of the one, and the powers and duties of the other, under the Constitution of Ohio.

In the examination of this grave question, we may dismiss all reference to the history of the past, the controversies, the persecutions, the dogmatic assumptions of any or all the sects to which reference has been made in the argument.

Nothing is gained by the assertion that the Bible is not the revealed will of God, or that science has so far modified or limited its statements, that the book itself is of doubtful authority. These objections are not of modern origin. There is nothing new or startling in the infidelity of the present day, for the same weapons are used now as in the past by the disciples of unbelief. We have been familiar with these discussions since our childhood, and while allowing to all the largest liberty of believing or disbelieving, we claim for ourselves the same privilege, and ever have, and trust we ever shall, be kindly but firmly the advocate of the plenary inspiration of that volume which is our only safe guide through this world and gives us the happy assurance of another and better when our lives and labors here are ended.

But we need not argue the point; for the old maxim, that the existence of the counterfeit conclusively proves there must be that which is genuine, is a sufficient answer to every cavil. Besides, the cause of truth is never advanced by satire upon the opinions or idiosyncracies of others, however sharp the attack or dark the picture.

There never can be any just denial of a fundamental truth, sustained only by reference to the faults or imperfections of those who believe and uphold it, and he who draws his conclusions of the verity of great truths from such a course of reasoning, will at last find himself in the position of one who, having examined the highest productions of art in statuary, should find at last that the only impression left on his mind was that the sculptures were naked.

Separated thus from the mass of irrelevant matter in which the question before us has been involved by the learning and the industry of the counsel who have addressed us, if we regard the different standpoints from which they have argued, the propositions to be solved are simply these: Had the defendants, in the exercise of the discretion given them to direct the course of study and decide upon the text books to be used, the legal right to declare he Bible should no longer be read in the schools, where for nearly half a century it had been used as the daily exercise, and, coupled with its exclusion, the denial of all religious instructions and the reading of religious books shall be prohibited.

If no such power existed, may we not adjudge the board has acted in "*ultra vires*," and their resolutions are void. What, then, does our present Constitution prescribe. By sec. 7, art. 1, it is ordained that "Religion, morality and knowledge being essential to good government, it shall be the duty of the General Assembly to pass suitable laws to protect all religious denominations in the peaceable enjoyment of their own mode of public worship, and to encourage schools and the means of instruction." The section commences with the assertion that "all men have a natural and indefeasible right to worship Almighty God according to the dictates of their own conscience. No persons shall be compelled to, erect or support any place of worship, or maintain any form of worship, and no preference shall be given by law to any religious society, nor shall any interference with the rights of conscience be permitted." This may be said to be a literal transcript of sec. 3, art. 8, of the Constitution of 1802, and that in substance is borrowed from art. 3 of the Ordinance of 1787. These are the affirmations of a great truth, and to vindicate which we believe they were inserted in our organic law.

They recognize the existence of a Supreme Being, and the fact is judicially admitted that religion, as well as morality and knowledge, are essential to good government, and consequently, make it imperative that schools and the means of education shall be regulated by the Legislature.

Now it will be admitted that no preference can be given to religious sects, as such, as difference of opinion upon religious subjects is not only tolerated, but the right to enjoy it is given to its fullest extent. There is a manifest distinction, however, between religion and religious denominations, as they present all shades of theoretic as well as practical belief. Hence it is we may recur to the clause so prominently presented in the section of our Bill of Rights that secures to all the worship of Almighty God, as the exponent of what we may rationally conclude the founders of the Constitution intended by the general term religion. This, moreover, is the definition of the word as we find it explained by the best lexicographers—Johnson and Richardson. Webster and

Worcester—and one may well conclude it can not be extended to those who know no other Divinity than that which was inscribed centuries ago upon the altar in Athens—"The Unknown God." If, then, the recognition of the Supreme Being is the true meaning to be applied in this connection let us inquire if the Legislation of our State, in very many instances, does not fully sustain the idea.

We find in the class of exemptions of personal property from execution, the family Bible is especially named, and this, too, before the homestead and the present privilege of the debtor were secured by law. So, in the Apprentice law, one of the conditions in the indenture binding on the master is that he shall give to the apprentice, at the close of his term, a new Bible; and in the statute regulating county jails, each prisoner is to be supplied with a copy of the Bible. (1 S. & C. 746.) By the 19th section of the Penitentiary law (1 S. & C. 918), it is made the duty of the Warden to furnish each criminal with a Bible—who shall permit, as often as he may think proper, regular ministers of the Gospel to preach to such convicts, and we are assured the same rule is adopted in the government of all of our benevolent institutions, including the House of Refuge and Reform School. Now, it must be recollected that all these institutions are sustained at the public expense, the property of every person in the State being taxed to furnish the necessary means. And yet, while the Scriptures are made indispensable for every penal, reformatory and benevolent institution, it is claimed they can not be introduced into the common schools of Cincinnati, and if found there, either used or read, shall thereafter be prohibited.

Nay, more, while that volume is found in every court of justice, and the two houses of the General Assembly, upon which we, the Judges of this Court, have been sworn to administer justice and uphold the Constitution and laws, it is expelled from our common schools, thus making it the only exception to its recognition as an exponent of religion and morality. There is, then, no express prohibition of the Bible, by law, as a book to be read or used in the education of our youth, nor do we think that it can be implied from the letter or the spirit of our organic law.

We have said that religion necessarily depends on the belief in the existence of a God—not the offspring of the imagination only or dependent for its authority upon what has been called certain fixed laws, nor yet limited to the narrow domain of reason, but an infinite power above us and over us, dealing with men as moral agents, imposing upon them His sanctions, while demanding obedience and accountability to His laws. This is the lowest view we can take of the Supreme Being. Still it is taught only by revelation, not of the rocks or the pride of the intellect, or the argument of the watch we find in Paley's Natural Theology, but by the answer of our own consciousness, that there is a divinity that stirs within us, which can not be satisfied with only cold demonstration, but adopts the beautiful sentiment: "Where reason fails there faith adorns." If we are challenged to prove what can not be demonstrated as an objective fact, we may well conclude with Bishop Berkley, "that the objections made to faith are by no means an effect of knowledge, but proceed rather from an ignorance of what knowledge is;" or the profound remark of Sir William Hamilton, that "no difficulty emerges in theology that had not previously emerged in philosophy."

Reason gains nothing by repudiating revelation, for the mystery of revelation is the mystery of reason also, is the profound observation of Henry Mansell, in his great work on the Limits of Religious Thought.

A religion of the intellect, disconnected with the supernatural, that has no other sanction than what is claimed to be reason, can not have been intended by those who framed our several Constitutions, or enacted the many statutes directly or remotely referring to the clause in the Bill of Rights, and we are pressed with the conviction that it was their purpose to authorize no other definition of the term "religion" than that which was understood to be the worship of Almighty God, who alone has endowed man with a conscience.

A further examination of the statute on the subject of grants for religious purposes and for the *support of the Gospel*—the title as given by the late Judge Swan, in his carefully compiled volume of the Laws of Ohio, published in 1825—we find that the whole space between pages 134 and 246 is devoted to the various enactments on the subject which we have referred to. These pages include the incorporation of colleges and academies, and expressly refer to the education of youth as important to morality, virtue, and religion; directing, also, how the income derived from section 29, in the Ohio Company's purchase, and the grant to John Cleves Symmes, set apart for religious purposes, should be appropriated and divided among the different denominations. And the law to incorporate the original surveyed townships, now in force (1 S. and C. 1580, sec. 13), provides that each and every denomination or religious society shall receive a dividend of the rents from the ministerial sections, according to their numbers, to be appropriated for the support of religion, at the discretion of the society. But the society must be formed and sustained for a religious purpose, as the language would seem plainly to import. Our Supreme Court, moreover, has given a judicial construction to the term in 7 O. S. 64, *The State* v. *The Trustees of Township* 9:

> "The society thus formed must be religious, and not for mere secular purposes; for the statute describes the society entitled to the fund as a religious society. Religious societies of sects and denominations are founded for the purpose of uniting together in public religious worship and religious services, according to the customary, habitual, or systematic forms of the particular sect or denomination, and in accordance with and to promote and enforce their common faith and belief."

From what we have already said, we are led to the conclusion that revealed religion, as it is made known in the Holy Scriptures, is that alone that is recognized by our Constitution, and has, by a long series of legislative enactments, been sustained by the General Assembly. On no other ground could blasphemy be made criminal, not merely against the Supreme Being, but extended as it is to the Son and the Holy Ghost, names to be found only in the Bible. Indeed, we are impressed with the belief that the Legislature merely expressed the great public sentiment, else the law against such profanity would long since have been repealed.

But it is said by one of the counsel who has so ably argued for the defendants, "that when the Constitution says religion and morality and knowledge are essential to good government, it simply means that the intuitive sense of right and wrong shall be brought out by exercise and developed; the only religion that it considers vital to the preservation of the State is that which is written upon human nature." This is a bold proposition, and one that is, it seems to us, most difficult to sustain upon any other ground than that which would justify the devotee to be crushed beneath the car of Juggernaut, the Hindoostan widow to cast herself upon the funeral pile of her husband, or the revolting cannibalism that once prevailed in the islands of the South Sea. Nay, further, on this hypothesis we may vindicate the orgies of the heathen temples in the most enlightened ages of the past, when the Roman could utter the exclamation, "*O, dii, immortales*," and yet sacrifice to Venus, to Bacchus, and to Mars.

To our apprehension it does not appear probable that our lawmakers would have sanctioned such a rule, if it had ever been proposed, and their silence as to such a suggestion is rationally conclusive that they never could have seriously entertained it. Without the teachings of the Holy Scriptures there is, we believe, no unvarying standard of moral duty, no code of ethics which inculcates willing obedience to law, and establishes human governments upon the broad foundation of the will of God. Hence, it was the great purpose of the clause in the Bill of Rights, to which we have already referred, to announce the deep conviction—we might say, the authoritative opinion—that religion was necessary to good government, not the shadowy view of man's duty which lets in upon the vision a faint ray of light to make the surrounding darkness more visible, but the recognition of an almighty power, demonstrable, it is true, by what meets our vision, but alone subjectively taught by his revealed will.

Yet, it is said the natural conscience is to be taught, the instinctive sense of right and wrong is to be brought out by exercise and developed; but we are not told what is to be the exercise, or how the development is to be effected. What is to be the process by which the minds of the young are to be cast into the crucible and refined from any innate or acquired impurity? What high and holy motive is to be addressed to the pupil, when his origin, the purpose of his probation on earth, and all knowledge of a hereafter, are not only to be withheld, but the volume which discloses them is ostracised as one not only unfit to be read, but as conflicting with the conscience that has never yet, perhaps, been enlightened by its truth?

It can not be claimed that good government can exist where there is no religion which embodies the idea of obedience to God; but on the contrary, the will of every man may be the true arbiter of his conduct and the measure of his responsibility; for if such a dogma should be allowed, all restraint upon human passion, every check upon the oppression of the few by the despotism of the many would cease, every individual being a law unto himself, defending his conduct by the assumption that he conscientiously believed he had the right to do so. In such a war of conflicting elements the strife of opinion would be uncontrolled, and the moral power of our republic be made to depend upon individual caprice, precipitating, at no distant day, the now freest and happiest government on earth into remediless ruin. We will not anticipate such a catastrophe; but if the shipwreck shall ever occur, it will a be fatal one.

The whole argument that seems to us reaches the real question before us is predicated upon the supposition that the Bible is a volume whose teachings lead to sectarianism, and which ought not, therefore, to remain in the schools.

We do not admit the assertion, either in whole or in part. What we understand by sectarianism is the work of man, not of the Almighty. We are taught in the Scriptures that we are all the children of a common Parent, who is our Father and our Friend, that we are all of the same blood, a common unity pervading the race. Such, however, is not the human lesson. Learned men are not satisfied with the plain statement of revelation. They have divided the human family into distinct parts, giving to each a separate origin. We learn from the Bible to forgive injuries, to deal justly, to elevate our conceptions above the objects that surround us, and feel we were born to be immortal. Not so are we thoroughly taught by the profoundest system of human philosophy.

A volume that unfolds the origin of men, the beginning of time, and the assurance of an eternity when the present dispensation shall end, can not, upon any rational principle, be said to indicate religious exclusiveness. It has, we admit, seen its dark days, and has contended with bitter foes, yet it has suffered as much, if it could suffer at all, from the mistaken zeal, or the dogmatism and intolerance, of its professed friends. If the Hebrew, the Samaritan or the Septuagint version of the Old Testament had not been burdened by the glosses and the traditions of men, and the book of the law been left untouched as it came from the hand of Moses, or as it was found in the Temple by Hilkiah, it would now be a clear, yet simple and conclusive record of the Divine will. And so of the decrees of councils as to what is or what is not to be believed, and the numerous commentaries that have been written in modern times upon every book and every verse of the New Testament, which have, many of them, obscured the meaning of the record, diluted its truths, or vindicated some favored theory—if all these had been omitted, we should find that "Scripture is given by inspiration of God, and is sufficient for doctrine, for reproof, for correction and instruction in righteousness."

We marvel not that the mixtures and devices of men have obscured revelation when scarcely a week passes by without the annunciation of some new annotation or analysis, or the defence of some peculiar dogma.

All these, we admit, tend to the same result, which is necessarily a devotion to a sect. But we can not admit that the Bible necessarily induces any such consequences.

If it is candidly examined, studied without preconceived prejudice, its truths admitted to the test of enlightened conscience, we doubt not the answer always will be as it ever has been, the acknowledgement of its sacred character, and a veneration for its truthfulness.

It is urged, however, that the conscience of the Catholic parent can not permit the ordinary version to be read as an exercise, as no religious teaching is permitted by this church, unless it is directed by the clergy or authorized by the church itself, and it is, therefore, offensive to the moral sense of those who are compelled to listen when any portion of the Bible is read; but the rule has long since been abolished requiring children to be present, or to read from the version now in use, if it should be the expressed wish of the parents first communicated to the teachers.

The reason of the objection, then, would seem to have ceased. More than this, it is in evidence before us that our Catholic friends have their own separate schools, and very few of their children attend the common schools, while in one of these schools the Douay translation of the Bible is read as a daily exercise.

The Catholic does not deny the inspiration of the Scripture, but does not admit the accuracy of what is called King James' version. Yet, with comparatively few exceptions, the omission of the Apocryphal Books, and the rendering of some peculiar passages, we do not suppose there is any very essential difference between the versions. Jerome was an accurate scholar, and has faithfully translated the Old Testament from the Septuagint, and the Gospels and the Epistles from the Greek, and we would freely say that no reasonable objection can be urged against the introduction into the schools of Wyckliffe's translation of the Vulgate, if its language was modernized, especially as it was the first attempt to render the Scriptures into English. As to the omitted Books, it is said that St. Jerome first called them Apocryphal, with the remark: "*Canonici sunt ad formandos mores non ad conformandos fidem.*"

But is it consistent with this claim of counsel that, even if the Bible should be prohibited, Catholic children would not attend the common schools, unless subject to the teachings of their spiritual guides? The schools have been denominated godless, while the Scriptures are yet read as a daily exercise. What must they become, and what will they be termed, when the Scriptures are forbidden?

What appears to us to underlie this view of the case, is the alleged injustice that Catholic parents, in common with other property-holders, should be taxed for the support of schools that are independent of the control of the Church, and consequently, opposed to its whole economy.

This has been pressed in argument, though no one of the counsel for the plaintiffs or defendants have intimated there should be a division of the school fund. With the justice or injustice, therefore, of the mode of taxation, we have nothing to do in deciding the questions submitted to us. If the point should ever arise, we trust we shall attentively consider all the objections that may be raised to the present organization of the schools; but it furnishes no ground of argument against the reading of the Bible that the taxes for the support of the schools are not equally assessed or properly distributed. We can not believe that any portion of the community, either from prejudice or the belief of wrong done, when the judicial tribunals are open, and their complaints may be heard, would imitate the strong man of old by laying their hands upon the pillars which support the temple, when the inevitable result would be a common ruin.

Nor do we perceive how the reading of the Old Testament can offend the conscience of a pious Israelite. That people have preserved intact the sacred record which so graphically and truthfully describes their origin, their dispersion, their wilderness journeyings, their persecutions, the proscription of their race for centuries, until they have found freedom in its truest sense in this Western world. They are no longer restricted in their industrial efforts, and are daily learning that the genius of our institutions proclaims the glorious equality of all men before the law. Their prophets have foretold, and their bards have sung what they now witness in fulfillment. Their children have been, and still are educated in the public schools, and in the higher departments of learning are exhibiting the ability and independence which their forefathers illustrated before their temple was destroyed, and Jerusalem was yet the joy of the whole earth.

Under the same resolutions that the conscience of the Catholic is protected, that of the Israelite is equally shielded from injury. When Voltaire, in his Philosophical Dictionary, vilified the Old Testament history, denied its authority, scorned its pure morals, claiming that the relations of the deluge, the exodus from Egypt, the passage of the Red Sea and the Jordan, were mythical, he was confronted boldly and sorely defeated by the noble arguments, the profound learning of the Portuguese Jews, then residing in Amsterdam. This work, of which we have an English translation, is well worthy the study of minister and layman.

It is urged for the defense that there is a class who cling to no particular sect, who do not regard the Scriptures as inspired, but, on the contrary, hold them to be human productions, and therefore their consciences are not consulted. If this is true, it is not perceived how disbelief is any objection to the reading of a book which may enlighten, if not improve, the moral faculties. The mere denial of a fact does not disprove it, and if we can not apprehend a truth, it is no ground to refuse the perusal of a volume that may remove doubt; at least none need be anticipated when the reader's faith and philosophy are also dependent on the fitness of things controlled, as he claims them to be, by fixed laws.

We therefore conclude upon this branch of the case, that the premises upon which the whole argument of the defendants depends as to the rights of conscience being violated, have been assumed, and not proved to exist. On the other hand, we may well suppose the consciences of the many thousands who protest against the resolutions of the Board of Education, if any wrong may have been done, have equal cause to complain.

Nor do we think that the mere reading of the Scriptures without note or comment, and in detached sentences, can be deemed an act of worship, in its commonly received definition. The lessons selected are, in all probability, those which elevate the mind and soften the heart—an exercise not only proper, but desirable to calm the temper of children, while it impresses the truth of personal responsibility for good or evil conduct. It furnishes a perfect standard of moral rectitude not to be found elsewhere, which is immutable as it is authoritative. No prayer is required of the teacher or the scholar, though the simple and beautiful *pater noster* would not, we believe, be out of place.

If, then, "no religious test," to use the language of the Bill of Rights, is required of teacher or scholar, if no act of worship, in a sectarian sense, is performed, if no sectarian or denominational teaching is introduced, and even the possibility of either is prevented by the resolution long since promulgated, that those who desire it may be exempted from the general rule, we can not see how the defendants can justify the exclusion from the schools of what has been permitted there for nearly half a century without rebuke. It can not be that a new revelation has been received by the Board of Education of what is their responsibility to the public, or that they, as a body, have become wiser, better informed, or have a clearer perception of moral duty than their predecessors, for these suppositions were not made, much less suggested, and we are consequently led to believe that there has been hasty, unnecessary and unauthorized legislation, neither demanded by the state of fact upon which that legislation is said to be based, nor yet the wish of those whose sons and daughters have heretofore been or are now being educated in the public schools.

Leaving these questions of secular teaching, and what is claimed to be worship, may it not be admitted that the Bible may properly be read for its moral teaching, its history, its geographical descriptions, its pure Saxon English, so simple that every ordinary capacity may be instructed, and the most exalted intellect find material for profound thought.

Where else do we find an intimation even of the origin of our world and of man, briefly stated, without explaining the mighty forces employed in the work of creation? When Longinus exclaimed that the true idea of the sublime was contained in the expression, "God said let there be light, and there was light," he gave but the echo of the same thought which has impressed the philosopher for ages. Such a gem would have established in his estimation the veracity of the volume, had it been questioned.

There has not been, we may assert, and never can be, a system of ethics that it not directly or remotely dependent on the lessons taught in the Scriptures, and to this source we may trace all that is "pure and lovely and of good report" among men. This, then, is not a dangerous volume to place in the hands of the young. Historically, it is the oldest record of past time. Centuries before Herodotus, the father of history, wrote his annals, all the books of the Old Testament, except that of Malachi, had been written, and were known and read wherever the Israelites were dispersed. We find here the earliest mention of Assyria, Babylonia and Egypt. The record of time is contemporaneous with the oldest dynasties, verified as they are by the cuneiform inscriptions found among the ruins upon the Tigris and Euphrates, and the hieroglyphs in the sarcophagi disinterred from the catacombs on the Nile. Palestine, with all her old associations, is revived, when the traveler uses the sacred volume as his text-book. It is a veritable itinerary, and alone has enabled the scholar to determine the places memorable for the demonstration of Jehovah's power, as when the sun stood still at Ajalon, or the shadow went back on the dial of Ahaz. Bethlehem, and Hebron, and Damascus, the whole valley of the Jordan, are here described accurately, and without which their former history would be imperfectly known.

Can it then be said that what the prophets of the Old Testament foretold of Nineveh and Babylon, when the excavations of

Leyard and Botta, and the researches of Rawlinson have confirmed the prediction, may not be perused by the children as a part of their education in the history and geography of the world? When Volney's travels in Syria, which describe the destruction of Tyre and Sidon, are not prohibited by the Board of Education, is it just to exclude what the Sacred Volume asserted would be their fate a thousand years before their destruction? There is to be no censorship over the Latin and Greek classics, or German and French literature, however exceptionable may be the production; the crusade is against the Bible only, the first printed volume after types were invented, and which, since 1450, has been regarded by millions as the word of God—a book which, from its first publication in Latin, has been translated, and is now circulated in more than two hundred languages; a volume recognized by every civilized government as sacred, and has ever retained, and, we trust, will ever retain, as contradistinguished from all other books, the name it bears—THE BIBLE.

As a work of history or geography, therefore, it bears the highest evidence of its accuracy, and commends itself to every intelligent mind as a faithful record of facts. Its prohibition, then, may, for like reasons as those given by counsel, include the works of Josephus, Pope's Essay on Man, Milton's Paradise Lost, Hallam's Middle Ages, Prescott's Phillip II., and Motley s History of the Netherland's, for each of these offend some conscience on the ground that private judgment is interfered with.

The resolution which dismisses the Bible forbids all religious instruction, as well as vocal music. It is a sweeping edict that comprehends not only the Holy Scriptures, but all other religious instruction, leaving the schools practically "without hope and without God;" not even natural religion is to be taught, the existence of a Deity, or the responsibility of man to his Creator. All is left a blank, if the inquiring pupil should interrogate the teacher as to his origin, he may be referred to the geologists, but not to Genesis. If he should be asked why it is that the Sabbath day is to be observed, he may be postponed until the teacher obtains the consent of the Board of Education to answer the question, thus leaving the scholar in doubt as to the meaning of what is constantly passing before his eye.

If, peradventure, at home, the pupil should have read of the Deluge, the instructor, if asked when and where it occurred, he may, if he is a mere humanitarian, assure the inquirer that the statement is a myth and not a verity. Such a state of moral discipline could not have been anticipated when the common schools were organized and the course of study prescribed, else we believe no pupil would have been taught, and no building been erected for his accommodation.

In this connection we can not well understand why the axe was not laid at the root, and the high schools which are equally supported by taxation, included within the terms of the excluding resolution. It is true that the Board could not, *ex officio*, have regulated the Trustees of those schools, but they might have intimated to them what they believed to be the true purpose of education. As it is, though the children in the preparatory department are forbidden to do what we believe they ought to do, whenever they enter the high schools, which it is their privilege to enter when properly prepared, they may read the Scriptures and receive such religious instruction as the spirit of the Constitution secures to them as individuals, and may well demand they should know that religion, morality, and knowledge are necessary to good government, without which there is no security for the public safety, or the protection of individual right.

Much stress is laid upon the idea that the former rule prescribing the reading of the Scriptures was compulsory upon the scholars, and so were all regulations in the course of instruction; but compulsory clauses do not make the rule illegal if right in itself. That it was right and proper we have already affirmed, and we need not again state the fact.

We have been referred to the opinions of many celebrated men, on theoretical questions, where public education is involved; and, while we have been instructed by their abstract notions, we can not defer to their judgment, unless we are satisfied they have investigated the subject from an American standpoint, where the largest liberty is to be tolerated, and unless the great principles that underlie our peculiar form of government are not endangered by the admixtures of a philosophy that would ignore religion.

In the progress of science the minds of many have become

greatly materialized, when questions of faith are involved, and it becomes us to be careful what we admit or affirm, as the result of dogmatic teachings, either in religion or morals. Until our trans-Atlantic brothers have become practically acquainted with the workings of our political system, their views of our social system, however learned, are entitled to but little weight.

On the whole case we are satisfied that we have complete jurisdiction of the subject before us, and of the parties; that the matters alleged by the plaintiffs and admitted by the defendants present just and equitable grounds for our interference. We so decide, because we are satisfied that the powers conferred on the defendants have been transcended; that the resolutions prohibiting the Bible and all religious instruction are *ultra vires*, and therefore void.

We have not referred to any adjudicated case, as those quoted by one of our colleagues fully justify us. We stand upon the admitted principles, as true in law as in equity, that the unauthorized acts of a corporate body or trustees, whose powers are prescribed by law, may be restrained. While we hold that every form of religious worship is to be alike protected by law, and the conscience of every man can not be questioned; while the broad shield of the Constitution is over all our citizens, without distinction of race or sect, we can not ignore the right of the petitioners to the relief they have sought, nor can we, with our views of legal duty, sustain the action of the defendants.

A majority of the Court are of this opinion, and a perpetual injunction will be therefore decreed, as prayed for in the petition.

OPINION OF JUDGE TAFT.

I.

I regret to find myself in a minority on this question. Nothing but a sense of duty has induced me to prepare a dissenting opinion.

The action in this case is brought to enjoin the Board of Education of the City of Cincinnati, from acting under the two following resolutions, which were adopted Nov. 1, 1869, viz.:

"*Resolved*, That religious instruction and the reading of religious books, including the Holy Bible, are prohibited in the common schools of Cincinnati, it being the true object and interest of this rule, to allow the children of the parents of all sects and opinions, in matters of faith and worship, to enjoy alike the benefit of the common school fund."

"*Resolved*, That so much of the regulations on the course of study and text-books in intermediate and district schools (p. 213, Annual Reports), as reads as follows: 'The opening exercises in every department shall commence by reading a portion of the Bible by, or under, the direction of the teachers, and appropriate singing by the pupils,' be repealed."

The injunction is sought against both resolutions, but on grounds which apply mainly, if not exclusively, to the first.

I propose to consider them separately, and in the order in which they were adopted. The object of this resolution is sufficiently indicated by its language, "it being the true object and intent of this rule, to allow the children of parents of all sects and opinions in matters of faith and worship, to enjoy alike the benefit of the common school fund."

I see no reason to suppose, the Board of Education intended anything more or less, than it has thus expressed. Its opinion evidently was, as the majority have said by their answer, that in the great diversity of religious faiths which exists among us, true conformity to the spirit and language of our Constitution could be best secured, by confining the instruction in the common schools which are supported by general taxation, to secular knowledge and moral and intellectual culture, leaving what is commonly understood by religious and doctrinal teachings, to other and more appropriate instrumentalities. By the words "religious instruction" as used in this rule, I understand special or formal religious teaching, such as would be in conformity to the views of some one, or more, of the numerous religious sects, and by consequence, would be offensive to some one, or more, of the other religious sects. The Board would probably have used the word sectarian, in connection with, or instead of "religious" instruction, but for the dispute that would have arisen, as to what was sectarian, each sect being likely to suppose its own views free from that objection. But, that its purpose might not be misunderstood, the explanatory clause is added, that the true object and intent of the rule was, "to allow the children of parents of all sects and opinions in matters of faith and worship, to enjoy alike the benefit of the common school fund." Whether this policy may or may not require any changes in the school books now used, beyond the omission of the reading from King James' version of the Bible, and the singing of hymns, can not now be determined, and if it could, would not in my judgment be material in the decision of the present case. But this first resolution does undoubtedly pledge the Board of Education as at present constituted, to all parents, that no religious doctrines shall be taught in the common schools, and no form of religious worship used, so far as it is practicable to avoid it, which is offensive to the religious convictions of any.

A fair construction, however, of this resolution does not require the exclusion of extracts from the Bible, or from other religious books, incorporated into the text-books of the schools for the purposes of instruction and practice in reading, and speaking, and composition, or for the purpose of scientific instruction. These books contain also numerous extracts from ancient classic authors. But we do not regard that as constituting these school readers and speakers, Pagan books, or the reading of them in the schools, as Pagan instruction. The passages so incorporated in the school books as lessons in reading and speaking, are not placed there, to give them authority as religious doctrines. A very considerable portion of the time of students in the high schools, and in colleges, is spent in translating Hesiod, Homer, Virgil, and other ancient authors, whose writings formed what might be denominated the Pagan Bible, and contained the popular mythological religion of their times. But it does not follow, that these students are in danger of becoming proselytes to Paganism.

It is obvious to my mind, that the Board intended to carry out the constitutional ideas contained in the seventh section of the Bill of Rights, "That all men have a natural and indefeasible right to worship Almighty God according to the dictates of their own conscience," "That no person shall be compelled to attend, erect, or support any place of worship, or maintain any form of worship, against his consent;" "That no preference shall be given by law to any religious society;" "That no interference with the rights of conscience shall be permitted;" and the kindred constitutional idea of the common schools, contained in the second section of the sixth article of the Constitution of Ohio, "That the General Assembly shall make such provision, by taxation or otherwise, as, with the income arising from the school trust fund, will secure a thorough and efficient system of common schools throughout the State: but no religious or other sect or sects shall ever have any exclusive right to, or control of, any part of the school funds of this State."

The Board has gone upon the theory, that to allow any sect or sects so to control the religious instruction or worship in the common schools as to exclude, or tend to exclude, any portion of the community from the enjoyment of them, would be, to the same extent, permitting such sect or sects "to have exclusive control of the school funds." And that the necessary secular education of all the children of suitable age, if they can be induced to attend the common schools, will afford ample opportunity to spend all the funds provided, or likely hereafter to be provided, for common school purposes; while the religious sects are left to support the teaching of religious tenets to their children, as they support public worship, on the voluntary principle.

Such, in general, is the logic of this proceeding. It evinces no hostility on the part of the Board of Education to the Bible, to religion, or religious teaching, but rather a neutrality toward all the sects, which could not be otherwise maintained, and which had become essential to religious peace. This proceeding is a natural result of the elements of our population. While these elements were quiet or acquiescing, no such proceeding was necessary, and it was natural that many should be surprised that the Board should regard this step as necessary now.

I see no evidence of any official oppression or abuse on the part of the Board, or of recklessness of duty, or of disregard of individual rights, or of sacred things, to justify the Court to interfere with its action, if it has acted within its legal power. It remains to decide whether the Board, in passing this first resolution, exceeded its lawful power.

The claim of the counsel for the plaintiff is, that the prohibition of religious instruction and of the reading of religious books, including the Holy Bible, in the common schools of Cincinnati, is in direct conflict with the last clause of the seventh section of the Bill of Rights, which provides, "That religion, morality and knowledge, however, being essential to good government, it shall be the duty of the General Assembly to pass suitable laws, to protect every religious denomination in the peaceable enjoyment of its own mode of worship, and to encourage schools and the means of instruction."

It is not claimed that the General Assembly has passed any law requiring religious teaching in the common schools. The absence of such a statute is an important feature, which can not be overlooked in deciding this case. But, I will first endeavor to ascertain what the framers of the Constitution intended to secure by this clause of the Bill of Rights, and afterward we may consider the means, by which it was to be done.

I will here remark at the outset, that I find no conflict between this clause and the preceding part of the section, which protects religious liberty and the rights of conscience.

It does not say what kind of "schools" are to be "encouraged," nor what "means of instruction." It does not designate "common schools," as "the schools," or "the means of instruction." And it is pertinent here to remark, that the provision in the old Constitution from which this section is derived, was adopted long before the common school system came into existence; and that it was the sixth article of our present Constitution of 1852, which *first* required the General Assembly, "by taxation or otherwise," "to secure a thorough and efficient system of common schools throughout the State;" and so far was it from associating the idea of religious teaching with this "efficient system of common schools," that it expressly provided "that no religious, or other sect or sects, shall ever have any exclusive right to, or control of, any part of the school fund."

There are other schools, which, under this clause in the Constitution, are entitled to encouragement by suitable laws from the General Assembly. Academies, seminaries for young ladies, high schools, colleges, universities, medical schools, law schools, theological schools, all of which and many more, are encouraged by suitable laws, under which they are incorporated, and hold property free from taxation. Nor are the schools the only "means of instruction," contemplated by the Constitution, all of which are embraced in this general provision.

If the framers of the Constitution had intended the "common schools" only, they would not have used such unlimited and general terms without referring in any manner to the system of common schools, which was provided for in the sixth article of the same Constitution, where the General Assembly was required, not merely to encourage by suitable laws, but "by taxation to secure a thorough system of common schools throughout the State." What occasion was there to require the General Assembly, by suitable laws to encourage common schools, when it had already been required "to secure an efficient system" of them, throughout the State? Nothing can be clearer, than that, if they had intended common schools only, they would have used the term "common schools," as the system of common schools was provided for in the same Constitution. This encouragement, therefore, provided for, is general and directory, enjoining upon the Legislature, a liberal policy toward all schools, and all means of useful instruction.

Is it necessary then, under this clause, that all kinds of schools in Ohio shall have religious instruction, and that every means of instruction shall be religious? Does this general provision requiring that the General Assembly shall "pass suitable laws, to protect every religious denomination in the peaceable enjoyment of its own mode of worship, and to encourage schools and the means of instruction," imply religious "schools," and religious "means of instruction?" If the Convention had so intended, it would have been natural, and very easy to have so said, and the entire absence of any expression of that purpose, affords a strong presumption that no such intention existed; and a singular intention it would be, to provide that laws should be passed, requiring all schools, and all the means of instruction to be religious, in the sense claimed by the plaintiffs in this case. But no such purpose appears to have been expressed, or intended.

The religion of the Bill of Rights, is not sectarian religion. I understand by that term, as there used, reverence and love toward God, and charity toward man—a sentiment cultivated in many ways, among which are, undoubtedly, the various sectarian forms of public worship, and, as I think also, all forms of useful secular education. The great discoveries of science for the last thousand years, have been but the results of searching God's works. The principles of His creation have been sought, and in many instances with great success. Our knowledge of the extent of the creation has been vastly enlarged by the same means, until the universe of the present day, compares with that of the Christian Era, as the vast solar orb of the Copernican system, compares with the flat disk of a Roman denarius, bearing the image and superscription of a Caesar. In this sense, scientific study is a truly religious work. The study of the works of the great Creators, and the principles or laws by which nature is uniformly, and with no mistakes or failures controlled, leads the student to the Author of all.

The fearful and wonderful structure of man's physical nature has been analyzed, and the processes of digestion, respiration, and circulation of the blood, have been by science revealed to mankind, forever to increase their reverence and adoration of the Divine Hand that made us.

These and similar researches in God's works have, by books of instruction, been brought within the reach even of the children in the common schools, as well as of the pupils of all the other schools in the land, and have been more or less incorporated into all the means of secular instruction. It is not, therefore, a violent presumption to suppose that the framers of our last Constitution thought that that religion and that morality, as well as that knowledge, of which they spoke in the Bill of Rights, would be promoted by encouraging schools and the means of instruction generally.

It was no part of their theory that such knowledge, even apart from that formal religious instruction which this first resolution was intended to dispense with, was godless or immoral in its tendencies. But, as I have said, the protection of every denomination in its form of public worship, also promoted the religion and the morality, of which they spoke in that section.

The Legislature has not omitted its duty toward religion, under this section of the Bill of Rights. It has done precisely what was enjoined upon it, passing suitable laws to protect every religious denomination in the enjoyment of its own form of public worship, and laws under which religious societies, as well as educational institutions, can hold property, free from taxation. The amount thus remitted every year to the churches is very large, and evinces an abiding purpose, on the part of the General Assembly and the public, to foster and strengthen all the instrumentalities by which religion, morality and knowledge can be promoted.

It is reasonable to suppose that knowledge and morality would be promoted by schools and the means of instruction. This clause, however, does not say that "schools, with religious teaching," or religious "means of instruction," are necessary to "religion, morality, and knowledge;" but, that "religion, morality, and knowledge, being essential to good government, suitable laws shall be passed to protect every religious denomination in its own mode of worship," so that they may flourish freely, without intruding their peculiar modes upon each other, "and to encourage schools and the means of instruction," *without limitation;* from which it may be safely inferred that the framers of the Constitution were satisfied that the encouragement of "schools and the means of instruction" in any and all branches of useful learning would tend to secure knowledge and morality, and religion in the sense in which that term was evidently used. If it is insisted that this constitutional provision for religion is not satisfied by "the protection of every religious denomination in its own mode of worship," but requires laws for the encouragement of "schools and the means of instruction" also, it does not follow that they are to be schools with special religious teaching; for the framers of the

Constitution expressed themselves as *satisfied* with the encouragement of schools and the "means of instruction" generally. This would be the natural and only construction which we could give this clause, even if the provision for the protection "of every religious denomination in its own form of worship" were omitted.

But, let us for a moment suppose that the term religion was used by the convention in the narrowest sense claimed for it, viz.: the Protestant Christian Religion. It would not follow that schools and means of instruction must necessarily be of that character. The words in the preamble of that clause, "religion, morality, and knowledge," and the subjects of the main declaration which follows, viz: The protection of the various forms of public worship, and "schools and means of instruction" would naturally be construed distributively, *singula singulis*, religion being the antecedent of the first part of the declaration, viz: The protection of the forms of worship, as knowledge would be the antecedent of the last; "schools and means of instruction" being of the same nature, and regarded as one. The insertion of this peculiarly religious instrumentality, viz: "the protection of every religious denomination in its own form of worship," which must be taken to refer to "religion" in the preamble, and can not possibly be taken to refer to "knowledge;" and designating no other "religious" instrumentality, and omitting to qualify "the schools and means of instruction" as religious, leaves them to refer directly to their proper antecedent, "knowledge," as an essential to good government, and only indirectly, if at all, to "religion," which was the proper antecedent of the other instrumentality, viz: the protection of religious worship. It is not material to determine by which of these instrumentalities morality was to be promoted, as it derives support from both.

But schools and the means of instruction, as here described, without including any special religious instruction or reading of the Bible, are as well adapted to promote "religion," one of the essentials to good government, as the protection of every religious denomination in its own mode of public worship, is adapted to promote knowledge, another essential to good government, while both may fairly be regarded as promoters of "morality."

This mode of construction can only become necessary or natural, by supposing the term religion, as used in the preamble, so restricted in its meaning as not to have relation to all of the subjects of the following declaration; in the same manner as the term knowledge may be supposed to have no particular relation to the protection of forms of denominational worship. As I understand "religion," however, in that clause of the Bill of Rights, it, as well as "morality" and "knowledge," has a direct relation to "schools and means of instruction," whether including special religious teaching or not. If the words "morality" and "knowledge" had been omitted from the preamble of the clause under consideration, and the words relating to religious denominations had been omitted also, in the declaration itself, so that it should read thus: "Religion, however, being essential to good government, it shall be the duty of the General Assembly to pass suitable laws to encourage schools and the means of instruction," it would not even then bear the construction claimed by the plaintiffs. It would only appear that the convention regarded the encouragement of schools and the means of instruction as favorable to the promotion of the religion which they deemed essential to good government; and it would not be possible to hold that the convention intended to impress a specially religious character upon all the schools in the State, and upon every means of instruction.

A fortiori, from the words as they stand, there is no sound reason to infer that the framers of the Constitution intended to fix a religious character upon all the schools and all the means of instruction, to be encouraged by suitable laws; especially upon the common schools, which are not named in that connection, but which are expressly provided for in another place, viz: art. 6, sec. 2, without any religious restriction whatever. They must be taken to have intended what they have expressed.

On what ground then can we interfere to compel the Board of Education to incorporate religious instruction in the exercises of the common schools?

If it is now in the common schools, it has been placed there by action of the Board. If it is to be, hereafter, incorporated with the other teaching in the schools, it will be through the same body, unless the Court should take the management of that department.

That the school laws contain no such requirement is conceded, and I find no foundation for it in the Bill of Rights.

If then, we interfere to restrain the discretion of the Board on this subject, as prayed for in the petition, we shall assume a power, expressly given to that body. For by section 9 of the school act of January 27, 1853,

> "The Board shall have the superintendence of all the common schools in the city, and from time to time to make such regulations for the government and instruction of the children therein, as shall appear to them proper and expedient."
>
> "And generally to do and perform all other matters and things pertaining to the duties of their said office which may be necessary and proper to promote the education, morals, and good conduct of the children in said schools."

And by the 12th section of the same act,

> "The common schools in the several districts of the city, shall at all times be equally free and accessible to all white children not less than six years of age, who may reside in said city, and subject only to such regulations for their admission, government, and instruction, as the Board of Education may from time to time provide."

No broader discretion could be given by a statute to a Board in the selection of the course of studies, and in the management of the schools generally. The statute requires no formal worship, nor does it require religious instruction in the schools, but gives the whole subject of their government and instruction, unqualifiedly, into the hands of the trustees, who are to be selected by the people. If the Board should exclude any particular branch of education, it would not justify the Court in interfering. For the selection of the instruction to be given and of the books to be read, has been entrusted, not to us, but to them. If we should find ourselves differing with the Board in our opinion of what its duty required it to incorporate in the course of instruction, we should have first to consider which of us is by law entitled to decide that question.

Neither of us can change the law. It is as binding on the Court, as on the Board of Education. The law has expressly conferred that discretion upon that body. I will not stop to give illustrations, which are obvious, and at hand, on this point.

But, if the plaintiffs were right, in construing the words "schools and the means of instruction," to mean "schools" with religious teaching and religious "means of instruction," it would not help the plaintiffs' case, because this clause in the Bill of Rights is made expressly to depend on legislation, and can have no force *proprio vigore:* and the Legislature has never given effect by law to any such construction of it as is now claimed.

This provision of the Constitution is addressed to the General Assembly, and that body is made the judge of what laws are suitable for the purpose. These school acts are the result of a judicial discretion in the General Assembly to decide what are "suitable laws," as well as of legislative power to pass them.

That this clause of the Bill of Rights is addressed to the General Assembly or law-making power, can not be disputed.

If the General Assembly should even neglect to act by passing laws encouraging schools, it might be great unfaithfulness to the Constitution on its part, but the judiciary could not interfere, because the Constitution has entrusted that duty to the General Assembly. For a non-performance of that duty, the General Assembly would be responsible to its constituents. If the General Assembly, instead of neglecting its duty on the subject, passes laws, these laws form the rule for the Board. The General Assembly has the discretion expressly conferred upon it judicial, as well as legislative, to accomplish a purpose by "suitable laws," and there is no other source from which "suitable laws," can be derived. Courts can not make them. And those which have been passed, must be taken to be "suitable." This principle is not novel, or unreasonable.

In the case of *Gillenwater* v. *Mississippi and Atlantic R. R. Co.*, 13 Ills. R. I., it was urged that a restriction upon railroad corporations by the general railroad law was a violation of the provision of the Constitution which enjoined upon the Legislature, "to encourage internal improvement by passing liberal general laws of incorporation for that purpose." The Court said: "This is a constitutional command to the Legislature, as obligatory on it as any other of the provisions of that instrument, but it is one which can not be enforced by counts or justice. It addresses itself to the Legislature alone, and it is not for us to say whether it has obeyed the behest in its true spirit. Whether the provisions of this law, are liberal, and tend to encourage internal improvements, is matter of opinion about which men may differ; and as we have no authority to revise legislation on this subject, it would not become us to express our views in relation to it."

The case of *Maloy* v. *The City of Marietta*, 11 O. S. R. 636, turns on the same principle. That case rose on the sixth section of article xiii, of the Constitution, which is, "The General Assembly shall provide for the organization of cities and incorporated villages by general laws, and restrict their power of assessment, so as to prevent the abuse of such power." It was claimed that the General Assembly had granted an "unrestricted" power of making such assessments.

The Court say, p. 638, "Were this true, it might be questionable whether the Courts could, for that reason, hold the grant of power to be void. The Constitution clearly imposes a duty upon the Legislature, but does not direct when or how it shall be exercised."

Speaking of this provision and the duty thereby enjoined, Judge Ranney, in *Hill* v. *Higdon*, 5 O. S. R. 248, says "a *failure* to perform this duty, may be of very serious import, but lays no foundation for judicial correction." It was further held that the "*mode and measure*" of restriction, rested with the Legislature, and could not be reviewed by the Courts.

The Supreme Court of the United States in the case of *Groves* v. *Slaughter*, 15 Peter's Rep. 449, which was very much considered, recognized and acted upon the same principle. The suit in that case was brought upon a note given for slaves imported into Mississippi, and the question was, whether the consideration was void under the Constitution of that State of 1832, which provided, "That the introduction of slaves into this State, as merchandize, or for sale, shall be prohibited, from and after the first day of May, 1833." The Constitution of 1817 had declared that the Legislature should have power to prevent slaves being brought into the State as merchandize. The time and manner in which it was to be done, was left to the discretion of the Legislature. By the Constitution of 1832, it was no longer left a matter of discretion when this prohibition was to take effect, bnt the first day of May, 1833, was fixed as the time.

The Court says, Judge Thompson giving the opinion: "But there is nothing in this provision which looks like withdrawing the whole subject from the Legislature." "It looked to legislative enactments to carry it into full operation." The Court proceeded to say: "Admitting the Constitution is mandatory upon the Legislature, and that they have neglected their duty in not carrying it into execution, it can have no effect upon the construction of this article. Legislative provision is indispensable to carry into effect the object of this prohibition. The enacting part of the article, '*Shall be prohibited*,' is addressed to the Legislature."

That was a strong case, because the injunction was direct upon the Legislature, that by a specified time a specific thing should be done, viz: The importation of slaves should be prohibited.

In the present case, the framers of the Constitution have conferred a large judicial discretion upon the General Assembly, to select such legislative provision as, in its judgment, shall be suitable to accomplish the purposes prescribed; and the General Assembly has, really, left no room for argument upon the proper means of accomplishing that purpose, because it has given an authentic and binding construction, when it passed the law under which the Board of Education was created and the common schools organized. Not only has it decided this question when it passed the common school laws without hinting at religious instruction, but it has decided the same question again and again, as often as laws have been passed for the encouragement of other schools and other means of instruction, by incorporation and otherwise, sometimes requiring, and sometimes not requiring, provision for religious culture.

Such a claim as that now made by the plaintiffs is sustained by no adjudications on like statutes, even where the construction of the constitutional provision was not doubtful, as it was in the case of *Groves* v. *Slaughter*. How can this Court make such a precedent in a case where the General Assembly has actually carried out the natural and the literal construction of the provision?

It has been suggested, that this reasoning does not apply, because the Board of Education were exercising legislative powers, and so were acting in the capacity of the General Assembly under the Constitution, and were bound by it. A moment's reflection will show that this can make no difference whatever. For, if we were to admit the suggestion that the Board was, for this purpose, the General Assembly, then it has the same power over the subject, and its construction is as binding as that of the General Assembly itself.

I hold, then—

That the defendants appear to have acted, in the adoption of this first rule, with due respect for the rights and opinions of all the people entitled to the benefit of the common schools.

That the rule is not in conflict with the seventh section of the Bill of Rights, by the fair and natural construction of the language of that section.

That, if the construction were doubtful, the General Assembly, on which the Constitution had devolved the power and duty of determining what were suitable laws under said section, has performed its duty by passing the common school laws, and has thereby made a decision, from which there is no appeal except to the people, that these are suitable laws "to encourage schools."

That it is our duty to ascertain what these school laws are, and abide by them, as we can not change them or make others, or decide even what they ought to be.

That the school laws thus enacted, confer on the Board of Education complete discretionary power over the government and management of the common schools, including power to adopt this rule, which is not in conflict with any law or constitutional provision; and

That this Court, in assuming to restrain the Board from carrying said rule into effect, is going beyond its proper sphere to decide a question which the law has placed within the exclusive discretion of the Board of Education.

II.

We come now to consider the second resolution.

In the absence of any statute whatever on the subject, the School Board, many years since, adopted the rule requiring the opening of the schools with the reading from King James' version of the Bible, and appropriate singing. In the like absence of any statute, the present Board, of which the defendants are the majority, repealed the same rule; and the injunction has been applied for against the Board, to restrain its action under the resolution. It is obvious that all the considerations which have been presented in support of the power of the Board to adopt the first rule, apply also to their power to adopt this; while the constitutional objection urged against the first, that it excluded all religious instruction from the common schools, has no application. Such seems to have been the view taken of the whole subject by the learned counsel for the plaintiffs, who have rested their entire argument on their objection to the first rule, and have presented none whatever against the second. Nor can this be regarded as an inadvertence; for the second rule was not overlooked. It was conceded that the Board had a discretion to regulate the course of studies and reading in the schools, but its power to exclude all religious instruction, as was done by the first rule, was denied. But it has not really been argued, and I am utterly at a loss to conceive how it can be argued, in view of our Constitution and laws, that the Board had exceeded its powers by passing the repealing resolution. If the Board of Education have not power to say, whether the schools shall be opened with the reading of the Bible and singing, who has that power? It is not claimed that the Legislature has prescribed any such opening of the schools. The Board itself made the rule, which no other person or body, under the laws, could do, and now has repealed it.

Whether this opening exercise be regarded as worship or as religious instruction, or simply as a lesson in reading and singing, it falls equally within the discretion of no person or body but the Board of Education. The plaintiffs, by their petition, say that a former Board removed all objection to this opening exercise, by excusing all children from joining in it whose parents made a request to that effect. If the Constitution requires the opening of all the schools by reading the Bible and singing, there can be no exceptions; and the repeal of the exercise as to all the children, is not less constitutional than its repeal as to part.

But there is no clause in the Constitution requiring that the schools shall be opened by reading of the Bible and singing, or that the Bible shall be read or not read in the schools. It is proper here to remark, that there is a plain and practical distinction between using the Bible as a book of reading lessons, and reading from it with appropriate singing as an opening exercise every morning. I shall have occasion to recur to this distinction in another connection.

The extent of the discretion of a school board or committee on the question of ruling the Bible in or ruling it out of the schools, as a book of reading lessons, was passed upon in *Donahue* v. *Richards*, 38 Maine R. 401, where the plaintiff had been expelled from the school because she refused to read in King James' version, but was willing to read in the Douay version. The Court sustained the power and discretion of the Board over the whole subject, holding that "both" versions "undoubtedly might be used in the schools, or both might be excluded therefrom." If religious instruction is to be given in the schools, the Board of Education is to provide for it; and if that body should prefer the religious instruction contained in McGuffey's Readers, or the other books which are supposed by the plaintiffs' counsel to contain religious instruction, it is not our province to determine which is the best plan. Nor is the Board accountable to the Court for the specific course of reading or study by which religious or other instruction is to be given. Nothing is clearer than that in the selection of the means of instruction in the common branches of science the Board of Education, and no other body, has complete and absolute discretion. It can try one plan, repeal it, and try another. In exercising such a discretion the Board would be at liberty to regard the opinions and conscientious scruples of the people whose children were entitled to the benefit of the schools.

In *Donohue* v. *Richards*, 38 Maine R. 413, to which I have referred, after an elaborate opinion fully sustaining the discretionary power of the school committee, the Court placed its decision distinctly upon that discretion, as not subject to judicial correction. The Court closed by declaring:

"That it was the duty of those to whom this sacred trust was confided, to discharge it with magnanimous liberality and Christian kindness: that while the law should reign supreme, and obedience to its commands should ever be required, yet in the establishment of the law which was to control, there was no principle of wider application and of higher wisdom, commending itself alike to the broad field of legislative, and the more restricted one of municipal action, than the precept, 'All things whatsoever ye would that men should do to you, do ye even so to them, for this is the law and the prophets.'"

The idea that the Christian religion was entitled to any higher or other privileges, before the law, than "the Pagan and Mormon, the Brahmin and the Jew, the Swedenborgian and the Buddhist, the Catholic and the Quaker," was rejected, and the Sabbath, and the use of the Bible in the schools, alike placed upon civil, and not religious, considerations, citing with approbation, and quoting from the opinion of the Supreme Court of Ohio, in *Bloom* v. *Richards*, 2 Ohio St. R. 388, on the subject.

There is, then, no hypothesis of fact or reason presented, or supposed, by any argument that has been made in this case, or which I can imagine, by which this Court can be justified in restraining the action of the Board of Education under the second rule. I hold that, whether the reading of the Bible and singing as practiced in the common schools be regarded as worship, religious instruction, or as simple reading and singing lessons, its introduction, continuance or discontinuance is entirely within the discretion of the Board of Education.

III.

Having come to the conclusion, that the Board was acting within its sphere, when it passed the resolutions, and so was not amenable to judicial censure, I might here stop and rest my opinion upon the power of the Board of Education.

But the defendants have not been content to rest the resolutions simply on their power to pass them. They insist that in passing them they discharged a solemn duty under the Constitution and laws of the State: a duty, which had become urgent by reason of the great and discordant variety of religious faiths in the city; that they had found it impossible to provide religious instruction, without offending the consciences of many; and that practically about one-third to two-fifths of the children entitled to the benefit of the schools, were excluded by the rules, as they stood before the resolutions were passed; that the compulsory reading from the King James' version of the Bible, with singing, as an opening exercise in the schools, daily, is regarded as a form of worship, and is in violation of that part of the seventh section of the Bill of Rights, which declares that:

> "No person shall be compelled to attend, erect or support any place of worship, or maintain any form of worship against his consent; and no preference shall be given by law to any religious society: nor shall any interference with the rights of conscience be permitted."

All sectarian forms of worship are clearly excluded by the Bill of Rights from the common schools, which are maintained at the expense of all, and for the equal benefit of all, unless such form of worship is acquiesced in by the parties interested.

It is to be observed here, that these provisions of the Bill of Rights, for the protection of rights of conscience, are not left for the enactment of suitable laws, by the General Assembly. They operate on the Legislature and people alike. The General Assembly is forbidden to pass laws giving religious preferences: and "no person shall be compelled to attend or maintain any form of worship, nor shall any interference with the rights of conscience be permitted."

No legislation is needed to give effect to these provisions; but they limit legislation, and form rules for Courts. In this respect, they differ from the last clause in the section, on which the plaintiffs rely.

What then is the character of the morning exercise of reading a passage in the Bible, and appropriate singing in the schools daily?

I think we are bound to regard it both as an act of worship, and a lesson of religious instruction. That it is an act of worship, the well known custom of the country, and indeed, of Christendom shows. For, by that custom, such formal reading and singing, at the opening of the duties of the day, uniformily mean worship.

It is intended to raise the thoughts of the participants to the Father of all, to read His Word, and to sing His praise. It is as a special message from Him that the passage from the Bible is read. And so I am bound to suppose the plaintiffs regard it. For if it was regarded simply as an ordinary reading lesson, it would not have been claimed that it was not subject, like other reading lessons, to be changed or discontinued under the rules of the Board.

The singing of Protestant hymns may be used to communicate dogmatic instruction as effectually as the Bible itself.

I can not doubt, therefore, that the use of the Bible with the appropriate singing, provided for by the old rule, and as practiced under it, was and is sectarian. It is Protestant worship. And its use is a symbol of Protestant supremacy in the schools, and as such offensive to Catholics and to Jews. They have a constitutional right to object to it, as a legal preference given by the State to the Protestant sects, which is forbidden by the Constitution.

And here, I again refer to the obvious distinction between the use of the Bible by way of worship, and its use as a reading book. The Court in *Donohue* v. *Richards*, 38 Me. R. already referred to, placed their decision upon the ground that the use of the Bible in that case was as a reading book, and not by way of worship or religious instruction. The question, whether the Board of Education under our Constitution could make the Bible a reading book in the schools, contrary to the conscientious scruples of the people, does not, in my opinion, arise in this case. For it is, as a form of worship and religious instruction only, and not as a reading book, that it is used in our schools, and as *such*, those who object to it, have a right to regard it; and that is the grouud, as I have understood these proceedings, on which this suit has been brought.

The answer states that the children of Roman Catholic parents, equal to at least half the entire number of children who attend the common schools, are kept away by reason of this rule; that a large number of Jews, who have children in the schools, object to the rule from conscientious reasons.

The counsel for the plaintiffs insist, that the Bible can, in no just sense, be regarded as sectarian, and that the conscientious scruples alleged, are not to be regarded.

The facts on which this question turns, are simple. The Roman Catholic uses a different version of the Bible and includes the Apocrapha, as part of it, which are excluded from the Protestant Bible. The Protestant Bible is the King James' version, which the Catholics regard as not only not a correct translation, but as distorted in the interest of the Protestant, as against the Roman Catholic Church. They object, therefore, on conscientious grounds, to having their children read it or hear it read. They say and believe, that it is a source of fatal religious error.

Nor is the incorrectness of the translation the only objection they entertain to the reading of the Bible in these schools. They hold, that the Bible is entrusted to the Church, and that it is not a suitable book to be read by, or to, children without explanation by persons authorized by the Church and of sufficient learning to explain and apply it.

We are not at liberty to doubt the conscientious objections, on the part of the Catholic parents to placing their children in the schools, while the schools are opened by the reading of the Protestant Bible and singing.

We have this unequivocal evidence of the reality of their conscientious scruples, that, when they have paid the school-tax which is not a light one, they give up the privilege of sending their children, rather than that they should be educated in what they hold to be, and what, without the adoption of one, or both of these resolutions, must be fairly held to be *Protestant schools.* This is too large a circumstance to be covered up by the Latin phrase *de minimis non curat lex*, to which resort is sometimes had. These Catholics are constrained every year to yield to others their right to one-third of the school money, a sum of money averaging not less than $200,000 every year, on conscientious grounds. That is to say, these people are *punished* every year for believing as they do, to the extent of $200,000, and to that extent, those of us who send our children to these excellent common schools, become beneficiaries of the

Catholic money. We pay for our privileges so much less than they actually cost. Mercantile life is supposed to cultivate in some a relish for hard bargains. But if it were a business matter, and not a matter of religious concern, could business men be found willing to exact such a pecuniary advantage as this? I think it would shock the *secular* conscience.

The authority of the Archbishop of Cincinnati was, however, used in this connection, to show that these resolutions, if carried out, would not be effectual to gather the children of Catholics into the public schools, which they, in common with other tax-payers, support. It appears that the Archbishop, like the plaintiffs, is not satisfied with secular education in the schools. In principle, he stands where they do, with the exception that they are in possession. Being out of possession, he would prefer to get out of the public treasury the share of the school fund, proportioned to the Catholic population, and apply it to the support of the parochial schools with Catholic religious instruction. If the Catholics were in possession, as the plaintiffs are, with the Douay version and Catholic forms of worship, perhaps he might still be willing to divide the money, and perhaps not, in which latter case he would occupy about the same position now occupied by the plaintiffs in this suit.

It is said that the Catholic clergy demand their share of the fund, to be used in carrying on schools under their control. That can not be done under the Constitution. But this affords no reason why the Board of Education should not grant to the Catholic people, what the Bill of Rights guarantees to every sect, that their rights of conscience shall not be violated, and that they shall not be compelled to attend any form of worship, or to maintain it against their consent, or be compelled to submit to religious preferences, shown by the government to other religious societies.

It is not for a court to anticipate, before judgment, that any party will not be satisfied with what the law gives him, nor are courts accustomed to withhold what is due because something else is asked.

Another numerous class of heavy tax-payers, the Jews, object to the old rule. But it is claimed on behalf of the plaintiffs, that the Jews have met with something like a conversion, and have become reconciled to the New Testament. That they held out for a while, but afterward came in, and there was no further difficulty with them; and that their case need not to have been further regarded. There is too much evidence of dissent on their part, from the old rule, to permit us to conclude that they have ever intended to waive their rights of conscience and of religious liberty. Like the majority of us, the Jews have received their faith from their ancestors, and according to that historic faith, the assertion in the New Testament that Jesus of Nazareth is God, is blasphemy against the God of Israel. If a Protestant Christian would object to have the common schools daily opened with the forms of worship peculiar to the Catholic Church, which worships the same triune God with him, how much more serious must be the objection of the Jew, to be compelled to attend, or support, the worship of a being as God, whose divinity and supernatural history he denies?

The truth in this matter undoubtedly is, that the Jews, like many others, have found out that our common schools are munificently endowed, and, in general, well conducted, so that the privilege of attending them is inestimable, and they have wisely concluded to secure for their children the secular education of the common schools, and attend to their religious nurture at home and in their own organizations. A faith which had survived so much persecution, through so many centuries, they may well have risked in the common schools of Cincinnati, though at some cost of religious feeling.

It is in vain to attempt to escape the foree of the clauses of the Bill of Rights by assuming that the Protestant Christian religion was intended in the Bill of Rights, and that the sects of Protestant Christians *only* were, therefore, entitled to protection. Between all forms of religious belief the State knows no difference, provided they do not transgress its civil regulations—a mighty contrast to some times and some countries, which have boasted of their religious liberality, because the ruling sects have tolerated the dissenting minority, as a nuisance, which they have magnanimously forborne to abate.

But the principle of equality of right, and nothing less than that, is now well established in Ohio, if not in all the other American States, by the unequivocal language of our Constitution and by judicial decisions.

In *Bloom* v. *Richards*,* 2 Ohio St. R. 390–1, our Supreme Court, by a unanimous opinion. in a case involving the validity of a contract made on Sunday, said:

"But the Constitution of Ohio having declared 'that all men have a natural and indefeasible right to worship Almighty God according to the dictates of conscience; that no human authority can, in any case whatever, control or interfere with the rights of conscience; that no man shall be compelled to attend, erect, or support any place of worship, or to maintain any ministry against his consent; and that no preference shall ever be given by law to any religious society or mode of worship, and no religious test shall be required, as a qualification to any office of trust or profit,' it follows that neither Christianity, or any other system of religion is a part of the law of this State.

We sometimes hear it stated, that all religions are tolerated in Ohio, but the expression is not strictly accurate; much less accurate is it to say, that one religion is a part of our law, and all others only tolerated.

It is not by mere toleration that every individual here is protected in his belief or disbelief. He reposes not upon the leniency of government, or the liberality of any class or sect of men, but upon his natural indefeasible rights of conscience which, in the language of the Constitution, are beyond the control or interference of any human authority. We have no union of Church and State, nor has our government ever been vested with authority to enforce any religious observance simply because it is religious. Of course, it is no objection, but, on the contrary, is a high recommendation to a legislative enactment based upon justice or public policy, that it is found to coincide with the precepts of a pure religion; but the fact is nevertheless true, that the power to make the law rests in the legislative control over things temporal and not over things spiritual. Thus the statute upon which the defendant relies, prohibiting common labor on the Sabbath, could not stand for a moment as a law of this State, if its sole foundation was the Christian duty of keeping that day holy, and its sole motive, to enforce the observance of that duty. For no power over things merely spiritual, has ever been delegated to the government, while any preference of one religion, as the statute would give upon the above hypothesis, is directly prohibited by the Constitution. Acts, evil in their nature, or dangerous to the public welfare, may be forbidden and punished, though sanctioned by one religion and prohibited by another; but this creates no preference whatever, for they would be equally forbidden and punished if all religions permitted them.

Thus no plea of religion could shield a murderer, a ravisher, or a bigamist, for the community would be at the mercy of superstition, if such crimes as these could be committed with impunity, because sanctioned by some religious delusion."

The same Court two years later, in *McGatrick* v. *Wasson*, 4 O. S. R. 571–2, again by unanimous opinion said:

"But was it a work of necessity within the meaning of the act? In answering this question, we must always keep in mind, that it is no part of the object of the act to enforce the observance of a religious duty. The act does not to any extent, rest upon the ground that it is immoral or irreligious to labor on the Sabbath any more than upon any other day. It simply prescribes a day of rest, from motives of public policy and as a civil regulation; and as the prohibition itself is founded on principles of policy, upon the same principles certain exceptions are made, among which are 'works of necessity and charity.' In saying this I do not mean to intimate, that religion prohibits works of necessity or charity on the Sabbath, but merely to show that the principles, upon which our statute rests, are wholly secular, and that they are none the less so because they may happen to concur with the dictates of religion. Thus the day of rest prescribed by the statute, is the Christian Sabbath, yet so entirely does the act rest upon grounds of public policy, that, as was said in *Bloom* v. *Richards*, 2 O. S. R. 391, 392, it would be equally constitutional and obligatory, did it name any other day, and it derives none of its force from the fact that the day of rest is Sunday. For, as was also said in that case, no power whatever is possessed by the Legislature over things spiritual, but only over things temporal; no power whatever to enforce the performance of religious duties, simply because they are religious; but, only within the limits of the Constitution, to maintain justice and promote the public welfare.

Unless then, we keep constantly in mind that the act rests upon public policy alone, we shall be in great danger of giving it a wrong construction: and instead of reading it in the light of the Constitution, which prohibits all religious tests and preferences, find ourselves led away from its meaning, by the influence of our own peculiar theological tenets."

The framers of our last Constitution were jealous of the ambition of sects. It forbids the imposition of their respective forms of worship on each other, and forbids that any one of them shall have any exclusive right to, or control of, any part of the school fund. Now, as they can not impose their respective forms of worship upon each other, and can not divide the school fund, it follows, that, while they may and ought to unite in the common schools, they must separate in their worship, unless waiving their religious differences, they agree to unite in their worship also. I am very far from depreciating the history and the usefuluess of the religious sects. They have roused the energies of nations to heroic achievements; and, beside cherishing earnest piety and strong faith in God, they have organized efficient charities for the poor and distressed. But they have not always been tolerant, and it is still one of their characteristics to ignore the conscientious scruples of each other.

Each sect feels a comfortable assurance that it is not mistaken in its faith, and must be excused, if it can not appreciate the faith, or want of faith, in others.

But nevertheless, the idea, that a man has less conscience because he is a Rationalist, or a Spiritualist, or even an Atheist, than the believer in any one of the accepted forms of faith, may be current, but it is not a constitutional idea, in the State of Ohio.

No sect can, because it includes a majority of a community or a majority of the citizens of the State, claim any preference whatever. It can not claim that its mode of worship or its religion shall prevail in the common schools. Nor does it make the case any better, if several sects agree in a certain degree and kind of religious instruction and worship, among themselves, though together forming a large majority of the community or State. So long as there are any, who do not believe in or approve of their mode of religious worship or instruction, they can not insist that it is not sectarian, or that any non-believing tax-payer shall be compelled to submit to it in the common schools.

While the Court will take cognizance of the existence of the Christian religion and of the Protestant religion, it is only for the purpose of preserving civil peace and order, and the welfare of the State; and for the same purpose, it will take cognizance of the existence of every sect. The State protects every religious denomination in the quiet enjoyment of its own mode of public worship. It protects them from blasphemy, when the public peace and order require it.

It is, therefore, an entire mistake, in my opinion, to assert, that the Protestant Christian religion has been so identified with the history and government of our State or country, that it is not to be regarded as sectarian under our Constitution; or, that, when the Bill of Rights says that "religion, morality and knowledge being essential to good government," it means the Protestant Christian religion. That would be a preference, which the same section expressly disclaims, and emphatically forbids.

To hold otherwise, and that Protestant Christians are entitled to any control in the schools, to which other sects are not equally entitled, or that they are entitled to have their mode of worship and their Bible used in the common schools, against the will of the Board of Education, the proper trustees and managers of the schools, is to hold to the union of Church and State, however we may repudiate and reproach the name. Nor is it to be presumed, that the cause of genuine religion, or of the Bible, can be permanently advanced by a struggle for this kind of supremacy. The government is neutral, and, while protecting all, it prefers none, and it *disparages* none. The State, while it does not profess to be Christian, exercises a truly Christian charity toward all. Its impartial charity extends to all kinds of Protestants, Roman Catholics, Jews and Rationalists alike, and covers them with its mantle of protection and encouragement; and no one of them, however numerous, can boast of peculiar favor with the State.

Nothing but the severset experiences of religious persecution in other countries, and in other times, could have planted liberty of religious opinion so deeply and so ineradicably in the American State governments. It was not realized under the Colonial government, which, though far removed from, were still closely allied to, the laws and religious institutions of the mother country. Roger Williams was greatly in advance of his time, and seemed to comprehend the principle of religious liberty. But even he dared not to claim its full realization, and what he claimed was not allowed.

"There goes many a ship to sea," said he, "with many hundred souls in one ship, whose weal and woe is common, and is a true picture of a commonwealth, or human combination, or society. It hath fallen out sometimes, that both Papists and Protestants, Jews and Turks may be embarked in one ship; upon which supposal, I affirm that all the liberty of conscience I ever pleaded for, turns upon these two hinges, that none of the Papists, Protestants, Jews or Turks be forced to come to the ship's prayers or worship, nor compelled from their own particular prayers or worship, if they practice any."

There is no more striking evidence of the advance which has been made in religious liberty, since the time of Roger Williams, than is to be found in the American State Constitutions of the present day, and in the most intelligent comments upon them by approved writers and jurists. The ideal is absolute equality before the law, of all religious opinions and sects, provided they do not infringe the laws enacted purely for civil government, with no symbols of the superiority of any faith over others, upheld by the power of the State. If this ideal has not been practically reached in all the older States, it may be ascribed to the fact that in several of them, as in Massachusetts and Connecticut, an established church was preserved till a comparatively recent period. And it is to be borne in mind that the adjudications of the Courts in a State with a church establishment maintained by law, are not applicable to the condition of religious equality existing in Ohio.

Mr. Cooley, in his valuable work, recently published, on Constitutional Limitations, discusses, with great intelligence and force, the subject of religious liberty and the rights of conscience, under the American State Constitutions. His opinion is strongly expressed in favor of secular instruction in the schools. In the course of the discussion of the American Constitutions on this subject, and of the adjudication thereunder, he makes an interesting statement of things not permitted under American Constitutions, in the interest of religious liberty and rights of conscience. He says:

"Those things which are not lawful under any of the American Constitutions may be stated thus:

"1. Any law respecting an establishment of religion. The Legislatures have not been left at liberty to effect a union of Church and State, or to establish preferences by law in favor of any one religious denomination or mode of worship. There is no religious liberty where any one sect is favored by the State and given an advantage by law over other sects. Whatever establishes a distinction against one class or sect is, to the extent to which the distinction operates unfavorably, a persecution; and if based on religious grounds, is religious persecution.

"It is not toleration which is established in our system, but religious equality.

"2. Compulsory support, by taxation or otherwise, of religious instruction. Not only is no one denomination to be favored at the expense of the rest, but all support of religious instruction must be entirely voluntary."

This great principle of equality in the enjoyment of religious liberty, and the faithful preservation of the rights of each individual conscience is important in itself, and is essential to religious peace and temporal prosperity, in any country under a free government. But in a city and State whose people have been drawn from the four quarters of the world, with a great diversity of inherited religious opinions, it is indispensable. When the Board of Education, therefore, which represents the civil power of the State in the schools, finds objection made to the use of the Protestant Bible and Protestant singing of Protestant hymns, on conscientious grounds, and concludes to dispense with the practice in the sehools, it is no just ground to charge on the Board hostility to the Bible, or to the Protestant religion, or to religion in general. The Bible is not banished, nor is religion degraded or abused. The Board have simply aimed to free the common schools from any just conscientious objections, by confining them to secular instruction, and moral and intellectual training. This, in my opinion, was, under the circumstances, just, and, under the Constitution of Ohio, a duty which they could not omit without violating the rights of conscience of those who, on conscientious grounds, objected to the practice under the old rule.

On the whole case, my conclusions are that the Board of Education had the power to pass both the first and the second of these Resolutions, and whether expedient or inexpedient, this Court has no lawful authority to restrain it from acting under either of them; that, upon the pleadings and the evidence in the case, the Board, in adopting the first of these resolutions, acted with a justice and liberality warranted by the Bill of Rights, and made necessary by the facts; and that, in adopting the second, it performed a duty imposed upon it by the language and the spirit of the Constitution of Ohio.

JUDGMENT.

February 18, 1870.

JOHN D. MINOR AND OTHERS *v.* THE BOARD OF EDUCATION OF CINCINNATI AND OTHERS	*Superior Court of Cincinnati.*

This cause was heard upon the pleadings, testimony, and arguments of the counsel of all the parties, and the Court having duly considered thereof, finds that the resolutions passed by the said Board of Education on the 1st day of November, A. D. 1869, and which are set forth in the petition, were passed without warrant or authority in law, and are in violation of the provisions of the seventh section in the first article or the Bill of Rights in the Constitution of this State, and are an abuse of the powers of said Board, and are, therefore, declared to be null and void; and the plaintiffs, as taxpayers of the City of Cincinnati, are entitled in behalf of said city, as well as in their own right, to the relief sought in their petition; to which the City of Cincinnati and said Board, and the members, defendants, who voted for said resolutions, except.

It is therefore adjudged and ordered, that the restraining order heretofore entered in this action be made perpetual, and that the City of Cincinnati, and said Board of Education, and the members and officers thereof, and teachers, and all other persons acting in aid or assistance of the said Board, be and are each and all commanded to refrain from promulgating, or in any wise, directly or indirectly, enforcing the said resolutions set forth in the petition as passed by said Board, on the 1st day of November, A. D. 1869, or any other measures of the like nature or effect, and are enjoined not to give or permit any force or effect to be given to said resolutions in the common schools of said city; and that the costs of this action be paid by the City of Cincinnati.

And thereupon the said defendants filed their motion for a new trial for causes therein alleged, which motion is overruled; and the defendants excepted to said overruling, and to said judgment, and tendered their Bill of Exceptions in that behalf, which is accordingly allowed, signed, and ordered to be filed as part of the record.

Ohio Valley Historical Series,

Robert Clarke & Co.

CINCINNATI.

Ohio Valley Historical Series.

In our Prospectus, issued in April, 1868, *we announced our intention of publishing, under this general title, a series of works relating to the early history of the Valley of the Ohio. It has not been our aim to give a consecutive history, but merely to collect and preserve by publication hitherto unpublished manuscripts of value relating to the subject, and to reprint some of the early works on Western history which are out of print and rare.*

In carrying out this design, we have already issued three works, which have been received with a favor beyond our most sanguine expectations, and on which a liberal patronage has been bestowed. We now announce as ready for delivery a fourth, which we hope may prove acceptable. We have two more volumes now in press, and others in active preparation, which will be announced in due time.

We take this opportunity of expressing our obligations to the gentlemen of the press for their uniformly kind and appreciative notices of our Series, and to numerous friends for the generous aid they have given us in procuring unpublished materials, as well as for many rare books, pamphlets, etc., relating to early times in the West, which we find exceedingly useful for editorial reference.

ROBERT CLARKE & CO.

Cincinnati, December, 1869.

Number Four.

McBride's Pioneer Biography, Vol. I.

PIONEER BIOGRAPHY: SKETCHES OF THE LIVES OF SOME OF THE EARLY SETTLERS of BUTLER COUNTY, OHIO. By the late JAMES MCBRIDE, of Hamilton. Vol. I. Containing the lives of JOHN REILY, THOMAS IRWIN, JOEL COLLINS, ISAAC ANDERSON, SAMUEL DICK, JOSEPH HOUGH, and JOHN WOODS, with a portrait of the author.

One volume, 8vo., pp. xiv, 352, finely printed on tinted paper, neatly bound in English cloth, gilt top, and uncut edges, or entirely uncut. Price, $3.50.

A few *large-paper* copies have been printed on extra-heavy tinted paper. Portrait on *India paper.* Cloth, gilt top, and uncut edges, or entirely uncut. Price, $7.00.

Vol. II will contain sketches of Capt. JOHN CLEVES SYMMES, with a full explanation of his celebrated theory of *Concentric Spheres;* ROBERT MCCLELLAN, one of Gen. Wayne's scouts during his campaign in Ohio; Judge HENRY WEAVER, ISAAC PAXTON, and other pioneers of note.

These sketches will be found to possess an interest beyond the mere details of the lives of the individuals. They were all of them men who took an active part in the settlement of the Miami country, were prominent in public affairs both civil and military, and participated in many of the early conflicts with the Indians in Ohio and Kentucky, and in the campaigns of Gens. Harmar, St. Clair, Scott, and Wayne; so that, interspersed in the narrative, will be found many details of interest concerning the early struggles, from the notes and recollections of eye witnesses, which have never before appeared in print.

Number One.

Bouquet's Expedition Against the Ohio Indians in 1764.

"AN HISTORICAL ACCOUNT of the EXPEDITION against the OHIO INDIANS, in the year MDCCLXIV, under the command of *HENRY BOUQUET, Esq., Colonel of Foot, and now Brigadier General in America*, Including his TRANSACTIONS with the INDIANS, RELATIVE to the DELIVERY of their PRISONERS, and the PRELIMINARIES of PEACE, with an INTRODUCTORY ACCOUNT of the Preceding CAMPAIGN, and BATTLE of BUSHY-RUN.

To which are annexed MILITARY PAPERS containing REFLECTIONS on the WAR with the SAVAGES; a METHOD of forming FRONTIER SETTLEMENTS; some ACCOUNT of the INDIAN COUNTRY; with a LIST of NATIONS, FIGHTING MEN, TOWNS, DISTANCES, and different ROUTES.

Published from authentic Documents by a *Lover of his Country*" (DR. WILLIAM SMITH, Provost of the *College of Philadelphia*).

With a Preface by FRANCIS PARKMAN, author of "*Conspiracy of Pontiac*," etc., and a translation of DUMAS' Biographical Sketch of GENERAL BOUQUET.

The MAP and PLATES are finely reproduced by the *Photo-Lithographic Process.*

One volume, 8vo., pp. xxiii, 162, finely printed on tinted paper, neatly bound in English cloth, gilt top, and uncut edges, or entirely uncut. Price, $3.00.

A few *large-paper* copies have been printed on extra-heavy tinted paper. Cloth, gilt top, and uncut edges, or entirely uncut. Price, $5.00

[From the Round Table.]

"A better initial volume to the *Ohio Valley Historical Series* could not be desired than this. Everything is in its favor—the beauty of the volume itself, an invariable characteristic of whatever leaves its publisher's press; the rarity of the work reprinted, the importance in the history of our anti-revolutionary colonizations of the events which occasioned the expedition; and, by no means the least, the brief explanatory preface added by Mr. Francis Parkman. * * * So that, while the antiquarian or historian will get most out of the work, the average reader will find in it no small pleasure along with the side light it throws upon the events of a period of which popular ideas are vague and undefined."

[From the Cincinnati Gazette.]

"It is, in short, a worthy beginning to an enterprise which must commend itself to all scholars and literary men, and which reflects credit upon Cincinnati, as well as upon the enterprise and tact of the publishers."

[From the New England Historical and Genealogical Register.]

"This is the first of the reprints of the *Ohio Valley Historical Series*, now in course of publication by Messrs. Clarke & Co., and is presented to us in a shape and style befitting the 'rarity of the volume, and its intrinsic value as an authentic and reliable narrative of one of the earliest British military expeditions into the territory North-West of the Ohio River.' * * * The volume is elegantly printed on tinted paper, has a good *index*, and is an honor to the enterprising publishers."

[From the American Literary Gazette and Publisher's Circular.]

"This is the first volume of the *Ohio Valley Historical Series*, just commenced by Robert Clarke & Co., Cincinnati. We have heretofore spoken of the plan of the projected series. It will undoubtedly form a valuable material for history. We can not too highly commend the admirable manner in which the publishers have produced the work. The paper and typography are unexceptionable. The original maps and plans are most successfully reproduced according to the 'Osborn Process,' by the American Photo-Lithographic Company, and the entire manufacture reflects credit on the skill and taste of Messrs. Clarke & Co."

[From the Atlantic Monthly.]

"The whole narrative is most entertaining for the interest of the subject, and for the quaintness of that highly literary style of the last century in which it is written. * * * *

"Its quaintness every one must relish, and none can help noticing the clearness and solidity of the narration. * * * It is an enterprise to which we heartily wish success, both for the valuable matter it will preserve for the use of the student and the pleasure it will afford the general reader."

Number Two.

Walker's History of Athens County, Ohio.

HISTORY OF ATHENS COUNTY, OHIO, and incidentally of the OHIO LAND COMPANY and the FIRST SETTLEMENT OF THE STATE at MARIETTA, with Personal and Biographical Sketches of the EARLY SETTLERS, NARRATIVES OF PIONEER ADVENTURES, etc. By CHARLES M. WALKER.

Illustrated with an original Map, showing the lands purchased by the Ohio Company, the Donation Tract, and Athens County, Past and Present, with fine Steel Portraits of Hon. Thomas Ewing, Sr., Bishop Ames, Judges Ephraim Cutler and Isaac Barker, and General John Brown.

One volume, 8vo., pp. viii, 600, finely printed on tinted paper, neatly bound in English cloth, gilt top, and uncut edges, or entirely uncut. Price, $6.00.

A few *large-paper* copies have been printed on extra-heavy tinted paper. Portraits on *India paper*. Cloth, gilt top, and uncut edges, or entirely uncut. 2 vols. Impl. 8vo. Price, $12.00.

[From the Historical Magazine.]

"We have never found a more complete local history, nor one in which the author has more successfully labored to present the annals, the statistics, and the local biographies of a community, with fidelity and elaborate minuteness; and as a specimen of really elegant typography, it is worthy of all praise."

[From the Cincinnati Commercial.]

"It is a work so thorough, so complete, so carefully prepared, that it will remain for many years the history of the territory embraced within the early limits of the county. The typography is superb, and the portraits are executed in the best style of steel line engraving."

[From the New York Tribune.]

"The publication of the *Ohio Valley Historical Series,* of which this elegant work forms the second volume, is an enterprise for which men of letters are under deep obligation to the good sense and good taste of the publishers. * * * The present volume, though modest in its pretensions, claiming little more than a local interest, is far more valuable in its contents than its title or its unpretending preface might lead one to suppose. It embraces a history of the great Ohio Land Company and the first settlement of the State at Marietta, with biographical sketches of the pioneers of that part of Ohio, and a map which possesses considerable historical interest. Quite apart from its intrinsic value, the work also deserves to be prized as a dainty specimen of handiwork, rarely surpassed by the best New York and Boston booksellers, to say nothing of those of the West. The type is sumptuous, the paper heavy, the binding neat and strong, and the general typographical arrangement extremely tasteful."

[From the New England Historical and Genealogical Register.]

"After years of patient and intelligent industry, Mr. Walker has succeeded in gathering together and presenting to us, in a very condensed form, the history of the county of Athens from its first feeble beginning, with sketches and statistics relating to the bloody Indian wars, the war of 1812, and the late civil war. It is also full of statistics relating to the several towns, such as the names of the officers, county and municipal; a history of its churches, schools, libraries, newspapers; with a description of its agricultural products, and of its mineral, manufacturing, and railway resources. All this must make a volume of surpassing interest and value to the inhabitants of the county and to the people of the State generally.

"Besides the above, Mr. Walker gives us his biographical sketches of the leading men connected with the settlement and history of the county, and this feature of the work gives it a peculiar interest for us; for the larger number of these were natives of New England, and many of them men of high character and standing here. In fact, the whole enterprise, begun and carried on by the Ohio Land Company, was the work of some of the leading spirits of New England, who had been active participators in the Revolutionary war. We know not where else so much information can be obtained relating to the origin and history of this company. The men engaged in it, and the emigrants they led to the North-West Territory, gave to the population of Ohio much of the character of its present population and many of the elements of their extraordinary prosperity.

"The volume is beautifully printed, and is in all respects one of the handsomest and most complete local histories we have ever seen."

[From the Cincinnati Chronicle.]

"The volume is one of the most admirable local histories we have ever seen. * * * Mr. Walker has done his work well and thoroughly. He has exhibited excellent taste and judgment, and his style is free from the objectionable features which too often mar and render comparatively valueless histories of this class."

[From the Cleveland Leader.]

"A book full of interest to every citizen of Athens county, and incidentally to every inhabitant of Ohio, as a record of the first settlement of the State. * * * * Mr. Walker seems to have enjoyed unrestricted facilities for the collection of data, and has worked up his subject with evident care and judgment. The result is, perhaps, the best county history ever written in the State."

Number Three.

Clark's Campaign in the Illinois in 1778–9.

COL. GEORGE ROGERS CLARK'S SKETCHES of his CAMPAIGN IN THE ILLINOIS IN 1778–9, with an Introduction by Hon. HENRY PIRTLE, of Louisville, Ky., and an Appendix containing the *Public and Private Instructions to Col. Clark* and *Maj. Bowman's Journal of the Taking of Post St. Vincents.*

One volume, 8vo., pp. viii, 119, finely printed on tinted paper, with a Portrait of General Clark, neatly bound in English cloth, gilt top and uncut edges, or entirely uncut. Price, $2.00.

A few *large-paper* copies have been printed on extra-heavy tinted paper. Portrait on *India paper*. Cloth, gilt top, and uncut edges, or entirely uncut. Price, $4.00.

[From the Atlantic Monthly.]

"The publishers of the *Ohio Valley Historical Series* here follow the narrative of Colonel Bouquet's Expedition (already noticed in these pages) with another volume possessing the same curious interest for the student of history, and the same fascination for the lover of exquisitely printed books; for the series, so far, is luxurious in paper and binding, and in typographical execution is surpassed by few productions of the American press.

"Colonel Clark's campaign was a very brief one, and in fighting not particularly arduous, as would appear from his own showing; but it was full of daring and heroic endurance; it resulted immediately in the reduction of the British military posts between the Ohio and the Mississippi, thus giving tranquility to all the frontier settlements, and it finally secured to us all this vast territory. * * * *

"A little of the romance which belongs to all French colonial history hangs about Colonel Clark's unconscious page, and his sketch affords here and there a glimpse of the life of the *habitans* in the old seventeenth-century settlements of the French at Kaskaskias, Cahokia, and St. Vincents; but for the most part it is a plain and summary account of the military operations, and depends for its chief interest upon the view it affords of the character of as brave and shrewd a soldier and as bad a speller as ever lived. Some of his strokes of orthography are unrivaled by the studied grotesqueness of Artemus Ward or Mr. Yellowplush; he declares with perfect good faith that on a certain occasion he was very much "adjutated;" and it is quite indifferent to him whether he write privilidge, happiniss, comeing, attacted, adjutation, sucksess, leathergy, intiligence, silicit, acoutriments, refutial, and anctious, or the more accepted forms of the same words, as like a *bona fide* bad speller, he is quite as apt to do. * * * *

"The letter is now printed for the first time. We heartily commend it to all who love to taste history at its sources, or who enjoy character. It is a curious contrast to the polite narrative of Colonel Bouquet, but it is quite as interesting, and the deeds it records have turned out of vastly greater consequence than those which the brave Swiss performed."

[From the Historical Magazine.]

"The importance of the expedition of Colonel Clark is known to every well-informed person as that to which we are mainly indebted for our possession, to-day, of the immense range of country west of the Alleghanies; and this personal narrative of that expedition, from the pen of its commander, it will be seen, is necessarily a paper of great historic interest, both as a portion of the local history of the West and as an element in the history of our relations with Great Britain, France, and Spain. The typography of the volume is excellent."

[From the Nation.]

"A very original and striking revolutionary character is portrayed by himself in 'Col. George Rogers Clark's Sketch of his Campaign in the Illinois in 1778–9.' * * * Clark's military capacity was certainly of a high order, and it is seldom one reads of a commander possessing such boldness, resources, and tact. He understood perfectly, for military purposes, the Indian nature, and how to exhibit at the right time courageous defiance and magnanimity. * * * The operations at Kaskaskia and Vincennes are described in a very graphic but truly modest manner—the march from the former post to take the latter being one of extraordinary hardship and enterprise. The odd spelling of the French, Spanish, and Indian names mentioned by Clark, and his ordinary orthography, too, make his narrative quite amusing. Some persons may guess what 'Messicippa,' 'La prary de rush' (La Prairie du Rocher), 'Canoweay' (Kanawha), 'adjutated,' and 'adgetation,' stand for. * * The notes of the editor of this volume add very much to its readableness and historical completeness."

[From the New Albany Ledger.]

"The quaint style of the original is faithfully retained, with Clark's orthography, punctuation, capital letters, and other peculiarities. The narrative is exceedingly interesting, and bears the impress of truth upon its pages. * * * The volume should find a place in the library of every Indianian who takes an interest in the events which had such momentous influence on the destinies of the region of country in which we now live."

[From the Louisville Courier-Journal.]

"The volume is gotten up in antique, and realizes all that the antiquary could desire. Judge Pirtle's preface is not the least valuable of the contents, which are in every way rare and valuable. It presents the reader with a distinct and graphic picture of Clark and his times."

In Press.

Dr. Drake's Pioneer Life in Kentucky.

PIONEER LIFE IN KENTUCKY: A Series of REMINISCENTIAL LETTERS addressed to his Children, giving a Faithful and Graphic Description of Pioneer Life. By the late DANIEL DRAKE, M. D., author of "Cincinnati in 1815," etc. Edited, with a Memoir, by his son, Hon. CHARLES D. DRAKE, of St. Louis.

Smith's Captivity with the Indians.

A REPRINT OF "AN ACCOUNT of the REMARKABLE OCCURRENCES in the Life and Travels of Col. JAMES SMITH (now a citizen of Bourbon county, Ky.), during his Captivity with the Indians in the years 1755, '56, '57, '58, and '59. In which the Customs, Manners, Traditions, Theological Sentiments, Mode of Warfare, Military Tactics, Discipline and Encampments, Treatment of Prisoners, etc., are better explained and more minutely related than has been heretofore done by any author on that subject. Together with a Description of the Soil, Timber, and Waters, where he traveled with the Indians during his captivity.

"To which is added a Brief Account of some very Uncommon Occurrences, which transpired after his return from captivity; as well as of the Different Campaigns carried on against the Indians to the Westward of Fort Pitt, since the year 1755 to the present date.

"Written by himself. Lexington; printed by John Bradford, on Main street, 1799."

ROBERT CLARKE & CO.

ALSO PUBLISH

Reprints of the following Rare American Tracts:

AN APPEAL TO THE PUBLIC ON BEHALF OF CAMERIA (AMERICA), *A Young Lady who was almost Ruined by the Barbarous Treatment of her own Mother.* London. Printed in the year 1781.

The edition consists of 124 small-paper copies, octavo, finely printed on tinted paper, sewed, uncut, price 75 cents; 25 large-paper copies, also on tinted paper, sewed, uncut, price $1.50.

SOME ACCOUNT of an EXISTING CORRESPONDECE now Carrying on Between the INHABITANTS OF THE MOON (*America*) and the NATIVES OF THIS COUNTRY; To which is subjoined a List of such Articles as are immediately wanted for the Export Trade. By some Merchants just arrived from that Planet. Interspersed with several useful and valuable Hints, particularly adapted to the use of those Gentlemen who are fond of Speculation. A Work strongly recommended to the Perusal of the Merchants, Bankers, Manufacturers, Wholesale Tradesmen, Shopkeepers, Underwriters, Insurance Brokers, and Ladies of Great Britain. London: Printed and sold by H. Fry, Finsbury-Place, Finsbury-Square, 1800.

The edition consists of 132 small-paper copies, octavo, finely printed on tinted paper, sewed, uncut, price 75 cents; 27 large-paper copies, also on tinted paper, sewed, uncut, price $1.50.

[From the Round Table.]

"We have just now before us a pamphlet (*Cameria*) from the press of Robert Clarke & Co., of whose beauty we remain within bounds when we say it is surpassed not merely by nothing we have seen from the best Boston, New York, or Philadelphia presses, but that, in simple elegance, it is not inferior to the finest workmanship of London or Edinburgh. * * * * But aside from its merits for a half hour's amusement, or whatever value it has as a historical curiosity, its beauty alone should make it prized."

[From the Cincinnati Chronicle.]

"It is a *fac simile* of the original *brochure*, most beautifully executed, in the highest style of the typographical art. It is very creditable to the good taste and judgment of the firm. * * * The *Cameria* appeared in the Edinburgh *Evening Post* of the 4th of March, 1781; and, said the original publishers, 'as it bears a lively resemblance to the manner of the late admirable DEAN SWIFT, and contains some striking allegorical passages, it is hoped that it will afford the reader some rational entertainment.'"

THE

Bible in the Public Schools.

ARGUMENTS

IN THE CASE OF

John D. Minor et als.

Versus

The Board of Education of the City of Cincinnati et als.

SUPERIOR COURT OF CINCINNATI.

WITH THE

OPINIONS AND DECISION

Of the Court.

1 vol., 8vo., cloth, - - - - -	$2.00
On tinted paper, gilt top, cloth extra, - -	2.50

Sent by mail, prepaid, on receipt of the price.

ROBERT CLARKE & CO.,
PUBLISHERS,
Cincinnati, Ohio.

www.ingramcontent.com/pod-product-compliance
Lightning Source LLC
LaVergne TN
LVHW021145110826
845150LV00005B/1129

* 9 7 8 1 4 2 5 5 4 7 3 8 7 *